OXFORD STUDIES IN AFRICAN AFFAIRS

General Editors
JOHN D. HARGREAVES *and* GEORGE SHEPPERSON

THE ỌYỌ EMPIRE

THE OYO EMPIRE
c.1600–c.1836

A West African Imperialism
in the Era of the
Atlantic Slave Trade

BY
ROBIN LAW

CLARENDON PRESS · OXFORD
1977

Oxford University Press, Walton Street, Oxford OX2 6DP

OXFORD LONDON GLASGOW NEW YORK
TORONTO MELBOURNE WELLINGTON CAPE TOWN
IBADAN NAIROBI DAR ES SALAAM LUSAKA ADDIS ABABA
KUALA LUMPUR SINGAPORE JAKARTA HONG KONG TOKYO
DELHI BOMBAY CALCUTTA MADRAS KARACHI

Oxford University Press 1977

British Library Cataloguing in Publication Data
Law, Robin
    The Oyo Empire, c. 1600–c. 1836.—(Oxford
    studies in African affairs).
    1. Oyo—Civilization
    I. Title II. Series
    966   DT474

ISBN 0–19–822709–4

Printed in Great Britain by
Western Printing Services Ltd., Bristol

To
Russell Meiggs

Preface

THIS book is the direct, if by now somewhat remote, descendant of a doctoral thesis submitted at the University of Birmingham in 1971. It has come to differ from its ancestor substantially in both form and content, as second thoughts and the discovery of new evidence have prompted reinterpretation and reorganization of the original material. That I have now finally moved from the stage of modification to that of publication reflects, alas, less any conviction that I am at last in a position to offer a definitive interpretation of the subject than a feeling that, after ten years, the attractions of continual rewriting have perhaps begun to pall. There should in principle be an optimum point at which to publish, when one is sufficiently distant from the original work of research to be able to view the subject fruitfully in its general historiographical context, yet close enough to it to be restrained from flights of imaginative fancy. Whether I have by good fortune approximated to this optimum point, the reader can judge.

The subject of the book is the history of the Ọyọ empire, which was one of the most powerful states in the coastal area of West Africa during the seventeenth and eighteenth centuries, but disintegrated in civil war during the first four decades of the nineteenth century. The principal interest of the history of Ọyọ in this period, and the respects in which its study contributes to understanding of issues of general importance in the historiography of Africa, can be found in two areas: the involvement of Ọyọ in the Atlantic slave trade, and the process of political change which occurred in the kingdom during its period of imperial expansion. With regard to the first, it is argued here that Ọyọ benefited materially from its participation in the slave trade, though at the expense of its neighbours who actually provided most of the slaves, and that the wealth derived from the trade was an important factor in the success of the kingdom's imperial expansion. It is also, however, suggested that, by an agreeable nemesis, the civil wars in the Ọyọ kingdom in the early nineteenth century were exacerbated by the European demand for slaves, as the Ọyọ themselves became for the first time the principal victims of local slave-raiding. With regard to the second, it is argued that the process of imperial expansion gave rise in Ọyọ to increasing political centralization, as its kings used their imperial and commercial revenues to build up a personal administrative staff, recruited largely from slaves, to govern their expanding empire. However, this growth of royal power was opposed and resisted by the non-royal chiefs of Ọyọ, and these tensions inside the Ọyọ polity led ultimately to the civil wars which brought about the collapse of the empire.

In working on this subject I have accumulated numerous debts of gratitude to individuals and institutions which should be recorded here. Before all others, my thanks are due to Dr. S. O. Biobaku, under whose guidance I first became acquainted with Ọyọ and its history, to Robert Smith, from whose advice and assistance in the early stages of the work I benefited enormously, and to Professor J. D. Fage, who supervised my original thesis. I also owe a major debt to Dr. A. G. Hopkins, who read parts of the work in typescript. Others from whom I have received invaluable information and ideas include Dr. Bọlanle Awẹ, Solomon Babayẹmi, Paulo Farias, the late Musa Baba Idris, Marion Johnson, Dr. Peter Lloyd, Dr. Michael Mason, Christian Merlo, Professor Peter Morton-Williams, Dr. Agneta Pallinder-Law, Professor John Peel, and Professor Abdullahi Smith. For assistance in the course of my fieldwork in Nigeria, I should also thank Mr. B. Ajuwọn and Mr. J. J. Ọjọade.

Thanks are also due to the staff of the libraries and archives in which I have worked in the course of the research for this book. In particular, I should thank the staff of the Public Record Office, London; the British Library, London; the Church Missionary Society Library, London; the Archives Nationales, Paris; the National Archives, Ibadan; the National Archives, Kaduna; Rhodes House Library, Oxford; and the libraries of the Universities of Lagos, Ibadan, Birmingham, and Stirling. For financial support received at various stages during the work of research and writing, I have to record my thanks to the University of Lagos, the Department of Education and Science, the University of Birmingham, the University of Stirling, the British Academy, and the Sir Ernest Cassel Educational Trust.

Stirling,   ROBIN LAW
August 1976

Contents

List of Maps

Abbreviations

ADLA	Archives Départementales de la Loire-Atlantique, Nantes.
AHU	Archivo Historico Ultramarino, Lisbon.
AN	Archives Nationales, Paris.
APB	Archivo Publico, Bahia.
ARA	Algemeen Rijks Archief, The Hague.
BNRJ	Bibliotheca Nacional, Rio de Janeiro.
CMS	Church Missionary Society, London.
JAH	*Journal of African History.*
JHSN	*Journal of the Historical Society of Nigeria.*
NAI	National Archives, Ibadan.
NAK	National Archives, Kaduna.
PP	Parliamentary Papers.
YHRS	Yoruba Historical Research Scheme.

Note on transcription of non-English words

In transcribing Yoruba words and names, I have used diacritical marks to distinguish the open vowels ɔ and ε (ọ and ẹ) and the sound *sh* (ṣ). I have not indicated accents. With regard to non-Yoruba words and names, I have not attempted to work out a systematic mode of transcription, and have generally used the forms which I found in my sources.

The Yoruba do not distinguish number, and I have followed this, writing, for example, 'the Ọyọ' rather than the awkward anglicized plural 'the Ọyọs'. For the sake of simplicity, I have also arbitrarily extended this disregard of number to other African languages, writing, for example, 'Hausa' and 'Nupe' instead of the strictly correct plurals 'Hausawa' and 'Nupecizi'.

Glossary of principal non-English words and titles used in the text

All words are Yoruba, except where indicated.

abọbaku	'those who die with the *ọba*', those customarily required to commit suicide at the death of the *Alafin*.
ade	crown of superior status, distinguished by a fringe of beads which covers the wearer's face.
afin	palace.
ajẹlẹ	representatives of the *Alafin* resident in the sub-ordinate towns of the Ọyọ kingdom.
Alafin	title of the *ọba* of Ọyọ.
Arẹmọ	title normally given to the eldest son of the *Alafin*.
Arẹ Ọna Kakamfo	title of the commander-in-chief of the provincial army of the Ọyọ kingdom.
Arọkin	the official historians of the Ọyọ court.
balẹ	ruler of a town of inferior status, without the right to wear a crown. (Distinguish *bale*, head of a lineage.)
Baṣọrun	the principal non-royal chief of Ọyọ, the head of the *Ọyọ Mesi*.
bẹrẹ	type of grass used as roof thatch; Bẹrẹ festival—annual festival at which *bẹrẹ* was brought for the thatching of the *Alafin*'s palace in token of homage.
ẹkun	province.
Ẹṣọ	the seventy junior war-chiefs of the Ọyọ capital.
Etsu (Nupe)	title of the king of Nupe.
ilari	category of slaves of the *Alafin*, serving principally as his messengers.
jihad (Arabic)	holy war of Muslims against non-Muslims.
mallam (Hausa)	Muslim scholar.
ọba	ruler of a town of superior status, with the right to wear a crown; *ọba alade—ọba* with the right to an *ade*.
Okẹrẹ	title of the *ọba* of Ṣaki.
Ologbo	title of the head of the *Arọkin*.
Olu	title of the *ọba* of Ilaro.
Oluwo	title of the *ọba* of Iwo.
Oluwoye	title of the *ọba* of Iwoye.

ọmọ ọba	member of the royal lineage.
Ọni	title of the *ọba* of Ifẹ.
Onikoyi	title of the *ọba* of Ikoyi.
Oniṣarẹ	title of the *ajẹlẹ* resident at Ijanna.
oriki	descriptive epithet or praise-name, often in the form of a long poem.
oriṣa	deity.
Osi Iwẹfa	title of one of the principal eunuch officials of the *Alafin*.
Ọwa	title of the *ọba* of Ileṣa and of Idanre.
Ọyọ Mesi	council of the seven principal non-royal chiefs of Ọyọ.
Ṣabiganna	title of the *ọba* of Iganna.
Timi	title of the *ọba* of Ẹdẹ.

Note on Yoruba royal titles:
The titles of Yoruba *ọba* are usually formed by adding a prefix to the name of the town concerned. The commonest prefix is *Oni* (owner of): e.g. the *Onikoyi* of Ikoyi. This is often contracted to *Ol-* (e.g. the *Olowu* of Owu), which, through the influence of vowel harmony, can become *Ọl-* (e.g. the *Ọlọfa* of Ọfa), *El-* (e.g. the *Elere* of Ere), *Ẹl-* (e.g. the *Ẹlẹgbẹ* of Ẹgbẹ), or *Al-* (e.g. the *Alake* of Ake). Other common prefixes are *A-* (e.g. the *Akirun* of Ikirun) and *Olu-* (e.g. the *Oluwo* of Iwo).

PART I

PROLEGOMENA

CHAPTER 1

Introduction

THE kingdom of Ọyọ as it existed at the end of the nineteenth century, when the area was brought under British rule, is represented today by the Ọyọ Division[1] of the Ọyọ State of the Federation of Nigeria.[2] The ruler of the kingdom, who has the title *Alafin*, has his capital, also called Ọyọ, at a town in the extreme south of the Ọyọ Division, about 30 miles north of Ibadan, the modern capital of the Ọyọ State. Even at the end of the nineteenth century, Ọyọ was a considerable kingdom—Ọyọ Division has an area of over 8,000 square miles. The Ọyọ capital was likewise a considerable city, with a population of over 40,000 in the census of 1911.[3] But the power and extent of Ọyọ at the end of the nineteenth century were but a shadow of what they had been earlier, during the seventeenth and eighteenth centuries. The kingdom had then included not only the present Ọyọ Division, but also much of the Ilọrin and Igbomina Divisions of the Kwara State to the north-east, the Ibarapa and Ọṣun Divisions of the Ọyọ State to the south, and part of the Ẹgbado Division of the Ogun State in the south-west.[4] In addition, tribute was levied by the Ọyọ from several neighbouring kingdoms. It is with this earlier period of Ọyọ power, which came to an end with the collapse of the Ọyọ empire in the 1830s, that the present study is concerned.

The capital of Ọyọ during this period of power was not at the modern site in the south of Ọyọ Division. The modern city of Ọyọ is a recent foundation, which only became the Ọyọ capital after the

[1] Strictly, the old Ọyọ Division no longer exists, having been divided into a Northern and a Southern Ọyọ Division, but for the sake of simplicity references to Ọyọ Division have been left unchanged.

[2] The Ọyọ State was created as part of the reorganization of the Nigerian States in 1976: earlier, the area formed part of the Western State.

[3] A. L. Mabogunjẹ, *Yoruba Towns* (Ibadan, 1962), 1. Earlier estimates, in the 1850s and 1890s, put the population of the Ọyọ capital at 25,000 and at 60,000: T. J. Bowen, *Central Africa: Adventures and Missionary Labours* (Charleston, 1857), 218; J. O. George, *Historical Notes on the Yoruba Country and its Tribes* (Lagos, 1895), 20.

[4] For a reconstruction of the boundaries of the Ọyọ kingdom at its greatest extent, see below, Ch. 6, pp. 85–90.

collapse of Ọyọ power in the 1830s.[5] Earlier, the capital of the
kingdom had been a town some 80 miles further north, in what is
now the extreme north-eastern corner of Ọyọ Division. The site is
now totally uninhabited, but vestiges of its former occupation,
notably the earthen city walls, with a circuit of some 15 miles, may
still be seen.[6] This earlier capital is sometimes called Katanga or
Katunga, in origin the name by which the Hausa people of northern
Nigeria referred to the city.[7] Since its abandonment in the 1830s, the
site has also been known as Ọyọ Ile, or 'Old Ọyọ'.[8]

The Ọyọ people are sometimes described as a 'sub-tribe' of the
Yoruba, but this calls for some comment. The name Yoruba is today
applied to a group of peoples who inhabit a large area of south-
western Nigeria (in terms of modern political geography, the Ọyọ,
Ondo, and Ogun States, most of the Lagos State, and a part of the
Kwara State) and parts of the neighbouring Republics of Benin
(formerly Dahomey[9]) and Togo to the west. The Ọyọ, who occupy
the north of this area, are the largest of the Yoruba sub-groups.
Other principal groups are, in the east, the Igbomina, Yagba, Ijẹṣa,
Ekiti, and Ondo; in the south, the Ifẹ, Ijẹbu, Ẹgba, Awori, Ẹgbado,
and Anago; and in the west, the Ketu, Ṣabẹ, Idaṣa, Iṣa, and Ana.[10]
The Yoruba are distinguished primarily on linguistic criteria, the

[5] Before becoming the Ọyọ capital the town was called Agọ Ọja, and it is
sometimes referred to as Agọ d'Ọyọ, 'Agọ become Ọyọ'.
[6] For descriptions of the site and its material remains, see: J. D. Clarke, 'A
Visit to Old Oyo', *The Nigerian Field*, 7.3 (1938), 139–42; id., 'Carved Posts at
Old Oyo', *Nigeria Magazine*, 15 (1938), 248–9; id., 'Ancient Pottery from Old
Oyo', *Nigeria Magazine*, 18 (1939), 109; R. G. Watters, 'A Visit to Old Oyo',
Nigeria Magazine, 44 (1958), 346–9; F. Willett, 'Investigations at Old Oyo,
1956–7: An Interim Report', *JHSN* 2.1 (1960), 59–77; id., 'A Terra-Cotta Head
from Old Oyo, Western Nigeria', *Man*, 59 (1959), no. 286; R. Smith and D.
Williams, 'A Reconnaissance Visit to Ọyọ-Ile', *Odu*, 2nd series, 3.1 (1966), 56–60.
Further investigation of the site is currently in progress, under the direction of
R. C. Soper of the University of Ibadan.
[7] This is the name used in the earliest European accounts of the city: e.g.
T. E. Bowdich, *A Mission from Cape Coast to Ashantee* (London, 1819), 208;
D. Denham and H. Clapperton, *Narrative of Travels and Discoveries in Northern
and Central Africa* (London, 1826), Denham's Narrative, 278. It is presumably
derived from the Hausa *katanga*, 'wall', alluding perhaps to the massive city
walls.
[8] Lit. 'Home Ọyọ'.
[9] The Republic of Dahomey was renamed Benin in 1975: it should be distinguished from the historical kingdom of Benin, which is situated in the Bendel
State of Nigeria.
[10] On the Yoruba in general, see D. Forde, *The Yoruba-Speaking Peoples of
South-Western Nigeria* (London, 1951).

various groups speaking closely related, if not wholly mutually intelligible, dialects.[11] They also share to a degree a common culture, and most of them have traditions of a common origin by migration from the southern Yoruba town of Ile Ifẹ, though this tradition is also shared by the non-Yoruba kingdom of Benin, in the Bendel State of Nigeria to the south-east of Yorubaland. But the application of the name Yoruba to this large group is a modern usage, strictly anachronistic for the period dealt with in this study. Originally the name designated only the Ọyọ, being the name by which the Hausa of northern Nigeria referred to the Ọyọ kingdom.[12] The extension of the term to its present general signification, to refer to the linguistic group, was the work of the Christian missionaries in Sierra Leone who first studied these languages, among freed slaves of Yoruba origin there, in the nineteenth century.[13] Even today the word is sometimes understood to refer specifically to the Ọyọ, who are commonly known as the 'Yoruba Proper'. In this study, however, except in direct quotations from sources, the word will be used throughout in its modern sense, to refer to the linguistic group.

It is a fact of considerable interest and importance that before the nineteenth century the name Yoruba was not used to designate the larger group of which the Ọyọ form part. Nor, as far as the evidence goes, was this large group distinguished by any other name.[14] It must, indeed, be doubtful whether the various 'Yoruba' groups were conscious of forming, on linguistic or other grounds, any sort of

[11] 'Primarily', because the Itsekiri of the Bendel State of Nigeria, who belong to the same linguistic group, are usually distinguished from the Yoruba on cultural and historical grounds.

[12] As noted by H. Clapperton, *Journal of a Second Expedition into the Interior of Africa* (London, 1829), 4. The term Yoruba is regularly used in African Arabic sources referring to Ọyọ. It also occurs in European accounts based on information from northern sources: e.g. Bowdich, *Mission from Cape Coast to Ashantee*, 208–9; J. Dupuis, *Journal of a Residence in Ashantee* (London, 1824), esp. lxxxv; Denham and Clapperton, *Narrative of Travels and Discoveries*, Denham's Narrative, 278, and Clapperton's Narrative, 42, 87. It never occurs in the early European sources, whose knowledge of Ọyọ derived from coastal informants.

[13] The term was first used in its modern, general sense by J. Raban, *The Eyo Vocabulary*, vol. iii (London, 1832), 10. The usage was not established without opposition. The linguist Koelle objected that the name Yoruba properly belonged only to the Ọyọ, and proposed instead as a general name for the linguistic group 'Aku', the usual name for Yoruba-speakers in Sierra Leone: S. W. Koelle, *Polyglotta Africana* (London, 1854), 5.

[14] At least by themselves. It appears that their western neighbours used the term 'Anago', strictly the name of a specific western Yoruba group, as a general term to cover all Yoruba-speakers, including the Ọyọ: e.g. A. Le Herissé, *L'Ancien Royaume de Dahomey* (Paris, 1911), 318–20.

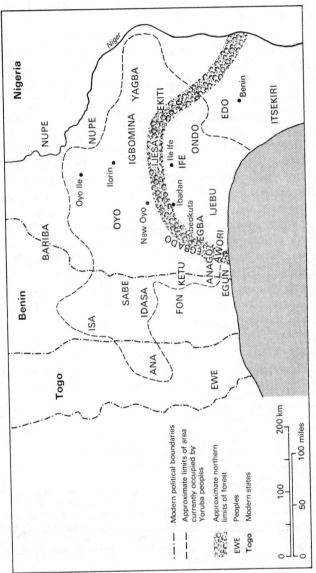

Map 1. Yorubaland.

unity or community. Certain traditions do allege that the various kingdoms which traced their origins to Ile Ifẹ, which included the non-Yoruba Benin as well as the principal Yoruba kingdoms, formed some sort of political entity or confederacy, but in practice there was certainly no such effective unity.[15] The numerous kingdoms of the Yoruba area were normally quite independent of, and not infrequently at war with, each other. Consciousness of a common Yoruba identity seems to have emerged only during the nineteenth century, probably initially among freed slaves of Yoruba origin in Sierra Leone.[16] In studying the history of the Ọyọ empire it is therefore necessary to think away the notion of a Yoruba 'tribe' and of the Ọyọ as a 'sub-tribe' of it.

It has also been customary to classify Ọyọ, along with such kingdoms as Benin, Dahomey, and Asante, among the 'states of the Guinea forest',[17] and this too is misleading. The area occupied by the Yoruba peoples includes both densely forested and more open savanna country. The forest area is in the south, extending along and for some distance inland from the coast, though in the west (beyond the River Yewa in Ẹgbado country) the open savanna country reaches to the coast. The bulk of the Ọyọ in fact live in the more open savanna country to the north. The modern town of Ọyọ is, indeed, situated at the northern margins of the forest, but before the nineteenth century this area lay at the southern marches of the Ọyọ kingdom. The original core of the kingdom was situated further north in the savanna, the old capital at Ọyọ Ile being situated in the extreme north of the Yoruba country. While the Ọyọ empire did ultimately embrace parts of the forest area, Ọyọ was thus more truly a savanna than a forest state.

It should also be pointed out that the modern aspect of the Yoruba country is in many ways a misleading guide to the conditions which existed during the period of the Ọyọ empire. The contemporary political geography of the country evolved out of the wars in which the Ọyọ empire collapsed in the nineteenth century. The removal of

[15] For further discussion, see below, Ch. 7.

[16] Certainly, it was in Sierra Leone that the Yoruba first acquired a common name—'Aku'—and a common political organization, with the election of an 'Aku King': C. Fyfe, *A History of Sierra Leone* (Oxford, 1962), 172, 292–293.

[17] e.g. J. D. Fage, 'States of the Guinea Forest', in R. Oliver (ed.), *The Dawn of African History* (2nd edn., London, 1968), 68–74; M. Crowder, *The Story of Nigeria* (2nd edn., London, 1966), Ch. 3.

the *Alafin*'s capital from Ọyọ Ile to the present town of Ọyọ was only one of a number of dramatic changes. Many other important towns of the Ọyọ kingdom were destroyed and abandoned.[18] The former Ọyọ town of Ilọrin became the seat of a dynasty of foreign (Fulani) origin, in allegiance to the Muslim Caliphate of Sokoto in northern Nigeria, and detached from the *Alafin*'s control much of the north-eastern provinces of the Ọyọ kingdom.[19] Ọyọ refugees from these disturbances moved south to occupy territory which had earlier been held by other Yoruba groups, in particular seizing from the Ẹgba the towns of Ijaye and Ibadan. After the 1830s Ijaye and Ibadan, though nominally subject to the *Alafin* at New Ọyọ, were the real powers among the Ọyọ, and assumed effective authority over the southern portions of the Ọyọ kingdom.[20] The movement of the Ọyọ into their territory drove the Ẹgba in turn towards the south-west, and led to the establishment of their modern capital at Abẹokuta.[21]

These disturbances involved a substantial displacement of population from north to south. Today the southern areas of Yorubaland are markedly more densely populated than the north, Ọyọ Division in particular being relatively sparsely populated.[22] Before the nineteenth century it appears that the reverse was the case, the south, with the important exception of the Ijẹbu area, being less densely populated than the north. Yoruba tradition affirms that originally 'the centre of life and activity, of large populations and industry, was . . . in the interior, whilst the coast tribes were scanty in number.'[23] This is corroborated by the contemporary impressions of Richard Lander, who travelled through the Yoruba country from Badagry on the coast to Ọyọ Ile in 1825–6, and who observed that 'the further we penetrated into the country, the more dense we found

---

[18] On the ruined towns of the Ọyọ kingdom, see W. Abimbọla, 'The Ruins of Ọyọ Division', *African Notes*, 2.1 (1964), 16–19; S. O. Babayẹmi, 'Ọyọ Ruins', *African Notes*, 5.1 (1968), 8–11.

[19] For these events, see below, Chs. 12 and 14.

[20] For the history of Ibadan, see B. Awẹ, 'The Ajele System: A Study of Ibadan Imperialism in the Nineteenth Century', *JHSN* 3.1 (1964), 47–60, and 'The End of an Experiment: The Collapse of the Ibadan Empire, 1877–93', *JHSN* 3.2 (1965), 221–30. For Ijaye, see R. Smith, 'Ijaiye: The Western Palatinate of the Yoruba', *JHSN* 2.3 (1962), 329–49.

[21] For Abẹokuta, see S. O. Biobaku, *The Egba and their Neighbours 1842–1872* (Oxford, 1957).

[22] P. C. Lloyd, *Yoruba Land Law* (London, 1962), 52–3.

[23] S. Johnson, *The History of the Yorubas* (London, 1921), 40.

the population to be.'[24] This change in the distribution of population, it should be noted, must have had a significant effect on the
vegetational character of the country also. Many areas in the south
will have been more densely forested before they began to be farmed
on a substantial scale by the refugee colonists of the nineteenth
century. This seems to be the case, for example, in the area of the
modern city of Ọyọ.[25] And many areas in the north, for example
around Ọyọ Ile, will have been more open when they were regularly
farmed by large populations, before the depopulation effected by
the nineteenth-century wars.[26]

The wars of the nineteenth century probably modified the pattern
of settlement in Yorubaland in other ways less immediately obvious.
In recent times the Yoruba have been characterized by a remarkable
degree of urbanization. Though the bulk of the population is employed in agriculture rather than in 'urban' crafts and industries,
most Yoruba live in large permanent towns. Town-dwellers may
have to travel considerable distances to their farms, but even at
quite remote farms no permanently organized settlements, but only
temporary hamlets (abule) are maintained.[27] This pattern of settlement was evidently already established by the 1850s, when a visiting
missionary estimated populations of 20,000 or more for no less
than seventeen Yoruba towns.[28] But it is doubtful to what extent
this was also the situation under the Ọyọ empire. Although urbanism
is probably an ancient feature of Yoruba civilization, it is clear that
the concentration of the population in large urban settlements was
considerably stimulated by the wars of the nineteenth century,
which caused people to seek security in large towns. Many of the
largest Yoruba towns, such as Ibadan, Abẹokuta, Ile Ifẹ, Iwo, and
Ogbomọṣọ, are known to have been either founded or substantially
augmented by the incorporation of refugees during the nineteenth
century,[29] and it appears that this did not represent merely the

[24] R. Lander, *Records of Captain Clapperton's Last Expedition to Africa*
(London, 1830), i. 95.
[25] P. A. Allison, 'Historical Inferences to be Drawn from the Effect of Human
Settlement on the Vegetation of Africa', *JAH* 3 (1962), 246.
[26] Cf. R. W. J. Keay, 'Notes on the Vegetation of Old Oyo Forest Reserve',
Farm and Forest (1947), 36–46.
[27] On Yoruba urbanism, see Lloyd, *Yoruba Land Law*, 50–9; Mabogunjẹ,
Yoruba Towns; E. Krapf-Askari, *Yoruba Towns and Cities* (Oxford, 1969);
G. J. A. Ojo, *Yoruba Culture* (London, 1966), 104–30.
[28] Bowen, *Central Africa*, 218.
[29] Mabogunjẹ, *Yoruba Towns*, 8–10.

replacement of old urban centres by new, but also an increase in the degree of urbanization. The most obvious instance of this is the case of the Ẹgba, who had earlier lived dispersed among some 150 small towns and villages, but came together in the single city of Abẹokuta in around 1830.[30] A similar, if less dramatic, transformation probably took place elsewhere. It is, at any rate, suggestive that among the Ijẹbu, who suffered least of the major Yoruba groups from the nineteenth-century wars, a less urbanized pattern of settlement is found, with the principal city surrounded by substantial and permanently organized dependent villages.[31] The Ijẹbu perhaps preserve a pattern of settlement formerly more widespread in Yorubaland.[32]

In the case of the Ọyọ kingdom, we have the contemporary evidence of Clapperton, who travelled through the area with Richard Lander in 1825–6, on the settlement pattern before the nineteenth-century wars. Clapperton's observations certainly indicate the existence of large towns, but not on a scale comparable to that attested later. For example, he estimated the population of Ijanna, apparently the largest town in the Ẹgbado area, at between 8,000 and 10,000.[33] Kuṣu, a now abandoned town in the north of the Ọyọ kingdom which he credits with a population of 20,000, he describes as 'much the largest town we have seen'.[34] The capital was presumably larger, but no figure is given.[35] There is also on this point the retrospective evidence of Clarke, a missionary active in the area in the 1850s. Clarke was told that although there had been several large towns in the Ọyọ kingdom before the wars of the nineteenth century—notably the capital itself, Ilọrin, Igboho, and Ikoyi—most

[30] Krapf-Askari, Yoruba Towns and Cities, 41.

[31] Lloyd, Yoruba Land Law, 56–7.

[32] As was suggested by a visiting missionary in the 1850s: CMS, CA2/049b, Revd. D. Hinderer, Journal, 13–14 Dec. 1854. However, Lloyd would connect the distinctive settlement pattern of the Ijẹbu with differences in kinship structures: P. C. Lloyd, 'Agnatic and Cognatic Descent among the Yoruba', Man, new series, 1 (1966), 484–500.

[33] Clapperton, Journal of a Second Expedition, 13.

[34] Ibid. 27. For the site of Kuṣu, cf. R. Smith, 'The Alafin in Exile: A Study of the Igboho Period in Oyo History', JAH 6 (1965), 64–5 and n. 24.

[35] A Frenchman who claimed to have visited the Ọyọ capital a little earlier is reported to have described its population, unhelpfully, as 'considerable, but by no means equal to what he had been taught to expect': J. Adams, Remarks on the Country Extending from Cape Palmas to the River Congo (London, 1823), 93. A modern scholar has suggested a population of 50,000 for Ọyọ Ile: P. C. Lloyd, The Political Development of Yoruba Kingdoms in the Eighteenth and Nineteenth Centuries (London, 1971), 13.

of the population had lived in small towns, with populations of about 1,000 each.[36]

In order, therefore, to visualize accurately the conditions of the time of the Qyọ empire, we have to imagine a Yorubaland very different from that of today—an Qyọ kingdom ruled from Qyọ Ile and incorporating substantial territory to the east and south of the present Qyọ Division, a population less urbanized and concentrated mainly in the north of the kingdom.

[36] W. H. Clarke, *Travels and Explorations in Yorubaland (1854–1858)* (Ibadan, 1972), 194.

CHAPTER 2

The Sources

IT cannot be claimed that the sources available for a study of the history of the Ọyọ empire are altogether satisfactory, either in quantity or in quality. There is, in particular, an almost total lack of first-hand evidence. This does not make the reconstruction of Ọyọ history impossible, though it does make it more difficult and increases the margin of uncertainty which exists in all historical reconstruction. In view of the deficiencies of the available evidence, it seems desirable, before proceeding to a reconstruction of the history of the Ọyọ empire, to consider in some detail the character of the sources used in this reconstruction. This, it is hoped, will give readers some guidance as to how far they need accept the conclusions offered in the main body of the work.

§1. CONTEMPORARY SOURCES: INTERNAL

No written records of the Ọyọ themselves survive from the period before the collapse of the Ọyọ empire in the 1830s, though it is likely that some once existed. The Ọyọ empire was certainly not a wholly illiterate society. It is known that Islam began to spread among the Ọyọ from the countries to the north as early as the sixteenth or seventeenth century,[1] and individual Ọyọ could well have acquired literacy in Arabic[2] along with the Islamic religion. The Ọyọ also imported numbers of slaves from the Muslim countries to the north. Some of these were certainly literate in Arabic, and some Ọyọ probably used literate northern slaves as secretaries. The French trader Landolphe records that a party of Ọyọ ambassadors whom he met in the Benin area in *c.* 1787 were literate in Arabic:[3] such ambassadors would probably have been royal slaves, and those met by Landolphe may well have been northerners. It is also noteworthy

[1] For the introduction of Islam in Yorubaland, see G. O. Gbadamọsi, 'The Growth of Islam among the Yoruba, 1841–1908' (Ph.D. Thesis, University of Ibadan, 1968), 8–17.

[2] The Arabic script has also been used to transcribe the Yoruba language.

[3] J. F. Landolphe, *Mémoires du Capitaine Landolphe* (Paris, 1823), ii, 86.

that the Muslim secretary of the king of Asante whom Bowdich met at Kumasi in 1817 had 'resided some time in Hio [Ọyọ]', though it is not stated whether he had held any similar post there.[4] But if any written records were kept at Ọyọ Ile, they were presumably lost when the city was abandoned in the 1830s.

If the existence of written records in the Ọyọ capital during the imperial period is somewhat speculative, there can be no question that such records were kept in Ilọrin, the subordinate town of the Ọyọ kingdom whose revolt in the late eighteenth century played a crucial role in the collapse of the Ọyọ empire. In 1817 the ruler of Ilọrin incited a rebellion of the Muslim elements in the Ọyọ kingdom, and in c. 1823 the Muslims seized control of Ilọrin, which became an emirate of the Sokoto Caliphate, under the immediate authority of the Emir of Gwandu.[5] The Ilọrin emirate certainly had a literate administration, and its records, if located, would throw considerable light on the last years of the Ọyọ empire. To date, however, the only Ilọrin document which has come to light from this period is a letter to 'Abd al-Salām, the Emir of Ilọrin, from 'Abdullāh, the Emir of Gwandu, written in 1829, which deals with the illegality of castration.[6]

The only first-hand accounts of the Ọyọ kingdom from the inside which we possess consist of reminiscences by individuals who were sold abroad as slaves during the last troubled years of the empire, but liberated by the British navy and settled in Sierra Leone. There are two of these. Ali Eisami, a native of Bornu in north-eastern Nigeria, who lived at Ọyọ Ile as a slave in c. 1813–17, related the story of his life in his native language, Kanuri, to the linguist Koelle in c. 1850.[7] Ajayi, better known under his adopted English name Samuel Crowther, later famous as a missionary in the Nigerian area, who was a native of the Ọyọ town of Osogun and enslaved at its destruction in 1821, wrote an account of his early life in English in 1837.[8]

[4] Bowdich, *Mission from Cape Coast to Ashantee*, 296.
[5] For these events, see below, Ch. 12, pp. 255–60.
[6] M. Last, *The Sokoto Caliphate* (London, 1967), 92 n.
[7] S. W. Koelle, *Native African Literature* (London, 1854), 115–21 (Kanuri text), 248–56 (English translation). The English translation is also reproduced in P. D. Curtin (ed.), *Africa Remembered: Narratives by West Africans from the Era of the Slave Trade* (Madison, 1967), 199–216.
[8] Published as an appendix in J. F. Schön and S. Crowther, *Journals of the Rev. James Frederick Schön and Mr. Samuel Crowther* (London, 1842), 371–85; also in Curtin, *Africa Remembered*, 289–316.

14   PROLEGOMENA

§2. CONTEMPORARY SOURCES: EXTERNAL

(1) *African*

Failing sources of local provenance, we are dependent for contemporary accounts of the Ọyọ empire on the literate societies
which had some contact with it. The Islamic societies to the north of
Ọyọ had a tradition of literacy in Arabic extending back over
several centuries, but the amount of material which they provide on
Ọyọ is disappointingly meagre. They do, however, provide two early
references to Ọyọ, in the seventeenth century. A passing reference to
Ọyọ (under the name 'Yoruba') occurs in a work of the Timbuktu
scholar Aḥmad Baba, the *Al-Kashf wa'l Bayān li Asnāf madjlūb
al-Sudān*, a treatise on slavery written in 1615–16: the Yoruba are
included in a list of non-Muslim peoples whom it is legitimate to
enslave.[9] Later in the seventeenth century, a scholar of Katsina in
Hausaland, Abū 'Abdullāh Muhammad b. Masanih (Ibn Masanih),
who died in 1667, wrote a work entitled *Shifā' rubā fī tahrīr fuqahā'
Yurubā*, 'A reply to the learned men of Yoruba'. The work is said to
have been concerned with the method of determining the time of
sunset, but it apparently also contained incidental information on
Yorubaland, and it is also cited under the title *Azhar al-rubā fī
akhbār Yurubā*, 'On the wonders of Yoruba'. But no manuscript of
this possibly invaluable work has yet been recovered.[10]

In addition to these early references, there is some material on Ọyọ
in the literature of the Sokoto Caliphate, in the early nineteenth
century. 'Uthmān dan Fodio, the founder and first ruler of the
Caliphate, refers twice to 'Yoruba', in works written in 1806 and
1811, but only to cite Aḥmad Baba's classification of them among
the Unbelievers.[11] More substantial is the brief account of Yoruba
included in the *Infāq al-Maisūr* of Muhammad Bello, the son of
'Uthmān, written in 1812. Bello's account, which is partly derived

[9] Quoted in T. Hodgkin, *Nigerian Perspectives* (2nd edn., London, 1975), 156.
[10] A. D. H. Bivar and M. Hiskett, 'The Arabic Literature of Nigeria to 1804:
A Provisional Account', *Bulletin of S.O.A.S.*, 25 (1962), 116; H. F. C. Smith,
'Arabic Manuscript Material Bearing on the History of the Western Sudan: A
Seventeenth Century Writer of Katsina', Historical Society of Nigeria *Bulletin
of News*, Suppl. to 6.1 (1961), 3.
[11] The two works are *Bayān wujūb al-hijra 'alā'l-'ibād* (1806) and *Tanbīh
al-ikhwān 'alā ahwāl ard al-Sudān* (1811): for the former, see F. H. El Masri, 'A
Critical Edition of Dan Fodio's *Bayān wujūb al-hijra 'alā'l-'ibād*' (Ph.D. Thesis,
University of Ibadan, 1968), 371; for the latter, see H. R. Palmer, 'An Early
Fulani Concept of Islam', *Journal of the African Society*, 14 (1915), 54

from the lost work of Ibn Masanih, consists mainly of a fanciful account of the migrations of the Yoruba to their present homeland.[12] There is also an account of the battles of the 1830s which led to the final abandonment of Ọyọ Ile, in which forces from the Sokoto Caliphate took some part, in the *Nubdha li-izar ba'd manaqib Shaikhina Khalil* of 'Umar b. Muhammad Bukhari b. al-Shaikh, a history of the reign of Khalil, Emir of Gwandu, written in *c.* 1850.[13]

(2) European

Considerably more material can be derived from European sources. European traders were active along the coast to the south of Ọyọ from the late fifteenth century, but for a long time they appear to have heard little or nothing of Ọyọ. It has sometimes been claimed that Ọyọ is referred to, under the name 'Licosaguou', in a Portuguese account of the kingdom of Benin, to the south-east, in the early sixteenth century, but this is unwarranted.[14] Probably Europeans became acquainted with Ọyọ only later, during the seventeenth century, when Ọyọ became a principal supplier of slaves for sale to the Europeans through Whydah and other ports of the 'Slave Coast'.[15] During the seventeenth century, the Dutch, French, and English all established permanent trading stations in the Whydah area, and they were followed by the Portuguese in the early eighteenth century.[16] The unpublished records relating to these trading stations

[12] Translated by E. J. Arnett, as *The Rise of the Sokoto Fulani* (Kano, 1922), 16; the passage is also quoted in Hodgkin, *Nigerian Perspectives*, 78–9.
[13] Cf. Last, *Sokoto Caliphate*, 85. This work was used by Aḥmad b. Sa'd in his *Ta'rikh Gwandu*, which in turn is the source of the account of the battles of the 1830s given by E. J. Arnett, *Gazetteer of Sokoto Province* (London, 1920), 38–9.
[14] Duarte Pacheco Pereira, *Esmeraldo de Situ Orbis* (Lisbon, 1905), 119, gives the name 'Licosaguou' to a powerful ruler in the interior 100 leagues east (*sic*) of Benin. This ruler has been identified with the *Alafin* of Ọyọ, e.g. by P. A. Talbot, *The Peoples of Southern Nigeria* (London, 1926), i. 281–2. The grounds for this identification are that Licosaguou's realm is said to be near that of another ruler called 'Hooguanee', which name is usually interpreted as *Oghene*, the usual Bini name for the *Ọni* of Ifẹ. But there is no reason to suppose that Ọyọ was especially powerful at this time, and the reference might equally be to another of the Yoruba kingdoms. Even the identity of Hooguanee with the *Ọni* of Ifẹ is questioned by A. F. C. Ryder, 'A Reconsideration of the Ife-Benin Relationship', *JAH* 6 (1965), 25–37.
[15] The name commonly given by European traders to the coast between the River Volta and Lagos.
[16] The Dutch had a factory at Offra, east of Whydah, by the 1650s, and established one at Whydah itself in 1682, but they withdrew from the area in the

contain much information,[17] and there are also several published accounts by individual European traders. For the seventeenth century, evidence relating to Ọyọ is rare. There are several references to a hinterland kingdom or people called 'Lucumies', 'Licomin', 'Ulcuim', 'Ulkami' and other variants, of which the earliest is that of Sandoval (1627)[18] and the most substantial that of Dapper (1668)[19], and these should probably be taken to relate to Ọyọ.[20] But the earliest unequivocal references to Ọyọ by name occur later, in the works of de Clodoré (1671)[21] and Barbot (1688),[22] and in a French document of 1690.[23] From the 1720s, when the Ọyọ army overran the kingdom of Dahomey, behind Whydah, there is much more material. The period of Ọyọ history best documented from Slave Coast sources is, roughly, *c*. 1770–90.

The major problem involved in utilizing the Slave Coast material

---

1730s. The French established a factory at Offra in 1669, but moved to Whydah in 1671. The English established factories at Offra in 1674, and at Whydah in 1683. The Portuguese installed themselves at Whydah in 1721.

[17] I have not myself consulted the Dutch and Portuguese records. For the former, I have relied upon the collection by A. Van Dantzig, *Dutch Documents Relating to the Gold Coast and the Slave Coast 1680–1740* (cyclostyled, Legon, 1971); for the latter, on the extensive verbatim citations in P. Verger, *Flux et reflux de la traite des nègres entre le golfe de Bénin et Bahia de Todos os Santos* (Paris, 1968).

[18] P. E. H. Hair, 'Ethnolinguistic Continuity on the Guinea Coast', *JAH* 8 (1967), 261.

[19] O. Dapper, *Naukeurige Beschrijvinge der Afrikaensche Gewesten* (Amsterdam, 1668), 491–5. Other seventeenth-century references include an account by a French missionary written in 1640, quoted by A. F. C. Ryder, *Benin and the Europeans 1485–1897* (London, 1969), 100; and the map of 'La Guinée et pays circomvoisins', in N. Sanson d'Abbéville, *L'Affrique en plusieurs cartes nouvelles et exactes* (Paris, 1656).

[20] These names probably represent 'Olukumi', a term applied to Yoruba-speakers in modern times in Cuba and in Igbo country in the Bendel State of Nigeria: W. Bascom, 'The Yoruba in Cuba', *Nigeria Magazine*, 37 (1951), 14–20; H. U. Beier, 'Yoruba Enclave', *Nigeria Magazine*, 58 (1958), 238–51.

[21] J. de Clodoré, *Relation de ce qui s'est passé dans les Isles et Terre-ferme de l'Amérique* (Paris, 1671), iii. 557, 558: apparently based on information obtained from an ambassador of the coastal kingdom of Allada who visited France in 1670.

[22] J. Barbot, 'Description des côtes de l'Affrique' (unpublished manuscript of 1688, in the Ministry of Defence Navy Library, London: ms. 63) 3e Partie, 133, 136, 139: Barbot visited the Slave Coast in 1682, but his references to Ọyọ are in part, and perhaps in their entirety, borrowed from the earlier work of de Clodoré.

[23] A list of slaves on an estate in French Guyana in 1690 includes one slave from Ọyọ, who had been brought from Africa in 1682: G. Debien and J. Houdaille, 'Les Origines des esclaves aux Antilles. No. 32: Sur un sucrerie de la Guyane en 1690', *Bulletin de l'I.F.A.N.*, série B, 26 (1964), 173.

is that little of it is based on first-hand observation. At this period Europeans seldom, if ever, penetrated into the hinterland to obtain first-hand knowledge of the Ọyọ kingdom itself. A French trader is said to have visited Ọyọ in the late eighteenth century, but his account of it, preserved only at second hand, is brief and uninformative.[24] The seventeenth- and eighteenth-century material which we possess is, therefore, mainly hearsay. In any case, even at its most generous, the documentation of Ọyọ history from these sources is far from lavish. It is also limited in scope, being mainly concerned with the involvement of Ọyọ in the Atlantic slave trade and with its relations with Dahomey and other states in the coastal area. There are only occasional allusions to events inside Ọyọ itself or to Ọyọ activities in other areas of the interior.

The decline of European interest in the Slave Coast in the early nineteenth century, due to the decline in its commerical importance following the abolition of the slave trade,[25] leaves the last years of the Ọyọ empire poorly documented from Slave Coast sources. This is, however, partly compensated for by the fact that Europeans at this period were beginning to penetrate for the first time into the interior of Africa, so that various explorers were picking up information about Ọyọ in several adjacent areas—for example, at Kumasi to the west in 1817[26] and in Bornu and Hausaland to the north in 1824.[27] Still more important, at this period European travellers finally penetrated into Ọyọ itself. In 1825-6 Clapperton and Richard Lander travelled from Badagry on the coast through Ọyọ Ile on their way to the north, and in 1827 Richard Lander alone (Clapperton having died) made the return journey. The Journals of both were preserved and published.[28] Richard Lander again travelled north through Ọyọ Ile, accompanied by his brother John, in 1830. The two brothers published a composite Journal:[29] the original manuscript Journal of Richard, though not that of John,

---

[24] Adams, *Remarks on the Country Extending from Cape Palmas*, 93.

[25] The French factory at Whydah was abandoned in 1797, the Portuguese in 1807, and the British in 1812.

[26] Bowdich, *Mission from Cape Coast to Ashantee*, 208-9.

[27] Denham and Clapperton, *Narrative of Travels and Discoveries*, Denham's Narrative, 278; Clapperton's Narrative, 42, 87.

[28] Clapperton, *Journal of a Second Expedition into the Interior of Africa*; R. Lander, *Records of Captain Clapperton's Last Expedition to Africa*.

[29] R. Lander and J. Lander, *Journal of an Expedition to Explore the Course and Termination of the Niger* (London, 1832).

is also extant.[30] A minor problem in utilizing these Journals is the difficulty of identifying many of the towns of the Ọyọ kingdom through which Clapperton and the Landers passed.[31] There are more serious questions about how far Clapperton and the Landers, who knew no Yoruba and appear to have communicated with the local people through the Hausa language,[32] were in a position fully to understand conditions in Ọyọ. Their accounts are nevertheless invaluable, but they illuminate only a very brief period in Ọyọ history, and that at a time when the power of Ọyọ was already in decline.

The last years of the Ọyọ empire are also illuminated by another important source, of a rather different character, which, though written by a Yoruba, belongs naturally to the same category as the European sources. This is an account by Samuel Crowther, first published in 1843, of, roughly, the last fifty years of the Ọyọ empire.[33] Crowther's account was presumably based on information gathered from freed slaves of Ọyọ origin in Sierra Leone, among whom he could easily have found eyewitnesses of the events which he recounts.

The records of the European missionary societies and of the British administration in Southern Nigeria, which have often been drawn upon in reconstructions of nineteenth-century Yoruba history, are of less help in a study of the Ọyọ empire, since both missionaries and administrators arrived in Yorubaland only in the 1840s, after the empire had already collapsed.[34]

§3. ORAL TRADITIONS

There is thus a singular paucity of contemporary evidence, even of a

---

[30] In the Wellcome Historical Medical Library, London: MS. 1659.

[31] For the identification of these towns, see W. Bascom, 'Lander's Routes through the Yoruba Country', *The Nigerian Field*, 25.1 (1960), 12–22; and cf. P. A. Allison, 'The Last Days of Old Oyo', *Odu*, 1st series, 4 (n.d.), 16–27; P. Morton-Williams, 'The Ọyọ Yoruba and the Atlantic Trade, 1670–1830', *JHSN* 3.1 (1964), 35–7; Smith, 'The Alafin in Exile', 64–5; and the map in S. O. Babayẹmi, 'Upper Ogun: An Historical Sketch', *African Notes*, 6.2 (1971), 75.

[32] For the use of Hausa by Clapperton and the Landers, cf. Clapperton, *Journal of a Second Expedition*, 119.

[33] S. Crowther, *A Vocabulary of the Yoruba Language* (London, 1843), iii–vii; the account is repeated in id., *A Grammar of the Yoruba Language* (London, 1852), iv–vii.

[34] The first Yoruba town to receive a missionary visit was Abẹokuta, in 1842; the missionaries reached New Ọyọ in 1853. A British Consul for the Bight of Benin, resident at Fernando Po, was appointed in 1849, and a separate consul for Lagos in 1852.

hearsay character, for all but the last years of the history of the Ọyọ empire. This necessitates a considerable reliance upon oral traditions in the reconstruction of Ọyọ history. It is, perhaps, no longer necessary to justify the use of oral traditions in the study of African history, since both the problems and the possibilities of using such material have been analysed at some length.[35] It is, however, useful to examine the nature of the traditional evidence on the Ọyọ empire in some detail, since a knowledge of the conditions under which traditions have been preserved and transmitted can assist in assessing their historical value.

Vansina, in his classic study of the historical use of oral tradition, has drawn attention to the importance of the distinction between traditions that are preserved and transmitted in a fixed verbal form and those that comprise merely a body of information which may be verbalized in a variety of ways.[36] Traditions that have fixed texts, it may be assumed, will have been transmitted with less alteration than those with free texts. In Yorubaland traditions of historical value that have fixed texts are represented primarily by two categories of oral poetry. There is, first, the immense corpus of poems connected with the cult of Ifa, the god of divination, many of which contain allusions to historical events. These poems are recited as part of the ritual of divination, and their transmission is closely controlled by the priests of Ifa.[37] Second, there are the numerous *oriki*, traditional praise-names or epithets associated with particular towns, titles, families, or individuals. An *oriki* may consist of a brief descriptive phrase, or of a poem of many lines. The *oriki* of individual kings and chiefs can be especially informative, sometimes recording at considerable length their exploits and ancestry.[38] Transmission of *oriki*

---

[35] The classic study is J. Vansina, *Oral Tradition: A Study in Historical Methodology* (London, 1965). Minor studies dealing specifically with Yoruba traditions include: S. O. Biobaku, 'Myths and Oral History', *Odu*, 1st series, 1 (n.d.), 12–17; id., 'The Problem of Traditional History, with special reference to Yoruba traditions', *JHSN* 1.1 (1956), 43–7; H. U. Beier, 'The Historical and Psychological Significance of Yoruba Myths', *Odu*, 1st series, 1 (n.d.), 17–25; P. C. Lloyd, 'Yoruba Myths—A Sociologist's Interpretation', *Odu*, 1st series, 2 (n.d.), 20–8; cf. also S. O. Biobaku (ed.), *Sources of Yoruba History* (Oxford, 1973).

[36] Vansina, *Oral Tradition*, 63.

[37] W. Abimbọla, 'Ifa Divination Poems as Sources for Historical Evidence', *Lagos Notes and Records*, 1.1 (1967), 17–26; see also the chapter by Abimbọla in Biobaku, *Sources of Yoruba History*.

[38] B. Awẹ, 'Praise Poems as Historical Data: The Example of the Yoruba *Oriki*', *Africa*, 44 (1974), 331–49.

B

is less closely controlled, but they are regularly recited by specialist groups of professional chanters.[39] It seems likely that careful study of this oral poetry would yield a great deal of information on the history of the Ọyọ empire. However, although the potential value for historical studies of Ifa poems and *oriki* has long been recognized, as yet little systematic use has been made of them in the reconstruction of Yoruba history.[40] Nor, it may be suggested, has adequate attention yet been directed to the problems of textual criticism involved in the use of such traditional poetry.[41] The present writer lacks the technical competence to undertake a study of Yoruba oral poetry, and only occasional and unsystematic use of *oriki* has been made in this work.

For the history of the Ọyọ empire, therefore, we have to rely primarily upon traditions that do not possess a fixed text. The basic narrative of events in Ọyọ history is provided by the traditions transmitted by the official historians of the kingdom, the *Arọkin*. The *Arọkin*, who are headed by an official entitled the *Ologbo*, are hereditary title-holders attached to the court of the *Alafin* and residing in a special apartment of the palace at Ọyọ, whose function is to recite the *oriki* of the successive *Alafin* on public occasions.[42] Their knowledge of history evidently derives mainly from these *oriki*, and the narrative of Ọyọ history which they offer is best regarded as an explanatory commentary on the *oriki*. The existence of official custodians of tradition such as the *Arọkin* can in general be regarded as a guarantee of the accurate transmission of traditions, but it also increases the likelihood of deliberate falsification of the traditions for political purposes. As Vansina remarks, 'an official tradition is less trustworthy as a historical source than a private one in so far as it is official, but more trustworthy in so far as it is much more carefully transmitted.'[43]

The official history of the *Arọkin* can be supplemented by traditions

[39] For a study of one of these groups, see S. A. Babalọla, *The Content and Form of Yoruba Ijala* (Oxford, 1966).

[40] For one exceptional, if not wholly convincing, venture, see J. A. Adedeji, 'The Origin of the Yoruba Masque Theatre: The Use of Ifa Divination Corpus as Historical Evidence', *African Notes*, 6.1 (1970), 70–86.

[41] Textual comparisons will have to take account of the numerous citations of traditional poetry in early local histories and similar works, dating in some cases from as early as the 1880s and 1890s. For the Ifa divination corpus, in particular, there are extensive quotations in the works of E. M. Lijadu, *Ifa* (Lagos, 1897) and *Ọrunmla* (Lagos, 1908).

[42] For the *Arọkin*, see Johnson, *History of the Yorubas*, 58, 125–6; B. A. Agiri, 'Early Oyo History Reconsidered', *History in Africa*, 2 (1975), 3.

[43] Vansina. *Oral Tradition*, 85.

collected from other title-holders of the capital and from subordinate towns of the Ọyọ kingdom. The oral traditions collected by the present writer have come mainly from these sources, and have been concerned with general information on the organization of the Ọyọ empire rather than with the narrative of events.[44]

It needs to be stressed that much of the 'oral tradition' used in the study of the Ọyọ empire has not been collected in the field by academically trained researchers, but comes at second hand from the writings of amateur historians. Of particular importance are the numerous local histories written by educated Yoruba, which include works in both English and Yoruba. Despite the early example of Samuel Crowther, mentioned above, historical studies by literate Yoruba were rare until the 1880s and 1890s, the first substantial work being the *Historical Notes on the Yoruba Country* of John O. George, written in 1895.[45] The first local historian to collect a significant body of oral traditions on the Ọyọ empire was Andrew L. Hethersett, who died in 1896, and whose material was posthumously incorporated in a school reading book, *Iwe Kika Ẹkẹrin*, published in 1912.[46] By far the most important work in this category is the *History of the Yorubas* of the Revd. Samuel Johnson, which though published only in 1921 was actually completed in 1897.[47] Johnson was a Sierra Leonean of Ọyọ extraction who served as Anglican Pastor at New Ọyọ in 1888–1901.[48] The early part of the *History*, which deals with the Ọyọ empire, is based primarily upon oral tradition (Johnson's main informants being the *Arọkin*), though Johnson also obtained information from people who claimed (perhaps falsely) to have first-hand recollections of the final period at Ọyọ Ile.[49] It would be difficult to exaggerate the importance of

[44] For details of informants interviewed, see below, Appendix on Sources.

[45] For the development of Yoruba historiography, see R. Law, 'Early Yoruba Historiography', *History in Africa*, 3 (1976), 69–89.

[46] A. L. Hethersett, in *Iwe Kika Ẹkẹrin li Ede Yoruba* (2nd? edn., Lagos, 1952), 49–78.

[47] Johnson, *History of the Yorubas*. Samuel Johnson died in 1901, and his book was prepared for publication by his brother, Dr. Obadiah Johnson.

[48] J. F. A. Ajayi, 'Samuel Johnson, Historian of the Yoruba', *Nigeria Magazine*, 81 (1964), 141–6.

[49] For Johnson's sources, see Johnson, *History of the Yorubas*, vii–viii. He names David Kukọmi of Ibadan as an informant who was 'a young man' during the reign at Ọyọ Ile of *Alafin* Abiọdun. But Abiọdun died probably in 1789 (cf. below, Ch. 4, p. 54), whereas Kukọmi died in 1895 at a reputed age of only 98: *Lagos Weekly Record*, 7 Sept. 1895. It is probable enough, however, that Johnson could have spoken to eyewitnesses of the events of the 1820s and 1830s.

Johnson's account of the Ọyọ empire, which inevitably forms the principal basis of any study of the period. Less substantial, but of interest as representing traditions collected independently of Johnson, is a brief history of Ọyọ by M. C. Adeyẹmi, a local schoolmaster, written in 1914.[50] There is also a more recent (c. 1961) history of Ọyọ, by Chief Samuel Ojo, the Bada of Ṣaki, one of the subordinate towns of the Ọyọ kingdom.[51] Chief Ojo's work, like many recent local histories, is primarily a conflation of earlier published accounts, including both local histories and European sources, but it also contains occasional items of original material. In addition to these histories of Ọyọ, there are several local histories of subordinate towns of the Ọyọ kingdom,[52] and of neighbouring kingdoms.

There is also a tradition of local historiography of Islamic inspiration in Yorubaland, centred on the Muslim town of Ilọrin. The most important work is an Arabic history of Ilọrin, the Ta'līf akhbār al-qurūn min 'umarā' bilād Ilūrin of Aḥmad b. Abī Bakr (alias Abū Ikọkọrọ), written in 1912.[53] Abū Ikọkọrọ claims to have been the first to write a history of Ilọrin,[54] but this is not altogether accurate, since a manuscript containing an account in Hausa of the foundation of the Ilọrin emirate was obtained in 1901 by the German explorer Mischlich from al-Hajj 'Umar, a scholar of Kete Krachi in northern Ghana.[55]

The records of the British colonial administration established over Yorubaland at the end of the nineteenth century also contain a

---

[50] M. C. Adeyẹmi, Iwe Itan Ọyọ-Ile ati Ọyọ Isisiyi abi Agọ-d'Ọyọ (Ibadan, 1914).

[51] S. Ojo, Iwe Itan Ọyọ, Ikoyi, ati Afijio (Ṣaki, n.d. but c. 1961). Chief Ojo has also written several other historical works, which are listed in the Bibliography.

[52] Useful histories exist of the towns of Ogbomọṣọ, Ẹdẹ, and Ṣaki: N. D. Oyerinde, Iwe Itan Ogbomọṣọ (Jos, 1934); E. A. Olunlade, Ẹdẹ: A Brief History (Ibadan, 1961); S. Ojo, Iwe Itan Ṣaki (Ṣaki, n.d. but c. 1967). Local histories of the towns of Iwo, Ọfa, and Isẹyin are also reported to exist, but I have not been able to see copies of these: E. A. Kẹnyọ, Itan Isẹdalẹ Iwo (Ibadan, 1962); J. B. Ọlafimihan, Iwe Itan Ọfa (Ọfa, 1950); W. Adeleke, Iwe Itan Ilu Isẹyin (Ibadan, 1964).

[53] For this work, see B. G. Martin, 'A New Arabic History of Ilorin', Centre of Arabic Documentation, University of Ibadan, Research Bulletin, 1.2 (1965), 20–7. A section of it is quoted in Hodgkin, Nigerian Perspectives, 279–82.

[54] Martin, 'A New Arabic History of Ilorin', 23.

[55] A German translation of this manuscript is given in A. Mischlich and J. Lippert, 'Beiträge zur Geschichte der Haussastaaten', Mittheilungen des Seminars für Orientalische Sprachen zu Berlin, 6 (1905), Dritte Abtheilung, 241–2. An English translation of the German translation is given in J. A. Burdon, Northern Nigeria: Historical Notes on Certain Emirates and Tribes (London, 1909), 98.

substantial amount of traditional material on the history of the Ọyọ empire, partly because historical precedents were frequently cited in the local disputes which it had to adjudicate. In particular, administrators often prepared formal reports on their districts, which regularly include historical sections recording the local traditions. An example of especial importance is the Intelligence Report on Ọyọ Division by J. MacRae Simpson, written in 1938.[56]

The use of oral traditions recorded in written local histories and administrative records might perhaps be questioned. Vansina, after all, has warned us to beware of informants who have created a personal interpretation of history out of traditions from different sources.[57] Ideally, it might be argued, oral traditions should be collected in the field only, and not taken at second hand from written sources. But this is an unrealistic attitude. These written sources preserve many traditions which are no longer current in oral form, and researchers in the field will in any case often find themselves referred by informants to the written histories. The intervention of a further intermediary in the chain of transmission certainly complicates the evaluation of oral traditions, particularly where local historians produce a conflation of traditions from different sources, and of material from written sources also, rather than a straightforward recension of the local traditions. But these problems are no greater than, indeed no different from, those regularly faced by Classical or Medieval historians working entirely from written sources.

As regards the general issue of the use of traditional evidence, it may be that too much has sometimes been made of the supposed difficulty and novelty of making use of material of this sort. The use of oral traditions, after all, goes back to the 'father of history' himself, Herodotus. The principal sources of inaccuracy in oral traditions are by no means mysterious, and can be allowed for in evaluating them. There is, first, the relatively obvious problem of patriotic and similar bias. Official court historians such as the *Arọkin* will evidently present the official court view of history, and in general informants will give the version of events which reflects best upon their own kingdom, town, or family. Discreditable episodes, such as defeats in war, tend to be forgotten. But this sort of bias, which is by

---

[56] J. MacRae Simpson, 'An Intelligence Report on the Oyo Division of the Oyo Province', 1938 (Rhodes House Library, Oxford: MSS. Afr. s. 526).
[57] Vansina, *Oral Tradition*, 191–2.

no means confined to oral traditions, can often be detected and allowed for by comparing accounts of the same events from different sources. It is also likely that accounts which reflect discredit upon the informant's group represent authentic traditions, since the informant would have no motive to fabricate such an account. Second, it must be remembered that the desire to preserve a record of the past for its own sake has been a relatively minor motivation in the preservation and transmission of historical traditions, and the ulterior motives involved in each case may have led to falsification of the tradition. For example, traditions may be repeated for purposes of entertainment or moral edification, in which case they may be recast for greater dramatic or didactic impact. More interesting are those cases where the traditions fulfil a political function, being cited as precedents or proofs in support of political claims or in justification of existing political arrangements. This sort of bias, too, is not difficult to detect and control, if the political function of the particular tradition concerned is known or can be surmised. Even traditions which are demonstrably tendentious, moreover, may be of great historical value, as evidence for past propaganda and ideology rather than for the actual events which they purport to describe.

Oral traditions no less than written sources can be subjected to rational appraisal, and made to yield information of value to the historian. Often, indeed, the two categories of material confirm and supplement each other. The historian of Ọyọ, moreover, must soon become aware that the crucial distinction is not between written and oral, or between contemporary and traditional, but between first-hand and hearsay sources. As has been seen, by far the greater part of the *contemporary* material on the Ọyọ empire consists of hearsay reports. It is not clear that the oral traditions deserve less credence than this contemporary material. In both cases, the information was transmitted orally before being recorded in writing. That the transmission operated in one case across space and in the other through time is not obviously a distinction of fundamental importance.

§4. CONCLUSION

The foregoing sources of evidence, it is suggested, do provide the basis for a meaningful reconstruction of the history of the Ọyọ empire. However, the present writer cannot but be aware of the deficiencies of the available evidence, and that what follows cannot be offered as in any sense a 'definitive' history of the Ọyọ empire. No historian ever reconstructs history 'as it actually was':[58] he has to be content to present it, in the words of an early Greek historian, 'as it seems to him'.[59] The inherent temptation of the historian to imaginative fancy is controlled by the discipline of the evidence. Clearly, the poorer and sparser the evidence, the less solid is the historical reconstruction erected upon it.

The state of the evidence also imposes a particular approach to the subject. It would have been preferable to present the history of the Ọyọ empire in the form of a coherent narrative of its rise and fall, with analytical excursuses interpolated as the requirements of interpretation demanded. In the event, this seemed impossible, without begging far too many of the controversial questions. It is therefore only for the pre-imperial period, for which the evidence, being entirely traditional, is fairly coherent (Chapter 3), and for the last forty or fifty years of the empire (c. 1790–c. 1836), for which evidence is relatively abundant (Chapters 12–14), that I have ventured to adopt a narrative framework. For the greater part of the imperial period (c. 1600–c. 1790), it has been necessary to adopt a topical approach, with detailed analyses of different aspects and areas of the empire: first, in Chapter 4, an attempt is made to construct a chronological framework; then, in Chapter 5, the political institutions and internal history of the Ọyọ capital are considered; in Chapters 6, 7, and 8 the geographical extent and administrative character of Ọyọ rule over the different categories of subjects in the empire are analysed; while Chapters 9 and 10 explore the military and economic bases of Ọyọ power. Only after the numerous problems in each of these individual fields have been resolved, or at least aired, is some attempt made, in Chapter 11, to present a synthesis and to offer a general perspective on the rise and expansion of the Ọyọ empire.

[58] *wie es eigentlich gewesen* (Leopold von Ranke).
[59] ὡς ἐμοὶ δοκεῖ (Hekataios).

CHAPTER 3

The Early History of Ọyọ

THE history of the Ọyọ 'empire', properly speaking, begins only in the early seventeenth century. Earlier, it does not appear that Ọyọ was a state of great importance or territorial extent. The history of the 'pre-imperial' period is nevertheless of interest, since it provides an essential background for the understanding of the subsequent development of the empire, and in this chapter an attempt is made to delineate at least the most significant features of the history of Ọyọ before the seventeenth century. It needs to be stressed, however, that the history of this earlier period, which has to be reconstructed entirely from oral traditions, is in many respects confused and obscure. The reconstruction offered in this chapter is, therefore, even more speculative than the rest of the book.

§1. ILE IFẸ AND THE ORIGINS OF KINGSHIP

Archaeological evidence demonstrates the antiquity of human settlement in Yorubaland,[1] while linguistic evidence suggests that the Yoruba (in the sense of speakers of the Yoruba language) have long occupied their present homeland.[2] The Yoruba have probably lived in Yorubaland for some thousands of years. The development of organized states, ruled by kings (ọba), is no doubt much more recent, but precision in this matter is impossible. Oral traditions do, however, present an account of the origins of kingship in Yorubaland, and we shall begin by considering this.

The traditions of the Yoruba peoples, including the Ọyọ, trace the origins of kingship to the town of Ifẹ, or Ile Ifẹ. The royal dynasties of the principal Yoruba kingdoms, and also of the neighbouring non-Yoruba kingdom of Benin, are supposedly descended from a

[1] An excavation at Iwo Eleru, near Akurẹ in eastern Yorubaland, has yielded evidence of settlement dating from about the eleventh or tenth century B.C.: F. Willett, 'A Survey of Recent Results in the Radiocarbon Chronology of Western and Northern Africa', *JAH* 12 (1971), 354.

[2] R. G. Armstrong, 'The Use of Linguistic and Ethnographic Data in the Study of Idoma and Yoruba History', in J. Vansina, R. Mauny, and L. V. Thomas (eds.), *The Historian in Tropical Africa* (London, 1964), 127–44.

common ancestor, Oduduwa, who reigned as king at Ile Ifẹ. Of the arrival of Oduduwa at Ile Ifẹ, different accounts are given. In some traditions, Ile Ifẹ is presented as the site of the creation of the habitable world, from which all mankind dispersed over the earth. The surface of the earth was covered with water, and Oduduwa descended by a chain from heaven to create the dry land.[3] Other traditions make Oduduwa an immigrant from outside Yorubaland who settled at Ile Ifẹ. An early example of such traditions of migration is given by the Sokoto scholar Muhammad Bello, according to whom the Yoruba were 'remnants of the Banū Kan'ān, which is the tribe of Nimrūd' who had been expelled from Iraq.[4] Ọyọ tradition, as represented by Johnson, claims that Oduduwa was a son of Lamurudu (Nimrūd?), a king of Mecca, and had been expelled from Mecca for apostasizing from Islam,[5] while another version makes the ancestors of the Yoruba come from Medina.[6] Other accounts locate the original homeland of the Yoruba rather nearer, for example in Nupe[7] or in Hausaland.[8] Some traditions appear to represent a conflation of the creation and migration accounts: according to these, the Yoruba migrated from another land, came to a vast expanse of water across which they set out either by wading or by canoe, and ultimately created dry land in the middle of it.[9]

During Oduduwa's lifetime, or soon after his death, his sons and grandsons are said to have dispersed from Ile Ifẹ to found their own kingdoms. Various lists are given of the original kingdoms founded at this time. Several versions name six original kingdoms,[10] Johnson names seven,[11] and other versions name sixteen.[12] There is considerable disagreement about the identity of the original kingdoms, but most versions agree in including among them Ọyọ, Ketu, and Benin.

---

[3] The legend of the creation of mankind at Ile Ifẹ was first recorded at Ọyọ Ile in 1830: R. and J. Lander, *Journal of an Expedition*, i. 180. Johnson, *History of the Yorubas*, 143, describes this as the Ifẹ tradition.

[4] Arnett, *Rise of the Sokoto Fulani*, 16; Hodgkin, *Nigerian Perspectives*, 78.

[5] Johnson, *History of the Yorubas*, 3–5.

[6] Adeyẹmi, *Iwe Itan Ọyọ*, 5.

[7] E. M. Lijadu, 'Fragments of Ẹgba National History', *Ẹgba Government Gazette*, 1904, no. 1.

[8] George, *Historical Notes on the Yoruba Country*, 29.

[9] Crowther, *Vocabulary of the Yoruba Language*, i–ii; George, *Historical Notes on the Yoruba Country*, 18.

[10] e.g. Bowen, *Central Africa*, 266; George, *Historical Notes on the Yoruba Country*, 16; Lijadu, 'Fragments of Ẹgba National History'.

[11] Johnson, *History of the Yorubas*, 7–8.

[12] e.g. E. A. Kẹnyọ, *Founder of the Yoruba Nation* (Lagos, 1959), 26.

The principal importance of the dynastic link with Ile Ifẹ lay in the fact that descent from a son or grandson of Oduduwa was considered necessary to validate a king's claim to wear an *ade*, or crown with a beaded fringe.[13]

It is difficult to assess what degree of truth, if any, there is in these traditions. However, the suggestion that Ile Ifẹ was the centre of an early monarchy seems to be supported by archaeological evidence from that city, principally the remarkable brass and terracotta sculptures found there, which appear to be associated with some form of sacred kingship.[14] The date at which this monarchy emerged is as yet uncertain, but radiocarbon dates indicate that the 'classical' period of Ifẹ culture, during which the terracotta sculptures were being made, extended from about the twelfth to the fourteenth century.[15] It seems very likely that Ile Ifẹ was, in fact, the first place in the Yoruba area where the institution of kingship emerged, and it may well be that the diffusion of kingship from Ile Ifẹ was effected at least in part by the migration of Ifẹ princes. It is not, however, necessary to believe that, as the traditions claim, the dissemination of kingship from Ile Ifẹ took place at a single stroke, in a single generation: the genealogical tidiness of the traditions is probably artificial.[16] Nor is it necessary to believe in the historicity of the dynastic link with Ile Ifẹ in every case where it is claimed. Since origin from Ile Ifẹ was necessary to secure recognition of kingly status, it is very likely that the claim of descent from Oduduwa was sometimes fabricated by kings anxious to legitimate their rule.

If the early emergence of kingship at Ile Ifẹ can probably be accepted, it is less easy to explain. Certain traditions, as has been seen, associate the origins of kingship with immigrants from outside Yorubaland. Those versions which bring these immigrants from Mecca or Medina can certainly be dismissed as reflecting no more than the desire of some Yoruba kings to connect themselves with

[13] Johnson, *History of the Yorubas*, 8.

[14] For these sculptures, see F. Willett, *Ife in the History of West African Sculpture* (London, 1967).

[15] M. Posnansky and R. McIntosh, 'New Radiocarbon Dates for Northern and Western Africa', *JAH* 17 (1976), 169.

[16] For a parallel case, cf. the traditions relating to the foundation of the kingdoms of Dahomey and Porto Novo by princes of Allada. These assert that the founders of the two kingdoms were brothers: e.g. Le Herissé, *L'Ancien Royaume de Dahomey*, 276–9. In fact, it appears that something like a century separated the foundation of the two states: cf. I. A. Akinjogbin, *Dahomey and its Neighbours 1708–1818* (Cambridge, 1967), 21–2.

the prestigious civilization of Islam;[17] the apparently anti-Islamic implications of the version recorded by Johnson, in which Oduduwa is expelled from Mecca for relapsing into paganism, probably reflect an attempt to legitimize Ọyọ resistance to the militantly Islamic Sokoto Caliphate in the early nineteenth century.[18] But the versions claiming origin from less distant areas to the north of Yorubaland are less easy to discount. Some modern scholars have therefore sought the explanation of the emergence of kingship in Yorubaland in the arrival of conquering immigrants from the north, from Nupe and Borgu.[19] However, Yoruba traditions offer claims of autochthonous origins, in the 'creation' versions of the Oduduwa legends, as well as stories of immigration, and it is not clear why these should be given less weight than the others. It may be that originally the 'creation' and 'migration' traditions referred to distinct autochthonous and immigrant elements in the Yoruba population; and it will be argued below that Ọyọ, in particular, may well have received immigrant royal dynasties from the north. But there seems little reason for crediting these hypothetical immigrants with any formative role in the evolution of Yoruba kingship.

A possibly more profitable approach to the problem of the origins of Yoruba kingship might be to connect this problem with that of the development of Yoruba urbanism. It is admittedly uncertain how early large urban settlements were established in Yorubaland.[20] But it is noteworthy that the existence of towns in Yorubaland seems to be correlated with the existence of kings: the north-eastern (Yagba, Bunu, and Ajumu) Yoruba, who do not live in towns, also lack

[17] Cf. the concern of Christian Yoruba such as Samuel Johnson to connect the Yoruba with Biblical history: e.g. Johnson, *History of the Yorubas*, 6–9; George, *Historical Notes on the Yoruba Country*, Introduction.

[18] Cf. the interpretation of the analogous traditions about Kisra, the dynastic ancestor of the Bariba kingdoms, by P. Stevens, 'The Kisra Legend and the Distortion of Historical Tradition', *JAH* 16 (1975), 185–200. It is significant that according to Johnson, *History of the Yorubas*, 3, Oduduwa had two brothers who were expelled with him from Mecca, and who became the kings of Gobir (a kingdom in Hausaland) and Kukawa (i.e. Bornu), two states prominent in the resistance to the Sokoto *jihad* in northern Nigeria.

[19] J. D. Fage, *A History of West Africa* (Cambridge, 1969), 42; cf. R. Oliver and B. M. Fagan, *Africa in the Iron Age* (Cambridge, 1975), 183–4.

[20] W. Bascom, 'Les Premiers fondements historiques de l'urbanisme Yoruba', *Présence africaine*, 23 (1959), 22–40, attempts to demonstrate the early existence of towns in Yorubaland from contemporary sources, but most of the references which he cites strictly attest the continuity only of political units, not of urban settlements. Note, however, that Ijẹbu Ode is described as a 'large city' as early as c. 1505: Pacheco Pereira, *Esmeraldo de Situ Orbis*, 117.

powerful monarchies.[21] The precise character of the connection between urbanism and kingship is not easy to determine. It has been suggested that towns grew up around the palaces of pre-existing sacred kings.[22] But it is perhaps more likely that the institution of kingship was evolved in response to the problems of administering heterogeneous urban communities.[23] The development of kingship, on this argument, could be seen as a consequence of urbanization. This is perhaps not all that helpful, since the historical origins of Yoruba urbanism are notoriously obscure. Those who believe in the crucial role of northern immigrants argue that urban settlement in Yorubaland had a military origin, being devised for the defence of foreign conquerors against hostile natives,[24] and it is certainly the case that Yoruba towns had important military functions, being regularly furnished with defensive walls.[25] But Yoruba towns had commercial as well as military functions,[26] and it seems probable that their development was related primarily to their role as markets for local and long-distance trade. Ancient Ile Ifẹ was certainly a commercial centre, since the brass used in its sculptures must have been imported from the north, and there is archaeological evidence for the manufacture there on a substantial scale of glass beads.[27]

§2. THE FOUNDATION OF ỌYỌ

The traditions of Ọyọ claim that the kingdom was founded by Ọranyan, or Ọranmiyan, one of the sons of Oduduwa who dispersed

[21] For the political organization of the north-eastern Yoruba, and the suggestion that this resembles that which existed among other Yoruba groups before the emergence of powerful monarchies, see esp. A. Obayẹmi, 'The Yoruba and Edo-speaking peoples and their Neighbours before 1600', in J. F. A. Ajayi and M. Crowder (eds.), *History of West Africa*, vol. i (2nd edn., London, 1976), 201–8.

[22] P. Wheatley, 'The Significance of Traditional Yoruba Urbanism', *Comparative Studies in Society and History*, 12 (1970), 393–423.

[23] Cf. the argument of Abdullahi Smith on the origins of kingship in Hausaland: A. Smith, 'Some Considerations Relating to the Formation of States in Hausaland', *JHSN* 5.3 (1970), 329–46.

[24] Fage, *History of West Africa*, 42; Oliver and Fagan, *Africa in the Iron Age*, 184.

[25] Cf. J. F. A. Ajayi and R. Smith, *Yoruba Warfare in the Nineteenth Century* (2nd edn., Cambridge, 1971), 23–8.

[26] For the commercial functions of Yoruba towns, see e.g. Krapf-Askari, *Yoruba Towns and Cities*, 99–105.

[27] For the bead-making industry at Ile Ifẹ, see Willett, *Ife in the History of West African Sculpture*, 106–8.

from Ile Ifẹ.[28] It is noteworthy that another of the kingdoms whose dynasties claim derivation from Ile Ifẹ, that of Benin, also claims Ọranyan as a royal ancestor.[29] The primary associations of Ọranyan, however, seem to be with Ile Ifẹ rather than with Ọyọ or Benin. Ọyọ and Benin traditions concede that Ọranyan returned to Ile Ifẹ and was buried there, while Ifẹ tradition maintains that Ọranyan never reigned at Ọyọ or Benin, but was king at Ile Ifẹ, though he spent some time (before his accession) at both Ọyọ and Benin assisting the local rulers and left sons in these towns who subsequently became kings in them.[30] The Ọyọ and Benin traditions seem to represent attempts to appropriate a prominent figure from Ifẹ history as the local founder. In Ọyọ tradition, Ọranyan's son Ṣango, who was worshipped as the god of thunder, seems far more important than Ọranyan himself as the dynastic ancestor. Certainly, the cult of Ṣango was much more centrally associated with royal power.[31] In one version, indeed, which perhaps represents the original tradition, it is asserted that it was Ṣango, rather than Ọranyan, who migrated from Ile Ifẹ and founded Ọyọ.[32]

Although the dynastic link with Ọranyan and Oduduwa was of crucial importance in legitimating the *Alafin*'s claim to royal status, there are grounds for questioning the historicity of the traditional claim of derivation from Ile Ifẹ. In addition to the conventional story of foundation by a prince of Ile Ifẹ, there are other traditions which connect the royal dynasty of Ọyọ with its immediate northern neighbours, the non-Yoruba Nupe and Bariba.

The Nupe, called in Yoruba the *Tapa*, live to the north-east of Ọyọ. One tradition, recorded by the local historian Lijadu, asserts that Ọyọ Ile was founded by a hunter, named Mọmọ (Muhammad), who came from Ogodo, a Nupe town on the south bank of the River Niger.[33] A more common story, which appears, for example, in

[28] Johnson, *History of the Yorubas*, 8–12.
[29] J. U. Egharevba, *A Short History of Benin* (3rd edn., Ibadan, 1960), 6–8.
[30] NAI, OYOPROF. 1/203, Ọni of Ifẹ to District Officer, Ifẹ, 9 Oct. 1931; J. A. Ademakinwa, *Ifẹ, Cradle of the Yorubas* (Lagos, 1958), i. 45–6 and ii. 22–3.
[31] For the cult of Ṣango at Ọyọ, see P. Morton-Williams, 'An Outline of the Cosmology and Cult Organization of the Ọyọ Yoruba', *Africa*, 34 (1964), 255; J. Wescott and P. Morton-Williams, 'The Symbolism and Ritual Context of the Yoruba *Laba Shango*', *Journal of the Royal Anthropological Institute*, 92 (1962), 23–37.
[32] Johnson, *History of the Yorubas*, 150.
[33] Lijadu, 'Fragments of Ẹgba National History'.

Johnson's *History*, speaks merely of an early dynastic marriage alliance between Ọyọ and Nupe. According to this version, Ọranyan, the founder of Ọyọ, married a daughter of a Nupe king called Elempe, the issue of this marriage being Ṣango, who became the third ruler of Ọyọ.[34]

The Bariba occupy the land of Borgu, to the north-west of Ọyọ. One tradition, recorded by the local historian Adeyẹmi, asserts that the founders of Ọyọ, after migrating from Medina, lived for some time with the Bariba before moving south into the Ọyọ area.[35] This account is supported by the traditions of the Bariba themselves. Bariba tradition claims that the principal dynasties of Borgu are descended from the sons of Kisra, an immigrant prince from Mecca: the Ọyọ are represented as a junior branch of the migration under Kisra.[36] In some versions the king of Bussa, the senior Bariba ruler, is said to have given the founder of Ọyọ a magic serpent, which led him to the site of Ọyọ Ile.[37] This serpent is also recalled in the version of Ọyọ tradition given by Johnson, though he offers no hint of the alleged common descent of the Ọyọ and Bariba dynasties. In Johnson's account Ọranyan, having left Ile Ifẹ, sought the assistance in founding his kingdom of the king of the Bariba, and the latter gave him a boa constrictor which led him to the site of Ọyọ Ile.[38]

In view of the traditions recorded by Lijadu and Adeyẹmi, it seems probable that the account of the foundation of Ọyọ given by Johnson, according to which the founder of Ọyọ (Ọranyan) came from Ile Ifẹ, received assistance from a Bariba king, and married a Nupe princess, is the result of the fusion of three originally distinct traditions deriving the royal dynasty from Ile Ifẹ, from Borgu, and from Nupe. The existence of these rival traditions clearly requires explanation. Of the three traditions, scepticism seems most justified with regard to the one that connects the Ọyọ royal dynasty with Ile Ifẹ. Given the strong prejudice among the Yoruba that only descendants of Oduduwa could validly claim royal status, a tradition of

---

[34] Johnson, *History of the Yorubas*, 149. 'Elempe' cannot be identified with any historical Nupe ruler: the name seems to be a conventional Yoruba term for a Nupe King.

[35] Adeyẹmi, *Iwe Itan Ọyọ*, 5–6.

[36] O. Temple, *Notes on the Tribes, Provinces, Emirates and States of the Northern Provinces of Nigeria* (2nd edn., London, 1922), 376; L. Frobenius, *The Voice of Africa* (London, 1913), ii. 618.

[37] M. Crowder, *Revolt in Bussa: A Study of British 'Native Administration' in Nigerian Borgu, 1902–1935* (London, 1973), 29–30.

[38] Johnson, *History of the Yorubas*, 11.

origin from Ile Ifẹ might readily have been fabricated in order to claim a spurious legitimacy for the rulers of Ọyọ. On the other hand, the traditions attributing a foreign origin to the Ọyọ dynasty seem less likely to have been invented, precisely because they put in doubt the dynasty's legitimacy. The existence of apparently contradictory traditions of origin from Nupe and from Borgu is probably to be accounted for by the fact that Ọyọ received dynasties from both its northern neighbours in turn.[39] A tradition reported by Frobenius, in fact, does state explicitly that there were two successive dynasties of *Alafin* at Ọyọ Ile, of which the first originated from Nupe and the second from Borgu.[40] As will be argued below, there are grounds for suggesting that the imposition of a new dynasty from Borgu occurred during the sixteenth century.

It is not possible to assign a date to the foundation of the Ọyọ kingdom. The foundation of Ọyọ has been attributed, by different writers, to the tenth century,[41] to around 1300,[42] and to the late fourteenth or early fifteenth century.[43] But there is as yet no worthwhile evidence on this point.[44]

§3. ỌYỌ BEFORE THE SIXTEENTH CENTURY

Of the earliest period of Ọyọ history, before the sixteenth century, very little is known. It is questionable whether any credence should be accorded to the traditional accounts of the earliest *Alafin*. As will be seen below, the Ọyọ kingdom suffered a temporary collapse, and probably also a change of dynasty, during the sixteenth century, a circumstance which is likely to have confused and distorted the transmission of traditions about the earlier period. Certainly, the earliest portion of the Ọyọ king-list looks very suspicious. According to Johnson, Ọranyan was succeeded as *Alafin* by the elder of his two sons, called Ajaka or Dada. Ajaka was deposed in favour of his

---

[39] An essentially similar conclusion is reached by Agiri, 'Early Oyo History Reconsidered', 8–10, though his reconstruction differs considerably in detail from that offered here.

[40] Frobenius, *Voice of Africa*, i. 177, 210, and ii. 629.

[41] Ojo, *Iwe Itan Ọyọ*, 204, places the accession of Ọranyan as king at Ile Ifẹ in 892 and his death in 1042 (*sic*): his foundation of Ọyọ occurred at an unspecified time between these two dates.

[42] Oliver and Fagan, *Africa in the Iron Age*, 183.

[43] R. Smith, *Kingdoms of the Yoruba* (London, 1969), 103–4; P. Morton-Williams, 'The Influence of Habitat and Trade on the Polities of Oyo and Ashanti', in M. Douglas and P. M. Kaberry (eds.), *Man in Africa* (London, 1969), 89.

[44] See further below, Ch. 4, p. 59.

younger brother Ṣango, but was restored to the throne after Ṣango's death, and was succeeded by his son Aganju.[45] Another account, however, places these four kings in a different order, making Aganju the father of Ọranyan rather than, as does Johnson, his grandson.[46] Moreover, the fact that Ọranyan, Dada, Ṣango, and Aganju were all worshipped as gods must raise doubts about their historical existence.[47] After Aganju's death, Johnson relates that one of his wives, called Iyayun, ruled as Regent until the majority of her son Kọri, who became the next *Alafin*, and that Kọri in turn was succeeded by Oluaṣo.[48] Iyayun, Kọri, and Oluaṣo are very probably historical figures, though it is unclear how much genuine tradition was remembered about them. It appears, moreover, that some early *Alafin* are omitted from Johnson's account: in particular, a certain *Alafin* Oluodo, who is said to have been omitted from the official king-list because he was killed while campaigning against the Nupe.[49] The entire early portion of the king-list seems factitious, and was probably constructed at some point in or after the sixteenth century out of fragmentary traditional and mythological elements.

However, whatever doubts may exist about the historicity of individual *Alafin* in the earliest portion of the Ọyọ king-list, it is likely that some of the incidents which have become associated with their names are historical. There are, indeed, a number of elements in these traditions which seem acceptable. One of these is the assertion, in certain stories, that the capital of the Ọyọ kingdom was originally not at Ọyọ Ile but at a town called Oko, whence it is said to have been removed to Ọyọ Ile by Ṣango.[50] It is easier to understand the suppression of this detail in most versions than its

[45] Johnson, *History of the Yorubas*, 148–55.

[46] Bowen, *Central Africa*, 316; A. B. Ellis, *The Yoruba-Speaking Peoples of the Slave Coast of West Africa* (London, 1894), 43–5.

[47] For Dada, a little known deity described as the 'god of new-born babes and vegetables', see Ellis, *Yoruba-Speaking Peoples*, 76; for Aganju, an earth deity whose cult had 'fallen into disuse', ibid. 44.

[48] Johnson, *History of the Yorubas*, 155–8.

[49] R. Smith, 'List of Alafin of Ọyọ', *The African Historian*, 1.3 (1965), 53–4; id., 'The Alafin in Exile', 74, n. 52. Smith himself places the reign of *Alafin* Oluodo between those of Ọbalokun and Ajagbo, in the seventeenth century, apparently on the grounds that Ajagbo's *oriki* describes him as *ọmọ Oluodo*, 'son of Oluodo'; but the phrase *ọmọ Oluodo* has to be interpreted here as 'descendant of Oluodo', since it also appears in the *oriki* of two earlier *Alafin*, Oluaṣo and Ofinran. These *oriki* were recorded for the author at the palace in Ọyọ.

[50] Johnson, *History of the Yorubas*, 12, 144, 150.

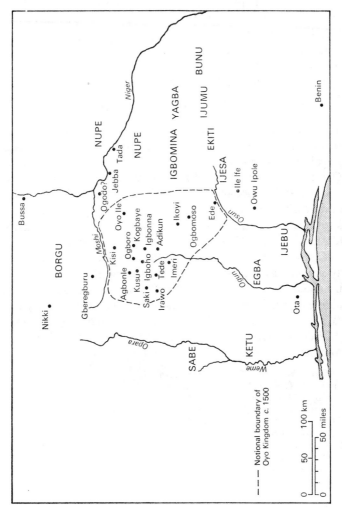

Map 2. Ọyọ in the pre-imperial period.

interpolation in one. Unfortunately the location of the site of the earlier capital at Oko is not known, though some have suggested that it was further north or closer to the River Niger than Ọyọ Ile.[51]

It is also possible to infer something about the extent of the Ọyọ kingdom in this period. Ọyọ tradition claims that Ọyọ was from its foundation the most powerful of the kingdoms in the Yoruba area,[52] but the detailed traditions relating to the early *Alafin* lend no support to this claim. These suggest rather that Ọyọ was engaged during this period in a struggle for hegemony with other towns situated quite close to Ọyọ Ile. There is, for example, a story that Ọranyan originally had no crown (*ade*), until he seized the crown belonging to the *Aladikun*, the ruler of Adikun, a town about 45 miles south-west of Ọyọ Ile.[53] *Alafin* Aganju is similarly said to have fought a successful war against the *Onisambo*, the ruler of Ọgbọrọ, about 50 miles west of Ọyọ Ile, in which the *Onisambo* was assisted by the neighbouring towns of Imẹri, Tede, and Igbọnna.[54] Ọgbọrọ tradition claims that the first *Onisambo* was an elder brother of Oranyan, implying that this town was once superior in status to Ọyọ,[55] and it seems likely that Aganju's war effected a transfer of the headship of the area from Ọgbọrọ to Ọyọ. The most distant Ọyọ venture recorded in this early period was the foundation of the town of Ẹdẹ, on the River Ọṣun about 80 miles south of Ọyọ Ile, which is said to have been established as a frontier post to check raids on Ọyọ territory by the Ijẹṣa, who lived across the Ọṣun. The foundation of Ẹdẹ is attributed, in different accounts, either to Ṣango[56] or to *Alafin* Kọri.[57]

Another very interesting tradition relating to this early period

---

[51] Morton-Williams, 'The Influence of Habitat and Trade on Oyo and Ashanti', 89; T. Shaw, 'A Note on Trade and the Tsoede Bronzes', *West African Journal of Archaeology*, 3 (1973), 236.

[52] On this claim, see further below, Ch. 7, pp. 123-6.

[53] Ojo, *Iwe Itan Ọyọ*, 23; Babayẹmi, 'Upper Ogun', 76-7.

[54] Johnson, *History of the Yorubas*, 155. The same war seems to be described in the local traditions of Ogbomọṣọ and Ṣaki, which claim that these towns supported Ọyọ, but these accounts name Agbọnle instead of Igbọnna among the towns allied against Ọyọ, and attribute the war to the reign of a later (seventeenth century) *Alafin*, Ajagbo: Oyerinde, *Iwe Itan Ogbomọṣọ*, 10-13; Ojo, *Iwe Itan Ṣaki*, 31.

[55] Babayẹmi, 'Upper Ogun', 77.

[56] Hethersett, in *Iwe Kika Ẹkẹrin*, 50-1; D. W. MacRow, 'Natural Ruler—A Yoruba Conception of Monarchy', *Nigeria Magazine*, 47 (1955), 229-31.

[57] Johnson, *History of the Yorubas*, 156. Another source reconciles the two versions by attributing to Ṣango the founding of Ẹdẹ and to Kọri the appointment of the first ruler of Ẹdẹ to bear the title *Timi*: Olunlade, *Ẹdẹ: A Brief History*, 2-3.

records that Ọyọ was at one time tributary to another of the Yoruba kingdoms, that of Owu. It is said that Ajaka in his first reign was compelled to pay tribute to the *Olowu* of Owu, but that Ọyọ was then liberated by Ṣango.[58] Whatever doubts there may be about the historicity of Ajaka and Ṣango, there seems no reason to doubt the essential truth of this story. At least, it is difficult to see what motive the Ọyọ could have had for inventing it. In the eighteenth century, the capital of Owu was situated in southern Yorubaland, over 100 miles from Ọyọ Ile,[59] but there is evidence suggesting that in earlier times the city of Owu had been located further north, in the Ọgbọrọ area.[60] The conflict between Ọyọ and Owu may therefore have been part of the struggle for supremacy between Ọyọ and the other towns in northern Yorubaland.

A final feature of the traditions about the early *Alafin* which can be accepted as historical is the occurrence of wars between the Ọyọ and the Nupe, their immediate north-eastern neighbours. Clashes with the Nupe are attributed to Ọranyan[61] and to Ajaka during his second reign.[62] There is also the story of *Alafin* Oluodo, who is said to have been drowned while fleeing across the River Niger during a campaign against the Nupe.[63] These wars were probably fought mainly against the Nupe groups to the south of the Niger, though the story of Oluodo suggests occasional forays across the river into the Nupe heartland. As we shall see, during the sixteenth century pressure from the Nupe was to lead to a temporary collapse of the Ọyọ kingdom.

§4. THE NUPE CONQUEST OF ỌYỌ

Under *Alafin* Onigbogi, the son and successor of Oluaṣo, the Nupe are said to have invaded the Ọyọ kingdom and destroyed the capital at Ọyọ Ile.[64] From the position of Onigbogi in the Ọyọ king-list,

[58] Johnson, *History of the Yorubas*, 149.

[59] At the site called Owu Ipole, about 20 miles south-west of Ile Ifẹ. By the early nineteenth century, the capital had been moved from Owu Ipole to Owu Ogbere, a site just east of Ibadan: R. Law, 'The Owu War in Yoruba History', *JHSN* 7.1 (1973), 143–4; A. L. Mabogunjẹ and J. Omer-Cooper, *Owu in Yoruba History* (Ibadan, 1971), 31–41.

[60] NAI, IBAPROF. 3/4, H. Childs, 'A Report on the Western District of the Ibadan Division of Oyo Province', 1934, §52; cf. Mabogunjẹ and Omer-Cooper, *Owu in Yoruba History*, 34–6; Law, 'The Owu War in Yoruba History', 144.

[61] Johnson, *History of the Yorubas*, 10.

[62] Ibid. 52.

[63] Smith, 'List of Alafin', 53–4; id., 'The Alafin in Exile', 74, n. 52.

[64] Johnson, *History of the Yorubas*, 159; Smith, 'The Alafin in Exile', 61.

this Nupe sack of Ọyọ may be supposed to have taken place early in the sixteenth century.[65] Around this same period, during the sixteenth century, the Nupe, who had earlier been divided into a number of small chieftaincies, are said to have been united into a single kingdom, by *Etsu* Edegi (Tsoede).[66] Some modern scholars have attributed the sack of Ọyọ Ile to Edegi, apparently on the grounds that before their unification under Edegi the Nupe would not have been powerful enough to effect it.[67] Nupe tradition, however, credits the sack of Ọyọ Ile to a certain *Etsu* Jiga, who is said to have lived before the time of Edegi.[68] Presumably this Jiga was the ruler of one of the small Nupe chieftaincies which existed before the unification.

The sack of Ọyọ Ile was apparently but one episode in a general process of Nupe expansion into Yoruba territory south of the Niger during the sixteenth century. *Etsu* Edegi himself is credited with raids against the Yagba and the Bunu, two north-eastern Yoruba groups.[69] Nupe power seems to have been felt some way to the south, for local traditions record that around this period Nupe forces sacked the town of Ẹdẹ, on the River Ọṣun,[70] and made two unsuccessful incursions across the Ọṣun into Ijẹṣa territory.[71] The Nupe apparently came to settle as well as to raid, for several northern Yoruba towns which later acknowledged the authority of Ọyọ claim

[65] For further discussion, see below, Ch. 4, pp. 56–59.

[66] For Edegi, see esp. S. F. Nadel, *A Black Byzantium: The Kingdom of Nupe in Nigeria* (London, 1942), 72–6. Edegi's reign is dated in different accounts to c. 1531–91 and to c. 1505–57: ibid. 406; Temple, *Notes on ... the Northern Provinces of Nigeria*, 525. For a sceptical view of the Edegi legends, see M. D. Mason, 'The Tsoede Myth and the Nupe Kinglists: More Political Propaganda?', *History in Africa*, 2 (1975), 101–12.

[67] C. R. Niven, *A Short History of the Yoruba Peoples* (London, 1958), 18; Crowder, *Story of Nigeria*, 61; cf. Smith, 'The Alafin in Exile', 61.

[68] NAK, BIDDIV. 2/1, B. 375, E. V. Rochfort-Rae, 'Introduction to certain notes collected from various Native Authorities, on the origins of the Bini, Kedawa, Agaba, Badeggi, Ebe and Gdwagbwazhi', 1921, Information from Sheshi Zagunla of Raba, §4; cf. M. D. Mason, 'The Nupe Kingdom in the Nineteenth Century: A Political History' (Ph.D. Thesis, University of Birmingham, 1970), 39 and n. 4.

[69] Nadel, *Black Byzantium*, 74.

[70] Olunlade, *Ẹdẹ: A Brief History*, 2–3.

[71] J. D. E. Abiọla, J. A. Babafẹmi and S. O. S. Ataiyero, *Iwe Itan Ijẹṣa-Obokun* (Ilesa, 1932), 44–5, 47–8. The date of these Nupe invasions is admittedly very uncertain. They are attributed to the reigns of *Ọwa* Yeyewaye and *Ọwa* Yeyeori (both female rulers), whom Abiọla and his co-authors place respectively thirteenth and sixteenth in the Ijẹṣa king-list, implying a period around the late seventeenth and early eighteenth centuries. However, an earlier recension of Ijẹṣa tradition, by H. Atundaolu, 'A Short Traditional History of the Ijesas and

to have been founded by Nupe immigrants.[72] It seems reasonable to posit a connection between these aggressions of the Nupe against their Yoruba neighbours and the political unification of the Nupe which Edegi effected in the same period. It may be speculated that the success both of Nupe expansion across the Niger and of the state-building enterprise of Edegi was due to the adoption by the Nupe of the use of cavalry. It appears that the Nupe had begun to import horses from Hausaland to the north during the fifteenth century,[73] and Nupe tradition credits Edegi with the ownership of many horses.[74] Ijẹsa tradition also records the use of cavalry by the Nupe in their invasions of Ijẹsaland.[75] In the open savanna country of northern Yorubaland, the use of mounted troops would have given the Nupe invaders a decisive military advantage over the Oyọ. In Ijẹsaland, however, the Nupe were entering forest country unsuitable for cavalry warfare, a circumstance which accounts for their defeats in this area.

The immediate result of the Nupe invasion of Oyọ was the total collapse of the latter state. After the sack of his capital, *Alafin* Onigbogi is said to have abandoned his kingdom and fled into exile in Borgu.[76] The city of Oyọ Ile was deserted, and the Oyọ kingdom ceased to exist as an effective political unit. In a very short time, however, the Oyọ kingdom had been reconstituted, and by the end of the sixteenth century the Oyọ had decisively checked the Nupe invaders.

§5. RECOVERY AND RECONSTRUCTION

The account of the reconstitution of the Oyọ kingdom after the flight of Onigbogi given by Samuel Johnson, on the basis of Oyọ tradition, is circumstantial and plausible, but probably highly tendentious. It is said that Onigbogi had married the daughter of a Bariba king, and that he now sought refuge with his father-in-law, who allowed him

---

Other Hinterland Tribes', *Lagos Weekly Record*, June and July 1901, lists the Ijẹsa rulers in a completely different order, placing Yeyewaye third in the list, implying a date in about the sixteenth century, and omitting Yeyeori.

[72] Babayẹmi, 'Upper Ogun', 77–9.

[73] The 'Kano Chronicle', in H. R. Palmer, *Sudanese Memoirs* (Lagos, 1928), iii. 111, records that Yakubu, ruler of Kano in 1452–63, sent ten horses to a Nupe ruler in exchange for eunuchs.

[74] 5,555 horses, according to Nadel, *Black Byzantium*, 74.

[75] Abiọla, Babafẹmi, and Ataiyero, *Iwe Itan Ijẹsa*, 47–8.

[76] Johnson, *History of the Yorubas*, 159.

to settle with his followers in the Bariba town of Gbere.[77] It is not clear to which of the Bariba kingdoms this tradition refers. The Bariba king involved is named as 'King Eleduwẹ', but this name seems to be used by the Yoruba without discrimination, to refer to any Bariba ruler.[78] Robert Smith, however, has established, from local traditions, that Gbere, where Onigbogi is said to have settled, is probably to be identified with Gberegburu, a small village about 60 miles north-west of Ọyọ Ile, which (at least in the nineteenth century) lay within the territories of the king of Nikki.[79] According to Johnson, Onigbogi died at Gbere, and was succeeded in the shadow dignity of *Alafin* by Ofinran, his son by the Bariba princess. From Gbere, Ofinran and his followers joined their Bariba hosts in raids into Ọyọ territory to the south, in the course of which they destroyed the town of Irawọ. But ultimately, Ofinran quarrelled with the Bariba, and withdrew again into Yorubaland, settling at Kuṣu, some 50 miles west of the old capital at Ọyọ Ile.[80] Ofinran's successor as *Alafin*, Egunoju, transferred his residence from Kuṣu to Igboho, about 10 miles further east. Igboho then remained the Ọyọ capital during the reigns of three further *Alafin*, namely Ọrọmpọtọ, Ajiboyede, and Abipa, until the last of these reoccupied the old capital at Ọyọ Ile.[81]

There are grounds for believing that this account is seriously misleading, and that it conceals the imposition of a new dynasty of *Alafin* of Bariba origin. It is illuminating to compare with Johnson's account the version of Ọyọ tradition recorded by Adeyẹmi. Adeyẹmi begins his account of the history of Ọyọ with the migration of the kingdom's founders from Medina to Borgu, and their movement from Borgu to settle at Igboho. The first *Alafin* at Igboho is named as Ọmọloju, a name which does not appear in Johnson's list of *Alafin*.[82] Ọmọloju is said to have been followed as *Alafin* by Egunoju, Ọrọmpọtọ, and Ṣopaṣan (i.e. Ajiboyede). Ṣopaṣan is said to have

---

[77] Ibid.; cf. NAI, OYOPROF. 4/7, 175/1918, 'History', by the *Ologbo* of Ọyọ, 9 Aug. 1918, encl. to *Alafin* of Ọyọ to Resident, Ọyọ, 10 Aug. 1918.

[78] For other references to Bariba kings called 'Eleduwẹ', cf. Johnson, *History of the Yorubas*, 166, 260.

[79] Smith, 'The Alafin in Exile', 62.

[80] Johnson, *History of the Yorubas*, 159–60. For the site of Kuṣu, see Smith, 'The Alafin in Exile', 64–5.

[81] Johnson, *History of the Yorubas*, 161–7.

[82] *Alafin* Ọmọloju is also mentioned in NAI, OYOPROF. 4/7, 175/1918, 'History', by the *Ologbo* of Ọyọ, 9 Aug. 1918, encl. to *Alafin* of Ọyọ to Resident, Ọyọ, 10 Aug. 1918.

been succeeded by Ofinran, who is credited with abandoning the settlement at Igboho, and he by Ogbolu (i.e. Abipa), who completed the move to Ǫyǫ Ile.[83] Of the discrepancies between Johnson and Adeyẹmi, the former's omission of *Alafin* Ǫmǫloju is not of great significance, since the confusion of this period, with its successive shifts of the capital, might easily have led to some *Alafin* being forgotten: there is, indeed, in addition to Ǫmǫloju, evidence for another *Alafin* of this period not mentioned by Johnson, called Apanpa, who is said to have been buried at the town of Kiṣi, about 20 miles north of Igboho.[84] The displacement of Ofinran in Adeyẹmi's list of *Alafin* might likewise be due simply to confusion between the various occasions when the Ǫyǫ capital was moved from one site to another.[85] But Adeyẹmi's omission of all the *Alafin* who according to Johnson reigned before the move from Borgu to Igboho is more difficult to explain away. It seems probable that Ofinran was the founder of the second dynasty of *Alafin*, originating from Borgu, whose arrival is recalled in the traditions recorded by Frobenius.[86] Johnson's story of the exile of Onigbogi and the return of his son to claim the Ǫyǫ throne is precisely the sort of tradition likely to be fabricated in order to conceal the imposition of a foreign dynasty.[87] By this means the new dynasty was affiliated to the old, and its legitimacy established.

The probable course of events may be tentatively reconstructed as follows. The destruction of Ǫyǫ power by the Nupe invasion left a political vacuum in northern Yorubaland, which the Bariba exploited by launching raids into Yoruba territory. Johnson's story of the Bariba attack on Irawǫ probably represents only one episode in a prolonged period of widespread raiding. A tradition of the destruction of Owu by the Bariba suggests that the displacement of the Owu kingdom from northern to southern Yorubaland may also have

[83] Adeyẹmi, *Iwe Itan Ǫyǫ*, 5–7. According to Adeyẹmi, Ofinran moved from Igboho to a place called Kogbaye, and Ogbolu (Abipa) from there to Ǫyǫ Ile. Johnson makes no reference to Kogbaye, but according to Ojo, *Iwe Itan Ǫyǫ*, 51, Abipa stayed briefly at Kogbaye during his move from Igboho to Ǫyǫ Ile. For the location of Kogbaye, about 10 miles east of Igboho, see Smith, 'The Alafin in Exile', 70–1.

[84] Smith, 'The Alafin in Exile', 63–4 and n. 19.

[85] Such confusion is evident elsewhere: cf. the account of Yoruba origins given by F. Ṣopẹin, 'A Chapter in the History of the Yoruba Country', *Nigerian Chronicle*, 17 Sept. 1909, places the temporary settlement at Kogbaye during the original move from Ile Ifẹ to Ǫyǫ Ile.

[86] Frobenius, *Voice of Africa*, i. 177, 210, and ii. 629.

[87] Cf. Vansina, *Oral Tradition*, 74.

occurred at this period, as a result of these Bariba raids.[88] Eventually, one group of Bariba raiders, perhaps from the frontier town of Gberegburu, succeeded in establishing itself permanently in Ọyọ territory, first at Kuṣu and then at Igboho. At the beginning, the Bariba at Igboho were probably only one of a number of Bariba groups which had settled in northern Yorubaland. The Ọyọ towns of Ogbomọṣọ, Ṣaki, and Kiṣi also have royal dynasties of Bariba origin, which were probably established around this period,[89] while another group of Bariba invaders seized control in the north-western Yoruba kingdom of Ṣabẹ.[90] But ultimately the Igboho group emerged as the most powerful, won recognition as the legitimate rulers of Ọyọ, and occupied the historic capital of the kingdom at Ọyọ Ile.

The *Alafin* at Igboho were not left undisturbed to establish their authority over the Ọyọ kingdom. Military pressure from the north, from both the Bariba and the Nupe, continued for some time. Under *Alafin* Ọrọmpọtọ a Bariba army is said to have invaded the kingdom and attacked Igboho, but to have been repulsed at Ilayi.[91] Ọrọmpọtọ's adversaries were perhaps simply a rival band of raiders, but they may have been an army from one of the major Bariba kingdoms (Bussa or Nikki) seeking to assert metropolitan authority over the new Bariba dynasty in the south. If so, the battle of Ilayi may have marked the assertion of effective independence by the Igboho dynasty. The threat of further invasion from the north-east, from the Nupe, also persisted. Under Ọrọmpọtọ's successor Ajiboyede, a Nupe army again invaded the Ọyọ kingdom, but on this occasion the invaders were decisively defeated, and their commander taken prisoner by the Ọyọ.[92] Johnson names the defeated Nupe commander as 'Lajọmọ, king of the Tapas', but it is not possible to

[88] Mabogunjẹ and Omer-Cooper, *Owu in Yoruba History*, 34–6; Law, 'The Owu War in Yoruba History', 144.

[89] For Ogbomọṣọ, see Oyerinde, *Iwe Itan Ogbomọṣọ*, 9–13; for Ṣaki, see Ojo, *Iwe Itan Ṣaki*, 20–1; for Kiṣi, see Smith, 'The Alafin in Exile', 64, n. 22, and Babayẹmi, 'Upper Ogun', 76.

[90] For the arrival of the Bariba dynasty in Ṣabe, see A. I. Aṣiwaju, 'A Note on the History of Ṣabẹ', *Lagos Notes and Records*, 4 (1973), 24–5. The date of its arrival is uncertain, but one account states that the founder of the dynasty came from Igboho, suggesting a close connection with the disturbances in the Ọyọ kingdom during the sixteenth century: George, *Historical Notes on the Yoruba Country*, 23.

[91] Johnson, *History of the Yorubas*, 161–2. Ilayi seems not to have been identified.

[92] Ibid. 162–3.

identify this man with any king known from Nupe sources. The name 'Lajọmọ' is in fact Yoruba, and it is idle to speculate which Nupe king the Ọyọ may have called by this name, especially as we might here again be dealing with the ruler of one of the pre-Edegian Nupe chieftaincies, and moreover the defeated commander may well have been in reality a subordinate general rather than a king.

Ajiboyede's victory apparently ended the Nupe threat to Ọyọ, and his successor Abipa was able, probably early in the seventeenth century,[93] to reoccupy the old capital at Ọyọ Ile without opposition. This dramatic recovery of Ọyọ power after the disastrous collapse under *Alafin* Onigbogi clearly requires explanation. There seems much plausibility in the conventional view that it was due to the adoption by the Ọyọ of the use of cavalry.[94] The principal evidence in support of this view is the fact that the earliest instance of the use of cavalry recorded in Ọyọ tradition relates to the reign of *Alafin* Ọrọmpọtọ.[95] It is also noteworthy that according to Frobenius, the practice of representing Ṣango, the early *Alafin* and principal royal deity, as a rider on horseback was introduced by the second dynasty of *Alafin* which originated from Borgu.[96] If, as was argued above, *Alafin* Ofinran was the founder of this dynasty, this would support the view that the Ọyọ adopted the use of cavalry during the sixteenth century. The initial military superiority of the Nupe over the Ọyọ may itself, as was suggested earlier, have been due to their use of cavalry. The balance of military power was redressed when the Ọyọ in turn adopted the new method of fighting.

The adoption of cavalry fighting was not the only innovation the Ọyọ accepted during this period. Ọyọ tradition also attributes to it the introduction of two important religious cults: the Egungun cult, of masqueraders representing the spirits of deceased ancestors, and the cult of Ifa, the god of divination. Of these, the Egungun cult is said to have been adopted from the Nupe invaders, the principal Egungun priest of Ọyọ, the *Alapini*, being a Nupe immigrant.[97] It does appear very likely that the Ọyọ would have been influenced by

[93] For the date, cf. below, Ch. 4, pp. 56–58.
[94] Ajayi and Smith, *Yoruba Warfare in the Nineteenth Century*, 3–4; Smith, *Kingdoms of the Yoruba*, 39–40; J. E. Flint, *Nigeria and Ghana* (New Jersey, 1966), 60; cf. R. Law, 'A West African Cavalry State: The Kingdom of Oyo', *JAH* 16 (1975), 3–4.
[95] Johnson, *History of the Yorubas*, 161.
[96] Frobenius, *Voice of Africa*, i. 210 and ii. 629.
[97] Johnson, *History of the Yorubas*, 160.

Nupe culture during this period, when they were militarily dominated by the Nupe and many Nupe were settling in Ọyọ territory. The
Ifa cult, on the other hand, is said to have been introduced from
southern Yorubaland, from the Awori town of Ọta, although its
arrival is also linked with the Nupe invasion. The mother of *Alafin*
Onigbogi, an Ọta woman, is said to have brought the cult to Ọyọ,
but the Ọyọ refused to accept it. The subsequent Nupe sack of Ọyọ
was believed to be a divine punishment for this refusal, and *Alafin*
Ofinran therefore officially adopted the cult at Kuṣu.[98] This story
cannot be accepted altogether at face value: the name of Onigbogi's
mother, Aruigba (Calabash-Bearer), is the name of a sort of carved
wooden bowl, in the form of a woman bearing a calabash, used in
Ifa ritual. The tradition may nevertheless be essentially historical,
and together with the Egungun story, it suggests that the Ọyọ saw the
Igboho period as a formative period of some importance in their
history.

The Nupe and Bariba invasions were also responsible for important population movements, and the foundation of important new
towns, within the Ọyọ kingdom. The temporary royal capitals,
Kuṣu and Igboho, remained considerable cities even after the
removal of the *Alafin* to Ọyọ Ile.[99] The town of Ikoyi, later considered the second town in the kingdom after the capital, is also
said to have been founded during the same period, as part of the
regrouping of the Ọyọ to resist the Nupe invasions.[100] The reorganization of the Ọyọ kingdom after the Nupe conquest can, indeed, be
plausibly seen as laying the foundations for the imperial expansion
of Ọyọ during the seventeenth and eighteenth centuries.

[98] Ibid. 158–60; cf. NAI, OYOPROF. 4/7, 275/1918, 'History', by the *Ologbo*
of Ọyọ, 9 Aug. 1918, encl. to *Alafin* of Ọyọ to Resident, Ọyọ, 10 Aug. 1918.
[99] Cf. the descriptions of these towns by Clapperton, *Journal of a Second
Expedition*, 26–7; R. and J. Lander, *Journal of an Expedition*, i. 109–15, 135–9.
[100] Ojo, *Iwe Itan Ọyọ*, 184; Babayẹmi, 'Upper Ogun', 77.

PART II

THE ỌYỌ EMPIRE (*c.* 1600–*c.* 1790)

CHAPTER 4

The Imperial Period:
A Chronological Framework

THE first need in studying the history of the Ọyọ empire is to establish some sort of chronological framework. The central problem is the correlation of evidence from contemporary European sources and from the indigenous traditions. The contemporary sources provide a certain amount of material on Ọyọ history, and the events to which they refer can, usually, be more or less precisely dated. But the amount of information that can be derived from contemporary sources is limited both as regards the period which they cover and as regards the aspects of Ọyọ history which they illuminate. The contemporary sources alone can hardly provide an adequate general picture of the development of the Ọyọ empire. For such a picture, we have to turn to oral tradition, which in the case of Ọyọ means primarily Samuel Johnson's *History of the Yorubas*. Johnson gives a coherent, though incomplete, account of the rise and fall of the Ọyọ empire, but one that suffers from a serious chronological vagueness. The oral traditions date events only by attributing them to the reigns of the successive *Alafin*. This is not only unsatisfactory in itself, but also makes it difficult to relate the events recorded in the contemporary sources to the general scheme of development provided by the traditions. It is therefore necessary to determine, as far as is possible, the probable dates of the reigns of the successive *Alafin*.

§1. THE ỌYỌ KING-LIST

The first prerequisite is to establish a complete list of *Alafin*. Samuel Johnson gives a list, derived from the *Arọkin* of Ọyọ, which includes thirty-five names from Oduduwa, counted as the first *Alafin* although he did not reign at Ọyọ, down to Oluewu, the last *Alafin* of the empire, in the 1830s. His list is as follows:[1]

    1. Oduduwa.
    2. Ọranyan (founder of Ọyọ).

[1] Johnson, *History of the Yorubas*, 669–70.

3. Ajaka, also called Dada.[2]
4. Ṣango.
– Ajaka (restored), second reign.
5. Aganju.
6. Kọri.
7. Oluaṣo.
8. Onigbogi (*Alafin* at the time of the Nupe sack of Ọyọ).
9. Ofinran.
10. Egunoju.
11. Ọrọmpọtọ.
12. Ajiboyede, *alias* Ṣopaṣan.[3]
13. Abipa, *alias* Ogbolu (reoccupied the old capital at Ọyọ Ile).
14. Ọbalokun.
15. Ajagbo.
16. Odarawu.
17. Karan.
18. Jayin.
19. Ayibi.
20. Ọsinyago.
21. Ojigi.
22. Gberu.
23. Amuniwaiye.
24. Oniṣile.
25. Labisi.
26. Awọnbioju.
27. Agboluaje.
28. Majẹogbe, *alias* Ojo Arẹsẹrena.[4]
29. Abiọdun.
30. Awolẹ, *alias* Aṣamu.[5]
31. Adebo.
32. Maku.
33. Majotu.
34. Amodo.
35. Oluewu (last *Alafin* at Ọyọ Ile).

This list is certainly incomplete. It is said that, conventionally,

---

[2] Johnson does not use the name Dada: it is given e.g. by Ojo, *Iwe Itan Ọyọ*, 28.
[3] For this alternative name, see e.g. Adeyẹmi, *Iwe Itan Ọyọ*, 7.
[4] For the second name, see ibid. 8.
[5] For the second name, see ibid. 9.

only those *Alafin* who were buried in the Bara, the royal burial place at Ọyọ, are enumerated in the official lists,[6] and that the names of many early *Alafin* who died in exile or for some other reason were not buried in the Bara have been forgotten.[7] A clear example of such an omission is the early *Alafin* Oluodo, whose case was discussed in the last chapter, who was not buried in the Bara because his body was lost when he was drowned while fleeing from the Nupe across the River Niger.[8] Other names may have dropped out of the list for the confused period following the Nupe sack of Ọyọ Ile under *Alafin* Onigbogi, when Ọyọ Ile was abandoned for some time and the *Alafin* resided at a series of temporary capitals: as has been seen, other sources provide the names of two *Alafin* of this period not mentioned by Johnson, an *Alafin* Ọmọloju who is said to have reigned immediately before Egunoju[9] and an *Alafin* Apanpa said to have been buried at Kiṣi.[10] Robert Smith was told that in all there had been over sixty *Alafin* before the final abandonment of Ọyọ Ile in the 1830s,[11] while Frobenius reports a more extreme claim that no less than 310 kings reigned at Ọyọ Ile.[12] These figures are no doubt fanciful, but we can accept that several names have been omitted from the received list.

There is also some disagreement about the order in which certain of the *Alafin* reigned. Here again, the most serious discrepancy relates to the period following the Nupe sack of Ọyọ. As was seen in the last chapter, Ofinran, according to Johnson the ninth *Alafin* and the immediate successor of Onigbogi, is placed by Adeyẹmi immediately after Ajiboyede, Johnson's twelfth *Alafin*.[13] This disagreement

---

[6] At the installation of an *Alafin*, sacrifices were offered at the tombs of his predecessors in the Bara: Johnson, *History of the Yorubas*, 44. This ceremony will have served to ensure that kings buried in the Bara were remembered. For a description of the Bara of New Ọyọ, see R. Smith, 'The Bara, or Royal Mausoleum at New Oyo', *JHSN* 3.2 (1965), 415–20. The Bara of Ọyọ Ile, which is said to be situated some distance north of the city, has not been located: Willett, 'Investigations at Old Oyo', 69.

[7] Smith, 'List of Alafin', 52; id., 'The Alafin in Exile', 74, n. 52.

[8] Smith, 'List of Alafin', 53–4; id., 'The Alafin in Exile', 74, n. 52.

[9] Adeyẹmi, *Iwe Itan Ọyọ*, 7; NAI, OYOPROF. 4/7, 275/1918' 'History', by the *Ologbo* of Ọyọ, 9 Aug. 1918, encl. to *Alafin* of Ọyọ to Resident of Ọyọ, 10 Aug. 1918.

[10] Smith, 'The Alafin in Exile', 63–4 and n. 19.

[11] Smith, 'List of Alafin', 52; id., 'The Alafin in Exile', 74, n. 52. Smith gives a total of 70 *Alafin*: this includes seven *Alafin* who reigned at New Ọyọ between the 1830s and 1960s.

[12] Frobenius, *Voice of Africa*, i. 177.

[13] Adeyẹmi, *Iwe Itan Ọyọ*, 7; cf. the somewhat confused account in NAI,

evidently reflects the confusion of this time of troubles in Ọyọ history. Adeyẹmi also reverses the order in which Majotu and Amodo, Johnson's thirty-third and thirty-fourth *Alafin*, reigned,[14] while another source transposes Adebo and Maku, thirty-first and thirty-second in Johnson's list,[15] but in these later instances Johnson is certainly correct.[16]

It is also likely that Johnson's king-list is in part spurious. In particular, it is difficult to accept the historicity of the earliest rulers listed. Johnson himself classifies Oduduwa, Ọranyan, Ajaka, and Ṣango as 'mythological kings and deified heroes', in contrast to Aganju and his successors, whom he describes as 'historical kings'.[17] These first four rulers are, in fact, all *orisa* (deities), and it seems probable that they are humanized gods rather than deified mortals.[18] More generally, the circumstances of the collapse and reconstruction of the Ọyọ kingdom after the Nupe sack of Ọyọ Ile, which possibly involved a change of dynasty,[19] must raise serious questions about the status of the entire early section of the king-list, including Johnson's first ten or twelve rulers. The early history of Ọyọ had probably to be pieced together by its official historians, the *Arọkin*, from exceedingly confused and fragmentary traditions.

In the present context, however, we are primarily concerned with the *Alafin* from Abipa, who reoccupied Ọyọ Ile after this period of confusion, onwards, since it was only after the reoccupation of the old capital that Ọyọ became a great imperial power. There seems much less reason to be suspicious of this later portion of the king-list.

§2. EARLIER CHRONOLOGIES

Only two earlier historians have attempted to produce a detailed chronology for the *Alafin* of the Ọyọ empire. In the 1920s Talbot suggested dates for the later *Alafin*, from Abipa onwards, and these dates were taken over, with minor modifications, by Chief Samuel

---

OYOPROF. 4/7, 275/1918, 'History', by the *Ologbo* of Ọyọ, 9 Aug. 1918, encl. to *Alafin* of Ọyọ to Resident of Ọyọ, 10 Aug. 1918.

[14] Adeyẹmi, *Iwe Itan Ọyọ*, 10.

[15] Hethersett, in *Iwe Kika Ẹkẹrin*, 71.

[16] Johnson's ordering of these *Alafin* is corroborated by the early account in Crowther, *Vocabulary of the Yoruba Language*, v–vi.

[17] Johnson, *History of the Yorubas*, 143, 155.

[18] Aganju is apparently also an *orisa*: cf. Ellis, *Yoruba-Speaking Peoples*, 44.

[19] Cf. above, Ch. 3, pp. 39–42.

Ojo, one of the local historians of Ọyọ.[20] The dates offered by Talbot and Chief Ojo are as follows:

	Talbot	Ojo
Abipa	1570–80	1570–80
Ọbalokun	1580–1600	1580–1600
Ajagbo	1600–55	1600–58
Odarawu	1655–60	1658–60
Karan	1660–5	1660–5
Jayin	1665–70	1665–70
Ayibi	1670–90	1676–90
Ọsinyago	1690–8	1690–8
Ojigi	1698–1732	1698–1732
Gberu	1732–5	1732–8
Amuniwaiye	1735–8	1738–42
Oniṣile	1738–50	1742–50
Labisi	1750	1750
Awọnbioju	1750	1750
Agboluaje	1750–72	1750–72
Majẹogbe	1772–5	1772–5
Abiọdun	1775–1801	1775–1805
Awolẹ	1801–11	1805–11
Adebo	1811	1811
Maku	1811	1811–12
(interregnum)	1811–16	1812–17
Majotu	1816–21	1817–18
Amodo	1821–32	1818
Oluewu	1832–5	1818–20

Talbot does not explain on what evidence he calculated these dates, but for the most part it is easy enough to reconstruct how he proceeded. The earliest dates, from Abipa to Ayibi, are evidently artificial, being constructed from arbitrary regnal units of five, ten, twenty, and in one instance (Ajagbo) fifty-five years. The attribution of an especially long reign to Ajagbo is based upon Ọyọ tradition, as recorded by Johnson.[21] Talbot's dates for the later *Alafin* are a little less arbitrary. He probably took from earlier writers (more or less accurately remembered) his dates for the accession of Abiọdun

---

[20] Talbot, *Peoples of Southern Nigeria*, i. 282–96; Ojo, *Iwe Itan Ọyọ*. Chief Ojo also gives dates for the *Alafin* before Abipa, back to Ọranyan, whose reign is dated to 892–1042.

[21] Johnson, *History of the Yorubas*, 168.

c

(1775),[22] the death of Abiǫdun (1801),[23] and the death of Oluewu (1835).[24] His dates for Ojigi (1698–1732) depend upon attributing to his reign two Ǫyǫ wars recorded (and dated) in contemporary sources, against Allada in 1698 and against Dahomey in 1726–30, while his dates for Oniṣile (1738–50) are similarly based upon the supposition that this ruler was responsible for campaigns against Dahomey recorded in a contemporary source as fought in 1738–47. The value of these various calculations and attributions will be considered in detail below. Talbot derives from recorded traditions the assigning of short reigns of less than one year each to Labisi, Awǫnbioju, Adebo, and Maku,[25] and the insertion of a five-year interregnum between Maku and Majotu.[26]

It is also possible to account for some of Chief Ojo's corrections to Talbot's dates. The contraction of Odarawu's reign to two years (1658–60) is probably based upon a tradition that his reign was especially short,[27] while the unexplained interpolation of a gap of six years (1670–6) between the reigns of Jayin and Ayibi is probably meant to take account of the fact that Ayibi is said to have acceded to the throne as a minor, so that a Regency was necessary.[28] The extension of Abiǫdun's reign to thirty years (1775–1805) similarly brings Talbot into line with recorded tradition.[29] The compression of the last three *Alafin* into a period of only three years (1817–20) is more curious, but Chief Ojo's belief that Amodo reigned for less than a year is based upon a tradition recorded earlier by Adeyǫmi.[30]

At any rate, it is clear that the dates offered by Talbot and Chief Ojo have no independent value whatever, and they should be discounted in any consideration of Ǫyǫ chronology.[31]

[22] Talbot quotes in this context A. Dalzel, *A History of Dahomy* (London, 1793), 156–7, who records not Abiǫdun's succession, but his victory in a civil war, and not in 1775, but in 1774.

[23] Ellis, *Yoruba-Speaking Peoples*, 10, probably following Crowther, *Vocabulary of the Yoruba Language*, v, had placed this in c. 1800.

[24] The same date had been given by R. F. Burton, *A Mission to Gelele, King of Dahome* (London, 1864), i. 197 n.

[25] Cf. Johnson, *History of the Yorubas*, 178, 193, 196.

[26] Cf. Ellis, *Yoruba-Speaking Peoples*, 11; Crowther, *Vocabulary of the Yoruba Language*, vi.

[27] Johnson, *History of the Yorubas*, 169.

[28] Ibid. 172.

[29] Cf. Hethersett, in *Iwe Kika Ękęrin*, 61.

[30] Adeyǫmi, *Iwe Itan Ǫyǫ*, 10.

[31] It seemed nevertheless necessary to refute their chronologies in detail, since experience suggests that university students tend to accord far too much respect especially to Chief Ojo's dates.

§3. THE EIGHTEENTH CENTURY: OJIGI TO ABIỌDUN

The only sure way to construct a dynastic chronology is to identify events attributed by the traditions to the reigns of particular *Alafin* with events recorded and precisely dated in contemporary sources. For the eighteenth century, four such equations between traditional and contemporary sources can be made with some confidence.

The first of these relates to *Alafin* Ojigi, whom tradition credits with the conquest of Dahomey.[32] The contemporary sources record a series of Ọyọ wars with the states in the Dahomey area: an invasion of Allada, the state which preceded Dahomey as the main power in the area, in 1698, and two protracted wars against Dahomey itself in 1726–30 and 1739–48.[33] There is no reason whatever to associate Ojigi with the first of these wars, against Allada in 1698. The tradition of Ojigi's conquest of Dahomey must relate either to the war of 1726–30, or to that of 1739–48 (or, conceivably, to both). Since, as will appear below, we have to find room for three *Alafin* (Gberu, Amuniwaye, and Oniṣile) between Ojigi's reign and the 1750s, it is more likely that the allusion is to the first war. *Alafin* Ojigi was therefore reigning in 1726–30. Talbot's attribution of the second Dahomian war to the reign of Oniṣile appears to be based on a much vaguer assertion in the traditions, that Oniṣile was 'a great warrior'.[34] No value can be attached to this equation.

The second fixed point in Ọyọ chronology is provided by a contemporary notice of internal dissensions in Ọyọ in 1754. In October of that year, it was reported: 'The King of Io is dead, and they are wrangling and fighting who shall have the throne. Two that have been seated on it within these two months are both killed.'[35] Tradition recalls two occasions in Ọyọ history when two successive *Alafin* were removed after very brief reigns. The immediate successors of *Alafin* Oniṣile, Labisi and Awọnbioju, are credited with reigns of only seventeen and 130 days,[36] while Adebo and Maku are said to have survived for only 130 days and three months respectively.[37]

[32] Johnson, *History of the Yorubas*, 174.

[33] For these wars, see below, Ch. 8, pp. 154–64. Talbot's dates for the second Dahomian war (1738–47) are now known to be incorrect.

[34] Johnson, *History of the Yorubas*, 176.

[35] PRO, T.70/1523, W. Devaynes to T. Melvil, 22 Oct. 1754 (extract), quoted in T. Melvil to Committee, 30 Nov. 1754; cf. Akinjogbin, *Dahomey and its Neighbours*, 146, n. 1.

[36] Johnson, *History of the Yorubas*, 178.

[37] Ibid. 193, 196; cf. Crowther, *Vocabulary of the Yoruba Language*, v–vi; Adeyẹmi, *Iwe Itan Ọyọ*, 10.

In view of the date of Ojigi's reign, it must be the earlier occasion which is in question here. The reigns of Labisi and Awǫnbioju can therefore be dated to 1754.

The removal of *Alafin* Labisi and *Alafin* Awǫnbioju was associated, according to Qyǫ tradition, with the usurpation of effective power at Qyǫ by a certain Gaha, who held the title of *Baṣǫrun*, the principal office in Qyǫ after that of the king. Gaha is said to have dominated the next two *Alafin*, Agboluaje and Majeǫgbe, but to have been overthrown and killed by Majeǫgbe's successor, Abiǫdun.[38] A contemporary source reports a civil war at Qyǫ between the king and his 'ministers', led by '*Ochenoo*, the prime minister', which ended in the defeat and death of the 'prime minister', as occurring in about May 1774.[39] This civil war can be identified with that between *Alafin* Abiǫdun and *Baṣǫrun* Gaha, 'Ochenoo' representing *Oṣǫrun*, a shorter version of the title *Baṣǫrun*.[40] *Alafin* Abiǫdun was therefore already on the Qyǫ throne in 1774.

The final contemporary reference in the eighteenth century which can be related to the traditions is a report of the death of a king of Qyǫ in early April 1789.[41] Since Abiǫdun is said to have had a 'long and prosperous reign' after overthrowing *Baṣǫrun* Gaha in 1774,[42] the king who died in 1789 must be identified with Abiǫdun. This admittedly gives an earlier date for the death of Abiǫdun than other evidence would lead us to expect. Samuel Crowther, in the 1840s, estimated that Abiǫdun died in c. 1800,[43] while some modern scholars have preferred an even later date, of c. 1810.[44] The contemporary report, however, must be accounted the best available evidence for the date of Abiǫdun's death, and the date of 1789 is therefore accepted in this work.[45] The attribution of Abiǫdun's

[38] Johnson, *History of the Yorubas*, 178–86; cf. Hethersett, in *Iwe Kika Ẹkẹrin*, 61–4; Adeyẹmi, *Iwe Itan Qyǫ*, 8–9.

[39] Dalzel, *History of Dahomey*, 156–7.

[40] Cf. Akinjogbin, *Dahomey and its Neighbours*, 145, n. 4.

[41] AN, C. 6/26, Gourg to Ministre de Marine, 8 June 1789, '. . . le Roy des Ailliots est mort, presqu'en même tems que le Roy Dahomet et même quelque tems avant, c'est à dire en Avril dernier . . .'; cf. Akinjogbin, *Dahomey and its Neighbours*, 175, n. 1. The king of Dahomey referred to, Kpengla, died on 13 April 1789.   [42] Johnson, *History of the Yorubas*, 186.

[43] Crowther, *Vocabulary of the Yoruba Language*, iv.

[44] See e.g. W. Bascom, 'The Fall of Old Oyo or Katunga', *Présence africaine*, 24–5 (1959), 321–7; P. Morton-Williams, 'The Yoruba Kingdom of Oyo', in D. Forde and P. M. Kaberry (eds.), *West African Kingdoms in the Nineteenth Century* (London, 1967), 66, n. 1.

[45] For further discussion of this problem, see R. Law, 'The Chronology of the

death to this year does raise problems for the chronology of events after his death, but these problems are not insoluble, and detailed consideration of them will be deferred to a later context, as part of the discussion of the decline and fall of the Ọyọ empire.[46] One tradition, it may be noted, asserts that Abiọdun reigned for thirty years in all:[47] it is just possible that Abiọdun succeeded as early as *c.* 1759, but it seems much more likely that the traditional report is exaggerated.

§4. THE LAST SIX KINGS: AWOLẸ TO OLUEWU

The chronology of Abiọdun's successors, the last *Alafin* of Ọyọ Ile, has been discussed by the author in detail elsewhere,[48] and will therefore be dealt with only briefly here.

There is no contemporary evidence relating to the chronology of Abiọdun's immediate successors, Awolẹ, Adebo, and Maku. However, traditional evidence recorded as early as the 1840s by Samuel Crowther offers figures for the lengths of the reigns of these three kings.[49] Awolẹ is said to have reigned for seven years, which would place his death in *c.* 1796. Adebo and Maku, as noted earlier, had very brief reigns, probably occupying less than a year altogether (*c.* 1796–7). The death of Maku was then followed by an interregnum of five years, which would indicate that the next *Alafin*, Majotu, was installed in *c.* 1802.

Majotu appears, on the basis of Ọyọ tradition, to have been the *Alafin* met by Clapperton and the Landers on their visits to Ọyọ Ile between 1826 and 1830,[50] an identification which gives him a surprisingly long reign of twenty-eight or more years.[51] For Majotu's successors, Amodo and Oluewu, there is again no contemporary evidence, but it is at least possible to assign a date to the campaign against Ilọrin in which the latter died, and which led to the final

---

Yoruba Wars of the Early Nineteenth Century: A Reconsideration', *JHSN* 5.2 (1970), 211–15.

[46] See below, Ch. 12, pp. 246–8.

[47] Hethersett, in *Iwe Kika Ẹkẹrin*, 61.

[48] Law, 'Chronology of the Yoruba Wars', 211–18.

[49] Crowther, *Vocabulary of the Yoruba Language*, v–vi. Partial corroboration of Crowther's figures is provided by later sources: Johnson, *History of the Yorubas*, 192–6; Hethersett, in *Iwe Kika Ẹkẹrin*, 69–70; Adeyẹmi, *Iwe Itan Ọyọ*, 10.

[50] Johnson, *History of the Yorubas*, 210.

[51] It is therefore necessary to reject the statement of Ellis, *Yoruba-Speaking Peoples*, 11, that Majotu reigned for 'about seven or eight years'.

destruction of Qyǫ power and the abandonment of the capital at Qyǫ Ile. Burton, in the 1860s, dated the fall of Qyǫ Ile to 1835.[52] While the basis for this calculation is not indicated, it is clear that it is approximately correct. Accounts based on Gwandu sources, which derive ultimately from nineteenth-century Arabic records, offer the date 1837, and it is at any rate clear that the fall of Qyǫ occurred early in the reign of Khalil, Emir of Gwandu, who succeeded in 1833.[53] A calculation based on a combination of evidence recorded by Crowther in 1841 and the later narrative in Johnson's *History* suggests that the death of Oluewu and the abandonment of Qyǫ Ile should be assigned to the dry season of 1835–6,[54] and this date is adopted in the present work. Calculating backwards from this date, Johnson's narrative of Oluewu's campaigns suggests that he probably came to the throne in *c.* 1833–4,[55] while to allow sufficient time for several campaigns which are said to have been fought under *Alafin* Amodo, the death of Majotu and the accession of Amodo have to be placed as early as possible, i.e. *c.* 1830–1.[56] The statement of Adeyǫmi that Amodo reigned only for five months[57] is difficult to reconcile with Johnson's narrative and must be rejected.

§5. THE SEVENTEENTH CENTURY AND EARLIER

There is no direct evidence to date the reign of any *Alafin* earlier than Ojigi. The only way to approach the chronology of the earlier period is the speculative one of calculating an average regnal length for the later *Alafin* and extrapolating this average back into the earlier period. Such calculations have been attempted by Smith, who worked out an average regnal length of 11·8 years for the seventeen *Alafin* who reigned between 1754 and 1956. On this basis, Smith calculated that the death of *Alafin* Abipa might have occurred in *c.* 1614 and the accession of *Alafin* Onigbogi in *c.* 1530, and therefore dated the reoccupation of Qyǫ Ile by Abipa to *c.* 1610 and the Nupe sack of the city under Onigbogi to *c.* 1535.[58]

---

[52] Burton, *Mission to Gelele*, i. 197, n.

[53] Arnett, *Gazetteer of Sokoto Province*, 38.

[54] Crowther, in Schön and Crowther, *Journals*, 317–18, reports being told in 1841 that the battle of Igbodo had been fought seven years earlier, i.e. *c.* 1834; Johnson, *History of the Yorubas*, 258–68, indicates that the death of Oluewu and the fall of Qyǫ occurred in the second dry season after the battle of Igbodo; cf. Law, 'Chronology of the Yoruba Wars', 217.

[55] Law, 'Chronology of the Yoruba Wars', 217–18.

[56] Ibid. 218.   [57] Adeyǫmi, *Iwe Itan Qyǫ*, 10.

[58] Smith, 'The Alafin in Exile', 72–4; id., *Kingdoms of the Yoruba*, 103.

Calculations based on the extrapolation of average regnal lengths are, of course, extremely hazardous.[59] The validity of the method depends upon the assumption that the factors which influenced the average length of reign, such as the mode of succession to the throne (which may affect the average age of kings at accession) and the incidence of premature terminations of reigns (for example, by assassination or deposition) remained constant throughout the period under study. In the case of Ọyọ, however, this was not so. The mechanics of royal succession at Ọyọ are only imperfectly known, but it appears that in early times the *Alafin*'s eldest son, who had the title *Arẹmọ*, normally succeeded, but that later it became customary for the *Arẹmọ* to commit suicide at his father's death and for the new *Alafin* to be selected from among a wide range of the members of the royal lineage. The change was possibly effected at the death of *Alafin* Ojigi, in the 1730s.[60] The earlier system of succession by primogeniture would produce relatively long reigns, the average regnal length approximating to the length of a generation. On the other hand, the later system of elective succession would tend to produce shorter reigns, since it encouraged the accession of mature or even elderly men.[61] Moreover, the traditions indicate that nearly all the *Alafin* from Odarawu to Oluewu were either murdered or compelled to commit suicide, whereas no such premature terminations of reign are recorded for the *Alafin* before Odarawu.[62] At New Ọyọ after 1836 the situation changed again. The practice of requiring the *Arẹmọ* to commit suicide was discontinued, although the *Arẹmọ* did not automatically succeed to the throne, and the assassination and deposition of *Alafin* became once more unfashionable.[63]

It is therefore likely that the average length of reign of the *Alafin* from, say, Odarawu to Oluewu was substantially shorter both than that of the earlier *Alafin* and than that of the *Alafin* who reigned at New Ọyọ after 1836. Closer study of Smith's figures reveals, indeed,

[59] The problems are discussed at length by D. P. Henige, *The Chronology of Oral Tradition: Quest for a Chimera* (Oxford, 1974), esp. Ch. 4.

[60] Cf. below, Ch. 5, pp. 66–67, 77–79.

[61] As noted by R. Lander, in Clapperton, *Journal of a Second Expedition*, 324: 'an elderly man is generally preferred'.

[62] The only early example is the mythical *Alafin* Ṣango, who is said to have committed suicide: Johnson, *History of the Yorubas*, 151. *Alafin* Ajaka is said to have been deposed, but subsequently restored: ibid. 148, 152.

[63] The only premature termination of a reign at New Ọyọ was the deposition of *Alafin* Adeniran in 1956.

that his average of 11·8 years for the period 1754–1956 breaks down into an average of 7·5 years for the last eleven *Alafin* of Qyq Ile (1754–1836) and one of twenty years for the first six *Alafin* of New Qyq (1836–1956).

Bearing these changes in mind, it is possible to make some tentative suggestions about the chronology of the earlier *Alafin*. According to Johnson, the nine *Alafin* from Odarawu to Onisile all had brief reigns.[64] It seems reasonable to apply to these nine *Alafin* the low average regnal length calculated for the period 1754–1836. On this basis, a notional date for the accession of Odarawu of c. 1687 is obtained. This date has no particular validity, but it seems justified to attribute the reign of Odarawu to the late seventeenth century. Odarawu is preceded in the king-list by Ajagbo, who is credited with a very long reign—according to tradition, no less than 140 years.[65] It seems likely that Ajagbo's reign occupied most of the latter half of the seventeenth century, and that his accession might be placed around or before the middle of the century. Only one name, that of Qbalokun, occurs in the king-list between Ajagbo and Abipa. This indicates that Abipa was probably reigning around the beginning of the seventeenth century. At this point, indeed, Smith's calculations and my own coincide. At any rate, we may place the reoccupation of Qyq Ile by Abipa in the early seventeenth century. The imperial period of Qyq history, which can conveniently be taken as beginning with this event, may therefore be taken as extending from, very roughly, c. 1600 to c. 1836.

Beyond Abipa, speculation becomes still more hazardous, but we may consider at least the problem of the date of the Nupe conquest of Qyq under *Alafin* Onigbogi. Talbot places this in c. 1550, a date hardly consistent with his placing of *Alafin* Abipa's accession in c. 1570, but nevertheless repeated by some recent writers.[66] Smith, as has been seen, suggests c. 1535. On Smith's own data, however, this seems too late. According to the genealogical relationships recorded by Smith, the six *Alafin* from Onigbogi to Abipa comprised four generations.[67] The 84 years which Smith allows these six

---

[64] Johnson, *History of the Yorubas*, 169–77.
[65] Ibid. 168. For the proverbial longevity of Ajagbo, cf. the traditional poem quoted by Bowen, *Central Africa*, 289–90.
[66] Talbot, *Peoples of Southern Nigeria*, i. 282; repeated by Niven, *Short History of the Yoruba Peoples*, 18; Flint, *Nigeria and Ghana*, 60; B. Davidson, *Africa in History* (3rd edn., London, 1974), 166.
[67] Smith, 'The Alafin in Exile', 63–9.

rulers (*c.* 1530–*c.* 1614) seems a little ungenerous: something more like the 120 years occupied by the first six *Alafin* of New Ọyọ (1836–1956) would appear more reasonable. On this basis, the Nupe sack of Ọyọ Ile would have occurred closer to *c.* 1500. This argument breaks down, however, if, as suggested earlier, the traditional genealogy of these kings, and indeed this whole section of the king-list, is factitious.[68] However, the confused conditions of the period are perhaps more likely to have produced telescoping than lengthening of the king-list, so that the earlier date should be preferred.

Earlier than this, it seems unprofitable to venture. Attempts have been made to use the king-list to calculate a date for the foundation of the Ọyọ kingdom.[69] But in view of the doubts which exist about the completeness, accuracy, and historicity of the earliest portions of the king-list, such calculations can have no value. Archaeological investigation may eventually establish at least the date at which Ọyọ Ile was first occupied, but the exploratory excavations so far carried out throw little light on this question.[70]

§6. SUMMARY OF CONCLUSIONS

For the purposes of this study, the imperial period of Ọyọ history is taken as extending from the reoccupation of Ọyọ Ile by *Alafin* Abipa, which is dated to around 1600, to the abandonment of Ọyọ Ile after the death of *Alafin* Oluewu in *c.* 1836. For the *Alafin* of this period, the following chronology is taken as being more or less approximately correct:

Abipa Ọbalokun	} 1st half of 17th century
Ajagbo	mid/late 17th century
Odarawu Karan Jayin Ayibi Ọsinyago	} late 17th/early 18th centuries

[68] Cf. above Ch. 3, pp. 40–41.

[69] Smith, 'The Alafin in Exile', 74; id., *Kingdoms of the Yoruba*, 103–4; Morton-Williams, 'The Influence of Habitat and Trade on Oyo and Ashanti', 89. Both Smith and Morton-Williams suggest, with reservations, the early fifteenth century.

[70] The earliest levels uncovered at Ọyọ Ile yielded pottery with impressions of maize-cobs, which must date from the sixteenth century or later: Willett, 'Investigations at Old Oyo', 75.

Ojigi	*floruit* 1726–30
Gberu	
Amuniwaiye	} 1730s–1754
Onişile	
Labisi	
Awọnbioju	} 1754
Agboluaje	
Majẹogbe	} *Başọrun* Gaha effective ruler
Abiọdun	1754–74
Abiọdun (effective rule)	1774–89
Awolẹ	1789–c. 1796
Adebo	
Maku	} c. 1796–7
interregnum	c. 1797–c. 1802
Majotu	c. 1802–30/1
Amodo	c. 1830/1–33/4
Oluewu	c. 1833/4–35/6

CHAPTER 5

The Capital

THE fundamental unit of Yoruba political organization was the town (*ilu*). Yoruba towns were largely autonomous communities, each with its own hereditary ruler, which may reasonably be termed 'city-states'. Large territorial kingdoms, like that of Ọyọ, comprised a number of such city-states, whose rulers recognized the over-all authority of the king of the capital city. The *Alafin* of Ọyọ was thus in the first place the king of the city of Ọyọ, and only secondarily the ruler of the Ọyọ kingdom. Consideration of the political organization of the Ọyọ kingdom must therefore begin with an examination of the government of the capital city.

To reconstruct in any detail the political institutions of the Ọyọ capital during the imperial period is, unfortunately, a matter of some difficulty. The only first–hand accounts of the city which we possess, those of Clapperton and the Landers in 1826–30, are not very informative about its system of government. The earliest substantial description of the political institutions of the capital is that of Johnson, written in 1897,[1] and on many points we are dependent upon works written still more recently.[2] It would be rash to assume that conditions attested for New Ọyọ in the late nineteenth or twentieth centuries also obtained at Ọyọ Ile. There is evidence that the shift of the capital from Ọyọ Ile to New Ọyọ was accompanied by significant modifications of the political system: in particular, it appears that the Ogboni society, an earth cult of considerable political importance at New Ọyọ,[3] did not exist at Ọyọ Ile.[4] Nor is it likely that the political institutions of Ọyọ Ile persisted unchanged throughout the imperial period. However, oral

[1] Johnson, *History of the Yorubas*, 40–74.
[2] Esp. Simpson, 'Intelligence Report on the Oyo Division', and Morton-Williams, 'The Yoruba Kingdom of Oyo'.
[3] Cf. P. Morton-Williams, 'The Yoruba Ogboni Cult in Ọyọ', *Africa*, 30 (1960), 362–74.
[4] This was suggested by Frobenius, *Voice of Africa*, i. 172–3, and has been argued in detail by B. A. Agiri, 'The Ogboni among the Ọyọ-Yoruba', *Lagos Notes and Records*, 3.2 (1972), 50–9, and by J. A. Atanda, 'The Yoruba Ogboni Cult: Did it Exist in Old Ọyọ?', *JHSN* 6.4 (1973), 365–72.

traditions and a few references in contemporary European sources provide an outline narrative of the internal history of the capital, which serves as some sort of control in the reconstruction of its political system, and they also either explicitly refer to, or indirectly attest, some of the institutional changes which took place. At least a tentative reconstruction can therefore be attempted.

The principal political institutions of the capital will first be delineated in general terms, with at least the notional intention of describing them as they may have operated at the beginning of the imperial period, in the early seventeenth century. Since this reconstruction depends in large part upon extrapolation from the post-imperial period, corroboratory references in contemporary European sources are cited wherever they are available. This essentially synchronic reconstruction will then be followed by an account of the internal political history of the city during the seventeenth and eighteenth centuries, with particular reference to the ways in which the political system was modified in this period.

§1. THE BASIS OF POLITICAL POWER: LINEAGES AND WARDS

We should begin, evidently, by making clear the practical basis of political power and influence in Qyǫ, but on this fundamental question there is very little direct evidence for the imperial period, and we have to proceed by assuming that the better-documented conditions of the nineteenth century can be projected backwards into earlier times. Political power normally lay with the senior 'chiefs', or holders of titles (*oloye*). However, generally speaking, these men were given senior titles in recognition of their power; political power did not derive from the possession of a title. Power was based ultimately on the control of resources, more specifically on the allegiance of followers and the accumulation of wealth—'men and means', to use an illuminating phrase of Samuel Johnson.[5] It is the allegiance of followers that should be especially stressed, since wealth was primarily important as a means of acquiring followers, being distributed in gifts to secure the loyalty of supporters or invested in the purchase of wives and slaves. A man might acquire wealth and a following by his own efforts, especially in warfare and in trade, but the large household that a powerful man built up during his lifetime normally passed intact after his death to his descendants, and power was perhaps more usually inherited than

[5] Johnson, *History of the Yorubas*, 279 etc.

created. In this, indeed, conditions during the imperial period certainly differed from those of the nineteenth century. The long period of confusion which followed the fall of the Ọyọ empire destroyed many existing chiefly households and afforded extended opportunities for able warriors and traders to build up wealth and power, so that the nineteenth century saw the rise of many self-made men.[6] The greater stability of Ọyọ during the imperial period will have meant that there were fewer such openings for individual achievement and social mobility. The fact, which is clear from the traditions, that the most powerful men in the politics of Ọyọ Ile were the holders of the principal *hereditary* chieftaincies evidently reflects the continuity and stability of the major chiefly households.

The political system of Ọyọ was thus founded upon the lineage, or *idile*, the large 'family' formed by the patrilineal descendants of a single man, the original founder of the lineage.[7] The city of Ọyọ can, indeed, be regarded as essentially a federation of lineages. The male members of a lineage, together with their wives and other dependants (such as slaves), normally shared a common residence in the *agbo ile*, or compound, though the larger lineages often occupied more than one compound. The average population of a compound would be about fifty.[8] The members of a lineage were also bound together by important economic interests, notably with regard to the ownership of land, which was vested collectively in the lineage as a whole, individual members enjoying only usufructuary rights. The eldest surviving male member of the lineage served as its head (*bale*). Much of the day-to-day administration of the city, including the maintenance of order and the adjudication of disputes, was the responsibility, in the first instance, of the *bale* and elders of the lineages involved. The lineages also played a crucial role in the politics of the city at a higher level, since all the most important chiefly titles of Ọyọ were the property of particular lineages. The

[6] Cf. J. F. A. Ajayi, 'The Aftermath of the Fall of Old Ọyọ', in J. F. A. Ajayi and M. Crowder (eds.), *History of West Africa*, vol. ii (London, 1974), 151–2.
[7] For the Yoruba lineage, see P. C. Lloyd, 'The Yoruba Lineage', *Africa*, 25 (1955), 235–51; id., *Yoruba Land Law*, 31–7; N. A. Fadipẹ, *The Sociology of the Yoruba* (Ibadan, 1970), 97–146.
[8] Simpson, 'Intelligence Report on the Oyo Division', Appendix on 'Oyo and its Environs', §4, gives an average compound population at New Ọyọ of about 50, with individual compounds ranging between 20 and over 100. Cf. Clapperton, *Journal of a Second Expedition*, 32, gives an average compound population of 30–40 for the Ọyọ town of 'Leobadda'; R. and J. Lander, *Journal of an Expedition*, i. 156, observe that compound populations varied between six or seven and 100.

succession to these titles was determined by the choice of the members of the lineages to which they belonged. The Ọyọ chiefs were thus representatives of the component lineages of the city, and served, to some degree, as spokesmen of lineage interests in the determination of national policy.

Adjacent compounds of the city were grouped together to form wards (*adugbo*), each of which was under the authority of an important chief resident in it. Each ward head was responsible for the maintenance of order in his ward, and adjudicated disputes referred to him by the lineages in it.[9] The effective power of a chief in Ọyọ depended not only on the size and wealth of his own lineage, but also on the extent of his ward, that is, on the number and size of the compounds acknowledging his authority as ward head.[10] The extent of a chief's ward was to some degree fluid, since compounds might transfer their allegiance from one chief to another, either by their own choice or at the orders of the *Alafin*. The major chiefly lineages of the city were thus in competition with each other for the allegiance of the smaller lineages, which could be secured in the long run only by the distribution of gifts and political favours.

The details of the ward structure of Ọyọ Ile are not known with any certainty.[11] It appears, however, that the city was divided into three main areas. First, there was the area of the king's palace (*afin*), known as Oke Afin. The palace itself occupied an immense area, according to Clapperton no less than a square mile,[12] and Oke Afin also included several compounds adjacent to the palace occupied by slave officials who performed ceremonial and administrative duties in the palace. Second, there were the wards of the city occupied by members of the royal lineage: there seem to have been three principal royal wards, headed by chiefs entitled the *Arẹmọ*, the *Ọna Iṣokun*, and the *Baba Iyaji*. And third, there were the wards occupied by the free Ọyọ of non-royal lineage, controlled by the most important

[9] Morton-Williams, 'The Yoruba Kingdom of Oyo', 50.

[10] Simpson, 'Intelligence Report on the Oyo Division', §48.

[11] For the ward structure of New Ọyọ, which does not replicate that of Ọyọ Ile, see NAI, OYOPROF. 6/1, 44/1914, 'List of Heads of Quarters', 2 Sept. 1914; Simpson, 'Intelligence Report on the Oyo Division', Appendix on 'Oyo and its Environs'.

[12] Clapperton, *Journal of a Second Expedition*, 58. This area included two 'large parks'. The *afin* at New Ọyọ is much smaller, only some 17 acres, but the entire area is built up: G. J. A. Ojo, *Yoruba Palaces* (London, 1966), 24–5. The difference is no doubt due to the fact that the New Ọyọ *afin* had to be fitted into a pre-existing town when the capital was moved there in the 1830s.

non-royal chiefs. The principal non-royal chiefs, who formed a council advisory to the *Alafin*, were the seven *Ọyọ Mesi*, headed by the *Bashọrun*.

§2. THE KING

The king, who had the title *Alafin*, or Owner of the *Afin* (Palace), was certainly the most important figure in the political system of Ọyọ. In theory, the *Alafin*'s power was absolute, and he alone decided major questions of national policy, but in practice his power was limited by the need to retain public confidence, and in particular he was expected to take account of the advice of the *Bashọrun* and the other *Ọyọ Mesi*. Among his specific administrative powers, two were of especial importance. First, the *Alafin* was the supreme judicial authority in Ọyọ. Disputes which could not be settled by the ward heads were referred to him, and only he could legally order an execution.[13] Second, the *Alafin* controlled the succession to all the chiefly titles of Ọyọ, since the choice of the lineage involved in each case had to be submitted to him for approval. He could also create and confer new titles. Johnson claims that he also enjoyed the right to depose a title-holder,[14] but no clear instance of the exercise of this right seems to be recalled in the traditions.[15]

Because of his importance, the *Alafin* was subject to a number of ritual restrictions. Most important, he was normally confined to the palace, and only appeared in public outside the palace at the three major annual festivals of the city: the Mọlẹ festival, in honour of Ifa, the god of divination; the Ọrun festival, at which the *Alafin* sacrificed to the gods to determine whether they approved the continuance of his reign; and the Bẹrẹ festival, at which he received from the Ọyọ chiefs a tribute of *bẹrẹ* grass for the thatching of the palace roofs.[16] His funeral ceremonies involved human sacrifices and enforced suicides of certain of his wives and slaves and of certain officials (known as the *abọbaku*, those who die with the king), to provide him with attendants in the afterlife.[17] The *Alafin* has sometimes been

[13] Morton-Williams, 'The Yoruba Kingdom of Oyo', 53, 62.

[14] Johnson, *History of the Yorubas*, 173.

[15] There is, however, the case of *Bashọrun* Akioso, who was placed under house arrest by *Alafin* Oluewu in the 1830s, pending the conclusion of the war against Ilọrin, but was then murdered by his own kinsmen 'to save him from a disgraceful death in public': ibid. 260.

[16] Ibid. 46–51. For the Bẹrẹ festival, see also S. O. Babayẹmi, 'Bẹrẹ Festival in Ọyọ', *JHSN* 7.1 (1973), 121–4.

[17] Johnson, *History of the Yorubas*, 56; Frobenius, *Voice of Africa*, i. 184;

described as a 'divine king',[18] and some writers, such as Frobenius, have argued that the *Alafin* was regarded specifically as the incarnation of Ṣango, the god of thunder and (according to tradition) one of the earliest *Alafin*.[19] The cult of Ṣango, which was controlled by the *Alafin*, was certainly an important prop of royal power in Ọyọ, but there is no evidence that the *Alafin* was ever regarded as divine in the strict sense of being worshipped as an *oriṣa* (deity). The *Alafin*'s traditional titulary described him more modestly as *ekeji oriṣa*, Companion of the Gods.[20]

The title of *Alafin*, like other important titles in Ọyọ, belonged to a particular lineage, supposedly descended from Ọranyan, the legendary founder of Ọyọ. The royal lineage had become segmented into three principal branches, whose titled heads were the *Ọna Iṣokun*, the *Ọna Aka*, and the *Ọna Ọmọ Ọla*, and eligibility for the throne was restricted to the Iṣokun branch.[21] The succession to the throne was determined in the first instance by the members of the royal lineage, known as the *ọmọ ọba* (children of the king). Their choice was discovered by the *Ọna Iṣokun*, the *Ọna Aka*, and the *Ọna Ọmọ Ọla*, and submitted by these chiefs to the *Ọyọ Mesi*, the council of senior non-royal chiefs, for approval.[22]

According to Johnson, in early times the *Alafin*'s eldest son, who had the title of *Arẹmọ*, normally succeeded to the throne, but later, owing to suspicions that some *Arẹmọ* had hastened their succession by parricide, it became customary for the *Arẹmọ* instead to commit suicide on the *Alafin*'s death.[23] It appears that during the early part of the imperial period it was still normal for the *Arẹmọ* to succeed his father. Such detailed evidence as we possess on the genealogical

---

cf. Clapperton, *Journal of a Second Expedition*, 49; R. Lander, *Records of Captain Clapperton's Last Expedition*, ii. 223–4.

[18] Ọyọ is cited as an example of 'divine kingship' in the classic study by J. Frazer, *The Golden Bough* (abridged edn., London, 1922), esp. 360–1.

[19] Frobenius, *Voice of Africa*, i. 183; cf. Simpson, 'Intelligence Report on the Oyo Division', §50.

[20] Morton-Williams, 'The Yoruba Kingdom of Oyo', 53.

[21] The division allegedly originated with the children of Oluaṣo, one of the early *Alafin*: Johnson, *History of the Yorubas*, 158.

[22] Ibid. 40, 42. Cf. R. Campbell, *A Pilgrimage to My Motherland* (New York, 1861), 50, also describes the *Ọna Iṣokun* as having 'the privilege of nominating a successor' to the *Alafin*; nowadays, however, the nominations of the *ọmọ ọba* are transmitted to the *Ọyọ Mesi* by another royal chief, the *Mọgaji Iyaji*.

[23] Johnson, *History of the Yorubas*, 41. The suicide of the eldest son of the *Alafin* is also mentioned by R. Lander, *Records of Captain Clapperton's Last Expedition*, ii. 223–4.

relationships of the successive *Alafin* before the eighteenth century tends to confirm that the succession normally passed from father to son (though not demonstrably to the *Aremo* among the sons) in this period.[24] The traditions relating to *Alafin* Jayin and *Alafin* Ayibi, around the beginning of the eighteenth century, also suggest that filial succession was still the norm. It is said that Jayin's unpopularity was mitigated by expectations of the succession of his popular son (*Aremo*?) Olusi, and that when Olusi predeceased his father the *Oyo Mesi* conferred the succession upon Olusi's son Ayibi, although he was still a minor.[25] Moreover, the earliest suicide of an *Aremo* specifically recorded in Oyo tradition was at the death of *Alafin* Ojigi, in the 1730s.[26] It seems probable, therefore, that the succession normally went by primogeniture until the early eighteenth century. The system we should envisage is one where the eldest son was normally designated as the heir apparent, but the *Oyo Mesi* retained the right to set aside his claims if he seemed unsuitable.[27]

§3. THE PALACE SLAVES

The *Alafin* controlled a large staff of officials who carried out the administrative and ceremonial tasks connected with the palace. These were known generally as *eru oba*, King's Slaves.[28] They resided either in the palace itself or in adjacent compounds of Oke Afin. In all, the palace slaves probably numbered several thousands.[29]

[24] The genealogy of the *Alafin* from Oluaso to Abipa, as given by Smith, 'The Alafin in Exile', 61–9, suggests that filial succession was normal in the sixteenth century: even if this geneaology is fictitious, it presumably reflects notions of how the succession ought to pass. There is little evidence for the later *Alafin*, but it is known that Odarawu was a son of his predecessor Ajagbo and that Jayin was a son of his predecessor Karan: *oriki* of Odarawu, recorded at the palace at Oyo; Johnson, *History of the Yorubas*, 170.

[25] Johnson, *History of the Yorubas*, 170–2.   [26] Ibid. 174.

[27] Cf. the situation in Dahomey, where the son first born to the king after his accession was recognized as heir-apparent, but could be rejected by the senior chiefs, the *Migan* and the *Mehu*, if he suffered from 'some defect or vice, of body or mind': R. Norris, *Memoirs of the Reign of Bossa Ahadee, King of Dahomy* (London, 1789), 4.

[28] On the palace slaves, see Johnson, *History of the Yorubas*, 57–67; Simpson, 'Intelligence Report on the Oyo Division', §§62–71; Morton-Williams, 'The Yoruba Kingdom of Oyo', 62–4; E. A. Oroge, 'The Institution of Slavery in Yorubaland' (Ph.D. Thesis, University of Birmingham, 1971), 49–80.

[29] At New Oyo in the 1930s, when the size of the palace organization had probably declined substantially from its pre-colonial level, the *afin* itself was estimated to have a population of 500, and there were forty-seven compounds of *eru oba* outside the *afin*: Simpson, 'Intelligence Report on the Oyo Division', Appendix on 'Oyo and its Environs', §17.

Johnson divides the palace officials into three categories: 'titled officers', eunuchs (*iwẹfa*), and *ilari*.[30] Of these three categories, the eunuchs were the highest in rank. The eunuchs were employed generally as guardians of the *Alafin*'s wives and children, but the senior titled eunuchs had much more extensive functions. The three principal eunuchs, who resided in their own compounds outside the palace, were, in order of rank, the *Ọna Iwẹfa* (Eunuch of the Middle), the *Ọtun Iwẹfa* (Eunuch of the Right), and the *Osi Iwẹfa* (Eunuch of the Left). These three were in charge respectively of judicial, religious, and administrative matters. The *Ọna Iwẹfa* normally took the *Alafin*'s place in giving judicial decisions; the *Ọtun Iwẹfa* had charge of the cult of Ṣango, and supervised the principal Ṣango shrine at the suburban hamlet of Koso; the *Osi Iwẹfa* was responsible for the collection of the *Alafin*'s revenues, and could also take the *Alafin*'s place in dealings with the Ọyọ chiefs.[31] Johnson observes that the *Osi Iwẹfa*, though nominally the least of the three, was in fact the most honoured, and attributes his rise in importance to an incident in the sixteenth century, when the *Osi Iwẹfa* saved the life of *Alafin* Ajiboyede in battle.[32] But possibly his rise was due rather to the increased importance of his sphere of responsibility with the expansion of the Ọyọ empire. 'Ebo', the 'chief eunuch' who was responsible for the maintenance of Clapperton and the Landers during their stays at Ọyọ Ile in 1826–30,[33] and whom the Landers described as 'next to the king . . . the most influential man in the place',[34] was presumably the *Osi Iwẹfa*.[35]

The *ilari* (also called the *arẹ*) were a special category of palace slaves, including both males and females, several hundreds in number.[36] The name *ilari*, meaning 'scar-head', alludes to the fact

[30] Johnson, *History of the Yorubas*, 57.

[31] For the *iwẹfa*, see esp. Johnson, *History of the Yorubas*, 59; Simpson, 'Intelligence Report on the Oyo Division', §§66–8; Morton-Williams, 'The Yoruba Kingdom of Oyo', 62–3.

[32] Johnson, *History of the Yorubas*, 59–60, 162–3.

[33] Clapperton, *Journal of a Second Expedition*, 37 etc.; R. Lander, *Records of Captain Clapperton's Last Expedition*, i. 109 etc.; R. and J. Lander, *Journal of an Expedition*, i. 169 etc.

[34] R. and J. Lander, *Journal of an Expedition*, i. 169.

[35] But the question of Ebo's office is complicated by the statement of R. Lander, *Records of Captain Clapperton's Last Expedition*, ii. 201, that during his absence from Ọyọ in 1826–7 Ebo 'had been taken into favour by his sovereign, and promoted to the highest office of state', referring presumably to promotion within the palace organization.

[36] Johnson, *History of the Yorubas*, 61, says that at New Ọyọ there were

that at their elevation to this rank, their heads were shaved and marked with incisions, into which magical substances were inserted. The male *ilari*, who came under the general authority of the *Osi Iwęfa*, served as the *Alafin*'s bodyguards, as his messengers to the world outside the palace, and as the collectors of taxes at the city gates. At the head of the *ilari*, under the *Osi Iwęfa*, were the *Arę Apeka* (also called *Olori Ęru*, or Head of Slaves), who was responsible for the activities of the *ilari* outside the palace, and the *Kudęfu*, who supervised the *ilari* inside the palace. The *Kudęfu* resided in the palace, but the *Arę Apeka* and several other senior *ilari* had their own compounds outside the palace.[37]

Johnson's third category of palace slaves, the 'titled officers', fulfilled a variety of administrative and ritual functions. Probably the most important of them was the *Olokun Ęsin*, or 'Master of Horse', who was responsible for the maintenance of the palace stables. The *Olokun Ęsin* resided in his own compound outside the palace, but went to the palace daily to supervise the stable slaves.[38] The Landers in 1830 met the 'Master of Horse' at Ọyọ, and describe him as 'an elderly man that possesses some influence over his master'.[39] The titled slave officials who resided inside the palace included such groups as the *Arọkin*, the official court historians, and the *Tętu*, the *Alafin*'s executioners.[40]

Although the palace officials were all slaves (*ęru*) in status, they were not all slaves in origin. In addition to bought slaves and war-captives (and descendants of these), it was not unknown for free Ọyọ to enter the palace service, or to be placed in it as children by their relatives.[41] Free men even occasionally volunteered to undergo emasculation in order to enter the ranks of the palace eunuchs.[42] Eunuchs were also recruited from among criminals: Johnson notes that the punishment of emasculation could only be imposed by the *Alafin* in the Ọyọ kingdom, and that offenders condemned to this punishment had to be sent to the capital, where they were taken

---

'several hundreds'; Talbot, *Peoples of Southern Nigeria*, iii. 270, says there were 200 male and 200 female *ilari*.

[37] For the *ilari*, see esp. Johnson, *History of the Yorubas*, 60–2; Simpson, 'Intelligence Report on the Oyo Division', §70–1; Morton-Williams, 'The Yoruba Kingdom of Oyo', 63–4.

[38] Johnson, *History of the Yorubas*, 57.

[39] R. and J. Lander, *Journal of an Expedition*, i. 177.

[40] For the 'titled officers', see esp. Johnson, *History of the Yorubas*, 57–9.

[41] Simpson, 'Intelligence Report on the Oyo Division', §63.

[42] Ibid., §68; cf. Johnson, *History of the Yorubas*, 163.

into the palace service.[43] Emasculation was imposed upon men
convicted of sexual offences, such as incest, bestiality, and adultery
with the wife of a king,[44] and according to Richard Lander also for
theft.[45] Eunuchs were also, however, recruited from among war-
captives.[46] The palace slaves probably included a large proportion
of non-Ọyọ, and a significant number of non-Yoruba. There are,
indeed, various references in the traditions to palace slaves originating from the countries to the north of Ọyọ—Nupe, Borgu, and
Hausaland.[47] It seems likely that some of these northerners were
literate in Arabic. It is noteworthy that the ambassadors from Ọyọ
whom Landolphe met in the Benin area in *c.* 1787 were literate in
Arabic.[48] Such ambassadors would normally be *ilari,* and these may
well have been of northern (perhaps Hausa) origin.[49]

Appointment to the senior palace titles was generally by promotion according to merit. Some titles, however, notably those of
the *Olokun Ẹsin* and the *Arọkin,* are said to have been hereditary,
meaning that the *Alafin* selected them from among descendants of
former holders of these titles.[50] Two of the most important palace
officials, the *Osi Iwẹfa* and the *Olokun Ẹsin,* were among the *abọbaku*
who were required to commit suicide at the death of the *Alafin,*[51] so
that these titles were always vacant to be filled according to the
choice of the new *Alafin.* In addition, the *ilari* titles lapsed at the
death of the *Alafin,* and could be confirmed or redistributed by his
successor.[52]

In addition to the palace slaves, there were a number of female
officials with important functions in the palace. The most important
of these was the *Iya Ọba,* or King's Mother. In early times, this was
apparently the *Alafin*'s real mother. The traditions certainly attest
the importance of the *Alafin*'s mother at the Ọyọ court, for on two

[43] Johnson, *History of the Yorubas,* 60.
[44] Ibid.
[45] R. Lander, *Records of Captain Clapperton's Last Expedition,* i. 283.
[46] PP, 1887 (c. 5144), vol. lx, p. 38, 'Report of Mr. Higgins, Acting Colonial
Secretary, and Mr. Oliver Smith, Queen's Advocate, Special Commissioners of
the Government of Lagos to the Tribes Interior of Lagos', 10 Feb. 1887.
[47] Johnson, *History of the Yorubas,* 149, 166, 168, 227.
[48] Landolphe, *Mémoires,* ii. 86.
[49] Some details of the account of their homeland which they gave to Landolphe
suggest Hausaland rather than Ọyọ, as noted by Ryder, *Benin and the Europeans,*
225.
[50] Johnson, *History of the Yorubas,* 57–8.
[51] Ibid. 56.
[52] Ibid. 67.

occasions when the *Alafin* had succeeded as a minor a regency was exercised by his mother: thus in the early years of *Alafin* Kọri's reign his mother Iyayun is said to have ruled as Regent,[53] while in the minority of *Alafin* Ofinran the kingdom was ruled by his mother Adasobo.[54] Later, however, it became customary for the *Alafin*'s mother, if still alive at his accession, to commit suicide, on the grounds that the *Alafin* should not have to abase himself before anyone.[55] The post of *Iya Ọba* was then filled by appointment from among the palace women. Second in importance to the *Iya Ọba* was the *Iya Kere* ('Little Mother'), who was the custodian of the *Alafin*'s regalia and also had charge of the female *ilari*.[56] The female palace officials, and the female *ilari*, were commonly known as *Ayaba* (*aya ọba*), or King's Wives. Richard Lander's statement, in 1827, that the *Alafin* had 2,000 wives,[57] should probably be understood as including these other categories of palace women as well as the *Alafin*'s wives properly speaking.

§4. THE ROYAL LINEAGE

Owing to the practice of large-scale polygyny by the successive *Alafin*, the royal lineage became very large, and the *ọmọ ọba*, the members of the royal lineage, probably formed a substantial minority of the population of the city. Several members of the royal lineage, moreover, held powerful positions in the city. The most important of these was the *Aremọ*: this title, as already noted, was normally given to the *Alafin*'s eldest son, but in the absence of adult sons it might be conferred upon another of the *Alafin*'s kinsmen.[58] The *Aremọ* controlled a large ward of the city, and generally shared in the powers of the *Alafin*. His position was enhanced by the fact that he was not, like the *Alafin*, restricted to the palace: as Johnson observes, 'the father is King of the palace, and the son the King for the general public.'[59] This situation could sometimes cause tension between the *Alafin* and the *Aremọ*: such tension apparently existed, for example, between *Alafin* Jayin and his son Olusi, leading to accusations that

[53] Ibid. 155.   [54] Smith, 'The Alafin in Exile', 64.

[55] Johnson, *History of the Yorubas*, 63.

[56] For the palace women, see esp. Johnson, *History of the Yorubas*, 63–7; Simpson, 'Intelligence Report on the Oyo Division', §72–3; Morton-Williams, 'The Yoruba Kingdom of Oyo', 64–5.

[57] R. Lander, *Records of Captain Clapperton's Last Expedition*, ii. 191.

[58] Johnson, *History of the Yorubas*, 47. Cf. *Alafin* Oṣinyago gave the title to a maternal cousin: ibid. 173.

[59] CMS, G.31 A.2/1888–9, S. Johnson to the Revd. J. B. Wood, 8 Nov. 1887.

Jayin murdered Oluṣi.[60] Under a senile or a weak *Alafin*, indeed, the *Arẹmọ* might become the effective ruler of Ọyọ.[61]

In addition to the *Arẹmọ*, there were several other members of the royal lineage who held important titles. Johnson distinguishes two principal groups of such titles, known conventionally as the 'fathers of the king' and the 'brothers of the king'.[62] The 'fathers' were the heads of the three principal branches of the royal lineage, already mentioned, the *Ọna Iṣokun*, the *Ọna Aka*, and *Ọna Ọmọ Ọla*. The 'brothers' were a group of junior titles, the most important of which was that of *Baba Iyaji*.[63] These lesser titles seem to have been created for segments of the Iṣokun branch of the royal lineage which had become excluded from eligibility for the throne:[64] certainly, it appears that the title of *Agunpopo*, one of this group, was created by *Alafin* Abiọdun, in the late eighteenth century, for his eldest son, who was barred from taking the title of *Arẹmọ* on grounds of illegitimacy.[65] Some of the 'brothers', including the *Baba Iyaji*, were among the *abọbaku* who died with the *Alafin*.[66] The *Ọna Iṣokun* and the *Baba Iyaji* served as heads of two large wards of the city, the other chiefs of the royal lineage being subordinate to them.

The relationship of the *ọmọ ọba*, particularly those holding important chieftaincies, to the *Alafin* was ambivalent. The existence of an immense royal lineage might be expected to provide a reservoir of supporters who would uphold the authority of the *Alafin* against the non-royal lineages of the capital. However, most of the *ọmọ ọba*, and all those holding senior titles with the exception of the *Arẹmọ*, belonged to sections of the royal lineage which were not eligible for the succession to the throne. Having no prospect of ever exercising the royal authority, they had no clear interest in upholding it. On the other hand, as the case of the *Arẹmọ* illustrates, those *ọmọ ọba* who were eligible for the succession might on occasions intrigue against the *Alafin* rather than supporting him, since the premature overthrow of an *Alafin* might open the way for their own accession to the throne. The power of the *Alafin* therefore rested less on the support

[60] Johnson, *History of the Yorubas*, 170–1.

[61] As occurred under *Alafin* Majotu in the 1820s: ibid. 212–15. Cf. also the case of *Alafin* Ojigi: ibid. 174.

[62] Ibid. 68–9.

[63] Nowadays more commonly called the *Mọgaji Iyaji*.

[64] Morton-Williams, 'The Yoruba Kingdom of Oyo', 61–2.

[65] Johnson, *History of the Yorubas*, 186–7; cf. Hethersett, in *Iwe Kika Ẹkẹrin*, 59.

[66] Johnson, *History of the Yorubas*, 56.

of the royal lineage than on that of the slave officials of the palace.

§5. THE NON-ROYAL CHIEFS

A number of titles in Ọyọ were held by free Ọyọ not of royal blood. Most of these titles belonged to particular lineages, and succession to them was decided by the choice of the members of the lineage, subject to the final approval of the *Alafin*. The most important of the non-royal chiefs were the seven who formed the council of the *Ọyọ Mesi*: these were, in order of rank, the *Baṣọrun*, the *Agbakin*, the *Ṣamu*, the *Alapini*, the *Laguna*, the *Akiniku*, and the *Aṣipa*.[67] Of these, the *Baṣọrun* was much the most important, and the most powerful chief in Ọyọ after the *Alafin* himself. It was the *Baṣọrun* who served as Regent (*adele*) during the interregnum between the death of one *Alafin* and the installation of his successor,[68] and on the one occasion during the imperial period when a minor was chosen to be *Alafin* (Ayibi) it was again the *Baṣọrun* who exercised the Regency.[69]

Individually, the *Ọyọ Mesi* had important functions. They probably served as the heads of the seven principal wards of the non-royal section of the city.[70] They also controlled some of the major religious cults. It was the *Baṣọrun* who divined at the annual Ọrun festival to determine whether the *Alafin*'s sacrifices were acceptable to the gods.[71] The *Agbakin* was in charge of the cult of Ọranyan, the founder of Ọyọ; the *Alapini* was the head of the Egungun, the masqueraders who represented the spirits of the deceased; the *Laguna* controlled the cult of Oriṣa Oko, the god of

[67] Ibid. 70–2; cf. ibid. 165, where the same seven chiefs are named as constituting the Ọyọ Mesi under *Alafin* Abipa, at the beginning of the seventeenth century. Nowadays, the *Ọna Mọdeke* (earlier considered one of the palace officials: cf. Johnson, *History of the Yorubas*, 58) is also regarded as one of the Ọyọ Mesi. J. A. Atanda, *The New Ọyọ Empire: Indirect Rule and Change in Western Nigeria 1894–1934* (London, 1973), 16 and n.4, suggests that this was also the case at Ọyọ Ile, while Morton-Williams, 'The Yoruba Kingdom of Oyo', 67–8, n.10, suggests that at Ọyọ Ile the *Ọna Mọdeke* held the place on the Ọyọ Mesi council later held by the *Aṣipa*.

[68] Johnson, *History of the Yorubas*, 46.

[69] Ibid. 172.

[70] At New Ọyọ, only the *Baṣọrun*, the *Alapini*, the *Laguna*, and the *Aṣipa* control large wards, but the decline of the other three Ọyọ Mesi was probably due to the dislocation which accompanied the shift of the capital from Ọyọ Ile to New Ọyọ: cf. Simpson, 'Intelligence Report on the Oyo Division', §48.

[71] Johnson, *History of the Yorubas*, 48; Morton-Williams, 'The Yoruba Kingdom of Oyo', 55. The title *Baṣọrun* means 'The lord (*iba*) who performs the ọrun'.

farming; and the *Aṣipa* that of Ogun, the god of war, iron, and hunting.[72] The *Ǫyǫ Mesi* also commanded the army of the Ǫyǫ capital, the *Baṣǫrun* serving as commander-in-chief.[73] One of the *Ǫyǫ Mesi*, the *Ṣamu*, was among the *abǫbaku* who were required to commit suicide when the *Alafin* died.[74]

Collectively, as has been seen, the *Ǫyǫ Mesi* served as advisers to the *Alafin*, and they also had the final voice in determining the succession to the throne. During the imperial period, as will be seen below, they also asserted a right to judge an *Alafin*'s conduct unsatisfactory, and formally to reject him, whereupon the *Alafin* was obliged to commit suicide.[75] This right presumably derived from the role of the *Baṣǫrun* in the annual Ǫrun festival, mentioned above.

References in an eighteenth-century source to the power of the king's 'ministers' in Ǫyǫ evidently refer to the council of the *Ǫyǫ Mesi*, while a reference to '*Ochenoo*, the prime minister' clearly alludes to the *Baṣǫrun*, 'Ochenoo' representing *Ǫṣǫrun*, a shorter form of the title *Baṣǫrun*.[76] It is a little surprising that Clapperton and the Landers in 1826–30 do not refer in unequivocal terms to the *Baṣǫrun* or the *Ǫyǫ Mesi*, though this may be partly due to the fact that they remained for the most part within the palace. It is probable, however, that we should recognize three of the *Ǫyǫ Mesi* in the 'three principal caboceers' whom Clapperton met in 1826, and who are also mentioned by the Landers in 1830 as 'three "head men"', as they are styled, who advise with the prince, and lead his soldiers to battle'.[77] Richard Lander also claims that in 1827 the *Alafin* offered him the post of 'Prime Minister', meaning presumably that of *Baṣǫrun*.[78]

There were numerous other titles of lesser rank than the *Ǫyǫ Mesi*. Of particular importance were the *Ęṣǫ*, the seventy junior war-chiefs, who acted as subordinate commanders of the army under the *Ǫyǫ Mesi*. Unlike most Ǫyǫ titles, these were not attached

[72] Johnson, *History of the Yorubas*, 72; Morton-Williams, 'The Yoruba Kingdom of Oyo', 56.

[73] For the military role of the *Ǫyǫ Mesi*, see further below, Ch. 9, pp. 190, 191.

[74] Morton-Williams, 'The Yoruba Kingdom of Oyo', 56.

[75] Johnson, *History of the Yorubas*, 70, 173; Morton-Williams, 'The Yoruba Kingdom of Oyo', 54.

[76] Dalzel, *History of Dahomy*, 12–13, 157.

[77] Clapperton, *Journal of a Second Expedition*, 42; R. and J. Lander, *Journal of an Expedition*, i. 183. The term 'caboceer', from the Portuguese *caboceiro* (head man), was commonly used by Europeans of African chiefs.

[78] R. Lander, *Records of Captain Clapperton's Last Expedition*, ii. 234.

to particular lineages, but conferred individually on merit. However, certain lineages apparently maintained a tradition of military service, and the *Ẹṣọ* titles were in practice normally conferred upon the descendants of former holders.[79] The *Ẹṣọ* were appointed by the *Ọyọ Mesi*, subject to the final approval of the *Alafin*.[80] They apparently occupied a special quarter of the city, known as Oke Ẹṣọ.[81]

Also worthy of mention among the non-royal chiefs was the *Parakoyi*, who was head of the Muslim ward of the city and commander of the Muslims in war.[82] Little is known of the development of the Muslim community in Ọyọ, but Islam seems to have been established in the kingdom by the seventeenth century, if not already in the sixteenth. A tradition reported by Johnson relates that when *Alafin* Ajiboyede, one of the kings of Igboho during the sixteenth century, executed some Ọyọ chiefs, a Muslim priest from Nupe who was resident at Igboho, called Baba Kewu, sent his son Baba Yigi to remonstrate with him, and induced him to make a public apology.[83] Another tradition, however, asserts that Islam was introduced into Ọyọ, by an Arab called Afa Yigi, only under *Alafin* Ajagbo, in the seventeenth century.[84] These two stories are not necessarily in contradiction, since the tradition relating to Ajagbo's reign probably records the establishment at Ọyọ of organized Islamic worship, and would not exclude the occasional presence of foreign Muslim clerics in earlier times. But it is difficult to place great confidence in the details of these traditions. In particular, it seems probable that the 'Baba Yigi' of Johnson's story and the 'Afa Yigi' of the second tradition are the same person, and while it is just possible that he could have been active under both Ajiboyede and Ajagbo, it seems much more likely that his name has become attached to traditions originally unconnected.[85] However, the attribution of the introduction of Islam to the reign of *Alafin* Ajagbo at least fits what little

---

[79] Johnson, *History of the Yorubas*, 79. At New Ọyọ, the surviving *Ẹṣọ* titles have tended to become hereditary: cf. Simpson, 'Intelligence Report on the Oyo Division', §§54–5.

[80] Morton-Williams, 'The Yoruba Kingdom of Oyo', 57.

[81] The Oke Ẹṣọ quarter of Ọyọ Ile is mentioned by Johnson, *History of the Yorubas*, 261. At New Ọyọ, there was no such quarter, the *Ẹṣọ* being scattered among the various wards of the city: Simpson, 'Intelligence Report on the Oyo Division', §§54–5.

[82] Oral evidence, from the *Parakoyi* of Ọyọ; cf. G. O. Gbadamọsi, 'The Imamate Question among Yoruba Muslims', *JHSN* 6.2 (1972), 230–1.

[83] Johnson, *History of the Yorubas*, 164.

[84] Gbadamọsi, 'The Growth of Islam among the Yoruba', 12–13.

[85] The very names 'Baba Kewu' and 'Baba Yigi' are suspicious, since *kewu*

evidence we have on this point from external sources. Whereas the Timbuktu scholar Aḥmad Baba in the early seventeenth century had classified the Yoruba (Ọyọ) among the non-Muslim peoples of West Africa,[86] the Hausa scholar Ibn Masanih of Katsina, who died in 1667, is recorded to have written a work on the method of determining the time of sunset addressed to 'the learned men (*fuqaha'*) of Yoruba', implying that Muslim clerics were by then active in the Ọyọ kingdom.[87] Certainly, by the end of the imperial period there was a substantial community of Muslims in the Ọyọ capital, though the great majority of the population of the city remained pagan. There is little hard information on which sections of the city's population were attracted to the new religion, though it is probable that Islam was especially strong among those involved in long-distance commerce[88] and it is known that the lineages who specialized in the craft of cloth-weaving were Muslims.[89] There is no evidence that any *Alafin* of Ọyọ Ile ever adopted Islam,[90] but a measure of official recognition was extended to the new cult. The *Alafin* appointed (or, rather, confirmed the selection of) the Imam, and the Imam in turn offered prayers for the *Alafin*.[91] Islam, in fact, functioned at first very much like the indigenous pagan cults of Ọyọ.

§6. THE STRUGGLE FOR POWER IN ỌYỌ

The traditions suggest that the imperial period was a time of bitter political strife inside the Ọyọ capital, with continual conflicts between the *Alafin* and the *Ọyọ Mesi*. The vague division of power between the *Alafin* and the *Ọyọ Mesi* was, perhaps, always likely to

---

and *yigi* are Yoruba words referring respectively to literacy in Arabic and the Muslim ceremony of betrothal: R. C. Abraham, *Dictionary of Modern Yoruba* (London, 1958), s.v. *kéú*, *yìgì*.

[86] Quoted in Hodgkin, *Nigerian Perspectives*, 156.

[87] Bivar and Hiskett, 'The Arabic Literature of Nigeria', 116.

[88] Cf. Ajayi, 'The Aftermath of the Fall of Old Ọyọ', 142; Gbadamọsi, 'The Imamate Question among Yoruba Muslims', 230.

[89] J. M. Bray, 'The Organization of Traditional Weaving in Iseyin, Nigeria', *Africa*, 38 (1968), 271.

[90] *Alafin* Amodo, in the 1830s, was obliged to make a profession of Islam under military compulsion from Ilọrin, and Atiba, the first *Alafin* at New Ọyọ, had been a Muslim before his accession but abandoned the religion on his accession to the throne: Johnson, *History of the Yorubas*, 217–18, 277. Otherwise, the first Muslim *Alafin* was Adeniran, who succeeded in 1945. Nowadays, Ọyọ is a predominantly Muslim town.

[91] Morton-Williams, 'The Influence of Habitat and Trade on Oyo and Ashanti', 92.

give rise to tension between them, and there are occasional glimpses of dissension even before the imperial period. *Alafin* Ajiboyede, as has been noted, is said to have executed some Qyọ chiefs, and to have averted an insurrection only by a public apology,[92] and the *Qyọ Mesi* are recorded to have opposed the transfer of the capital from Igboho to Qyọ Ile by Ajiboyede's successor Abipa.[93] However, the traditions indicate that an exceptionally bitter struggle for power began in the late seventeenth century, and continued throughout the imperial period, down to the fall of Qyọ in the 1830s.[94]

The long reign of *Alafin* Ajagbo, in the latter half of the seventeenth century, was followed by what Johnson calls 'a succession of despotic and short-lived kings', nine *Alafin* whose reigns were terminated by deposition or assassination.[95] Ajagbo's successor Odarawu was formally rejected by the *Qyọ Mesi* soon after his accession, and committed suicide. This is the earliest rejection of an *Alafin* recorded in Qyọ tradition: although a right of rejection might seem implicit in the *Başọrun*'s role in the Qrun festival, such a right had apparently not been exercised before the time of Odarawu. The overthrow of Odarawu therefore represented a significant institutional change which substantially strengthened the *Qyọ Mesi* against the *Alafin*. Odarawu's successor Karan attempted to challenge this newly claimed right of rejection, and refused a demand for his suicide, but he was killed in an insurrection. The next two *Alafin*, Jayin and Ayibi, were compelled to commit suicide; Ayibi's successor Qsinyago was allegedly murdered;[96] and Qsinyago's successor, Ojigi, also suffered rejection and suicide, probably in the 1730s.

The rejection of Ojigi was apparently accompanied by a further institutional modification in the interests of the *Qyọ Mesi*, namely an alteration of the system of succession to the Qyọ throne. The old system of filial succession was difficult to sustain when *Alafin* were removed in such rapid succession: Ayibi, who succeeded as a minor and reigned only briefly,[97] cannot have left any adult sons at his death, while Qsinyago seems also to have lacked adult sons, since he

[92] Johnson, *History of the Yorubas*, 164.
[93] Ibid. 164–6.
[94] Cf. R. Law, 'The Constitutional Troubles of Qyọ in the Eighteenth Century', *JAH* 12 (1971), 25–44.
[95] Johnson *History of the Yorubas*, 169–77.
[96] He is said to have been poisoned: such allegations of murder by poison should be treated with some reserve, since they might easily be made whenever an *Alafin* died suddenly, especially during a period of political tension.
[97] Johnson, *History of the Yorubas*, 172–3.

gave the title of *Arẹmọ* to a material cousin.[98] The *Ọyọ Mesi*, it appears, now completed the breakdown of the old system by insisting that in future the *Arẹmọ* should be excluded from the succession, and be required instead to commit suicide at the *Alafin*'s death. Johnson records that Ojigi was rejected in order to get rid of his *Arẹmọ*, who had behaved with great cruelty, and comments vaguely: 'for about this time the custom began to prevail for the Arẹmọs to die with the father.'[99] This is in fact the first recorded instance of the suicide of an *Arẹmọ*, and it seems probable that while the Ọyọ Mesi may always have enjoyed the right to set aside the *Arẹmọ*'s claim to the throne, they began to exercise this right systematically only from the 1730s. Tradition claims that the *Arẹmọ* was required to commit suicide in order to discourage parricide,[100] but while this may have been the official excuse it seems likely that the real purpose of the new system was to increase the influence of the *Ọyọ Mesi* in determining the succession, by opening it up to competition among a wider range of the *ọmọ ọba*. Unfortunately, the principles governing the royal succession in this later period are far from clear. A European source in the 1770s implies that the succession normally passed to a son of the late king,[101] but this is perhaps merely a careless projection of European norms onto the Ọyọ. Richard Lander in 1827, however, grasped the elective character of the Ọyọ kingship, though he exaggerated it by failing to realize that eligibility was restricted to a single lineage: 'We were mistaken in supposing the crown of Yariba to be hereditary, the chiefs invariably electing, from among the wisest and most sagacious of their own number, an individual who is invested with the supreme dignity.'[102] One account asserts that in this period, when an *Alafin* died, his successor was chosen 'from another branch of the royal family'.[103] This suggests the system, common in Yoruba kingdoms, whereby the king is chosen in rotation from different 'houses' (*ile*) of the royal lineage. Such a system operated at New Ọyọ in the post-imperial period,[104]

---

[98] Ibid. 173.   [99] Ibid. 174.   [100] Ibid. 41.

[101] Norris, *Memoirs of the Reign of Bossa Ahadee*, 12.

[102] R. Lander, *Records of Captain Clapperton's Last Expedition*, ii. 223.

[103] PP, 1887 (c. 5144), vol. lx, p. 39, 'Report of Mr. H. Higgins, Acting Colonial Secretary, and Mr. Oliver Smith, Queen's Advocate, Special Commissioners of the Government of Lagos to the Tribes Interior of Lagos', 10 Feb. 1887; repeated by Ellis, *Yorubas-Speaking Peoples*, 167.

[104] The first *Alafin* at New Ọyọ, Atiba, was succeeded by two of his sons, Adelu (1859–75) and Adeyẹmi (1875–1905): subsequently the succession alternated between two houses descended from Adelu and Adeyẹmi.

but the genealogical data available on the later *Alafin* of Qyǫ Ile do not confirm the operation of a rotational pattern of succession there.[105] Whatever the precise details of the new system, however, it clearly involved a choice between rival candidates, thereby enhancing the power of the *Qyǫ Mesi*, who had the final voice in the decision. It also appears that members of the royal lineage who were eligible for the throne were prevented from holding important titles in the capital.[106] This had the effect that they could not, like the *Arǫmǫ*, build up a following with which to press their claims to the succession, and guaranteed effective freedom of choice to the *Qyǫ Mesi*.

Ojigi's successor as *Alafin*, Gberu, attempted measures to restore royal power against the *Qyǫ Mesi*. When the title of *Baṣǫrun* fell vacant, he appointed a personal friend, called Jambu, to the post. This involved transferring the title to a new lineage.[107] It is doubtful whether there was any precedent for this exercise of royal prerogative.[108] The move, however, failed to resolve the problem of tension between the *Alafin* and the *Baṣǫrun*: like Henry II's appointment of Becket as Archbishop of Canterbury,[109] it served rather to demonstrate that the cause of this tension lay not in the personalities of individual kings and chiefs, but in the structure of the political system. *Baṣǫrun* Jambu was soon in opposition to *Alafin* Gberu, and eventually secured Gberu's rejection and suicide. The death of Gberu was followed by a brief interregnum, since the prince chosen to succeed him, Amuniwaiye, at first refused to be installed, out of fear of Jambu. Jambu therefore ruled Qyǫ as Regent for three years, until he in turn was compelled to commit suicide.[110] Jambu's lineage, however, retained possession of the title of *Baṣǫrun*. On

---

[105] There is little genealogical information on these *Alafin*, but note that Oniṣile was a son of his predecessor Amuniwaiye, while Majǫogbe was a brother of his predecessor Agboluaje: *Oriki* of Oniṣile, recorded at the palace at Qyǫ; Johnson, *History of the Yorubas*, 180.

[106] It seems, indeed, that eligible princes were usually required to live outside the capital altogether: Johnson, *History of the Yorubas*, 67–8.

[107] Ibid. 71–2, 175. It should be noted, however, that Gaha, the fourth *Baṣǫrun* of Jambu's line, is said to have been a descendant of Yamba, the last *Baṣǫrun* of the old line: I. A. Akinjogbin, 'The Oyo Empire in the Eighteenth Century: A Reassessment', *JHSN* 3.3 (1966), 454. It must be presumed that Jambu's lineage intermarried with that of Yamba.

[108] The *Baṣǫrun* title was transferred to new lineages on three further occasions in the early nineteenth century: Johnson, *History of the Yorubas*, 72.

[109] Cf. C. Greenway, *The Life and Death of Thomas Becket* (London, 1961), 61, for Henry's motives in appointing Becket.

[110] The episode of Jambu's regency is not mentioned by Johnson. See YHRS, Chief S. Ojo, 'Report on Qyǫ Yoruba History', n.d.; cf. Ojo, *Iwe Itan Qyǫ*, 62.

Jambu's death, Amuniwaiye was installed as *Alafin*, but he died after a brief reign, allegedly by murder.[111] His successor Oniṣile was rejected by the *Qyọ Mesi* and committed suicide.

The rejection of Oniṣile was followed by the usurpation of effective power in Qyọ by the *Baṣorun*, Gaha.[112] Gaha procured the deaths of the next two *Alafin*, Labisi and Awọnbioju, after very brief reigns, and compelled Awọnbioju's successor, Agboluaje, to accept his authority. During the period of his power, Gaha is reported to have appropriated the royal revenues, compensating the *Alafin* by a pension of ten heads of cowries (equivalent to about 10 dollars) per day.[113] He began with widespread support, a reaction to the tyrannical rule of the earlier *Alafin*,[114] but alienated much of this goodwill by his own despotic behaviour, and acquired a reputation for favouring only members of his own lineage.[115] *Alafin* Agboluaje eventually committed suicide in despair at the situation, and his successor Majẹogbe died in circumstances which prompted accusations that he had been murdered by Gaha.[116] The next *Alafin*, Abiọdun, for some years submitted to Gaha, but eventually organized his overthrow, with the aid of military forces from the subordinate towns of the Qyọ kingdom, under the *Arẹ Ọna Kakamfo*, or commander-in-chief of the provincial army, Qyabi of Ajaṣẹ. Gaha was abandoned by the other chiefs of the capital, who went over to Abiọdun, and even by some sections of his own lineage, who were bought off by the prospect of the succession to his title.[117] Gaha's compound was stormed and Gaha himself captured and executed.

While there may be doubts about details in this picture of internal strife presented in the oral traditions, there can be no question about its essential historicity, since it is confirmed by contemporary European sources. A report of 1754 refers to succession disputes in Qyọ, and to the killing of two kings within two months, alluding

[111] The murder was supposedly effected by magic: as with allegations of poisoning, scepticism is justified.

[112] For the rule of Gaha, see Johnson, *History of the Yorubas*, 178–86; Hethersett, in *Iwe Kika Ẹkẹrin*, 61–4; Adeyẹmi, *Iwe Itan Qyọ*, 8–9.

[113] Johnson, *History of the Yorubas*, 182.

[114] Ibid. 178.

[115] Hethersett, in *Iwe Kika Ẹkẹrin*, 61.

[116] It is said that Gaha and Majẹogbe both employed magicians in an effort to kill each other, and that Gaha succeeded: it is very probable that magicians were employed, but Gaha's magicians might easily have claimed credit for a death which was in fact natural.

[117] Johnson, *History of the Yorubas*, 184, refers to a brother of Gaha called Olubu who abandoned Gaha in the hope of obtaining the title of *Baṣorun*,

probably to *Baṣọrun* Gaha's murder of Labisi and Awọnbioju.[118]
The same picture emerges from the account of the English trader
Norris, written in the 1770s:

> The *Eyoes* are governed by a king; but not by one so absolute as the tyrant
> of *Dahomy*. If what report says of him be true, when his ill conduct gives
> just offence to his people, a deputation from them wait upon him, and
> represent to him, that the burden of government has been so fatiguing,
> that it is full time for him to repose from his cares, and to indulge himself
> with a little sleep. He thanks his people for their attention to his care,
> retires to his apartment as to sleep, where he gives directions to his women
> to strangle him; which is immediately executed, and his son [*sic*] quietly
> succeeds him, upon the same terms of holding the government no longer
> than his conduct merits the approbation of his people.[119]

This passage is repeated a few years later by Dalzel, with the addition
of a few details, notably a reference to the role of the king's 'ministers', i.e. the *Ọyọ Mesi*, in organizing demands for his suicide.[120]
Dalzel also records an unsuccessful demand for the suicide of the
Alafin in 1774, which led to a civil war in which the 'ministers' were
defeated and '*Ochenoo* [*Ọṣọrun*, i.e. *Baṣọrun*], the prime minister,'
was killed: evidently a reference to the overthrow of *Baṣọrun* Gaha
by *Alafin* Abiọdun.[121]

It is more difficult to be confident about the causes of the bitter
political struggles of the eighteenth century. The traditions offer
personal explanations, referring in stereotyped terms to the tyranny
of the successive *Alafin* and the ambition of *Baṣọrun* Gaha. This,
even if true, clearly does not get us very far: for why should tyranny
and ambition have been so much more rife in the eighteenth century
than earlier? One modern interpretation argues that the political
troubles of the eighteenth century arose out of disagreements over
national policy, the *Ọyọ Mesi* advocating a programme of military
expansion and the *Alafin* wishing to concentrate upon commercial
development.[122] But the evidence in support of this view is exiguous,

though in the event he was executed by Abiọdun. The *Baṣọrun* appointed to
replace Gaha belonged to the same lineage, and had presumably deserted him
in good season.

[118] PRO, T.70/1523, W. Devaynes to T. Melvil, 22 Oct. 1754 (extract), quoted
in T. Melvil to Committee, 30 Nov. 1754; cf. Akinjogbin, *Dahomey and its
Neighbours*, 146, n.1.

[119] Norris, *Memoirs of the Reign of Bossa Ahadee*, 11–12. For the date of
writing, see ibid. 1.

[120] Dalzel, *History of Dahomy*, 12–13.

[121] Ibid. 156–7.

[122] Akinjogbin, 'The Oyo Empire in the Eighteenth Century'.

and the assumed antagonism between the military and commercial interests in Qyọ seems unrealistic.[123] Probably we should think in structural rather than in personal or political terms, and relate the troubles to the changing distribution of power within the political system of Qyọ. On the face of it, the traditions attest a progressive increase in the influence of the *Qyọ Mesi*, culminating in 1754 in the seizure of power by the *Baṣọrun*. But this appearance is perhaps misleading. It is likely that royal power also was growing during the seventeenth and eighteenth centuries. The size and complexity of the *Alafin*'s staff of palace slaves was exceptional among Yoruba kingdoms,[124] and it seems probable that the elaboration of the palace organization was connected with the expansion of the Qyọ empire during this period. Certainly, as will be seen in the following chapters, the palace slaves played an important role in the administration of the expanding empire. This expansion of the *Alafin*'s staff of slaves tended to undermine the power of the *Qyọ Mesi*, since it freed the *Alafin* from dependence upon them in the execution of national policy. It may be, therefore, that the *Qyọ Mesi* were in fact attempting to resist this growth of royal power. The removal of individual *Alafin* proved to effect little, since it did not destroy the organization of palace slaves upon which royal power was based, and therefore in 1754 the *Baṣọrun* was obliged to seize effective power for himself.

The ability of the *Baṣọrun* and the *Qyọ Mesi* to offer such protracted and effective resistance to the development of royal autocracy remains to be explained. This was perhaps primarily due to the fact that although the *Alafin* had created an administrative machinery which dispensed with the need to rely upon the *Qyọ Mesi*, the latter still retained control of the metropolitan military system.[125] The balance of military power inside the capital was therefore still in their favour, and when an *Alafin* attempted to defy a demand for his rejection, as did Karan, he could be overthrown by force. *Alafin* Abiọdun was therefore able to overthrow *Baṣọrun* Gaha in 1774 only by calling in assistance from outside the capital, by bringing in the *Arẹ Ọna Kakamfo* and the military forces of the provincial towns of the Qyọ kingdom against the *Baṣọrun*. In this way, too, the empire became involved in the politics of the capital.

[123] For a fuller appraisal, see Law, 'The Constitutional Troubles of Qyọ', 34–6.   [124] Lloyd, *Political Development of Yoruba Kingdoms*, 11.
[125] Cf. below, Ch. 9, pp. 199–201.

CHAPTER 6

The Ọyọ Kingdom

THE empire over which the *Alafin* ruled comprised territories which were subjected to Ọyọ control in different ways and to varying degrees, and our consideration of it must begin by making clear the distinctions between the various categories of subjects. Two principal statements on this point are to be found in the primary sources. The informants of Clapperton in 1826 distinguished between 'the kingdom of Yoruba' and its 'tributaries', which are listed as Dahomey, Allada (Porto Novo), Badagry, and Mahi.[1] A more complicated account is given by Samuel Johnson. He distinguishes, first, between 'Yoruba Proper', i.e. the land of the Ọyọ Yoruba, which was closely controlled by the *Alafin*, and the other kingdoms whose dynasties derived from Ile Ifẹ, i.e. the other major Yoruba kingdoms and Benin, which acknowledged the *Alafin* as 'overlord' but otherwise 'lived more or less in a state of semi-independence'. He then goes on to add that at its greatest extent the empire 'also included the Popos [Egun, i.e. the peoples of the Badagry–Porto Novo area], Dahomey, and parts of Ashanti, with portions of the Tapas [Nupe] and Baribas.'[2] Both these accounts thus distinguish a central area under close control, which is evidently at least approximately equivalent in both versions ('the kingdom of Yoruba', 'Yoruba Proper'), from outlying dependencies more loosely subjected. But while Clapperton knows only one category of the latter (the 'tributaries'), Johnson introduces a second group, the kingdoms which acknowledged a common dynastic link with Ile Ifẹ.

Johnson's scheme of three categories of Ọyọ subjects has been elaborated and modified by Ajayi, who distinguishes, first, 'the metropolitan area consisting of those who spoke . . . the Ọyọ dialect, and who owed direct allegiance to the Alafin'; second, 'the other Yoruba people conquered or dominated by the Ọyọ-speaking ones', the most important of whom were the Ẹgba and Ẹgbado in the south; and third, 'the non-Yoruba people who were not directly

[1] Clapperton, *Journal of a Second Expedition*, 56.
[2] Johnson, *History of the Yorubas*, 40–1.

D

controlled but were forced to pay tribute from time to time', such as Dahomey, the Nupe, and the Bariba.[3] But three objections can be made to this analysis. First, it seems an unwarranted assumption that only speakers of the Ọyọ dialect could 'owe direct allegiance' to the *Alafin*.[4] Second, it is unclear why the Ọyọ should have made a distinction between 'Yoruba' and 'non-Yoruba' subjects, given that the use of the term 'Yoruba' to refer to the linguistic group nowadays so designated is a development of the nineteenth century, and that during the imperial period it was applied only to the Ọyọ.[5] And third, it seems implausible to lump together the Ẹgba and the Ẹgbado in the same category, since, as will be shown below, the former were only loosely subject to Ọyọ, while the latter were under very close control (more rigorous, indeed, than the Ọyọ Yoruba towns). In this connection, it is also to be noted that the Ẹgbado are included by Clapperton in his 'kingdom of Yoruba', which is said to extend south as far as the town of 'Puka' (Ipokia).[6]

The present writer, therefore, would propose a revision of the three categories of Ọyọ subjects, which can be characterized as follows:

1. The area that, to use Ajayi's phrase, 'owed direct allegiance to the Alafin', and was subject to a relatively centralized administration from the capital. The Ọyọ Yoruba formed the core of this area, but it also came to include some of the Igbomina and Ekiti Yoruba to the east and some of the Ẹgbado, Awori, and Anago Yoruba in the south.

2. The kingdoms whose dynasties were traditionally supposed to be descended from Oduduwa, the legendary king of Ile Ifẹ, and over whom the *Alafin* claimed authority as the legitimate successor to Oduduwa's kingship. Of these perhaps only the Ẹgba were in any real sense subject to Ọyọ, but others (such as the Ijẹṣa) were prepared to acknowledge loosely the suzerainty (or at least the senior status) of the *Alafin*.

---

[3] Ajayi and Smith, *Yoruba Warfare in the Nineteenth Century*, 4.

[4] Though no doubt people subject to Ọyọ for long periods tended to adopt the Ọyọ dialect. However, the 'Ọyọ dialect' comprises several distinct sub-dialects, such as those of the Ibarapa in the south-west and of the Ibọlọ in the south-east: T. J. Bowen, *Grammar and Dictionary of the Yoruba Language* (Washington, 1858), xv; Johnson, *History of the Yorubas*, 12.

[5] Cf. above, Ch. 1, pp. 4–5.

[6] Clapperton, *Journal of a Second Expedition*, 56; cf. ibid. 4. Clapperton does not mention the Ẹgba.

3. States outside the Ifẹ dynastic system which paid tribute to Ọyọ, such as Dahomey. It will be seen that the distinction between the second and third categories relates more to the basis upon which Ọyọ rule was justified than to the manner in which it was exercised.

In this study the terms 'kingdom' and 'provinces' will be used exclusively to refer to the first category of subjects, those in the central area under close Ọyọ control. The totality of Ọyọ subjects of all three categories will be referred to as the 'empire'.

§2. THE BOUNDARIES OF THE ỌYỌ KINGDOM

It is clearly desirable to establish the territorial extent of the Ọyọ kingdom, but its precise boundaries are not in every case easy to fix. Indeed, the very concept of a linear frontier may not always be applicable. In most areas, however, at least the approximate limits of the kingdom at its greatest extent can be determined with some probability.

In the north-west the Ọyọ kingdom marched with Borgu, the territory of the Bariba. In 1826–30 Clapperton and the Landers found that the boundary with Borgu to the north of the region of Kişi was the River 'Moussa', i.e. the Moshi.[7] Further west, however, the boundary does not appear, at this late period, to have followed the main stream of the Moshi. Bowdich was told at Kumasi in 1817 of a trade-route between Dagomba and Bornu which passed via Parakou, Tumbuya, Godeberi, and Kaiama, and learned that 'A river running to the Quolla [Niger] . . . called Leeasa, flows to the eastward of this path, and is crossed, going from Goodoobirree [Godeberi] southwards, to a large kingdom called Yariba [Yoruba] . . . Aquallie [Agbọnle?] is the frontier town of Yariba, one journey from Goodoobirree.'[8] The River 'Leeasa', which evidently formed the boundary between Ọyọ and Borgu in this area, seems to be the affluent of the main stream of the Moshi (confusingly, also called Moshi on modern maps) which flows north-east from a point near the town of Ilẹşa (whence, perhaps, the name 'Leeasa'). But in earlier times, the Ọyọ kingdom appears to have extended further to the north-west. The towns of Ilẹşa, Kenu, and Okuta, which are today occupied by the Bariba, are acknowledged by local tradition to have

[7] Ibid. 63; R. Lander, *Records of Captain Clapperton's Last Expedition*, ii. 184; R. and J. Lander, *Journal of an Expedition*, i. 181.
[8] Bowdich, *Mission from Cape Coast to Ashantee*, 208.

belonged originally to the Yoruba.[9] Probably, therefore, the boundary of the Ọyọ kingdom at its greatest extent had followed the main
stream of the Moshi along its entire length.

To the north-east, Ọyọ marched with the Nupe kingdom. The
boundary here appears to have followed the River Niger downstream
of its confluence with the Moshi for a short distance.[10] But there
was a Nupe province, of uncertain dimensions, on the south bank
of the Niger, whose capital was originally at Ogudu but was moved
in the early nineteenth century to Tsaragi.[11]

In the east, to the south of the Nupe province of Ogudu, the Ọyọ
kingdom incorporated a number of towns of the Igbomina Yoruba.
Most important of these was Ajaṣẹ Ipo, which is said to have been
founded by the son of a daughter of an *Alafin*.[12] At some period,
the River Ọṣin, to the east of Ajaṣẹ Ipo, may have formed the boundary of the Ọyọ kingdom in this area. This, at least, is asserted in the
traditions of the southern Igbomina town of Ila, which claims the
traditional headship of the Igbomina.[13] But ultimately the Ọyọ
kingdom certainly included several Igbomina towns east of the Ọṣin,
such as Igbaja, Oro, Isanlu Iṣin, Omu Aran, Oke Aba, Ora, and
Idọfin.[14] The northern Ekiti town of Osi, to the south-east of
Igbomina country, was also incorporated.[15] Idọfin and Osi probably

[9] NAK, DOB/HIS/35, H. L. Norton-Traill, 'South Borgu', 1908; cf. H. B.
Hermon-Hodge, *Gazetteer of Ilorin Province* (London, 1929), 145–8.
[10] Clapperton, *Journal of a Second Expedition*, 56, was told that the Ọyọ
kingdom was bounded by the Niger 'in the east'.
[11] For the Ogudu province of Nupe, see K. V. Elphinstone, *Gazetteer of
Ilorin Province* (London, 1921), 24.
[12] Elphinstone, *Gazetteer of Ilorin Province*, 11; Kẹnyọ, *Founder of the Yoruba
Nation*, 50–1.
[13] For the claim of Ila to the headship of the Igbomina, see George, *Historical
Notes on the Yoruba Country*, 25; Johnson, *History of the Yorubas*, 78; Atanda,
The New Ọyọ Empire, 8. The claim that the Ọṣin was the boundary between Ọyọ
and Ila is made in NAI, OYOPROF. 3.4895, Evidence of Chief Adeleke Onaolopo,
the *Babakekere* of Ila, to Select Committee of Western House of Assembly
(dealing with a petition for the inclusion of the northern Igbomina in the
Western Region), encl. to Clerk of Western House of Assembly to President
of Western House of Assembly, 1 Dec. 1949.
[14] NAK, SNP 7/13, 2570/1912, C. S. Burnett, 'Assessment Report, Igbadja
District, Offa Division', 1912, §11; SNP 7/13, 4706/1912, C. S. Burnett, 'Assessment Report, Isanlu District, Offa Division', 1912, §9; SNP 7/13, 4705/1912,
C. S. Burnett, 'Assessment Report, Omu District, Offa Division', 1912, §9;
SNP 7/13, 4705/1912, V. F. Biscoe, 'Assessment Report, Omu-Isanlu District',
1916, *passim*; Elphinstone, *Gazetteer of Ilorin Province*, 12–15; Kẹnyọ, *Founder
of the Yoruba Nation*, 51–3.
[15] NAK, SNP 7/13, 4705/1912, C. S. Burnett, 'Assessment Report, Omu

mark the extreme eastern limits of the Ọyọ kingdom. The town of
Obo, a few miles east of Osi, claims never to have been subject to
Ọyọ.[16] There is a possibility that Ọyọ rule in some form extended
still further east, into the country of the Yagba. The three western
Yagba towns of Ẹgbẹ, Ere, and Ẹri claim to have been founded by
immigrants from Ọyọ Ile, and their traditions suggest that they
maintained some sort of contact with Ọyọ.[17] It is evident, however,
that this area was at the periphery of Ọyọ influence.

In the south-east the Ọyọ kingdom marched with the territory of
the Ekiti (who were at times subject to Benin), the independent
Igbomina kingdom of Ila, the Ijẹṣa, and the kingdom of Ifẹ. The
traditions of Benin recall a war fought against Ọyọ, perhaps around
1600, which had as its issue the setting of a frontier between the two
empires at the northern Ekiti town of Ọtun.[18] This probably means
that Ọtun formed a sort of neutralized buffer state between the
Benin province in Ekiti and the Ọyọ province in Igbomina, rather
than that the Ọyọ kingdom extended as far as Ọtun. Further west,
towards Ila, the Ọyọ kingdom extended to include the town of
Ọyan.[19] Along the northern section of the boundary with the Ijẹṣa,
the Ọyọ kingdom included the towns of Ikirun, Ire, and Iragbiji,
while Ada was formally recognized as a frontier town, its *Balẹ* being
appointed alternately by the *Alafin* and by the *Ọwa* of Ilesa, the
paramount Ijẹṣa ruler.[20] Further south, the Ọyọ–Ijẹṣa boundary is
said to have followed the River Erinlẹ,[21] while the River Ọṣun,
downstream of its confluence with the Erinlẹ, formed its southern-

---

District, Offa Division', 1912, §9; cf. Temple, *Notes on . . . the Northern Provinces
of Nigeria*, 390.
   [16] Oral evidence, from the *Ọwal'Obo* of Obo Ile.
   [17] Oral evidence, from Ẹgbẹ, Ere, and Ẹri. Informants in these towns denied
that they were ever subject to the *Alafin*, but two stories told at Ere indicate
some contacts with Ọyọ: (a) The priesthood of the *oriṣa* Alaṣe (now defunct)
at Akata, the oldest quarter of Ere, is said to have been filled by women sent
from Ọyọ; (b) It is recalled that an *Elere* of Ere once quarrelled with his people
and fled to Ọyọ Ile; the people of Ere asked the *Alafin* to send him back, but the
Elere feared that they would poison him if he returned; the *Alafin* therefore sent
men with him to dig a well (which still exists at Ere) which would give him a
private water supply.
   [18] Egharevba, *Short History of Benin*, 32. For this war, see further below,
Ch. 7, pp. 129–30.
   [19] E. A. Kẹnyọ, *Yoruba Natural Rulers and their Origins* (Ibadan, 1964), 112.
   [20] Atanda, *The New Ọyọ Empire*, 6–7.
   [21] D. Oluganna, *Oshogbo* (Oṣogbo, 1959), 28.

most section.[22] The town of Ẹdẹ, which was founded by Ọyọ to guard the frontier against the Ijẹṣa,[23] is now situated on the south bank of the Ọṣun, but before the nineteenth century its site lay to the north of the river.[24] Further west, the traditions of Ifẹ claim that the Ifẹ kingdom extended northwards to include the towns of Iwo and Ejigbo.[25] But these two towns were certainly ultimately incorporated in the Ọyọ kingdom,[26] and the Ọyọ–Ifẹ boundary followed the River Ọṣun.[27]

To the west of the Ọṣun River Ọyọ had as its neighbours the kingdom of Owu and the territory of the Ẹgba. The River Ọba, a tributary of the Ọṣun, formed the boundary with Owu.[28] Ọyọ marched with Ẹgba territory in the area between the Rivers Ọba and Ogun: the Ọyọ kingdom extended approximately as far as the site of the present town of Ọyọ and also included Iṣẹkẹ to the south-east, while Ẹgba territory extended as far north as the town of Awe.[29]

In the west, the Ọyọ kingdom marched with the kingdom of Ṣabẹ, the boundary following the River Ọpara.[30] Further south, the kingdom included the Ibarapa towns in the triangle between the Rivers Ọyan and Ogun, such as Idiyan, Igangan, Idere, and Eruwa,[31] and marched with the kingdom of Ketu to the west at the Ọyan[32] and with the Ẹgba to the east probably at the Ogun.

The Ọyọ kingdom also extended across the River Ọyan, to include a large area between the Rivers Yewa and Ogun. In this area, the kingdom ultimately incorporated all the towns of the Ẹgbado,

---

[22] Atundaolu, 'Short Traditional History of the Ijesas', *Lagos Weekly Record*, 22 June 1901.

[23] Johnson, *History of the Yorubas*, 156.

[24] Olunlade, *Ẹdẹ: A Brief History*, 9, 18; MacRow, 'Natural Ruler', 231; cf. Clarke, *Travels and Explorations in Yorubaland*, 119.

[25] NAI, OYOPROF, 1.71, Resident, Ọyọ Division, to Secretary, Southern Provinces, 9 Feb. 1939; cf. W. Bascom, *The Yoruba of Southwestern Nigeria* (New York, 1969), 30.

[26] Tradition at Iwo, indeed, maintains that the town was always under the *Alafin*: Oral evidence, from D. A. Adeniji of Iwo.

[27] Atanda, *The New Ọyọ Empire*, 7.

[28] Oral evidence, from the *Balẹ* of Ẹrunmu (an Owu town).

[29] A. K. Ajiṣafẹ, *History of Abẹokuta* (2nd edn., Abẹokuta, 1924), 20.

[30] Oral evidence, from Chief S. Ojo, the *Bada* of Ṣaki; the *Oniwere* and Chiefs of Iwere; the *Ṣabiganna* and Chiefs of Iganna.

[31] NAI, IBAPROF. 3/4, H. Childs, 'A Report on the Western District of the Ibadan Division of Oyo Province', 1934, *passim*.

[32] A. I. Aṣiwaju, 'The Impact of French and British Administrations on Western Yorubaland, 1889–1945' (Ph.D. Thesis, University of Ibadan, 1971), 33.

Map 3. The Ọyọ Kingdom at its greatest extent (c. 1780).

including Ibara in the east[33] and Ilobi in the south,[34] and also the Awori town of ọta to the south-east.[35] To the west of the Yewa River, it included the Anago towns of Ihunmbọ, Ilaṣe, Ifọnyin, Ipokia, and Itakete.[36]

The total area of the ọyọ kingdom at its greatest extent cannot be calculated with any precision, given the uncertainty about the location of its boundaries in many sectors. It must, however, have been something of the order of 18,000 square miles. The population of this area in the early twentieth century seems to have been some-where around three-quarters of a million: the population of the ọyọ kingdom in the eighteenth century is likely to have been rather greater.[37]

§3. THE EXPANSION OF THE ọYọ KINGDOM

The precise stages by which the ọyọ kingdom expanded to attain the boundaries outlined above are only very imperfectly known. It seems a fair assumption that expansion into Igbomina and Ekiti country to the east and into ẹgbado, Awori, and Anago country to the south-west was subsequent to the consolidation of the central ọyọ Yoruba core, and that within the ọyọ Yoruba core the northern area around the capital represents the original ọyọ kingdom and the southern areas were later acquisitions. The evidence, however, is so

[33] K. Fọlayan, 'ẹgbado to 1832: The Birth of a Dilemma', *JHSN* 4.1 (1967), 16.

[34] E. V. S. Thomas, 'Historical Survey of the Towns of Ilaro, Ilobi, Ajilete, and Ilashe in the Ilaro Division', 1933 (microfilm in University of Ibadan Library), 53, 59; NAI, CSO 26/4, 30435, J. H. Ellis, 'Intelligence Report on the Ilobi, Okeodan, and Ajilete Groups of the Egbado People in the Ilaro Division, Abeokuta Province' (1935), 1, 5.

[35] CMS, CA2/087a, Revd. J. White, Journal, 9 Dec. 1855; NAI, CSO 26/2, 20629, F. C. Royce, 'Assessment Report on Otta District, Egba Division, Abeokuta Province' (1927), §22, 52, 368.

[36] Thomas, 'Historical Survey of the Towns of Ilaro, Ilobi, Ajilete, and Ilashe', 105–6; NAI, CSO 26/4, 31065, W. R. Hatch, 'Intelligence Report on the Ihumbo Group in the Ilaro Division of the Abeokuta Province' (1935), 1, 6; NAI, CSO 26/4, 30375, J. H. Ellis, 'Intelligence Report on the Ipokia Group of the Anago Tribe in the Ilaro Division, Abeokuta Province' (1935), 10; Morton-Williams, 'The ọyọ Yoruba and the Atlantic Trade', 30–1; Fọlayan, 'ẹgbado to 1832', 18–19; Aṣiwaju, 'The Impact of French and British Administrations on Western Yorubaland', 19–21. Ipokia and Ihunmbọ are the 'Puka' and 'Humba' of Clapperton, *Journal of a Second Expedition*, 2–6.

[37] Although there was probably significant population growth during the nineteenth century, there was also a substantial movement of population out of the old ọyọ kingdom, especially into the Ibadan and Ile Ifẹ areas.

exiguous that the process of expansion cannot be traced in any detail.

To the east of the River Ogun, as was seen in an earlier chapter, the tradition relating to the earliest *Alafin* suggest that the Ọyọ kingdom had already expanded to the south-east as far as the River Ọṣun, where the town of Ẹdẹ was founded as a frontier post against the Ijẹṣa, even before the Nupe conquest of Ọyọ in the sixteenth century.[38] Expansion eastwards, into Igbomina country, is likely to have been later. One of the Igbomina towns, Igbaja, is said to have been founded by the Ọyọ as a base to check Nupe raids, and on what had previously been Nupe territory.[39] This suggests that Ọyọ expansion into this area followed the final defeat of the Nupe invaders by *Alafin* Ajiboyede in the late sixteenth century.[40] On the other hand, the Benin tradition of a war against Ọyọ around 1600, resulting in the setting of a frontier at Ọtun in northern Ekiti,[41] would indicate that by that date the Ọyọ had already established at least military control over the Igbomina area, though not necessarily that they had incorporated it into their kingdom. There is also a record of a campaign against the Igbomina under *Alafin* Ojigi, probably in the 1720s or 1730s. This may have effected an extension of the Ọyọ kingdom in this area, but no details are given.[42]

To the west of the River Ogun the traditions relating to the earliest *Alafin* suggest that before the sixteenth century Ọyọ power was not felt south of the area of the towns of Tede and Imẹri.[43] The extension of Ọyọ rule further south can perhaps be attributed to the sixteenth and seventeenth centuries. Evidence relating to the Onko area of the Ọyọ kingdom, around the town of Iganna, points to the seventeenth century. Iganna itself is said to have been founded, by immigrants from the western Yoruba kingdom of Ṣabẹ, during the reign of *Alafin* Ọbalokun, in the first half of the seventeenth century.[44] Local tradition at Iganna maintains that the town was founded on land already belonging to the *Alafin*,[45] but it seems probable that the

[38] Cf. above, Ch. 3, p. 36.
[39] Kẹnyọ, *Founder of the Yoruba Nation*, 51.
[40] For which, see above, Ch. 3, pp. 42–3.
[41] Cf. above, p. 87.
[42] Johnson, *History of the Yorubas*, 174. Ojo, *Iwe Itan Ọyọ*, 62, states that Ojigi's forces were suppressing a revolt in Igbomina, but this is probably merely rationalization.
[43] Cf. above, Ch. 3, p. 36.
[44] Johnson, *History of the Yorubas*, 168.
[45] Oral evidence, from the *Ṣabiganna* and Chiefs of Iganna.

foundation of Iganna was connected with some sort of consolidation or reorganization of Ọyọ rule in the area. Ọbalokun's successor, Ajagbo, in the second half of the seventeenth century, is credited with a successful campaign in the Onko area, but no details are given.[46] To the south of the Onko area, in the Ibarapa area of the kingdom, evidence on the chronology and circumstances of Ọyọ expansion is even more exiguous. It is to be noted, however, that one of the major Ibarapa towns, Eruwa, is said to have been founded by a man from Igboho,[47] while another, Tapa, originated as a settlement of Nupe immigrants who had resided for some time at Ọyọ Ile and were then sent by the *Alafin* to the Ibarapa area.[48] This association with Igboho and the Nupe is suggestive, recalling the period in the sixteenth century when Igboho was the Ọyọ capital and Nupe immigrants were settling in northern Yorubaland.[49] The move into the Ibarapa area need not belong to the sixteenth century, but might have been part of a reorganization connected with the abandonment of Igboho as the royal capital in the early seventeenth century. This is all very speculative, but the combination of evidence from the Onko and Ibarapa areas does seem to point to the establishment or consolidation of Ọyọ rule in this region during the later sixteenth and seventeenth centuries.

The only area for which any sort of detailed chronology of Ọyọ expansion can be suggested is the extreme south-western portion of the kingdom, beyond the River Ọyan, and even here the evidence is at points contradictory. It is to be noted that Ọyọ tradition credits *Alafin* Ajagbo, in the second half of the seventeenth century, with sending an army to attack the Egun state of Wemẹ,[50] and that a contemporary European source records what appears to be an Ọyọ invasion of the kingdom of Allada in 1698.[51] These campaigns seem to indicate that Ọyọ had won military control of at least the northern Ẹgbado and Anago areas by the late seventeenth century, though the establishment of formal Ọyọ rule may have been later. Three stages

[46] Ajagbo is said to have 'destroyed Onko': Johnson, *History of the Yorubas*, 169.

[47] NAI, IBAPROF. 3/4, H. Childs, 'A Report on the Western District of the Ibadan Division of Oyo Province' (1934), §101.

[48] Ibid., §89. 'Tapa' is the usual Yoruba name for the Nupe.

[49] Cf. above, Ch. 3, pp. 37–44.

[50] Johnson, *History of the Yorubas*, 169. For this campaign, see further below, Ch. 8, p. 154.

[51] W. Bosman, *A New and Accurate Description of the Coast of Guinea* (London. 1705), 396–8. Cf. below, Ch. 8, p. 156.

of Ǫyǫ colonization in the area can be distinguished. The earliest
was apparently in the Anago area to the west of the River Yewa. Of
the Anago towns, Ifǫnyin and Ihunmbǫ are said to have been
founded by immigrants from Ǫyǫ: Ilaṣe was a later offshoot of
Ifǫnyin, while Ipokia and Itakete claim an independent derivation.[52]
A total of sixteen *Elewi Odo* (kings) of Ifǫnyin are recorded to have
reigned up to 1900, while the twenty-first *Onihunmbǫ* of Ihunmbǫ
was on the throne in 1964: Morton-Williams interprets these
figures as indicating that the two kingdoms were established 'around
1700', a date which cannot be regarded as more than very approximate.[53] It is at any rate clear that Ifǫnyin was in existence by the
reign of *Alafin* Agboluaje (1754– ?), since Ǫyǫ tradition recalls the
dealings of that monarch with an *Elewi Odo* of Ifǫnyin.[54] The
towns of Ipokia and Itakete were presumably brought under Ǫyǫ
rule when the colonies of Ifǫnyin and Ihunmbǫ were founded.

The second stage was the foundation in northern Ęgbado country
of the town of Ęwǫn, which became the base for the establishment of
further Ǫyǫ colonies at Imala, Tibǫ, Aibo, and other towns in the
area. Local tradition attributes the foundation of Ęwǫn to a certain
Ga.[55] This is presumably Gaha, the *Baṣǫrun*, who was the effective ruler
of Ǫyǫ between 1754 and 1774. The implied date is at least roughly
confirmed by the fact that the seventh *Amala* of Imala was reigning
when the Ęgba settled at Abęokuta to the east in the late 1820s.[56]

The third and final stage seems to have been the colonization of
the southern Ęgbado area, with the foundation of the towns of Ilaro,
Ibęṣe, Jiga, Idǫgǫ, and Ijanna. But over this there is a flagrant
contradiction in the traditions. It is agreed in all accounts that the

[52] For the origins of these towns, see Morton-Williams, 'The Ǫyǫ Yoruba
and the Atlantic Trade', 30–1; Fǫlayan, 'Ęgbado to 1832', 18–19; Aṣiwaju, 'The
Impact of French and British Administrations on Western Yorubaland', 18–24.
The founder of Ifǫnyin seems to have come from the Ibarapa town of Idere;
Ipokia and Itakete claim a connection with Benin.

[53] Morton-Williams, 'The Ǫyǫ Yoruba and the Atlantic Trade', 31; cf. Fǫlayan,
'Ęgbado to 1832', 18, without stating his grounds, places the foundation of these
towns in 'the sixteenth or seventeenth century'.

[54] Johnson, *History of the Yorubas*, 179–80.

[55] E. P. Cotton, 'Report on the Egba Boundary', 1905 (included as an Appendix
in Thomas, 'Historical Survey of the Towns of Ilaro, Ilobi, Ajilete, and Ilashe');
cf. Fǫlayan, 'Ęgbado to 1832', 17. Ęwǫn was destroyed in the nineteenth century,
and the headship of the area passed to Imala.

[56] NAI, ABEDIST. 1/1, 412, 'The History of Imala Town related by Akitunde
the Babamagba of Sango', 20 Oct. 1945; NAI, ABEPROF. 8/2, J. H. Blair,
'Abeokuta Intelligence Report' (1938), 1.

area was originally under the authority of the *Olu* of Ilaro, but that
later the *Alafin* established an official with the title *Oniṣarẹ* at
Ijanna to supersede him in control. Johnson states that the first
Oniṣarẹ was sent to Ijanna by *Alafin* Ọbalokun, i.e. during the first
half of the seventeenth century.[57] Adewale argued that this must be a
confusion for the sending of the first *Olu* to Ilaro, and suggested that
the first *Oniṣarẹ* was in fact appointed by *Alafin* Abiọdun after the
overthrow of *Baṣọrun* Gaha in 1774, as a measure to counter Gaha's
influence in the Ẹgbado country.[58] But Johnson's statement is
corroborated by an account collected later from the *Arọkin* at Ọyọ,
according to which the first *Olu* settled at Ilaro under *Alafin* Egunoju,
during the sixteenth century, and the first *Oniṣarẹ* at Ijanna under Ọbalokun.[59] Local Ẹgbado tradition, however, attributes the
founding of Ilaro and other towns in the area to the reign of *Alafin*
Abiọdun (1774–89).[60] A detailed examination of the Ẹgbado king-
lists seems decisive in favour of this later date. Thus, the fullest
king-list of Ilaro gives only eight *Olu* down to and including Aṣade
Agunloye, who was killed in an invasion of the Ẹgbado country by
the Ẹgba in c. 1833.[61] Moreover, tradition claims that originally
each *Olu* reigned for only three years at Ilaro before being recalled
to Ọyọ, and that Aṣade was the first *Olu* to reign longer.[62] It should
also be noted that the second, third, and fourth *Olu* are all described
as sons of *Alafin* Abiọdun.[63] In the case of Ijanna, only three
Oniṣarẹ are remembered to have reigned before the Ẹgba invasion of
c. 1833,[64] of whom the last is presumably to be identified with the
'governor' who had just arrived in the town when the Landers
passed through it in April 1830.[65] It seems, therefore, that the Ọyọ

[57] Johnson, *History of the Yorubas*, 168.

[58] T. J. Adewale, 'The Ijanna Episode in Yoruba History', in *Proceedings of
the Third International West African Conference, Ibadan 1949* (Lagos, 1956),
251–2; cf. Fọlayan, 'Ẹgbado to 1832', 16, 25.

[59] Thomas, 'Historical Survey of the Towns of Ilaro, Ilobi, Ajilete, and Ilashe',
83, 86.

[60] Morton-Williams, 'The Ọyọ Yoruba and the Atlantic Trade', 40.

[61] NAI, CSO 26/2, 19862, J. H. Kirk, 'Intelligence Report on Ilaro Division,
Abeokuta Province', 1927.

[62] Johnson, *History of the Yorubas*, 226, 248.

[63] NAI, CSO 26/2, 19862, J. H. Kirk, 'Intelligence Report on Ilaro Division,
Abeokuta Province', 1927.

[64] Adewale, 'The Ijanna Episode in Yoruba History', 251, citing the lost
'History of Ijanna' (1932), written by Salu, *Balogun* of Ijanna.

[65] R. and J. Lander *Journal of an Expedition*, i, 181. The former Governor
had died fifteen months earlier.

colonization of the Ilaro area has to be attributed to *Alafin* Abiọdun (1774–89), while the appointment of the first *Oniṣarẹ* at Ijanna presumably belongs to the late eighteenth or early nineteenth century. The peripheral Ẹgbado towns which were not Ọyọ colonies, such as Ilobi and Ibara,[66] and the Awori town of Ọta, also an independent foundation,[67] were probably brought under Ọyọ control at the same time as the colonization of the Ilaro area.

The case of Ẹgbado raises certain general points about the character of the expansion of the Ọyọ kingdom. The use of the term 'colonization' calls for some comment. Many towns of the Ọyọ kingdom claim to have been founded by settlers from the capital, and their ruling dynasties often claim descent from princes of the royal lineage of Ọyọ. These claims should be treated with some reserve, since a connection with the capital might be fabricated for purposes of prestige, and for local rulers in particular there were obvious attractions in claiming a spurious royal ancestry. And even in those cases where we believe such claims to be true, it may be misleading to speak of 'colonization', implying an organized movement directed by the authorities in the capital. State initiative was no doubt involved in some cases, such as those of Ẹdẹ and Igbaja, which are said to have been founded as military outposts to protect threatened frontiers.[68] But in many others the settlement may have been due to the individual enterprise of those concerned.[69] In the case of Ẹgbado it seems legitimate to speak of 'colonization', since such a large number of towns were established in a limited area over a short period of time.

One should also beware of assuming that the Ọyọ 'colonists' in every case moved into unoccupied land. Doubtless they often did, and tradition indicates that this was the case in Ẹgbado.[70] But it is likely that in some cases where traditions claim foundation by an Ọyọ prince, an Ọyọ dynasty was in reality installed over a pre-existing town when it was incorporated into the Ọyọ kingdom. There is, in any case, other evidence suggesting that the Ọyọ kingdom

---

[66] These towns claim origin from Ile Ifẹ: Fọlayan, 'Ẹgbado to 1832', 15–16.

[67] Ọta also claims foundation from Ile Ifẹ: NAI, CSO 26/2, 20629, F. C. Royce, 'Assessment Report on Otta District, Egba Division, Abeokuta Province', 1927, §19.

[68] For the case of Ẹdẹ, see Johnson, *History of the Yorubas*, 156; for Igbaja, see Kẹnyọ, *Founder of the Yoruba Nation*, 51.

[69] Traditions frequently describe the founders of towns as hunters.

[70] Cf. Adewale, 'The Ijanna Episode in Yoruba History', 251.

expanded by conquest and absorption as well as by colonization. Several towns of the Ọyọ kingdom are ruled by dynasties which claim an independent derivation, usually from Ile Ife. Claims to an Ife origin might equally be fabricated for purposes of prestige, but in some cases they may indicate that the town concerned existed as an independent political entity before being brought into the Ọyọ kingdom. It is at least suggestive that several important towns claiming an independent origin are located along the periphery of the kingdom. Besides Ipokia, Itakete, Ilobi, Ibara, and Ọta in the south-west, to which reference has already been made, there are Iwo and Ọyan on the south-eastern frontier,[71] and the Igbomina towns of Omu Aran and Isanlu Iṣin in the east.[72] In two instances, moreover, the traditions of neighbouring kingdoms claim suzerainty over towns of the Ọyọ kingdom, suggesting that Ọyọ had detached these towns from a previous allegiance. Thus, Ọyọ may have taken Iwo and Ejigbo from the Ife kingdom,[73] and the towns of the Igbomina from the kingdom of Ila.[74]

§4. THE GOVERNMENT OF THE ỌYỌ KINGDOM

A word of caution is in order before proceeding to a detailed examination of the manner in which the Ọyọ kingdom was governed. It is very probable that the catalogue of the *Alafin*'s rights of interference in the subject towns of the kingdom which is offered below presents a far more schematic appearance than the reality would have warranted. There was, after all, no written constitution in which these rights were listed and defined, and it may be that the very notion of seeking to identify the specific rights which the *Alafin* enjoyed is misleading. The present writer found that informants tended to state, if pressed, that in theory the *Alafin* might do anything he wished, and, of course, his orders would always be obeyed. The 'rights' he enjoyed were those that he chose to exercise and was able to enforce. In so far as there was a theoretical limitation to his powers, it was that of precedent. Old 'rights' might be lost by disuse, and new 'rights' acquired by the very act of asserting them. This

[71] Both towns claim an Ife origin: for Iwo, this statement depends on oral evidence, from D. A. Adeniji of Iwo; for Ọyan, see Kẹnyọ, *Yoruba Natural Rulers and their Origins*, 11.

[72] These towns also derive from Ile Ife: Elphinstone, *Gazetteer of Ilorin Province*, 12; Kẹnyọ, *Founder of the Yoruba Nation*, 51.

[73] Cf. above, p. 88.

[74] Cf. above, p. 86.

consideration, the importance of what the *Alafin* did in practice rather than what he might do in theory, may explain some of the discrepancies encountered in the evidence from different towns of the kingdom on the question of how far the *Alafin* could interfere in the internal affairs of these towns.

Clapperton and the Landers in 1826–30 provide some useful information on the government of the Qyǫ kingdom, but we are primarily dependent in this matter on oral traditions. There is a brief but invaluable account of the government of the kingdom in Johnson,[75] and additional information can be derived from the more recent local histories of some towns of the kingdom.[76] There is also relevant material in the records of the British colonial administration in Nigeria, including an Intelligence Report on Qyǫ written by Simpson in 1938.[77] The subject of the government of the Qyǫ kingdom has also received a certain amount of attention from modern scholars.[78] This material has been supplemented by oral evidence collected by the present writer, from palace officials at Qyǫ,[79] and from the provincial towns of Ṣaki, Iganna, Iwere, Iwo, and Iwoye.[80] A difficulty in using such traditional evidence is the fact that many of the towns involved have been subjected to Qyǫ rule during three distinct periods: the imperial period, when the capital was at Qyǫ Ile; the later nineteenth century, when many of the towns retained some sort of allegiance, often nominal or indirect, to the *Alafin* at New Qyǫ;[81] and the period of British administration, in which they were placed under the *Alafin* as the Native Authority of Qyǫ Province.[82]

---

[75] Johnson, *History of the Yorubas*, 75–6.

[76] Especially useful are Oyerinde, *Iwe Itan Ogbomǫṣǫ*, and Olunlade, *Ẹdẹ: A Brief History*.

[77] Simpson, 'Intelligence Report on the Oyo Division', §56, 75–9.

[78] See esp. Atanda, *The New Qyǫ Empire*, 22–6; Morton-Williams, 'The Yoruba Kingdom of Oyo', 40, 62, 64.

[79] The informants interviewed on this subject at the palace were the *Kudẹfu*, the *Qna Iwẹfa*, the *Qtun Iwẹfa*, the *Osi Iwẹfa*, and the *Ilusinmi* (a senior *ilari*).

[80] The informants interviewed were: at Ṣaki, Chief S. Ojo, the *Bada*, a local historian; at Iganna, the *Ṣabiganna* and his Chiefs; at Iwere, the *Oniwere* and his Chiefs; at Iwo, D. A. Adeniji, a local historian; and at Iwoye, the *Oluwoye* and his Chiefs.

[81] In this period, initially only the northern Qyǫ towns, such as Ṣaki, Kiṣi, and Igboho, were directly under the *Alafin*, the others being under the immediate authority of Ibadan and Ijaye: Johnson, *History of the Yorubas*, 282. After the fall of Ijaye in 1862, the *Alafin* also acquired direct control over the Iseyin-Iganna area west of the River Ogun: Ajayi and Smith, *Yoruba Warfare in the Nineteenth Century*, 122.

[82] For this period, see Atanda, *The New Qyǫ Empire*.

The mechanisms of Ọyọ rule differed in each period, and care must be taken to distinguish, as far as this is possible, how much of the evidence truly relates to the imperial period. A further problem is that the evidence provides the basis for little more than a static picture of the government of the Ọyọ kingdom: the changes which must have taken place during the imperial period are difficult to trace.

The general account of the operation of Ọyọ rule which is first offered below is principally applicable to the older areas of the kingdom in the north. The administration of the Ẹgbado area, which presents certain distinctive features, is then treated separately. And finally, an attempt is made to reconstruct in general terms the ways in which the machinery of Ọyọ administration in the kingdom may have developed during the course of the seventeenth and eighteenth centuries.

(a) The status of subordinate rulers

The subordinate towns of the Ọyọ kingdom all had their own hereditary rulers. The more important towns had rulers with crowns, known as *ọba*, while the lesser towns had rulers without crowns, or *balẹ*. Even those of the subordinate rulers who were *ọba*, however, were not recognized as equal in status to the *ọba* of Ọyọ itself, the *Alafin*. For only the *Alafin* in the Ọyọ kingdom had the right to wear an *ade*, or crown with a beaded fringe. The subordinate *ọba* had only bead-less crowns usually called *akoro*, but in the Onko area in the west of the kingdom known as *tomi*.[83] Today, indeed, several subordinate *ọba* of the Ọyọ kingdom wear *ade*, but this is generally recognized as a recent development, and often condemned as a usurpation.[84] A difficult case, however, is the *Olu* of Ilaro, the principal *ọba* of the Ẹgbado province of the kingdom, who seems to have been claiming the right to wear an *ade* as early as 1878.[85] But even the *Olu* is omitted from most authoritative lists of the *ọba alade* (*ọba* with *ade*), such as that submitted by the *Ọni* of Ifẹ at the request of the Governor of Lagos in 1903,[86] and it is probable that this

[83] For *akoro*, cf. Johnson, *History of the Yorubas*, 8, 75. The term *tomi* is used at Iganna and Iwere: Oral evidence.

[84] At Iwoye, it is admitted that the *Oluwoye* originally wore only an *akoro*, but it is claimed that an *ade* was brought to the town by the wife of one *Oluwoye*, who was a daughter of *Alafin* Abiọdun: Oral evidence.

[85] CMS, CA2/056, Revd. J. Johnson, 'Visit of Inspection to Ilaro', entry for 30 Aug. 1878.

[86] For this list, see Smith, *Kingdoms of the Yoruba*, 209–10.

king acquired his *ade* after the fall of the Ọyọ empire in the 1830s. It is to be noted that the rulers of those states which were tributary to Ọyọ, but were not incorporated into the Ọyọ kingdom, such as the Egba, were not downgraded in this way, and had an acknowledged right to wear *ade*.[87]

The inferior status of the subordinate *ọba* was also indicated by other restrictions. They were not, for example, allowed, like the *Alafin*, to have eunuchs in their service.[88]

(b) Tribute

Ọyọ rule over the towns of the kingdom involved, first, the payment of an annual tribute (in Yoruba, *asingba* or *isin*). The *ọba* and *balẹ* of the subordinate towns were required to bring their tribute to Ọyọ in person at the annual Bẹrẹ festival, at which they followed the chiefs of the capital in paying their homage and tribute to the *Alafin*.[89] According to Johnson, the Bẹrẹ festival took place around January, but this date seems to be only approximate, for Clapperton appears to have witnessed the preliminaries to a Bẹrẹ festival when he visited the Ọyọ capital in February 1826. The *Alafin* pressed Clapperton unsuccessfully to remain in Ọyọ until 'the customary fêtes or amusements' due 'in about two months', in which he would appear 'robed as a king',[90] and it was presumably in connection with this festival that Clapperton observed 'caboceers [chiefs] from distant provinces' arriving in the city and prostrating themselves before the 'chief eunuch' (*Osi Iwẹfa?*) and the *Alafin*.[91]

The basic element in the tribute paid by the provincial towns was the *bẹrẹ* grass used for the thatching of the palace roofs, the giving of which was symbolic of subordination to the recipient.[92] In some cases, the tribute may have consisted solely of this *bẹrẹ* grass. This is claimed, for example, at Iwo.[93] But usually the towns paid additional

[87] The three principal *ọba* of the Egba—the *Alake*, the *Oṣile*, and the *Agura*—are all included in the *Ọni*'s 1903 list of *ọba alade*: ibid.

[88] Johnson, *History of the Yorubas*, 60.

[89] Ibid. 41, 50-1. Some sources assert that the provincial rulers were required to attend the Bẹrẹ festival in person only on alternate years, or in the Yoruba idiom 'every three years': Simpson, 'Intelligence Report on the Oyo Division', §56; Oral evidence, from Chief S. Ojo, the *Bada* of Ṣaki.

[90] Clapperton, *Journal of a Second Expedition*, 41.

[91] Ibid. 47.

[92] For the significance of the *bẹrẹ* tribute, cf. the incident in 1866 when Ogunmọla of Ibadan demanded *bẹrẹ* from the *Alafin*: Johnson, *History of the Yorubas*, 372.

[93] Oral evidence, from the local historian D. A. Adeniji.

tributes in money (i.e. cowry shells) and kind. The town of Ṣaki is said to have paid two rams and ten bags of cowries (i.e. 200,000 cowries, or about 100 dollars).[94] Iganna contributed dried meat and yam flour.[95] The Igbomina town of Omu Aran paid 'one ram and some cowries'.[96] In the Anago area, the town of Ilaṣe paid a tribute of gunpowder, flints, and tobacco,[97] while Ifọnyin supplied 'cloths and other articles of European manufacture'.[98] The Awori town of Ọta provided locally made rush-mats.[99] In most cases the amount of the tribute was fixed, but from Igboho the *Alafin* received the proceeds of a tax in cowries imposed on goods passing through the town gates.[100]

In addition to the regular annual tribute, the *ọba* and *balẹ* of the subordinate towns were required to attend in person at the capital, bringing gifts, whenever a new *Alafin* was installed.[101]

(c) Military service

The towns of the Ọyọ kingdom were also required to supply forces to serve in the Ọyọ army.[102] *Alafin* Ajagbo, in the latter half of the seventeenth century, instituted the title of *Arẹ Ọna Kakamfo*, which was conferred on the ruler of a provincial town, to act as commander-in-chief of these provincial forces.[103]

(d) Control of foreign policy

The provincial towns could have no independent foreign policy: as Johnson observes, 'foreign relations ... were entirely in the hands of the central government at Ọyọ'.[104] In particular, local rulers could not undertake wars except on the instructions of the *Alafin*.[105]

---

[94] Oral evidence, from Chief S. Ojo, the *Bada* of Ṣaki.

[95] Oral evidence, from the *Ṣabiganna* and Chiefs of Iganna.

[96] Elphinstone, *Gazetteer of Ilorin Province*, 12.

[97] Thomas, 'Historical Survey of the Towns of Ilaro, Ilobi, Ajilete, and Ilashe', 106.   [98] Johnson, *History of the Yorubas*, 179.

[99] CMS, CA2/087a, Revd. J. White, Journal, 8 Dec. 1855.

[100] Smith, 'The Alafin in Exile', 71, n.40.

[101] This was stated by all informants: cf. Johnson, *History of the Yorubas*, 196.

[102] Oral evidence from Ṣaki, Iganna, and Iwo. This obligation of military service was denied at Iwere, while informants at Iwoye were unclear on this point.

[103] Johnson, *History of the Yorubas*, 74, 169. For the organization of the provincial army, see further below, Ch. 9, pp. 191–5.

[104] Johnson, *History of the Yorubas*, 40.

[105] Oral evidence from Ṣaki, Iganna, and Iwoye. Informants at Iwere and Iwo were uncertain on this point.

(e) Control of the succession of subordinate rulers

The *Alafin*'s hold on the provincial towns was secured by ensuring that their local administration was in reliable hands. Clapperton observes that the appointment of the provincial rulers 'depend[ed] on the will of the king',[106] while Johnson states: 'They are invested originally with power from Ọyọ, whither they usually repair to obtain their titles, the sword of state being given them by the Alafin at their installation.'[107]

Matters were not, in fact, quite as simple as these accounts suggest. The titles of the *ọba* and *balẹ* of the provincial towns regularly belonged to particular lineages, and succession to them was determined in the first instance by the members of the lineage concerned, in consultation with the local chiefs. But usually the local choice had then to be submitted to the *Alafin* at the capital for approval. This may not have been true in every case. At Ṣaki, for example, it is claimed that the *ọba*, the *Okẹrẹ*, was selected and installed without reference to the *Alafin*, messengers being sent to the capital only after the event to announce the succession of the new ruler.[108] But normally the *ọba* or *balẹ* designate had to travel to Ọyọ to obtain the *Alafin*'s approval for his installation, and the *Alafin* would then send some of his *ilari* to accompany him back to his town to witness the local installation ceremonies.[109] Usually the *Alafin* seems to have been presented with only one candidate for his approval, but if the succession was disputed locally the rival candidates might be sent to Ọyọ for the *Alafin* to choose between them.[110]

Several incidents recalled in local traditions add circumstantial colour to this procedure. At Ikirun, it is recorded that on one occasion a prince sent to Ọyọ to announce the death of the *Akirun* was arbitrarily appointed by the *Alafin* to succeed him.[111] At Iwo, it is said that an *Oluwo* designate who went to seek the *Alafin*'s approval died while at Ọyọ, and that the *Alafin* appointed a prince

---

[106] Clapperton, *Journal of a Second Expedition*, 57.

[107] Johnson, *History of the Yorubas*, 76.

[108] Oral evidence, from Chief S. Ojo, the *Bada* of Ṣaki.

[109] Oral evidence, from the *Kudẹfu* and other palace officials at Ọyọ, the *Ṣabiganna* and Chiefs of Iganna, the *Oniwere* and Chiefs of Iwere, the *Oluwoye* and Chiefs of Iwoye, and D. A. Adeniji of Iwo.

[110] Oral evidence, from the *Ṣabiganna* and Chiefs of Iganna.

[111] NAI, OYOPROF. 3.16, 24 vol. 1, 'Akirun of Ikirun', recommendation of Assistant District Officer, Ibadan Northern District, n.d., encl. to District Officer, Ibadan Division, to Senior Resident, Ọyọ Province, 13 Mar. 1940.

from his entourage to be *Oluwo* in his place. The people of Iwo, however, refused to accept the *Alafin*'s nominee, and elected another *Oluwo*: when the *Alafin* learned of this, he sent messengers to order the usurper to commit suicide, and his own nominee was restored.[112] Death on this initial journey to Ọyọ seems, indeed, to have been something of an occupational hazard for provincial rulers. In the case of the Igbomina town of Isanlu Iṣin, the death of an *Oluṣin* designate on his journey to Ọyọ is said to have caused the *Alafin* to decree that in future the *Oluṣin* should go to obtain approval for his installation from a prince of the royal lineage of Ọyọ who was resident in the Igbomina area.[113] Other instances are recalled also of disputes between the *Alafin*'s nominee for the throne and the choice of the local people. At Ẹdẹ, one *Timi* found on his return from obtaining the *Alafin*'s approval at the capital that in his absence a rival had claimed the title, and he had to drive the usurper out.[114] A similar situation arose at Ikoyi in the 1830s, though in this instance it was the *Alafin*'s nominee who was eventually driven out.[115]

(f) Deposition of subordinate rulers

The *Alafin* might also depose a provincial ruler of whose conduct he disapproved. Johnson describes the procedure: 'To dethrone a kingling, he is publicly divested of his robe and sandals and the announcement is made that XYZ having forfeited his title, he is deprived of it by AB his suzerain.'[116] This right of deposition is denied in some towns, but this perhaps indicates only that no ruler was ever deposed by the *Alafin* in those particular towns.[117] Instances of the deposition of provincial rulers are not lacking. Two are recalled in the traditions of Ogbomọṣọ. In about the 1790s, Ologolo, the *Balẹ* of Ogbomọṣọ, incurred metropolitan displeasure by revealing religious secrets to his wife, and for this reason was summoned to the capital and detained there permanently. His attendants were permitted to return to Ogbomọṣọ only upon payment of a ransom of 2,000 cowries for each of them.[118] Ologolo's

112 NAI, OYOPROF. 1.71, Resident, Ọyọ Province, to Secretary, Southern Provinces, 8 Feb. 1939; Oral evidence, from D. A. Adeniji of Iwo.
113 NAK, SNP 7/13, 4705/1912, V. F. Biscoe, 'Assessment Report, Omu-Isanlu District', 1916, §30; cf. Elphinstone, *Gazetteer of Ilorin Province*, 12.
114 Olunlade, *Ẹdẹ: A Brief History*, 17.
115 Johnson, *History of the Yorubas*, 219–20.
116 Ibid. 76.
117 It was denied at Ṣaki, Iganna, and Iwoye, but admitted at Iwere and Iwo.
118 Oyerinde, *Iwe Itan Ogbomọṣọ*, 24, 26.

successor, Olukan, quarrelled with his chiefs. The *Alafin*, hearing of this, summoned him to Ọyọ for questioning on the matter, and decreed that he should go into exile and the chiefs of Ogbomọṣọ elect another *Balẹ*.[119] At Ẹdẹ it is recorded that one *Timi* offended the *Alafin* by inadvertently appearing at the Ọyọ court with his war-staff. The *Alafin* instructed the chiefs of Ẹdẹ to depose him, and he was accordingly exiled from the town.[120] At Ilọrin *Balẹ* Alagbin is said to have been removed by *Alafin* Abiọdun (1774–89) in favour of his son Afọnja, because he was 'too weak to rule the town'.[121] And the Landers in 1830 heard that the ruler of 'Esalay', an unidentified town between Igboho and Ọyọ Ile, who had been abetting highway robbery on the local roads, had been ordered by the *Alafin* either to pay a fine of 120,000 cowries or to commit suicide.[122]

(g) *Judicial subordination*

A further aspect of metropolitan interference in the local admin-istration of the provincial towns was that in judicial matters their rulers were subordinated to the *Alafin*. Johnson observes: 'The [local] King's civil officers judge all minor cases, but all important matters are transferred to the Alafin of Ọyọ, whose decision and laws were as unalterable as those of the ancient Medes and Persians.'[123] Judicial reference to the *Alafin* meant in practice judgement by the *Ọna Iwẹfa*, the palace eunuch who regularly deputized for the *Alafin* in judicial matters. The precise categories of cases which had to be brought before the *Ọna Iwẹfa* are unclear. Disputes between pro-vincial rulers were naturally judged at the capital.[124] It is also generally agreed that disputes which could not be settled by the local ruler and his chiefs, or in which the disputants were not satisfied with their decision, might be taken to be judged at Ọyọ.[125] It is also claimed by informants at the capital that the provincial

[119] Ibid. 26.
[120] Olunlade, *Ẹdẹ: A Brief History*, 16.
[121] S. Ojo, *Short History of Ilorin* (Ṣaki, n.d.), 10.
[122] R. and J. Lander, *Journal of an Expedition*, i. 158. In the event, the delin-quent ruler took refuge in a neighbouring town.
[123] Johnson, *History of the Yorubas*, 77.
[124] Morton-Williams, 'The Yoruba Kingdom of Oyo', 62.
[125] Oral evidence from Ṣaki, Iganna, Iwere, and Iwo. This is confirmed by evidence from Ẹdẹ and Ipokia: Olunlade, *Ẹdẹ: A Brief History*, 10; NAI, CSO 26/4, 30375, J. H. Ellis, 'Intelligence Report on the Ipokia Group of the Anago Tribe in the Ilaro Division, Abeokuta Province' (1935), 11. Informants at Iwoye denied the existence of any such appeal procedure.

rulers did not have the authority to order an execution, and that all capital cases had to be referred to the *Alafin*.[126] This is admitted in some towns, but denied in others.[127] It may be that some towns had a privileged position in this respect, but it is more likely that recollections on this point have been contaminated by the conditions of the post-imperial period, when the towns were much more loosely subject to the *Alafin* at New Ọyọ. Another punishment which could not be imposed except at the capital was emasculation.[128]

The judicial subordination of the provincial rulers to the *Alafin* seems to have been motivated principally by considerations of status and prestige, and perhaps additionally by a desire for the revenues derived from court fees and bribes. There is no suggestion in the traditions that the system was intended to protect the *Alafin*'s supporters in the provincial towns against hostile decisions in the local courts.

(h) Religious sanctions

These administrative controls were reinforced by the sanction of religion, and in particular the cult of Ṣango, the god of thunder who had supposedly been one of the earliest *Alafin* of Ọyọ. The Ṣango cult played an important role in securing the loyalty of the provinces to the *Alafin*. Indeed, Biobaku has suggested that the cult of Ṣango in the Ọyọ empire 'assumed something of the force of emperor worship in the later Roman empire'.[129] The *Alafin*'s *ilari*, it is said, were often initiated priests of Ṣango, and those who were not regularly travelled with Ṣango priests in their entourage.[130] Moreover, the organization of the Ṣango cult in the provincial towns was controlled from the capital, and Ṣango priests in the provinces had to travel to Ọyọ to receive instruction and initiation from the *Mọgba*, the Ṣango priests of the royal shrine at Koso.[131]

---

[126] Oral evidence, from the *Kudẹfu* and other palace officials at Ọyọ.

[127] It was admitted at Iganna, but denied at Ṣaki, Iwo, and Iwoye, while informants at Iwere were unclear on this point. The referring of capital cases to Ọyọ is corroborated by evidence from Ẹdẹ: Olunlade, *Ẹdẹ: A Brief History*, 10.

[128] Johnson, *History of the Yorubas*, 60.

[129] Biobaku, *The Egba and their Neighbours*, 8.

[130] Morton-Williams, 'Cosmology and Cult Organization of the Ọyọ Yoruba', 255.

[131] Wescott and Morton-Williams, 'Symbolism and Ritual Context of the Yoruba *Laba Shango*', 27.

(i) The provinces

The Oyo kingdom was divided into a number of provinces (*ekun*), each under the authority of an important provincial ruler. The details of this division into provinces are, however, disputed. According to Johnson, there were four provinces: the Ekun Otun (Right-Hand Province), whose 'chief town' was Iganna, and which included all the towns on the right bank of the River Ogun from Saki in the north to the Ibarapa area in the south; the Ekun Osi (Left-Hand Province), whose chief town was Ikoyi, comprising the towns to the east from Igboho and Kisi to the Igbomina area, and including Ogbomoso and Ilorin; the Ibolo Province, under Iresa (a town destroyed in the wars of the nineteenth century, situated to the south of Ilorin[132]), lying to the south-east and including the towns of Ofa, Oyan, Ikirun, Ejigbo, and Ede; and the Epo Province, under Idode (a town north-east of modern Oyo, whose inhabitants were moved into the new capital in the 1830s[133]), including the area around modern Oyo and the town of Iwo.[134] Chief Ojo, however, states that there were in all eight *ekun*. These comprised, first, three Ekun Otun or Right-Hand Provinces to the west of the River Ogun and three Ekun Osi or Left-Hand Provinces to the east. The three Ekun Osi are delimited much as in Johnson's account: the Ekun Osi 'proper' under Ikoyi, the Ekun Ibolo under Iresa, and the Ekun Epo under Idode. Johnson's Ekun Otun, however, now becomes three provinces: the Ekun Otun proper, under Saki, comprising the towns in the north of the area, around Saki itself, and also Iseyin to the south-east; the Ekun Onko, or Onko Province, under Iganna, in the central area, including Ilaji, Iwere, and Isemi; and the Ekun Ibarapa, or Ibarapa Province, in the south, of which the most important towns were Eruwa and Igbo Ora.[135] In addition, according to Chief Ojo, the Igbomina and Egbado towns of the Oyo kingdom formed two further provinces, the Ekun Igbomina under Ajase Ipo and the Ekun Egbado under Ilaro.[136]

[132] For the site of Iresa, cf. CMS, CA2/066, the Revd. A. C. Mann, Journal, 1 Aug. 1855.

[133] Cf. Johnson, *History of the Yorubas*, 281.   [134] Ibid. 12–13.

[135] This reference to Igbo Ora is anachronistic, since Igbo Ora was an unimportant village until it was augmented by the incorporation of refugees from Ibarapa towns destroyed by the Fulani in the nineteenth century: NAI, IBAPROF. 3/4, H. Childs, 'A Report on the Western District of the Ibadan Division of the Oyo Province', 1934, §§67–75.

[136] Ojo, *Iwe Itan Oyo*, 7–8. For other reconstructions, cf. Simpson, 'Intelligence Report on the Oyo Division', §§17–18; Babayemi, 'Upper Ogun', 73.

It appears that Chief Ojo's reconstruction represents a closer approximation to the reality than Johnson's. In the Ẹkun Ọtun, the position of Ṣaki at the head of some sort of province is confirmed by the contemporary evidence of Clapperton, who was told in 1826 that the king of Ṣaki 'held great authority under the king of Eyeo, and had a great district, and many large towns, under his regency'.[137] The existence of separate Onko and Ibarapa provinces is also corroborated by other sources:[138] the boundary between the two is said to have followed the River Ofiki.[139] The headship of the Ibarapa province, about which Chief Ojo is silent, perhaps belonged to the town of Idere, since this was described to a visiting missionary in 1877 as 'an ancient royal town of all the Barapa territory'.[140] The position of Ajaṣẹ Ipo as the head, under the *Alafin*, of the Igbomina towns is likewise acknowledged in local traditions.[141] Of Ilaro and the Ẹgbado province more will be said below. But even Chief Ojo's account may suffer from anachronisms and oversimplifications. In the Epo province other sources attribute the headship not to Idodẹ but to Iṣẹkẹ, another of the local towns whose populations were incorporated into New Ọyọ in the 1830s.[142] This seems more probable, since the ruler of Iṣẹkẹ, the *Ẹlẹpẹ*, was an *ọba*, and therefore of superior status to the ruler of Idodẹ, who was merely a *balẹ*. Tradition at the town of Iwo, however, repudiates the suggestion of subordination either to Idodẹ or to Iṣẹkẹ.[143]

In any case, the structure of the *Ẹkun* no doubt suffered alteration from time to time. In the Ẹkun Ọtun it is said that the headship originally belonged to the town of Imẹri, and was transferred to Ṣaki only after a revolt by Imẹri which Ṣaki helped to suppress.[144]

---

[137] Clapperton, *Journal of a Second Expedition*, 25; cf. R. Lander, *Records of Captain Clapperton's Last Expedition*, i. 92.

[138] Simpson, 'Intelligence Report on the Oyo Division', §17; CMS, CA2/056, the Revd. J. Johnson, 'Itineraries', 1877.

[139] CMS, CA2/056, the Revd. J. Johnson, 'Itineraries', 1877.

[140] CMS, CA2/035, S. W. Doherty, Journal, 27 Jan. 1877.

[141] NAK, SNP 7/13, 4702/1912, C. S. Burnett, 'Assessment Report, Ajasse Po District, Offa Division' (1912), §11; NAK, SNP 10/4, 746P/1916, V. F. Biscoe, 'Assessment Report, Ajasse Po District' (1916), §1; cf. Hermon-Hodge, *Gazetteer of Ilorin Province*, 37; Temple, *Notes on . . . the Northern Provinces of Nigeria*, 390.

[142] Oral evidence, from the *Parakoyi* of Ọyọ; Simpson, 'Intelligence Report on the Oyo Division', Appendix on 'Ọyọ and its Environs', §17.

[143] Oral evidence, from D. A. Adeniji of Iwo.

[144] Ojo, *Iwe Itan Ṣaki*, 31–2. This episode is attributed to the reign of *Alafin* Ajagbo. in the second half of the seventeenth century, but the war against Imẹri

It is also recorded that during the reign of *Alafin* Awolẹ, in the late eighteenth century, the town of Iseyin repudiated its subordination to Ṣaki and secured the *Alafin*'s recognition of its status as a separate province.[145]

Information on the position of the head town within its *ẹkun* has been obtained principally at Ṣaki and Iganna.[146] Evidence from these towns indicates that there was a real measure of devolution of authority to the *ẹkun* heads. The *Okẹrẹ* of Ṣaki and the *Ṣabiganna* of Iganna are said to have received the personal homage and tribute of the rulers of the towns under them at their own annual festivals, which were held immediately after the *Alafin*'s Bẹrẹ festival. For the Bẹrẹ festival, the subordinate rulers assembled at the head town of the province before proceeding together to the capital, led by the *ẹkun* head. In war the *ẹkun* head was responsible for mustering the troops of the towns in his province, and commanded them in battle. When a subordinate ruler was installed, he had to obtain the approval of his *ẹkun* head for his succession before going to Qyọ to seek the approval of the *Alafin*. And judicial disputes in the subordinate towns were referred on appeal in the first instance to the court of the *ẹkun* head, whence they might be taken to the court of the *Alafin* at the capital. Little evidence from other provinces of the kingdom is available, but local tradition in Igbomina suggests that some towns there, including Omu Aran, while acknowledging the senior status of the *Olupo* of Ajaṣẹ Ipo, were not in any real sense subordinate to him.[147]

The heads of the various *ẹkun* were not all of equal status. The *Onikoyi* of Ikoyi was acknowledged as the leading provincial ruler, and it was he who led the others in homage to the *Alafin* at the annual Bẹrẹ festival.[148] It appears that the *Onikoyi* of Ikoyi and the

---

seems to be identical with a war attributed in Qyọ tradition to the much earlier *Alafin* Aganju: cf. above, Ch. 3, p. 36. [145] Ibid. 35–6.

[146] Oral evidence, from Chief S. Ojo of Ṣaki, and the *Ṣabiganna* and Chiefs of Iganna.

[147] NAK, SNP 7/13, 4705/1912, V. F. Biscoe, 'Assessment Report, Omu-Isanlu District' (1916), §4, states that the *Olomu* of Omu Aran held his title 'direct from the Alafin of Oyo', while Isanlu Iṣin, Ijara, Ala, and Oke Aba 'though independent of the Olupo of Ajasse Po administratively, recognized him as the biggest of the Igbona chiefs and used to go with him yearly to greet the Alafin of Oyo . . . [but] paid their tribute direct to the Alafin of Oyo and not through the Olupo of Ajasse Po.'

[148] Johnson, *History of the Yorubas*, 41; cf. CMS, CA2/066, the Revd. A. C. Mann, Journal, 28 July 1855, describes the *Onikoyi* as 'second after the king', i.e. the *Alafin*.

Okẹrẹ of Ṣaki functioned in some sense as the over-all heads respectively of the three Ẹkun Osi and the three Ẹkun Ọtun, the *Okẹrẹ*
standing second in status to the *Onikoyi*.[149] The missionary Mann
was told in 1855 that the *Arẹsa* of Irẹsa, the head of the Ibọlọ
province, was ranked next after the *Onikoyi*, but this probably
refers to his status within the Ẹkun Osi.[150] But it is unclear what the
over-all headship of the *Onikoyi* and the *Okẹrẹ* amounted to in
practice. At Ṣaki it is claimed that the *Ṣabiganna*, the head of the
Onko province, acknowledged his subordination to the *Okẹrẹ* of
Ṣaki by sending gifts to the latter at his annual festival, though not
by paying homage in person, but this is denied at Iganna.[151] It seems
probable that the ranking of the various *ẹkun* heads was more a
matter of status than of effective subordination.

(j) The role of the Ọyọ chiefs: the 'fief' system

The chiefs and officials of the capital played an important role in
the administration of the Ọyọ kingdom, as intermediaries between
the provincial towns and the *Alafin*. Johnson notes that 'Every one
of [the provincial *ọba*] as well as every important Balẹ has an official
at Ọyọ through whom he can communicate with the crown.'[152]
The 'officials' here referred to were important title-holders of the
capital, to whom the provincial towns were attached. These Ọyọ
chiefs were referred to by the people of the towns under them as
baba (father), usually rendered by modern scholars as 'patron'. The
patron chiefs served generally as spokesmen of their clients' interests
before the *Alafin*, and communicated their petitions to him. They
also transmitted their clients' tribute to the *Alafin* at the annual
Bẹrẹ festival, and received back a share of it from him.[153] It has
been suggested that the towns attached to a patron might be termed
a 'fief'.[154] This seems unexceptionable, provided that it is realized
that the Ọyọ 'fiefs' did not consist, as was usual in medieval Europe,

---

[149] Oral evidence, from Chief S. Ojo, the *Bada* of Ṣaki.

[150] CMS, CA2/066, the Revd. A. C. Mann, 31 July 1855.

[151] Oral evidence, from Chief S. Ojo of Ṣaki, and the *Ṣabiganna* and Chiefs of
Iganna.

[152] Johnson, *History of the Yorubas*, 76.

[153] Oral evidence, from the *Kudẹfu* and other palace officials at Ọyọ, Chief
S. Ojo of Ṣaki, and the *Ṣabiganna* and Chiefs of Iganna; Simpson, 'Intelligence
Report on the Oyo Division', §§76–7.

[154] Simpson, 'Intelligence Report on the Oyo Division', §76.

of property in land, but merely of rights to a share of tribute.[155] Nor does it appear that the Ọyọ 'fiefs', like those of medieval Europe, were granted specifically and explicitly in return for a promise of military service by the fief-holder.

Some towns of the Ọyọ kingdom claim that they were not attached to any patron, and that their rulers had direct access to the *Alafin*, but this seems improbable.[156] Towns were apparently allotted to the patronage of chiefs at the discretion of the *Alafin*, although chiefs might acquire a right to the clientage of towns by conquering them in war.[157] It is unfortunately impossible to reconstruct the distribution of client towns among the Ọyọ chiefs during the imperial period, but it is clear that the patrons included chiefs of all categories—palace slaves, titled women of the palace, chiefs of the royal lineage, and non-royal chiefs. Simpson suggests that the principal fief-holders in the imperial period were the *Baṣọrun*, the *Aṣipa*, the *Arẹmọ*, the *Iya Ọba* and the *Iya Kere*, the *Olokun Ẹṣin*, and the *Iwẹfa*, particularly the *Osi Iwẹfa*.[158] In detail, it is known that the *Iya Kere* was the patron of Iwo, Iseyin, and Ogbomọṣọ,[159] the *Alapini* of Ṣaki,[160] and the *Parakoyi* of Iṣẹkẹ.[161] There was perhaps a progressive tendency for the *Alafin* to deprive the non-royal chiefs of their client towns. Certainly, by the period of British colonial rule, when for the first time we possess comprehensive details of the distribution of client towns, the non-royal chiefs had been almost entirely squeezed out. The principal fief-holders in the 1920s and 1930s were the three senior *Iwẹfa*, some of the senior *ilari* (notably the *Ilusinmi*), and two royal chiefs, the *Arẹmọ* and the *Baba Iyaji*. The only non-royal chief to hold a fief was the *Baṣọrun*, and he had only one small town, Awẹ.[162] It is not clear how far the division of the kingdom into fiefs corresponded with its division into *ẹkun*.

---

[155] However, in medieval Europe also 'fiefs' sometimes consisted of tax-collecting rights: cf. F. L. Ganshof, *Feudalism* (3rd edn., London, 1964), 113–15.

[156] This is claimed at Iwo and Iwoye: in the case of Iwo, this is contradicted by the evidence of Johnson, *History of the Yorubas*, 64, that the *Iya Kere* was the 'feudal head' of Iwo.

[157] Simpson, 'Intelligence Report on the Oyo Division', §76.

[158] Ibid.   [159] Johnson, *History of the Yorubas*, 64.

[160] Morton-Williams, 'The Yoruba Kingdom of Oyo', 56.

[161] Oral evidence, from the *Parakoyi* of Ọyọ. The title *Parakoyi* is supposed to derive from *o para Ikoyi*, 'he goes frequently to Ikoyi', as the *Parakoyi* travelled annually to Ikoyi to meet the *Ẹlẹpẹ* of Iṣẹkẹ bringing his tribute to Ọyọ: this etymology, however, is fanciful, since the title *Parakoyi* is a common one among the Yoruba, occurring also e.g. in Ile Ifẹ, Ijẹbu, and Abẹokuta.

[162] NAI, OYOPROF. 3.1329, 'List of Native Authorities', submitted by

Probably the fiefs were deliberately constructed to cut across the structure of the *ẹkun*, so that rivalry for the allegiance of the provincial towns between the fief-holder and the *ẹkun* head might minimize the danger of either using his position to defy the *Alafin*.[163]

Although the granting of fiefs to the chiefs of the capital involved some sharing by the *Alafin* of the responsibility for the administration of the kingdom, the degree of delegation was limited. The only important aspect of provincial administration which the fief-holders controlled was the transmission of tribute. Moreover, the *Alafin* kept a very close watch over relations between the fief-holders and the provincial towns under them. The patron chief and his clients were obliged to communicate with each other only through officials called *baba kekere* (little fathers), who were appointed by the *Alafin* from among his palace slaves and were responsible to him.[164] As an additional precaution, there was normally a separate *baba kekere* for each town within a chief's fief.[165]

(k) The king's agents: the role of the palace slaves

The *Alafin* did not depend solely upon the fief-holders to keep him informed of conditions in the provincial towns. In most, if not all, of the provincial towns of the kingdom there were official Ǫyǫ representatives permanently stationed to watch over their loyalty. These representatives were called *asoju ǫba* (those who serve as the king's eyes), or *ajẹlẹ*.[166] The term *ajẹlẹ*, it may be noted, was not restricted to the Ǫyǫ kingdom, being used also in the neighbouring kingdom of Nupe,[167] and in the Yoruba states which in the nineteenth century succeeded to the power of Ǫyǫ—Ilǫrin, Ibadan, and

District Officer, Ǫyǫ, to Senior Resident, Ǫyǫ Province, 27 Aug. 1923; Simpson, 'Intelligence Report on the Oyo Division', §76.

[163] This suggestion is based on the situation in the 1920s and 1930s: in what had earlier been the Ẹkun Ǫtun, Ṣaki was under the *Kudẹfu*, Iseyin under the *Osi Iwẹfa*, Tede under the *Ǫna Iwẹfa*, Ipapo under the *Ǫtun Iwẹfa*, and Ǫkaka under the *Arẹmọ*; in the Ẹkun Onko, Iganna was under the *Ǫna Iwẹfa*, Iwere under the *Ǫbanimowu* (an *ilari*), and Oke Iho under the *Arẹmọ*.

[164] Morton-Williams, 'The Yoruba Kingdom of Oyo', 64; Simpson, 'Intelligence Report on the Oyo Division', §§79–80. The term *baba kekere* is sometimes also used of the patron himself.

[165] Simpson, 'Intelligence Report on the Oyo Division', §79

[166] Oral evidence, from the *Kudẹfu* and other palace officials at Ǫyǫ, Chief S. Ojo of Ṣaki, the *Ṣabiganna* and Chiefs of Iganna, and the *Oniwere* and Chiefs of Iwere; Simpson, 'Intelligence Report on the Oyo Division', §§77–8.

[167] For the *ajẹlẹ* of the Nupe kingdom, see Nadel, *Black Byzantium*, 115–16; Mason, 'The Nupe Kingdom', 439–40.

Abẹokuta.[168] It has been stated that the term *ajẹlẹ* is derived from the Arabic *ajala*, 'to dispatch',[169] but Yoruba etymologies are also offered.[170] The Landers appear to have met an *ajẹlẹ* in 1830 at the town of Igboho. They speak of the local ruler's 'head man or minister', and observe: 'This man has been placed in his present situation by the King of Katunga as a kind of spy on the actions of the governor, who can do nothing of a public nature without, in the first place, consulting him and obtaining his consent to the measure.'[171]

It is not certain how many of the provincial towns suffered the imposition of *ajẹlẹ*. In the Ẹkun Qtun province it is said that the *Alafin* had an *ajẹlẹ* only in Ṣaki, the head town of the province, while the *Okẹrẹ* of Ṣaki placed his own *ajẹlẹ* in the subordinate towns.[172] In the Onko province, however, it is said that the *Alafin* had *ajẹlẹ* not only in Iganna, the head town, but also in subordinate towns such as Iwere, and it is denied that the *Ṣabiganna* of Iganna had any *ajẹlẹ* of his own.[173] This apparently contradictory evidence can perhaps be accepted in both instances, since it is by no means improbable that there were such differences in the closeness of the *Alafin*'s control in the various *ẹkun*. The towns of Iwo, in the Epo province, and Iwoye, in the Ibọlọ province, also claim not to have suffered the imposition of *ajẹlẹ*.[174] In these cases, lacking evidence from other towns in these areas, it must remain uncertain whether the claim is true or there is some confusion with the post-imperial period.

The *ajẹlẹ* were normally appointed by the *Alafin* from among the slaves of the palace.[175] When *Baṣọrun* Gaha seized power in Qyọ in

[168] For the Ibadan *ajẹlẹ*, see Awẹ, 'The Ajele System'; for Ilọrin, cf. Lloyd, *Political Development of Yoruba Kingdoms*, 44; for Abẹokuta, cf. A. Pallinder-Law, 'Government in Abẹokuta 1830–1914' (Fil. Dr. Thesis, University of Göteborg, 1973), 20.

[169] Nadel, *Black Byzantium*, 115.

[170] Abraham, *Dictionary of Modern Yoruba*, s.v. *jẹ* (= 'to reply'); Awẹ, 'The Ajele System', 53, n.1, offers the translation 'owner of the land'.

[171] R. and J. Lander, *Journal of an Expedition*, i. 147.

[172] Oral evidence, from Chief S. Ojo, the *Bada* of Ṣaki.

[173] Oral evidence, from the *Ṣabiganna* and Chiefs of Iganna, and the *Oniwere* and Chiefs of Iwere.

[174] Oral evidence, from D. A. Adeniji of Iwo, and the *Oluwoye* and Chiefs of Iwoye.

[175] Oral evidence, from Chief S. Ojo of Ṣaki, the *Ṣabiganna* and Chiefs of Iganna, and the *Oniwere* and Chiefs of Iwere; Simpson, 'Intelligence Report on the Oyo Division', §77.

1754–74, he appears to have replaced the *Alafin*'s slaves by members of his own lineage. Johnson states of the period of his rule: 'His sons were scattered all over the length and breadth of the kingdom, they resided in the principal towns and all the tributes of those towns and their suburbs was paid to them. No tribute was paid to the Alafin.'[176] The *coup d'état* by which *Alafin* Abiǫdun overthrew Gaha in 1774 began with a massacre of these sons of Gaha who were resident in the provincial towns.[177]

It has sometimes been stated that the *ajęlę* were selected by the *Alafin* from among the *ilari* of the palace,[178] but this seems to be a confusion. The *ilari* served as the *Alafin*'s messengers to the provincial towns, not as his permanently resident representatives in them. The *ilari* have been more accurately described as 'travelling intendants',[179] and their role in the administration of the kingdom is felicitously characterized by Robert Smith, who observes that the *ajęlę*, who supervised the local rulers, 'were in turn supervised by the *ilari*, the royal messengers from Ǫyǫ.'[180]

It is sometimes suggested that either the *ajęlę* or the *ilari* were responsible for the collection of taxes in the Ǫyǫ kingdom.[181] In fact, as has been seen, the tribute of the provincial towns was normally carried to Ǫyǫ at the Bęrę festival by the local rulers, and the *Alafin*'s agents did not usually function as tax-collectors. A major exception was the Ęgbado province, which will be discussed below, where the collection of taxes was organized by the palace slaves.[182] It is also possible that the Igbomina province was an exception: at any rate, local tradition records that the *Alafin* placed a 'messenger' (*ilari*?) at Ijara in Igbomina to receive taxes.[183] But in the older provinces of the kingdom the palace slaves do not appear

[176] Johnson, *History of the Yorubas*, 180.

[177] Ibid. 183–4.

[178] Crowder, *Story of Nigeria*, 110; J. B. Webster and A. A. Boahen, *The Revolutionary Years: West Africa since 1800* (London, 1967), 92.

[179] Atanda, *The New Ǫyǫ Empire*, 26.

[180] Smith, *Kingdoms of the Yoruba*, 45.

[181] Crowder, *Story of Nigeria*, 58, 108; Flint, *Nigeria and Ghana*, 61; Atanda, *The New Ǫyǫ Empire*, 26.

[182] The eunuch whom the Landers met at 'Chaadoo', an unidentified town south of Irawǫ, who 'was recently sent by the King of [Ǫyǫ] to receive the customary tribute from the governors of the various towns on the road between Katunga and Jenna [Ijanna]', was probably on his way to collect tribute in the Ęgbado area: R. and J. Lander, *Journal of an Expedition*, i. 129.

[183] NAK, SNP 7/13, 4705/1912, V. F. Biscoe, 'Assessment Report, Omu-Isanlu District' (1916), §32.

to have collected any taxes. *Baṣọrun* Gaha in 1754–74, according to Johnson, had the tribute of the provincial towns collected locally by his kinsmen whom he had appointed to replace the *Alafin*'s *ajẹlẹ*,[184] but this was not the normal practice.

Other functions also have been wrongly attributed to the Ọyọ *ajẹlẹ*. It has been suggested that they adjudicated local disputes,[185] but there seems to be no recollection of any such judicial functions in the traditions. An important function of the later Ibadan *ajẹlẹ* was the supervision of foreign visitors, who had to report first to the *ajẹlẹ* on arriving in any town.[186] But this can hardly have been true of the Ọyọ *ajẹlẹ*, or we would have heard much more of them from Clapperton and the Landers.[187] The functions of the Ọyọ *ajẹlẹ* seem, in fact, to have consisted, as succinctly described by the Landers, in the general supervision of the local ruler's conduct, and additionally in keeping the *Alafin* informed of any developments in the town bearing upon the interests of Ọyọ.[188]

(*l*) *The government of the Ẹgbado province*

The system of administration which the Ọyọ applied to the Ẹgbado area of their kingdom is in some respects better documented than the one that operated in the older provinces in the north. Clapperton and the Landers are much more informative on Ẹgbado than on the areas further north, and local traditions have been more systematically recorded in Ẹgbado than elsewhere.[189] The administration of the Ẹgbado area has also received more detailed study from modern scholars.[190] This is fortunate, since Ẹgbado presents certain distinctive features of considerable interest.

The successive stages in the extension of Ọyọ control over the Ẹgbado area and their probable chronology have been discussed

[184] Johnson, *History of the Yorubas*, 180.

[185] Simpson, 'Intelligence Report on the Oyo Division', §76; Webster and Boahen, *West Africa since 1800*, 168.

[186] Awẹ, 'The Ajele System', 55.

[187] And in the one instance where the Landers met an *ajẹlẹ*, at Igboho, they went first to the residence of the local ruler, and were introduced by him to the *ajẹlẹ*: R. and J. Lander, *Journey of an Expedition*, i. 144.

[188] Oral evidence, from the *Kudẹfu* and other palace officials at Ọyọ, Chief S. Ojo of Ṣaki, the *Ṣabiganna* and Chiefs of Iganna, and the *Oniwere* and Chiefs of Iwere.

[189] See esp. Thomas, 'Historical Survey of the Towns of Ilaro, Ilobi, Ajilete, and Ilashe'.

[190] Esp. Morton-Williams, 'The Ọyọ Yoruba and the Atlantic Trade'; Fọlayan, 'Ẹgbado to 1832'.

above. There is no reason to believe that the administration of Ọyọ rule over the earliest dependencies in the area, the Anago towns in the west, which initially formed a small province under the *Elewi Odo* of Ifọnyin,[191] differed in essentials from the system described above for the older provinces of the kingdom. A minor variation was that when an *Elewi Odo* was installed, although his name had to be communicated to Ọyọ for the *Alafin*'s approval, he went to receive his title not to Ọyọ but to the near-by kingdom of Ketu, where he was crowned by the *Alaketu*.[192] Whether this was a concession due to the great distance of Ifọnyin from the capital, or a recognition of Ketu's prior rights in the area (or both), is not clear. However, new elements were introduced into the government of the Ẹgbado area, with the appointment, first, of the *Olu* of Ilaro, probably by *Alafin* Abiọdun (1774–89), and later, of the *Onişarẹ* of Ijanna, a few miles north of Ilaro.[193]

The *Olu* of Ilaro was appointed by the *Alafin* to serve as the provincial head of the Ẹgbado area.[194] His authority apparently covered Imala and the other towns in northern Ẹgbado founded by *Başọrun* Gaha,[195] but probably not the older Anago towns in the west. The *Olu*'s position as *ẹkun* head does not seem to have been in any way exceptional,[196] but the *Alafin* secured a greater degree of control by making the post of *Olu* tenable only for a limited period, and filled by appointment by the *Alafin* from among the *ọmọ ọba* of the capital. According to Johnson,

The ancient custom was for the Alafin to crown a new Olu every three years. After the expiration of his term of office the retiring Olu was to take ten of his young wives, and whatever else he chose, and proceed to the metropolis, and there spend the rest of his days in peace. There was a quarter of the city assigned to them known as Oke Olu.[197]

[191] Fọlayan, 'Ẹgbado to 1832', 19; Aşiwaju, 'Impact of French and British Administration on Western Yorubaland', 19–20.

[192] Morton-Williams, 'The Ọyọ Yoruba and the Atlantic Trade', 30–1.

[193] The *Onişarẹ* did not reside at the modern village of Ijanna (which is called Ijanna Ejẹgun, after its founder Ejẹgun), but at a now deserted site (called Ijanna Eyọ, or Ijanna of the Ọyọ) about two miles from it. When Ijanna Eyọ was destroyed by the Ẹgba in c. 1833, some of its people moved into Ijanna Ejẹgun, whose *Balẹ* is nowadays chosen alternately from two houses, descended from Ejẹgun and from the last *Onişarẹ*: Oral evidence, from the *Balẹ* of Ijanna.

[194] Cotton, 'Report on the Egba Boundary'.

[195] The authority of the *Olu* is acknowledged, reluctantly, at Imala: Thomas, 'Historical Survey of the Towns of Ilaro, Ilobi, Ajilete and Ilashe', 83.

[196] See the account given by Fọlayan, 'Ẹgbado to 1832', 23.

[197] Johnson, *History of the Yorubas*, 226.

To this tradition can be related the statement of Clapperton in 1826 that the ruler of Ilaro 'told us that he had a house at Eyeo, and that over half of his wives were there.'[198] It is said that the first *Olu* to reign for more than three years was Aṣade Agunloye, the eighth to hold the title, who was killed in an invasion of Ẹgbado by the Ẹgba in *c.* 1833.[199]

But by the 1820s the *Olu* had been superseded in effective authority over the Ẹgbado province by the *Oniṣarẹ* at Ijanna. The appointment of the *Oniṣarẹ* was even more closely controlled by the *Alafin*, since he was chosen by the *Alafin* from among the palace slaves.[200] The explanation for this which was given to the Landers in 1830 was no doubt correct:

This is the invariable rule with the sovereigns of that country, of which Jenna [Ijanna] is a province, for they fear that its distance from the capital being very great, a person of higher rank, if possessed of talents and spirit, could easily influence the natives to throw off the yoke, and declare themselves independent of Yariba.[201]

As an additional precaution, the *Oniṣarẹ* was selected from among the *Alafin*'s non-Yoruba slaves: Johnson states that the *Oniṣarẹ* was always a Nupe, but according to the Landers the *Oniṣarẹ* appointed in 1830 was a Hausa.[202] And perhaps a further guarantee of the *Oniṣarẹ*'s loyalty was the arrangement, reported by Clapperton and the Landers, whereby he was included among the *abọbaku* who had to take their own lives when the *Alafin* died.[203]

It seems probable that one reason for the appointment of the *Oniṣarẹ* was doubt about the loyalty of the *Olu*. Adewale suggested that this might be connected with the discontinuance of the three-year limitation on the *Olu*'s rule, and this seems very plausible. Adewale speculated that the change might have occurred in the aftermath of

[198] Clapperton, *Journal of a Second Expedition*, 10.
[199] Johnson, *History of the Yorubas*, 249. Current tradition at Ilaro does not recall the limitation of the *Olu*'s rule to three years, but admits that the early *Olu* were buried at Ọyọ Ile and that Aṣade Agunloye was the first *Olu* to be buried locally: Oral evidence, from the *Olu* and others at Ilaro.
[200] Clapperton, *Journal of a Second Expedition*, 39; R. and J. Lander, *Journal of an Expedition*, i. 81.
[201] R. and J. Lander, *Journal of an Expedition*, i. 81.
[202] Johnson, *History of the Yorubas*, 168, 227; R. and J. Lander, *Journal of an Expedition*, i. 81.
[203] Clapperton, *Journal of an Expedition*, 49; R. and J. Lander, *Journal of an Expedition*, i. 93. Some of the palace slaves who served under the *Oniṣarẹ* in Ẹgbado were likewise obliged to commit suicide when the *Oniṣarẹ* died: R. and J. Lander, *Journal of an Expedition*, i. 94–5.

E

the civil war between *Alafin* Abiǫdun and *Baṣǫrun* Gaha in 1774.[204]
This involves rejecting the tradition that Aṣade Agunloye, who
died in *c.* 1833, was the first *Olu* to exceed the three-year limit. But,
as has been argued earlier, the *first Olu* was probably appointed
only under *Alafin* Abiǫdun. Perhaps Aṣade found his opportunity to
perpetuate his rule at Ilaro in the confusion occasioned by the
political troubles of the capital after the death of Abiǫdun in 1789,
while the reorganization of the Ẹgbado province under the *Oniṣarẹ*
represents a subsequent reassertion of metropolitan control, in the
late eighteenth or early nineteenth century. The *Olu* evidently
resented his subordination to the *Oniṣarẹ*, and sought solace in his
nominal superiority of status. The Landers report that the *Olu* in
1830 'said he was a greater man than the Governor of Jenna, inso-
much as the latter was a slave to the King of Katunga, but himself a
free man.'[205] The delicacy of relations between the *Olu* and the
Oniṣarẹ is perhaps indicated by the tradition that they used to meet
once a year, sitting back to back in the middle of a field and com-
municating through messengers.[206]

Johnson describes the *Oniṣarẹ* as an *ajẹlẹ*,[207] but he was a much
more powerful figure than the *ajẹlẹ* in the towns of the older provinces of the kingdom. The normal arrangement by which the
tribute of the Ẹgbado towns was carried to Ǫyǫ by the local rulers,
led by the *Olu*, was now ended, and the tribute was instead collected
locally by the *Oniṣarẹ*, and forwarded by him to the *Alafin*.[208] The
Oniṣarẹ also transmitted judicial appeals and other petitions from
the local rulers to the *Alafin*.[209] It appears, however, that the local
rulers continued to travel to the capital to obtain the *Alafin*'s
approval at their installation.[210]

In addition to usurping the traditional functions of the *ẹkun*
head, the *Oniṣarẹ* was also charged with organizing, through a staff of
subordinate slaves, a new system of provincial taxation, the collection of taxes on local trade. The Landers observed in 1830, as
they approached Ilaro: 'Turnpikes are as common from Badagry to

---

[204] Adewale, 'The Ijanna Episode in Yoruba History', 252–3; followed by
Fǫlayan, 'Ẹgbado to 1832', 24–5.

[205] R. and J. Lander, *Journal of an Expedition*, i. 76.

[206] Johnson, *History of the Yorubas*, 227.

[207] Ibid. 168.

[208] Morton-Williams, 'The Ǫyǫ Yoruba and the Atlantic Trade', 37; Fǫlayan,
'Ẹgbado to 1832', 25.   [209] Fǫlayan, 'Ẹgbado to 1832', 25.

[210] Cf. evidence from Ǫta: NAI, CSO 26/2, 20629, F. C. Royce, 'Assessment
Report on Otta District, Egba Division, Abeokuta Province', 1927, §52.

this place, as on any public road in England. Instead of horses, carriages, &c., people carrying burdens alone are taxed; but as we are under the protection of the government, no duty has been exacted for any of our things.'[211] They also noted 'a kind of turn-pike' at the southern approaches to Ijanna,[212] and remark of their journey between Ibeṣe and 'Chow' further north: 'Several strangers accompany us from town to town, in order to evade the duty which is exacted at the turnpike-gates, by stating themselves to be of the number of our attendants.'[213] The existence of such 'gates' (in Yoruba, *ibode*), and the location of some of them, are also recalled in local traditions. These seem to indicate that the new system of tax-collection under the *Oniṣarẹ* embraced the whole south-western area of the kingdom, including the Anago and Awori towns as well as the Ẹgbado proper.[214] Two villages which, as their names indicate, were the sites of *ibode* were Bode Aṣe, just outside Ipokia to the north,[215] and Eyọ Bode Igbo, just north of Ilobi.[216] Tibọ in northern Ẹgbado was also a toll-collecting station,[217] and the existence of locally resident Ọyọ agents who collected taxes for the *Alafin* is also recalled in the traditions of Ihunmbọ[218] and Ọta.[219]

(m) Change through time: a process of centralization?

In the case of Ẹgbado it was possible to trace a growth of effective royal control over the province, culminating in the establishment of a highly centralized administration staffed by the *Alafin*'s palace slaves. It is less easy to trace any similar process of centralization in the older provinces of the kingdom, but there are grounds for suggesting that in these too the imperial period saw a progressive growth of royal power.

[211] R. and J. Lander, *Journal of an Expedition*, i. 68.

[212] Ibid. i. 79.   [213] Ibid. i. 104.

[214] But cf. Thomas, 'Historical Survey of the Towns of Ilaro, Ilobi, Ajilete, and Ilashe', 107, argues that Ilaṣe did not come under the *Oniṣarẹ*.

[215] Morton-Williams, 'The Ọyọ Yoruba and the Atlantic Trade', 37.

[216] Thomas, 'Historical Survey of the Towns of Ilaro, Ilobi, Ajilete, and Ilashe', 4, 59; NAI, CSO 26/4, 30435, J. H. Ellis, 'Intelligence Report on the Ilobi, Okeodan, and Ajilete Groups of the Egbado People in the Ilaro Division, Abeokuta Province' (1935), 1.

[217] Abẹokuta Divisional Archives, 'The History of Tibo Town in the Egba District', 1 July 1938, encl. to petition of *Balẹ* of Tibọ and others, asking for separation from Imala, 17 July 1947.

[218] NAI, CSO 26/4, 31065, W. R. Hatch, 'Intelligence Report on the Ihumbo Group in the Ilaro Division of the Abeokuta Province' (1935), 6.

[219] NAI, CSO 26/2, 20629, F. C. Royce, 'Assessment Report on Otta District, Egba Division, Abeokuta Province' (1927), §§52, 368.

In other, smaller Yoruba kingdoms, it appears that the administration of subject towns was normally left entirely to the chiefs of
the capital, to whom the subject towns were attached as clients.[220]
Such a system of 'fiefs' also existed, as has been seen, in the Ǫyǫ
kingdom, and it seems likely that this was the original mechanism by
which the Ǫyǫ kingdom was administered. However, in Ǫyǫ the
Alafin was able to establish closer royal control over the provinces,
by three means, all of which involved the use of his palace slaves.
First, many important 'fiefs' were granted to the senior palace
officials rather than to the non-royal chiefs of the capital: whether
this was effected by a transfer of towns from the latter to the former,
or merely by assigning newly conquered towns to the palace officials,
is not certain. Second, the *baba kekere* were introduced, in order to
establish royal control over the relations between the fief-holders and
their client towns. And third, the *ajẹlẹ* were placed in the provincial
towns as the *Alafin*'s permanent representatives, thus dispensing
altogether with the need to depend on the chiefs of the capital for
communication with the provinces. In the older provinces this
process of centralization does not seem to have been carried further,
but in the two provinces which were organized latest the role of the
palace slaves was even more important. Thus, in the Igbomina
province, there is evidence suggesting that the *Alafin*'s agents were
responsible for collecting local taxes; while in Ẹgbado, not only
did the palace slaves take over local tax collection, but an *ajẹlẹ* in
effect became the provincial head.

In the light of this, it is perhaps easier to understand the protracted
period of political troubles inside the capital during the eighteenth
century, described in the previous chapter. What the *Ǫyǫ Mesi* were
seeking to resist, it may be suggested, was the increase in royal
power which the expansion of the palace organization of slaves and
its increasing role in the administration of the empire represented.[221]
This suggestion would add significance to the action of *Baṣǫrun* Gaha
in 1754–74 in replacing the *Alafin*'s *ajẹlẹ* in the provincial towns
by members of his own lineage. The political troubles of the capital
were thus closely bound up with the expansion of the Ǫyǫ empire.

[220] Cf. the study of Ado Ekiti by P. C. Lloyd, 'Sacred Kingship and Government among the Yoruba', *Africa* 30 (1960), 231.

[221] Cf. Crowder, *Story of Nigeria*, 108; Lloyd, *Political Development of Yoruba
Kingdoms*, 14.

CHAPTER 7

The Heritage of Oduduwa: the Ọyọ Hegemony in Yorubaland

THE second category of Ọyọ subjects distinguished at the beginning of the last chapter comprised those over whom the *Alafin* claimed authority as the successor to the kingship of Oduduwa, the legendary founder and first king of Ile Ifẹ. The kingdoms whose royal dynasties claimed descent from Oduduwa included not only all the principal Yoruba kingdoms, but also the neighbouring Edo kingdom of Benin. According to Ọyọ tradition, all these kingdoms formed some sort of confederacy, and the *Alafin* of Ọyọ was the acknowledged head of this confederacy. The present chapter will first examine, in general terms, the claim of the *Alafin* to this position of primacy, and then attempt a detailed reconstruction of the actual extent of the *Alafin*'s effective authority over Yorubaland and Benin.

§1. THE POSITION OF IFẸ

Consideration of this question must start out from the fact that there is another, and on the face of it more plausible, claimant to the primacy among the kings descended from Oduduwa, namely the *Ọni* of Ifẹ. If the kingdoms ruled by the descendants of Oduduwa did indeed form a political unit, it would seem natural that the headship of the confederacy would devolve upon the occupant of the ancestral throne at Ile Ifẹ. This is, indeed, precisely what is claimed by Ifẹ sources. According to an account given by the *Ọni* of Ifẹ in 1931, when Oduduwa, shortly before his death, conferred crowns on his sons, he first crowned his eldest son as the *Ọni* of Ifẹ, and ordered his other sons, the founders of the other kingdoms, 'to show filial obedience to their eldest brother.' In consequence, it is claimed, 'The Ọni is still regarded by his younger brothers as their father.'[1] This conception of the *Ọni* of Ifẹ wielding an acknowledged paternal authority over the family of dynasties descended from Oduduwa has been elaborated by Ademakinwa, the local historian of Ifẹ.[2] It

[1] NAI, OYOPROF. 1/203, *Ọni* of Ifẹ to District Officer, Ifẹ, 9 Oct. 1931.
[2] Ademakinwa, *Ifẹ, Cradle of the Yorubas*.

has also been adopted in recent years by Professor Akinjogbin. In his words,

> . . . the person occupying the throne of the original ancestor was regarded as the 'father' of all the other kings and all the other kings regarded one another as 'brothers' . . . The 'father' king had to give the final sanctions to the appointments of any of the kings, who in turn took an oath never to attack his territory. In the Yoruba country . . . the election of the kings of all the most important kingdoms was sanctioned at Ifẹ with the presentation of symbolic objects, among which swords and cutlasses feature prominently.[3]

Akinjogbin calls this conception of inter-state relationships in terms of the genealogical links between dynasties the 'ẹbi [family] social theory'. The confederacy comprising the 'father' king and his 'sons' he christens an 'Ẹbi Commonwealth'.[4]

Plausible as this Ifẹ view might appear, it is difficult to find supporting evidence for the claim that the Ọni of Ifẹ exercised any such 'paternal' authority over the other kings. Even the Ifẹ sources, indeed, leave the precise character of this authority very unclear. The one tangible expression of it which is mentioned, and particularly stressed by Akinjogbin, is the custom of making reference to Ile Ifẹ in the installation rituals of the kings of the derivative kingdoms. At Ọyọ, when a new *Alafin* was installed, a sword supposed to have belonged to Ọranyan, the founder of Ọyọ, had to be taken to Ile Ifẹ to be reconsecrated before being used in the ceremonies at Ọyọ.[5] Similarly, in the case of Benin, parts of the bodies of deceased kings had to be taken to Ile Ifẹ for burial, and the Ọni sent messengers with gifts to the local installation ceremonies.[6] However, such institutional expressions of the traditional dynastic link with Ile Ifẹ were by no means universal. The *Alaketu* of Ketu merely sent messengers to inform the Ọni of Ifẹ of his accession,[7] while no reference to Ile Ifẹ of any sort appears to have been made at the installation of the *Olowu* of Owu,[8] the *Awujalẹ* of Ijẹbu,[9] or the Ọwa

---

[3] Akinjogbin, *Dahomey and its Neighbours*, 14–17.

[4] Ibid. 16. *Ẹbi* is a Yoruba word for 'family': it is used by Akinjogbin, not on the authority of informants, but (as he explains, ibid. 16, n.1) to avoid the connotation of a European-type family.

[5] Johnson, *History of the Yorubas*, 10.

[6] R. E. Bradbury, *The Benin Kingdom and the Edo-Speaking Peoples of South-Western Nigeria* (London, 1957), 22.

[7] G. Parrinder, *The Story of Ketu* (2nd ed., Ibadan, 1967), 85.

[8] Oral evidence, from the *Olowu* of Owu Ipole.

[9] Oral evidence, from Chief O. Odutọla, the *Olotu'fore* of Ijẹbu.

of Ilẹṣa.[10] And even in the cases of Ọyọ and Benin, there is no suggestion that the Ọni's role in the installation rituals gave him any voice in the selection of the king. No instance is recalled of the Ọni refusing to sanction the installation of the local choice. Beyond this, it does not appear that the Ọni received any tribute from his 'sons', or exercised any sort of control over their actions. He certainly did not prevent them from fighting wars against each other. It is very difficult, therefore, to accept that the Ọni's 'paternal' status can have meant very much in practice.

Unfortunately, there is little detailed evidence on relations between Ifẹ and Ọyọ before the nineteenth century. One episode, however, towards the end of the eighteenth century, is recorded in the traditions, and is used by Akinjogbin to illustrate Ifẹ overlordship over Ọyọ. During the reign at Ọyọ of *Alafin* Abiọdun (1774–89), there was an outbreak of kidnapping in the area of Apomu, an important market town in the west of the Ifẹ kingdom, and several Ọyọ traders were enslaved. Abiọdun, according to Johnson, therefore sent orders to the *Olowu* of Owu and the *Ọni* of Ifẹ to suppress these kidnappings, and these two kings passed on these orders to the *Balẹ* of Apomu, who took action against the practice. One of those who were punished by the *Balẹ* was the Ọyọ prince Awolẹ, and when Awolẹ succeeded Abiọdun as *Alafin* (1789) he sought revenge by ordering an expedition against Apomu. According to Johnson, the *Balẹ* of Apomu fled for protection to the *Ọni* of Ifẹ, but the *Ọni* could not save him 'as the offence was against the Suzerain [i.e. the *Alafin*].' The *Balẹ* therefore committed suicide, in order to save his town from attack, and the Ọyọ expedition was called off.[11] Johnson's account, based presumably on Ọyọ sources, is evidently tendentious in describing the *Alafin* as the 'suzerain' of the *Ọni*. The traditions of Apomu give a slightly different account of the incident. They assert that the *Balẹ* fled to Ile Ifẹ, but that after negotiations with Awolẹ the *Ọni* assured him that he could return to Apomu in safety: however, the *Balẹ* committed suicide out of cowardice.[12] There is nothing in either account which suggests that Ifẹ was in any sense the overlord of Ọyọ. Akinjogbin, however, gives a very different interpretation of the episode. He points out that Awolẹ's decision to attack Apomu was a violation of the oath which the *Alafin* took at

---

[10] Personal communication from Dr. Bọlanle Awẹ, reporting oral evidence from Ilẹṣa.   [11] Johnson, *History of the Yorubas*, 189.
[12] YHRS, D. A. Adeniji, 'History of Apomu', n.d.

his installation, in return for the reconsecration of the sword of Qranyan at Ile Ifẹ, never to attack the *Qni*'s territory, and suggests that the expedition was abandoned because the Qyọ chiefs for this reason refused to carry it out.[13] But it does not appear that this rewriting of the episode is based on any explicit evidence in the traditions. At least, Akinjogbin cites no other source than Johnson, and would appear to be arguing simply from the existence of the installation oath. Against this, it can be argued that the fact that the traditions make no reference to the oath is a prima facie reason for doubting that it was regarded as of any practical significance.[14] At any rate, the traditional accounts of the Apomu incident lend no support to the notion of an Ifẹ overlordship over Qyọ.

Besides the difficulty of putting any concrete content into the *Qni*'s claims to authority, there is the additional objection that the *Qni*'s dynastic status is disputed. Ifẹ tradition, as has been seen, makes the *Qni* descend from the eldest son of Oduduwa, but this claim is not universally accepted. A very widespread story asserts that the first *Qni* was not a son of Oduduwa at all, but a slave who was left as caretaker of the palace at Ile Ifẹ when the sons of Oduduwa dispersed to found their kingdoms. Versions of this story are told, for example, in Qyọ,[15] in Ijẹbu,[16] in Ilẹsa,[17] and apparently in Ketu.[18] Very probably this version is secondary, and the *Qni*'s claim to descent from Oduduwa represents the original tradition. And very probably the revised version became current precisely because kings such as the *Alafin* of Qyọ, the *Awujalẹ* of Ijẹbu, the *Qwa* of Ilẹsa, and the *Alaketu* of Ketu wished to evade the implication in the original tradition that they were junior in status to the *Qni* of Ifẹ. But, however spurious such traditions, they do demonstrate the unreality of Ifẹ pretensions to an accepted 'paternal' primacy among the dynasties descended from Oduduwa.

---

[13] I. A. Akinjogbin, 'The Prelude to the Yoruba Civil Wars of the Nineteenth Century', *Odu*, 2nd series, 1.2 (1965), 32–4.

[14] Similarly the oath does not appear to have been invoked when the Owu attacked Apomu and other western Ifẹ towns in c. 1812, or when Ile Ifẹ itself was attacked, by Qyọ refugees settled nearby at Modakẹkẹ, in 1852 and 1882. This suggests that the oath is in fact a recent innovation, inspired precisely by these attacks on Ifẹ during the nineteenth century.

[15] Johnson, *History of the Yorubas*, 11–12.

[16] Oral evidence, from Chief O. Odutọla, the *Olotu'fore* of Ijẹbu.

[17] Abiọla, Babafẹmi, and Ataiyero, *Iwe Itan Ijẹsa*, 23–5; cf. Johnson, *History of the Yorubas*, 24–5.

[18] Crowther was told at Ketu in 1853 that the *Alaketu* was the 'rightful pro-

It may well be that the *Ọni*'s claims to authority had some reality in an early period, but any effective Ifẹ overlordship must be supposed to have faded by the period with which this study is concerned, when Ọyọ became the principal power in Yorubaland. It is possible that the decline of Ifẹ authority was, at least in part, a consequence of the rise of Ọyọ.[19] As has been seen, there is evidence suggesting that Ọyọ expanded at the expense of the Ifẹ kingdom, taking from it the towns of Iwo and Ejigbo.[20] Certainly, by the eighteenth century at least, the only plausible candidate for the paramountcy among the Ifẹ derivative kingdoms was Ọyọ.

§2. THE ỌYỌ CLAIM TO PARAMOUNTCY

The denial of royal ancestry to the *Ọni* of Ifẹ opened the way for the *Alafin* of Ọyọ to put himself forward as the rightful paramount among the kings descended from Oduduwa.[21] According to a common tradition, Ọranyan, the founder of Ọyọ, had been the youngest of Oduduwa's children.[22] This probably reflects a period when Ọyọ was one of the least important of the kingdoms connected with Ile Ifẹ, presumably before the seventeenth century. At a later stage, however, the growth of Ọyọ power evidently made the traditionally junior status of the *Alafin* seem inappropriate, and the claim was formulated that the *Alafin*, rather than the *Ọni* of Ifẹ, was the true successor to the paternal primacy of Oduduwa. This, it must be stressed, was in direct contradiction to the Ifẹ claim. The common theory that the Ọyọ and Ifẹ claims to paramountcy were complementary, the *Ọni* being the religious and the *Alafin* the political head of Yorubaland,[23] is a modern fiction, the result of an attempt to harmonize contradictory evidence attributing the same sort of authority to two different rulers.

According to Ọyọ tradition, it was Ọranyan who had succeeded Oduduwa as king of Ile Ifẹ, and when Ọranyan later founded Ọyọ, this represented a transfer of the seat of government from Ile Ifẹ to

---

prietor' of the palace at Ile Ifẹ, and the *Ọni* merely its 'keeper': CMS, CA2/031b, the Revd. S. Crowther, Journal, 16 Jan. 1853.

[19] Cf. Smith, *Kingdoms of the Yoruba*, 23–4.

[20] Cf. above, Ch. 6, pp. 88, 96.

[21] See further R. Law, 'The Heritage of Oduduwa: Traditional History and Political Propaganda among the Yoruba', *JAH* 14 (1973), 207–22.

[22] Bowen, *Central Africa*, 266; George, *Historical Notes on the Yoruba Country*, 18; Johnson, *History of the Yorubas*, 8, 23.

[23] e.g. Frobenius, *Voice of Africa*, i. 171–2; R. E. Dennett, *Nigerian Studies, or the Religious and Political System of the Yoruba* (London, 1910), 91.

Qyọ.[24] A supplementary tradition asserts that when Oduduwa's property was divided among his children, Ọranyan inherited the land, so that the other kings became his tenants and paid him tribute in return for permission to live on the land.[25] In this conception, since the foundation of Qyọ by Ọranyan, all the other kingdoms derived from Ile Ifẹ were subject to the *Alafin* of Qyọ. This claim of the *Alafin* to the heritage of Oduduwa is presumably the basis for Johnson's assertion that the Qyọ empire at its greatest extent was bounded by the River Niger in the east and by the sea to the south, that is, including all the Yoruba kingdoms and Benin.[26] It also probably lies behind a somewhat more limited claim, recorded in other traditions, which described Qyọ, Ketu, Owu, and Ijẹbu as the 'Four Corners of Yorubaland', which formed some sort of confederacy under the headship of the *Alafin* of Qyọ.[27]

Qyọ lordship over the Ifẹ derivative kingdoms was allegedly given a practical expression under *Alafin* Ojigi in the early eighteenth century, when 'in order to show his undisputed sovereignty over the whole of the Yoruba country, including Benin' the *Alafin* sent an expedition which sailed down the Niger from Borgu to the sea, then westwards along the coast to the Popo (Egun) country, before returning overland to Qyọ.[28] Precisely what the *Alafin*'s 'undisputed sovereignty' amounted to in practice is left vague. Johnson concedes that the other kingdoms 'lived more or less in a state of semi-independence, whilst loosely acknowledging [the *Alafin* as] an overlord'.[29] It is, however, asserted that the other kingdoms all paid tribute to Qyọ.[30]

It is clear that the *Alafin*'s claim to the heritage of Oduduwa was bogus, both in the sense that the traditional headship belonged, if to anyone, to the *Ọni* of Ifẹ, and in the sense that the *Alafin* never in fact exercised authority over the extensive area claimed. The second

[24] Johnson, *History of the Yorubas*, 11.

[25] Ibid. 8–9.

[26] Ibid. 179.

[27] PP, 1887 (c. 4957), vol. lx, p. 6, A. Moloney to Sir S. Rowe, 12 May 1881; cf. Ellis, *Yoruba-Speaking Peoples*, 10; Johnson, *History of the Yorubas*, 574. These accounts name the 'four corners' as Qyọ, Ketu, Ijẹbu, and Ẹgba, but Dennett, *Nigerian Studies*, 91–2, names Owu instead of Ẹgba. Dennett evidently preserves the original version, Ẹgba having been substituted for Owu after the destruction of the latter kingdom in the 1820s.

[28] Johnson, *History of the Yorubas*, 174.

[29] Ibid. 40; cf. ibid. 9.

[30] Ibid. 179; CMS, CA2/031a, the Revd. S. Crowther to T. J. Hutchinson, 10 Sept. 1856.

of these assertions will be justified in detail below. In the present context, however, it needs to be stressed that the *Alafin*'s claim, and the divergence between his claim and the effective extent of his authority, has had a seriously distorting effect on the view of Ọyọ history presented in Ọyọ tradition. Since the *Alafin* is supposed to have ruled a vast empire since the time of Ọranyan, Ọyọ traditions do not present a coherent account of the rise of Ọyọ from insignificance to greatness. Indeed, since the effective authority of the *Alafin* in the eighteenth century was so much less extensive than the fictitious authority bequeathed by Ọranyan, Ọyọ traditions had to present the power of Ọyọ as declining rather than increasing. Thus, Bowen in the 1850s was assured that although the *Alafin* had originally been 'sovereign' of Benin and the other Yoruba states, 'After a while, Benin . . . became independent, and in course of time, the other four tribes withdrew from the confederacy, leaving Yoruba [Ọyọ] alone.'[31] The claim to authority over Benin seems to have been recognized as being especially absurd: Johnson also concedes that Benin was one of the first of the subordinate kingdoms to become independent of Ọyọ,[32] while another source asserts that on Ọranyan's death his empire was divided between two of his sons, Yorubaland being allotted to the *Alafin* of Ọyọ and the area further east to the King of Benin.[33] After the collapse of Ọyọ power in the 1830s, in some traditions the disintegration of Ọranyan's fictitious empire became confused with the collapse of the historical Ọyọ empire of the eighteenth century. Hence, it could be claimed that the whole of Yorubaland and Benin had remained tributary to Ọyọ until after the death of Abiọdun, the last strong *Alafin*, in 1789.[34] Johnson offers a compromise version: in his account, although Benin had defected earlier, the whole of Yorubaland remained united under the suzerainty of Ọyọ until the death of Abiọdun.[35]

Insistence on the unhistorical character of the Ọyọ claim to the heritage of Oduduwa should not be taken to imply that the claim was unimportant. It provided a justification for Ọyọ aggressions against the kingdoms of Yorubaland—the *Alafin*, after all, was merely reclaiming an authority which was rightfully his. It might

[31] Bowen, *Central Africa*, 266.
[32] Johnson, *History of the Yorubas*, 40.
[33] Ojo, *Iwe Itan Ọyọ*, 23.
[34] CMS, CA2/037, Mrs. J. Faulckner, 'A True Story of the Yoruba Country', 11/12 July 1874.
[35] Johnson, *History of the Yorubas*, 187; cf. ibid. 642.

also provide a basis upon which the rulers of Yoruba kingdoms could be induced to acknowledge Ọyọ primacy. How far the *Alafin* succeeded in turning his claim into effective authority will now be examined. It is convenient to divide the study of this problem into three sections, dealing with Ọyọ relations with, first, the kingdoms of eastern Yorubaland and Benin, second, the kingdoms of southern Yorubaland, and third, the western Yoruba kingdoms of Ṣabẹ and Ketu.

§3. EASTERN YORUBALAND AND BENIN

To the south-east the Ọyọ kingdom had as its immediate neighbours the Ijẹṣa, who formed a single kingdom under the *Ọwa* of Ilesa, the Igbomina kingdom of Ila, and the Ekiti, who were divided into several (conventionally, sixteen) independent kingdoms. To the south of the Ekiti, along the south-eastern border of the Yoruba country, were the kingdoms of Akurẹ, Ọwọ, Ondo, and Idanre. And beyond these in turn was the non-Yoruba kingdom of Benin.

Throughout the period of Ọyọ imperial power, much of eastern Yorubaland was dominated by Benin. Benin expansion in this area apparently began under *Ọba* Ẹwuare, who reigned at Benin in the second half of the fifteenth century. Benin tradition credits Ẹwuare with conquering Ọwọ and Akurẹ,[36] while local tradition in Ekiti indicates that his forces penetrated even further, and conquered the Ekiti kingdom of Ado.[37] Akurẹ, where Ẹwuare placed a Bini political resident, appears to have served as the headquarters of Benin rule in the area.[38] Benin tradition also claims Ondo as part of the Benin empire in this period.[39]

Ọyọ influence in eastern Yorubaland is unlikely to have been significant before the end of the sixteenth century. Ọyọ had been in contact from quite early times with the Ijẹṣa kingdom, and the foundation of Ẹdẹ, probably in the pre-imperial period, is said to have been intended to safeguard the frontier of the Ọyọ kingdom against raids by the Ijẹṣa.[40] However, the extension of the Ọyọ

---

[36] Egharevba, *Short History of Benin*, 15–16. For the date of Ẹwuare's reign, cf. R. E. Bradbury, 'Chronological Problems in the Study of Benin History', *JHSN* 1.4 (1959), 277–80; id., *Benin Studies* (London, 1973), 32–6.

[37] A. Oguntuyi, *A Short History of Ado-Ekiti* (Akurẹ, n.d.), 18.

[38] Egharevba, *Short History of Benin*, 16, 82. For Bini rule over eastern Yorubaland, see further S. A. Akintoye, 'The North-Eastern Districts of the Yoruba Country and the Benin Kingdom', *JHSN* 4.4 (1969), 539–53.

[39] Egharevba, *Short History of Benin*, 37, 82.

[40] Cf. above, Ch. 3, p. 36.

kingdom eastward beyond Ẹdẹ, into Igbomina country, probably followed the recovery of Ọyọ after the Nupe invasions of the six-teenth century.[41] This expansion probably involved fighting against Ila, whose ruler, the *Ọrangun*, claimed the traditional headship of the Igbomina, but no details of this are preserved in the available traditions.

Various pieces of evidence combine to suggest that Ọyọ made a considerable, but unsuccessful, attempt to conquer eastern Yoruba-land around the beginning of the seventeenth century. There was, first, an Ọyọ invasion of the Ijẹṣa kingdom, under *Alafin* Ọbalokun, whose reign probably fell during the first half of the seventeenth century. According to Johnson, Ọbalokun

sent an expedition into the Ijẹṣa country which was ambushed and defeated by the tribe known as Ijẹṣa Arẹra, the Ọyọs being then unaccustomed to bush fighting. So great was the loss of life in this expedition that the *Ologbo* was sent out as a town crier to inform the bereaved of their losses in the war.[42]

Johnson's reference to the inexperience of the Ọyọ in 'bush fighting' perhaps alludes to their use of cavalry, which would be ineffective in the forests of Ijẹṣaland.[43] Johnson apparently believed that the name 'Arẹra' designated a sub-group of the Ijẹṣa, but it is explained today as an epithet of the Ijẹṣa as a whole.[44] Other sources also refer to an 'Ijẹṣa Arara' or 'Ijẹṣa Rẹrẹ' War, which is presumably to be identified with Ọbalokun's expedition. One account claims that during the war the *Ọwa* of Ilẹṣa expanded his territory, founding several towns in the Ikirun area.[45] The traditions of Ikirun itself confirm that this town came under pressure from the Ijẹṣa during the war: the people of Ikirun are said to have been driven from the original site of their town by an Ijẹṣa raid.[46] Whether such raids on Ọyọ territory preceded or followed the defeat of Ọbalokun's invasion of Ijẹṣaland is not indicated.

The traditions do not make clear the circumstances which led to Ọbalokun's war against the Ijẹṣa. Chief Ojo, it is true, presents it as a

[41] Cf. above, Ch. 6, p. 91.

[42] Johnson, *History of the Yorubas*, 168.

[43] For the Ọyọ use of cavalry, cf. below, Ch. 9, pp. 183–7.

[44] Personal communication from Dr. Bọlanle Awẹ, reporting oral evidence from Ilẹṣa.

[45] Abraham, *Dictionary of Modern Yoruba*, s.v. Oṣogbo, (4) (d). This account, which is presumably derived from administrative records now lost, places the war in *c.* 1760.

[46] YHRS, D. A. Adeniji, 'History of Ikirun', n.d.

revolt of the Ijẹṣa against Ọyọ rule, claiming that Ọbalokun's expedition was dispatched because the Ijẹṣa had failed to send tribute to his predecessor Abipa when the latter reoccupied the old Ọyọ capital at Ọyọ Ile.[47] But this evidence should be disregarded, since Chief Ojo is probably merely rationalizing the traditions in the light of the official Ọyọ view that the *Alafin* was originally the overlord of all Yorubaland. The traditions of the Ijẹṣa themselves appear not to recall Ọbalokun's invasion.[48] They do, however, provide a plausible context for it, by suggesting a period of competition for influence in Ijẹṣaland between Ọyọ and Benin. An early Ijẹṣa ruler, *Ọwa* Ọwaluṣẹ (or Ọwaniṣẹ), who is credited with having moved the Ijẹṣa capital to Ilẹṣa, is said to have been the son of an Ọyọ princess, to have spent some time at Ọyọ before his accession, and to have gained the Ijẹṣa throne with the support of Ọyọ: the *Alafin* is said to have posted a mounted envoy at Ilẹṣa to warn him of any military move by Ọwaluṣẹ's opponents. Ọwaluṣẹ's successor, *Ọwa* Atakunmọsa, on the other hand, is closely identified with Benin, where he is said to have spent several years in exile.[49] These traditions appear to record the replacement of a predominant Ọyọ influence at Ilẹṣa by a predominant Benin influence.[50] The change seems to have taken place around the end of the sixteenth century. *Ọwa* Atakunmọsa is remembered in Benin tradition as a contemporary of *Ọba* Ehẹngbuda of Benin:[51] the local historian of Benin, Chief Egharevba, dates the reign of Ehẹngbuda to 1578–1606, and while it cannot be shown that these dates are precisely accurate it is clear that they are not wildly wrong.[52] This brings the accession of

---

[47] Ojo, *Iwe Itan Ọyọ*, 52.

[48] It is not mentioned, e.g. in Abiọla, Babafẹmi, and Ataiyero, *Iwe Itan Ijẹṣa*. However, this work does record two unsuccessful invasions of Ijẹṣaland by the Nupe, and it is conceivable that there has been some confusion between the Ọyọ and the Nupe in Ijẹṣa tradition: ibid. 44–5, 47–8; cf. above, Ch. 3, p. 38 and n.71.

[49] J. O. Oni, *A History of Ijeshaland* (Ilẹṣa, n.d.), 25, 29, 72. For Ọwaluṣẹ, cf. Ojo, *Iwe Itan Ọyọ*, 39. For Atakunmọsa, cf. Kẹnyọ, *Yoruba Natural Rulers and their Origins*, 77–82; Egharevba, *Short History of Benin*, 33.

[50] The significance of these traditions was pointed out to me by Professor J. D. Y. Peel.

[51] Egharevba, *Short History of Benin*, 33.

[52] Cf. Bradbury, 'Chronological Problems in Benin History', 274–6; id., *Benin Studies*, 30–2. It is interesting to note that one Ijẹṣa local historian independently dates the reign of *Ọwa* Atakunmọsa to about the same period (1575–1655): Atundaolu, 'Short Traditional History of the Ijesas', *Lagos Weekly Record*, 20 July 1901. The Ọyọ local historian Chief Ojo makes *Ọwa* Ọwaluṣẹ, Atakunmọsa's predecessor, a contemporary of *Alafin* Aganju of Ọyọ, implying a date in the

Atakunmọsa and the consequent establishment of Benin influence at Ilẹsa so close in time to Ọbalokun's invasion of Ijẹsaland that it seems reasonable to posit a connection between the two events. It may also be noted that in one version of Ijẹsa tradition Atakunmọsa is said to have been succeeded as Ọwa of Ilẹsa by a certain Uyi Arẹrẹ,[53] whose name prompts comparison with the name 'Arẹra' or 'Rẹrẹ' given to Ọbalokun's war in Ọyọ sources. If Ọbalokun's invasion occurred in the reign of Ọwa Uyi Arẹrẹ, it might have been intended to reassert Ọyọ influence in Ilẹsa after its eclipse under his predecessor Atakunmọsa.

The suggestion that Ọbalokun's invasion of Ijẹsaland was a response to the penetration of Benin influence is supported by the fact that Benin tradition also records a direct confrontation between Ọyọ and Benin forces as occurring around this time in the neighbouring area of Ekiti. Ọba Ehẹngbuda of Benin, the contemporary of Ọwa Atakunmọsa, is said to have fought a war against the Ọyọ, which was ended by a treaty fixing the boundary between the two powers at Ọtun, in northern Ekiti.[54] It is possible that this war is also referred to in a European source, the work of Dapper, which was published in 1668. Dapper's informants, who visited Benin at an uncertain date during the first half of the seventeenth century, perhaps in the 1640s,[55] were told that during the reign of the then king's father, named as 'Kombadje', Benin had been attacked by a large army of cavalry from a country to the north-west called 'Isago'. Kombadje had defeated the invaders, foiling their cavalry by digging concealed pits in the battlefield, into which their horses stumbled.[56] The Ọyọ are known to have made considerable use of cavalry, and it has been suggested that 'Isago' might be identified with Ọyọ, and 'Kombadje' with Ehẹngbuda.[57] Against this, it has

fifteenth century, but this must be rejected as incompatible with the Benin evidence on the date of Atakunmọsa: Ojo, *Iwe Itan Ọyọ*, 39.

[53] Atundaolu, 'Short Traditional History of the Ijesas', *Lagos Weekly Record*, 20 July 1901. However, the version of the Ijẹsa king-list given by Abiọla, Babafẹmi, and Ataiyero, *Iwe Itan Ijẹsa*, places this ruler (here called Bilayiarẹrẹ) much later, being separated from Atakunmọsa by the reigns of six intervening rulers.

[54] Egharevba, *Short History of Benin*, 32.

[55] His information on the neighbouring Itsekiri kingdom relates to the year 1644: Dapper, *Naukeurige Beschrijvinge der Afrikaensche Gewesten*, 507.

[56] Ibid. 505.

[57] Bradbury, 'Chronological Problems in Benin History', 274–6; id., *Benin Studies*, 30–2.

been argued that the use of cavalry might equally indicate the Nupe, who are known to have dominated northern Yorubaland during the sixteenth century,[58] but since a war with Qyọ at about the right time is recorded in Benin tradition, the identification with the Qyọ is more plausible. It may be inferred that the war between Qyọ and Benin was fought for control of the Ekiti area, and the establishment of a frontier at Qtun in northern Ekiti marked the abandonment of Qyọ claims in the area. Dapper includes 'Isago' among the tributaries of Benin,[59] but while Qyọ may well have made payments to Benin in negotiating a settlement, it seems improbable that it became permanently tributary.

Two other episodes recorded in local traditions, although less precisely datable, can probably be connected with the war between Qyọ and Benin in the time of Ehẹngbuda. First, the traditions of Idanre record that under the third Qwa of Idanre, Beyọja, the kingdom was attacked by an Qyọ army, mounted on horses, which was ambushed and driven off. The purpose of the Qyọ attack is said, in a suggestive but enigmatic phrase, to have been 'to recover the original Oduduwa crown'.[60] Second, the traditions of Ondo record that the third Oṣemọwe of Ondo, Luju, established friendly relations, marked by the exchange of presents, with the Alafin of Qyọ, but that under Luju's son Lẹyọ, the seventh Oṣemọwe, the Qyọ attacked Ondo 'through no just cause' and were defeated.[61] There is also a story, not attached to the reign of any particular Oṣemọwe, that Ondo was once tributary to Qyọ, until the Ondo placed charms inside the bundles of tribute which killed all who tried to open them, thus inducing the Alafin to release them from their obligation to pay tribute.[62]

Unfortunately, interpretation of these traditions of Idanre and

---

[58] Ryder, Benin and the Europeans, 15.

[59] Dapper, Naukeurige Beschrijvinge der Afrikaensche Gewesten, 501.

[60] YHRS, I. A. Akinjogbin, 'Report on Idanre History', n.d. The most probable meaning of the reference to 'the original Oduduwa crown' is that Oduduwa's crown was supposed to be in the possession of the Qwa of Idanre; but it is possible that there is an allusion here to the claim of the Alafin to dynastic primacy as the successor to Oduduwa's kingship.

[61] J. A. Leigh, The History of Ondo (Ondo, 1917), 26. Leigh dates the reign of Luju to 1561–90 and that of Lẹyọ to 1649–68, but no value can be attached to these dates.

[62] Ibid. 7–8. Chief S. Ojo, Iwe Itan Ondo (4th impression, Ondo, 1962), 28–31, records this story together with a variant attributing the ending of the tribute to Qjọmu Nla, the national hero of Ondo tradition; according to Leigh, History of Ondo, 20–2, Qjọmu Nla lived in the time of Oṣemọwe Luju.

Ondo has been complicated by the way in which they have been handled by Chief Ojo. In the first place, Chief Ojo attributes these incidents to the reigns of specific *Alafin*: the Idanre war to the reign of *Alafin* Kọri,[63] the ending of Ondo's tribute to that of *Alafin* Ajiboyede,[64] and the expedition defeated by Ọṣemọwe Lẹyọ to that of *Alafin* Ayibi.[65] This would suggest dates for these incidents in, respectively, the fifteenth century, the sixteenth century, and the early eighteenth century. It is unlikely, however, that any value whatever should be attached to these chronological equations, for Chief Ojo's attempts to synchronize the king-lists of the different Yoruba kingdoms are frequently arbitrary.[66] It seems more reasonable to take the two Ondo stories as relating to the same or closely connected events, attesting a single Ọyọ attempt, temporarily successful but ultimately a failure, to bring Ondo under Ọyọ rule. And it is probable that both this attempt and the attack on Idanre were part of the Ọyọ encroachment into eastern Yorubaland which was checked by *Ọba* Ehẹngbuda of Benin around the beginning of the seventeenth century. Chief Ojo also offers an explanation of the expedition against Idanre, asserting that it was sent because Idanre had ceased to send tribute to Ọyọ during the period of *Alafin* Kọri's minority, when Kọri's mother Iyayun ruled Ọyọ as Regent.[67] But as in the case of the Ijẹṣa war of *Alafin* Ọbalokun, this is probably merely a reinterpretation in the light of Chief Ojo's belief that originally the *Alafin* ruled all Yorubaland.

Probably the Ọyọ operations against the Ijẹṣa, in Ekiti, and against Ondo and Idanre, all formed part of a systematic attempt to establish Ọyọ control over eastern Yorubaland. The attempt failed, not only because of the opposition of Benin, but also because the Ọyọ, in moving into eastern Yorubaland, were entering forested and hilly country where their cavalry could not operate effectively. At any rate, after their decisive defeats around the beginning of the seventeenth century, it does not appear that the Ọyọ made any further

[63] Ojo, *Iwe Itan Ọyọ*, 45.
[64] Ojo, *Iwe Itan Ondo*, 28–31, 41–2.
[65] Ibid. 48.
[66] In the case of Ondo, it is probable that Chief Ojo has simply taken Leigh's dates for Ọṣemọwe Luju (1561–90) and Ọṣemọwe Lẹyọ (1649–68), and compared them with his own dates for the *Alafin* of Ọyọ (as given in *Iwe Itan Ọyọ*), according to which Ajiboyede was reigning in 1562–70 and Ayibi in 1670–90: the minor discrepancy between the dates of Lẹyọ and Ayibi may simply represent an error on Chief Ojo's part.
[67] Ojo, *Iwe Itan Ọyọ*, 45.

attempts at military expansion in the east. After the reign of *Ọba*
Ehẹngbuda, the rulers of Benin appear to have neglected their
Yoruba dependencies, and effective Bini control in eastern Yorubaland declined,[68] but there is no evidence that the Ọyọ sought to
exploit this. In the early nineteenth century, from *c.* 1818, Benin
control over Ọwọ and Akurẹ, and over Ekiti as far as Ọtun, was
again reasserted by force of arms.[69] Hence it was that Clapperton
could still be told in 1826 that the Ọyọ kingdom marched in the
south-east with 'Accoura [Akurẹ], a province of Benin'.[70]

However, although Ọyọ attempts at military conquest in the east
were defeated, it appears that at least some of the eastern Yoruba
kingdoms eventually acknowledged in some sense the suzerainty of
Ọyọ. One tradition reported by Johnson describes the north-eastern
Yoruba rulers, the *Ọwa* of Ileṣa, the *Ọrangun* of Ila, the *Ore* of Ọtun,
and the other Ekiti kings, as 'younger brothers' of the *Alafin* of Ọyọ,
and claims that:

> The Ọwa and his brothers used to pay the Alafin annual visits, with
> presents of firewood, fine locally-made mats, kola nuts and bitter kolas;
> the Owore of Ọtun with sweet water from a fine spring at Ọtun—this
> water the Alafin first spills on the ground as a libation before performing
> any ceremonies. The other Ekiti kings used also to take with them suitable
> presents as each could afford, and bring away lavish presents from their
> elder brother.[71]

In another passage Johnson repeats the assertion that the first *Ọwa*
of Ileṣa was a younger brother of the *Alafin*, and comments:

> This relationship was acknowledged by the Ọwa paying a yearly tribute
> of a few heads of cowries, mats, and some products of his forests to the
> Alafin, while the latter sent him presents of robes, vests, and other superior
> articles well worthy of him as an elder brother.[72]

The claim that the *Alafin* exchanged gifts with the rulers of these
north-eastern kingdoms is corroborated by evidence from Ileṣa,[73]

[68] After the reign of Ehẹngbuda, no further Benin campaigns in eastern
Yorubaland are recorded in Benin tradition until the early nineteenth century.
[69] Egharevba, *Short History of Benin*, 45–7; Oguntuyi, *Short History of
Ado-Ekiti*, 36–9; Bradbury, 'Chronological Problems in Benin History', 270–1;
id., *Benin Studies*, 25–6.
[70] Clapperton, *Journal of a Second Expedition*, 56.
[71] Johnson, *History of the Yorubas*, 25, quoting Ijẹṣa tradition.
[72] Ibid. 10.
[73] Personal communication from Dr. Bọlanle Awẹ, reporting oral evidence
from Ilesa.

Ila,[74] and Ọtun.[75] It is doubtful, however, whether the kings of these towns ever went in person to Ọyọ to deliver their gifts, as Johnson in the first passage cited claims. The *Alafin*'s seniority of status as an 'elder brother' is also admitted in both Ileṣa[76] and Ila.[77] (Evidence on this point from Ọtun is lacking.) It is denied, however, that this recognition of the *Alafin*'s seniority meant that these kingdoms were subject to Ọyọ, or that the gifts sent to Ọyọ were regarded as tribute (*asingba*). In the 1880s, the Ijeṣa offered to resume the payment of these gifts, proposing 'that the Ọwa, being the Alafin's younger brother, would still acknowledge him by a yearly gift, which is not to be taken for tribute, but as a token of respect.'[78] There is no doubt that this is an accurate characterization of the relationship of Ileṣa and Ila (and perhaps also Ọtun) to the Ọyọ empire. The *Alafin*'s claim to the heritage of Oduduwa was formally recognized, but these kingdoms remained effectively independent.

There is no reason to suppose that Benin, even after the decline of its power in the seventeenth and eighteenth centuries, ever felt compelled to make a similar acknowledgement of the *Alafin*'s status. There is, unfortunately, little evidence on relations between the two kingdoms after Ẹhẹngbuda's war against Ọyọ. Diplomatic contacts certainly continued, for Landolphe in *c.* 1787 met an Ọyọ embassy which had come to Benin 'on political business'.[79] Another source, of the early nineteenth century, suggests, though not without ambiguity, that the *Ọba* of Benin regularly sent envoys with gifts to the *Alafin* of Ọyọ.[80] The *Alafin* in 1826 even told Clapperton that he 'had sent to his friend the king of Benin for troops to assist him in the war' against Ilọrin.[81] This seems very improbable. Indeed, it appears that the civil wars in the Ọyọ kingdom had disrupted communications between the two states: certainly, the Landers in

[74] Atanda, *The New Ọyọ Empire*, 3.
[75] NAK, SNP 7/13, 4705/1912, C. S. Burnett, 'Assessment Report, Awtun District, Offa Division' (1912), §10; repeated by Temple, *Notes on . . . the Northern Provinces of Nigeria*, 453.
[76] Personal communication from Dr. Bọlanle Awẹ, reporting oral evidence from Ileṣa.
[77] Atanda, *The New Ọyọ Empire*, 8.
[78] Johnson, *History of the Yorubas*, 497; cf. ibid. 528.
[79] Landolphe, *Mémoires*, ii. 85–7; cf. Ryder, *Benin and the Europeans*, 224–5.
[80] Dupuis, *Journal of a Residence in Ashantee*, liv. This account actually reports the sending of gifts by Benin to 'Zogho', which seems to be the western Bariba kingdom of Djougou, but throughout Dupuis's book 'Zogho' is consistently confused with Ọyọ: cf. below, Ch. 8, p. 172.
[81] Clapperton, *Journal of a Second Expedition*, 41.

1830 were told that 'not the slightest intercourse or communication' was maintained with Benin.[82]

§4. SOUTHERN YORUBALAND

In the south, to the west of the Ifę kingdom, the Ǫyǫ kingdom marched with the kingdom of Owu and the territory of the Ęgba. Further south, beyond these, was the kingdom of Ijębu. Of these three states, it will be recalled that Owu and Ijębu were listed among the 'Four Corners of Yorubaland' which acknowledged the leadership of the *Alafin* of Ǫyǫ. However, there is not much in the way of supporting evidence for the view that these two kingdoms were subject to Ǫyǫ.

In an early period, it will be remembered, the kingdom of Owu had exacted tribute from Ǫyǫ, the liberation of Ǫyǫ being attributed to the legendary *Alafin* Şango.[83] During the period of the Ǫyǫ empire, if we can believe Ǫyǫ tradition, the relationship was reversed, and Owu became subject to Ǫyǫ. Johnson, writing of Owu in the early nineteenth century, observes: 'from the days of Şango they have been very loyal to the Alafin of Ǫyǫ.'[84] Even if we discount the projection of the subjection of Owu back to the time of Şango (as no doubt we should), it is not clear whether this claim can be accepted. Current Owu tradition certainly denies that Owu ever paid tribute to Ǫyǫ, or even that there was any regular exchange of gifts between the rulers of the two kingdoms.[85] However, if Owu was not a subject, perhaps it was an ally or friend of Ǫyǫ. There are a few hints of this in some sources. There is an enigmatic phrase in the *oriki* of *Alafin* Gberu, who reigned probably in the 1730s or 1740s: *O jagun Ibadan, o f'Olowu sęri* ('He fought Ibadan, he made the Olowu a witness').[86] This indicates that Owu was in some way involved in a campaign by Gberu against the Ęgba town of Ibadan, but whether as an active ally, and if so on which side, is unclear. Other evidence is less ambiguous. A later *Olowu* of Owu is said to have married a daughter of *Alafin* Abiǫdun,[87] while Abiǫdun himself

---

[82] R. and J. Lander, *Journal of an Expedition*, i. 176. Cf. the story that Adele, the exiled king of Lagos then at Badagry, had attempted to communicate with Benin through Ǫyǫ, but that his messenger had not proceeded beyond Ǫyǫ: ibid. i. 186.

[83] Cf. above, Ch. 3, p. 37.

[84] Johnson, *History of the Yorubas*, 206.

[85] Oral evidence, from the *Olowu* of Owu Ipole.

[86] *Oriki* collected at the palace at Ǫyǫ.

[87] Ojo, *Iwe Itan Ǫyǫ*, 68.

is said, as has been seen, to have sent instructions to the *Olowu* to suppress the kidnapping of traders in the Apomu area.[88]

There is rather more evidence on the relations of Ọyọ with Ijẹbu. In Ijẹbu, as in eastern Yorubaland, Ọyọ seems to have been competing for influence with Benin. The power of Benin certainly extended along the lagoon to the south of Ijẹbu as far west as Lagos, where a Bini dynasty was established probably during the later sixteenth century.[89] Benin tradition claims that even before this, under *Ọba* Ozolua around the end of the fifteenth century, the Bini had conquered Ijẹbu.[90] The antiquity, if not the historicity, of the Benin claim to authority over Ijẹbu is demonstrated by the fact that Dapper's informants in the seventeenth century listed Ijẹbu among the dependencies of Benin.[91] However, it appears that from the seventeenth century, Ijẹbu was drawn under the influence of Ọyọ.

The main evidence for Ọyọ influence in Ijẹbu is a story of an intervention there by Ọyọ forces under *Alafin* Ajagbo, during the latter half of the seventeenth century. The campaign is alluded to in Ajagbo's *oriki*:

T'Ajagbo gb'ogun de 'jẹbu Ode
Ipanpa ati Oṣugbo mọ to nwọn nke pe o dọwọ Ilamurẹn
Ilamurẹn yi sile o tamora
Ayun wọn ni a ri, a ko r'abọ wọn.

When Ajagbo brought war to Ijẹbu Ode,
The Ipanpa and Oṣugbo shouted that they were in the hands of the
                              Ilamurẹn.
The Ilamurẹn went home to prepare themselves.
We saw their going, but not their coming back.[92]

A detailed account of the circumstances leading to this war is given by Chief Ojo. According to him, the king of Ijẹbu, Ayọra, was deposed, and appealed for assistance to *Alafin* Ajagbo at Ọyọ. Ajagbo sent two *ilari* to Ijẹbu Ode, the Ijẹbu capital, to reinstate

[88] Johnson, *History of the Yorubas*, 189.

[89] Egharevba, *Short History of Benin*, 30–1; J. B. O. Loṣi, *History of Lagos* (2nd edn., Lagos, 1967), 4–7; for the date, cf. R. Law, 'The Dynastic Chronology of Lagos', *Lagos Notes and Records*, ii.2 (1968), 51–2.

[90] Egharevba, *Short History of Benin*, 24; for Ozolua's date, cf. Bradbury, 'Chronological Problems in Benin History', 277–80; id., *Benin Studies*, 32–6.

[91] Dapper, *Naukeurige Beschrijvinge der Afrikaensche Gewesten*, 501; a later source, G. A. Robertson, *Notes on Africa* (London, 1819), 301, also reports that Ijẹbu was subject to Benin.

[92] Quoted in Ojo, *Iwe Itan Ọyọ*, 56. *Ipanpa*, *Oṣugbo* and *Ilamurẹn* are the names of groups of Ijẹbu chiefs.

Ayọra, but soon afterwards Ayọra was assassinated. Ayọra's partisans again appealed to Ọyọ, and Ajagbo dispatched an army which succeeded in entering Ijẹbu Ode through their treachery. The ringleaders against Ayọra were seized and carried off to Ọyọ, and a certain Fasọjoye was installed as king.[93] Partial corroboration of Chief Ojo's account was obtained from an Ijẹbu informant, who admitted that Ayọra plotted with the *Alafin* to bring an Ọyọ army against Ijẹbu, but asserted that he was murdered before this could be effected, and disclaimed any knowledge of a king called Fasọjoye.[94] Probably Chief Ojo's account should be accepted, for it would be readily intelligible if Ijẹbu tradition, by a process of patriotic censorship, had chosen to suppress the unpleasant fact that the Ọyọ army actually entered the Ijẹbu capital, and to omit from the king-list the name of a ruler imposed by a foreign conqueror. The position of Ayọra in the Ijẹbu king-list seems consistent with his having reigned during the latter half of the seventeenth century.[95]

A second tradition concerning Ọyọ relations with Ijẹbu is, however, less easy to believe. According to Johnson, *Alafin* Jayin, who reigned in the early eighteenth century, sent an *ilari* to the Ijẹbu area, to arbitrate in a land dispute between Owu and another town, and this *ilari* became the king of Ijẹbu: the royal title of Ijẹbu, *Awujalẹ*, being supposedly derived from *Agbejailẹ* ('arbiter of a land dispute'), an Ọyọ *ilari* title.[96] This story is rejected in Ijẹbu, where it is claimed that the title *Awujalẹ* dates back to the beginnings of the kingdom. This claim is supported by a Portuguese account of *c.* 1505, in which the king of Ijẹbu appears already to be referred to by the title *Awujalẹ*.[97] What historical basis, if any, there might be behind Johnson's story is a matter of conjecture. *Alafin* Jayin might well have sent an *ilari* to Ijẹbu on diplomatic business, and perhaps an authentic tradition to this effect was elaborated in order to imply the subordination of Ijẹbu to Ọyọ.

[93] Ibid. 53–4.

[94] Oral evidence, from Chief O. Odutọla, the *Olotu'fore* of Ijẹbu.

[95] Ayọra is thirty-first in a list whose fortieth king, Fusẹngbuwa, was reigning at the time of the Owu War of *c.* 1817–22: Oral evidence, from Chief O. Odutọla, the *Olotu'fore* of Ijẹbu; cf. Chief Odutọla's book, *Iwe Kini Ilọsiwaju Ẹkọ Itan Ijẹbu* (Ijẹbu Ode, 1946), 5.

[96] Johnson, *History of the Yorubas*, 20, 171–2

[97] Pacheco Pereira, *Esmeraldo de Situ Orbis*, 117. The text as published reads, 'ho Rio d'esta terra aguora em nossas dias se chama Agusale' (the *River* of this land in our time is called Agusale), but probably *Rey* (King) should be read for *Rio* (River), and *Agusale* taken as the title *Awujalẹ*.

Whether Ọyọ authority was established over Ijẹbu on any permanent basis is uncertain. Tradition in Ijẹbu, as in Ilẹṣa and Ila, concedes the *Alafin*'s claim to senior status as an 'elder brother', but denies that the kingdom was ever subject to Ọyọ.[98] It is disputed whether the *Awujalẹ* of Ijẹbu exchanged gifts with the *Alafin* of Ọyọ, though it seems probable that they did.[99] It is noteworthy that in 1826, when Clapperton was told of the kingdom of 'Jaboo' to the south of Ọyọ, his informants do not appear to have claimed that it was subject to Ọyọ.[100]

The evidence for Ọyọ influence in the third of the southern Yoruba states, Ẹgbaland, is much stronger. The Ẹgba, it should be noted, did not constitute a strong, centralized kingdom like Owu or Ijẹbu. They comprised a loose confederacy, being divided into three distinct groups or provinces, the Ẹgba Agura (or Gbagura) in the north, the Ẹgba Alake in the south-west, and the Ẹgba Oke Ọna in the south-east, each group with its own paramount *ọba*. The *ọba* of the Ẹgba Alake group, the *Alake* of Ake, exercised only a vague suzerainty over the others.[101] Johnson claims that the Ẹgba were 'an offshoot of the Yorubas proper [i.e. Ọyọ]', having their origins in a settlement of some of the *Ẹṣọ* (war-chiefs) of Ọyọ during the campaigns of Ọranyan, the founder of Ọyọ. The first *Alake* was the commander of these *Ẹṣọ*, and a half-brother of Ọranyan.[102] Certainly, some towns of the northern Ẹgba, the Gbagura, notably Ilugun, are said to have been founded by immigrants from Ọyọ,[103] but this is not true of the majority of the Ẹgba towns, while the *Alake* himself is claimed to have come to the Ẹgba area immediately from Ketu, and ultimately from Ile Ifẹ.[104] It is also claimed that the *Alafin* and the *Alake* were full brothers, being both born to Oduduwa by his principal wife, Ọmọnidẹ. According to Ẹgba tradition, indeed, Ọmọnidẹ accompanied the *Alake* to Ẹgbaland, and died and was buried at Ake. Consequently, it is claimed, the *Alafin* at their installation used to send gifts of slaves, oxen, beads, and clothes to

[98] Oral evidence, from Chief O. Odutọla, the *Olotu'fore* of Ijẹbu.

[99] It is denied by Chief Odutọla; but cf. Mabogunjẹ and Omer-Cooper, *Owu in Yoruba History*, 13.

[100] Clapperton, *Journal of a Second Expedition*, 56.

[101] For the political organization of the Ẹgba, see Johnson, *History of the Yorubas*, 17; Ajiṣafẹ, *History of Abẹokuta*, 18–20; Biobaku, *The Egba and their Neighbours*, 3–4; Pallinder-Law, 'Government in Abẹokuta', 2–4.

[102] Johnson, *History of the Yorubas*, 17.

[103] Ajiṣafẹ, *History of Abẹokuta*, 11; Lloyd, *Yoruba Land Law*, 228.

[104] Ajiṣafẹ, *History of Abẹokuta*, 9–10.

the *Alake* 'to invoke the spirits of his ancestral mother'.[105] Ẹgba tradition nevertheless acknowledges that the Ẹgba were for a long time tributary to Ọyọ.

The Ẹgba account of how the Ẹgba came to be tributary to Ọyọ is of great interest. Ajiṣafẹ, a local historian of Ẹgbaland, relates that the first *Alafin*, being the youngest of Oduduwa's children, was still a minor when Oduduwa died. His brothers, the kings of the other Yoruba states, therefore gave him annual presents to enable him to support himself. Later, when these brothers had died, leaving the *Alafin* alone of the original kings, the *Alafin* compelled their successors, his nephews, to continue to pay these annual presents 'as a matter of right', so that they became tributaries of Ọyọ.[106] This story appears to represent an amusing half-acceptance of the official Ọyọ version: the projection of Ọyọ overlordship back to the days of Ọranyan is accepted, but it is presented as a usurpation.

It is difficult to determine the date at which the Ẹgba in reality became tributary to Ọyọ. Ọyọ influence in the area was probably already considerable in the later sixteenth and early seventeenth centuries. During this period, an Ọyọ king or prince married the daughter of an *Alake* of Ake, who became the mother of *Alafin* Ọbalokun.[107] Ọbalokun's successor, Ajagbo, also had an Ẹgba mother, from the Gbagura town of Ikereku Iwere.[108] The foundation of the Ẹgba town of Ilugun by immigrants from Ọyọ may belong to the same period, since its founder is said to have come from Igboho, suggesting that it was founded during the period when Igboho was the Ọyọ capital.[109] However, none of this need imply that any part of Ẹgbaland had yet been brought under Ọyọ rule. There is no suggestion of Ọyọ conquest, rather than merely Ọyọ influence, in Ẹgbaland until the reign of *Alafin* Ajagbo, who is said to have attacked and destroyed Ikereku Iwere, although it was his maternal town.[110] This is the earliest recorded Ọyọ campaign in Ẹgbaland, and it may be that it was Ajagbo, in the latter half of the seventeenth century, who began the reduction of the Ẹgba to Ọyọ rule. Possibly Ajagbo's

[105] Ibid. 14; J. B. O. Loṣi, *History of Abẹokuta* (Lagos, 1923), 2; cf. George, *Historical Notes on the Yoruba Country*, 18. Johnson, *History of the Yorubas*, 9, agrees that the mother of the *Alafin* and the *Alake* died at Ake, but says nothing of any gifts.

[106] Ajiṣafẹ, *History of Abẹokuta*, 13.

[107] Johnson, *History of the Yorubas*, 168.

[108] Ibid. 169.

[109] Lloyd, *Yoruba Land Law*, 228.

[110] Johnson, *History of the Yorubas*. 169.

Egba campaign was linked in some way with his war in Ijebu, discussed above. Two later campaigns in Egbaland are also recorded in Oyo tradition. As mentioned earlier, the *oriki* of *Alafin* Gberu, who reigned in the 1730s or 1740s, credits him with a campaign against the Gbagura town of Ibadan.[111] This can perhaps be connected with the local tradition that Ibadan was destroyed on the orders of an *Alafin* because its *Bale* had revealed the secret of the Egungun cult to his wife.[112] Later in the eighteenth century, *Alafin* Abiodun (1774–89) is said to have ordered the destruction of another Gbagura town, Ijaye, in revenge for an insult suffered by him from the wife of the *Bale* when he visited the town as a trader before his accession.[113]

For information on the mechanisms of Oyo rule in Egbaland we are dependent on Egba tradition. The Egba local historians, however, are not entirely in agreement on this matter. George states that the *Alafin* used to send messengers (*onise*) every year to collect gifts (*ebun*) from the Egba towns.[114] Folarin corroborates this, but calls the messengers *ilari* and speaks of 'tribute' rather than gifts.[115] Ajisafe, however, asserts that the *Alafin* placed resident representatives (*ajele*) in the Egba towns to collect the annual gifts.[116] Modern historians seem to prefer Ajisafe's version,[117] but on balance it seems rather more likely that the *Alafin* merely sent *ilari* annually to collect tribute, and that there was no resident Oyo administration in Egbaland. Another local historian, Losi, adds the interesting observation that 'the Oyo . . . forced the people by cunning and deceitful means to give them gifts by representing themselves as the chief priests of the Sango worshippers.'[118] This shows that the cult of

[111] *Oriki* collected at the palace at Oyo.

[112] I. B. Akinyele, *Iwe Itan Ibadan ati Iwo, Ikirun ati Osogbo* (3rd edn., Ibadan, 1959), 16: this account, however, attributes the destruction of Ibadan to the mythical *Alafin* Sango. The reason given for the destruction of Ibadan is a traditional stereotype: cf. the similar allegation against a *Bale* of Ogbomoso, recorded by Oyerinde, *Iwe Itan Ogbomoso*, 23–4.

[113] Johnson, *History of the Yorubas*, 187.

[114] George, *Historical Notes on the Yoruba Country*, 71. George writes of 'messengers (*onise*), who would nowadays be called *ajele*': this is a little misleading, since the term *ajele* was normally used of resident officials, whereas George evidently refers to messengers sent periodically to Egbaland.

[115] A. Folarin, *Short Historical Review of the Life of the Egbas, from 1829 to 1930* (Abeokuta, 1931), 7.

[116] Ajisafe, *History of Abeokuta*, 14. The term *ajele* is used in the Yoruba version of this book, *Iwe Itan Abeokuta* (2nd edn., Abeokuta, 1972), 12.

[117] Biobaku, *The Egba and their Neighbours*, 8; Smith, *Kingdoms of the Yoruba*, 83–4. [118] Losi, *History of Abeokuta*, 4.

Ṣango, the Ọyọ god of thunder, was exploited to buttress the *Alafin*'s authority outside as well as inside the Ọyọ kingdom proper.[119]

It does not appear that Ọyọ rule over the Ẹgba involved any interference beyond the annual collection of tribute by the *Alafin*'s *ilari*. There is no record of the Ẹgba being required to supply forces for the Ọyọ army, or of any provision for appeal from the judicial decisions of the local rulers to the *Alafin*.[120] Townsend in 1849 wrote that: 'Originally the [Ẹgba] formed a province of the Yoruba kingdom [i.e. Ọyọ], governed by a chief, elected by themselves, and confirmed by the Yoruba Monarch [*Alafin*].'[121] This suggests that the *Alafin*'s consent was necessary for the installation of the *Alake*. But there is no corroboration of this in any other source, and perhaps it should be discounted. However, although the Ẹgba may have suffered no more than the exaction of tribute, there was no question that this *was* tribute, unwillingly given, and that the Ẹgba were subject to Ọyọ. The status of Ẹgbaland was, therefore, altogether different from that of, for example, the Ijẹṣa, who had contrived to concede a nominal recognition of the *Alafin*'s seniority without losing the substance of their independence. The differing fates of these two peoples are readily explicable: although the Ẹgba as well as the Ijẹṣa lived in forest country which offered no advantage to the Ọyọ cavalry, the political fragmentation of the Ẹgba will have made them easier to dominate than the centralized Ijẹṣa kingdom. It is, perhaps, rather more surprising that the Ẹgba escaped with such a loose form of subjection, while the Ẹgbado across the River Ogun were brought under a very close Ọyọ control, being incorporated within the Ọyọ kingdom proper. The reason for this is probably that the Ẹgbado area was of great commercial importance, since it controlled the approaches to the slave-trade ports of Badagry and Porto Novo. Ẹgbaland did not have a comparable commercial importance.[122]

[119] For the Ṣango cult in the Ọyọ kingdom, cf. above, Ch. 6, p. 104.

[120] The latter seems to be excluded by the Ẹgba proverb, *Ejọ ku Ake* (A dispute dies at Ake), alluding to the role of the *Alake*'s court as the final appeal court in Ẹgbaland: NAI, ABEPROF. 8/2, J. H. Blair, 'Abeokuta Intelligence Report' (1938), 4.

[121] H. Townsend, 'Abbeokuta and its Inhabitants', *Church Missionary Intelligencer*, 1.6 (1849), 138.

[122] At least until the rise of Lagos as a major slave trade port, from the 1790s: but by then, the Ẹgba were probably already independent of Ọyọ rule.

§5. THE WESTERN KINGDOMS: KETU AND ṢABẸ

The immediate neighbours of Ọyọ to the west, beyond the Rivers Opara and Ọyan, were two Yoruba kingdoms, Ketu in the south and Ṣabẹ in the north. Both were states of considerable size and power.[123] The relations of Ọyọ with Ketu and Ṣabẹ must have been a matter of considerable importance for the Ọyọ, since these two states formed buffers between Ọyọ and the non-Yoruba peoples beyond—the Mahi and the kingdom of Dahomey—whom the Ọyọ were to seek to dominate during the eighteenth century.[124] However, evidence on these relations is disappointingly meagre.

Ketu, it will be remembered, was counted with Owu and Ijẹbu among the 'Four Corners of Yorubaland' which followed the *Alafin*. Ọyọ sources claim Ketu as a dependency: Crowther asserts that Ketu paid tribute to Ọyọ,[125] while tradition in the Anago area of the Ọyọ kingdom recalls that the *Alaketu* of Ketu used to travel in company with the *Elewi Odo* of Ifọnyin and the other Anago rulers to attend the annual Bẹrẹ festival at Ọyọ.[126] The traditions of Ketu itself, however, 'do not recognize any obligation to Ọyọ.'[127] A straightforward conflict of evidence such as this is difficult to resolve, but there is at least ample evidence that friendly relations were maintained between Ketu and Ọyọ. The rulers of the two kingdoms used to send messengers to each other to announce their accession.[128] There was also a measure of practical co-operation, in connection with the Ọyọ colonization of the Anago area to the south of Ketu around the end of the seventeenth century. When the kingdom of Ifọnyin was founded in this area by immigrants from Ọyọ, the *Alaketu* is said to have given permission for its founders to pass through Ketu territory on their way south; and moreover, the *Elewi Odo* of Ifọnyin, although he was subject to Ọyọ and had to seek the approval of the *Alafin* for his accession, was actually crowned by the *Alaketu*.[129] On the other hand, it is to be noted that during the later eighteenth century Ketu came under pressure from Dahomey, itself a

---

[123] For the history of Ketu, see Parrinder, *The Story of Ketu*; for Ṣabẹ, see Aṣiwaju, 'Note on the History of Ṣabẹ'.

[124] Cf. below, Ch. 8.

[125] Crowther, *Vocabulary of the Yoruba Language*, iii.

[126] P. Morton-Williams, Review of Parrinder's *The Story of Ketu*, in *Odu*, 1st series, 7 (1959), 42–3.

[127] Parrinder, *The Story of Ketu*, 11.

[128] Ibid. 85.

[129] Morton-Williams, 'The Ọyọ Yoruba and the Atlantic Trade', 30–1.

tributary of Qyọ, and suffered Dahomian attacks in *c.* 1760[130] and in 1789,[131] without apparently provoking any protective reaction from Qyọ. This suggests that the degree of co-operation between Ketu and Qyọ fell short of formal alliance.[132] We may also note that when Clapperton in 1826 learned that the Qyọ kingdom marched in the west with 'Ketto', he was not told that Ketu was subject to Qyọ.[133] The precise status of Ketu *vis-à-vis* Qyọ must, therefore, remain doubtful. There was clearly friendship and at least occasional co-operation, and it seems probable enough that gifts were exchanged, though less likely that the *Alaketu* travelled in person to Qyọ to pay homage. An exchange of gifts could be seen merely as a matter of courtesy, and it is possible that such an exchange could be interpreted somewhat differently at Qyọ and at Ketu. Beyond this, it would be hazardous, on the evidence at present available, to speculate.

Evidence on the relations of Qyọ with Ṣabẹ is equally sparse. There is a suggestion of early hostility between the two kingdoms, since the traditions of Ṣaki, in the north-west of the Qyọ kingdom, recall a war against Ṣabẹ, perhaps in the seventeenth century.[134] Later, however, on at least one and probably on two occasions we find Ṣabẹ in active alliance with Qyọ, against Dahomey. When Dahomey revolted against Qyọ rule in 1823, the Qyọ army which was sent in an unsuccessful attempt to suppress the revolt passed through Ṣabẹ on its way to Dahomey, and was reinforced by troops supplied by Ikoṣoni, the ruler of Ṣabẹ.[135] There is also a story that

---

[130] Parrinder, *The Story of Ketu*, 39.

[131] Ibid. 41–3; Dalzel, *History of Dahomy*, 201–2.

[132] Akinjogbin, *Dahomey and its Neighbours*, 166, states that forces from Ketu aided Qyọ and Dahomey in an attack on Badagry in 1784, but Dalzel, *History of Dahomy*, 182–3, which he cites, refers only to '*Anago* auxiliaries' and to '*Kossu*, a Nago chief belonging to Eyeo', who supplied provisions: though the term Anago is often used to refer to Yoruba-speakers in general, including the Ketu, the reference here is probably to the Anago proper, the inhabitants of the extreme south-western area of the Qyọ kingdom, in the hinterland of Badagry.

[133] Clapperton, *Journal of a Second Expedition*, 56.

[134] Ojo, *Iwe Itan Ṣaki*, 32. The date of this war is uncertain: Chief Ojo dates the reign of *Okẹrẹ* Otiti, under whom it took place, to 1675–1745, and also makes this ruler a contemporary of *Alafin* Ajagbo of Qyọ.

[135] E. Dunglas, 'Contribution à l'histoire du Moyen-Dahomey', t. II, *Études dahoméennes*, 20 (1957), 57. For the revolt of Dahomey in 1823, cf. below, Ch. 13, pp. 271–2. The account of Ikoṣoni's war against Dahomey given by T. Moulero, 'Histoire et légende de Chabe', *Études dahoméennes*, new series, 2 (1964), 66–7, identifies his allies not as the Qyọ, but as the Ilọrin: this presumably results from confusion between Ajanaku, the Qyọ commander in this war, and another famous Ajanaku, who was a general of Ilọrin.

an earlier king of Ṣabẹ, Akikanju, fought against the Dahomians when they revolted against Ọyọ:[136] this probably refers to a different occasion, in the 1790s.[137] It should also be noted that the Ọyọ had invaded Dahomey on several occasions before the 1790s, the earliest being perhaps during the latter half of the seventeenth century.[138] It is likely that all these invasions were mounted from the north,[139] and presumably involved the passage of Ọyọ troops through Ṣabẹ territory. This argues some sort of alliance or understanding between Ọyọ and Ṣabẹ as early as the later seventeenth century. Whether Ṣabẹ paid tribute to Ọyọ, or in any sense recognized the *Alafin*'s overlordship or seniority, cannot be determined from the available evidence.

§6. CONCLUSION

We are now in a position to attempt an evaluation of the *Alafin*'s claim to the heritage of Oduduwa. The claim was unhistorical, and has to be understood as propaganda, an attempt to rationalize and legitimize the position of hegemony which Ọyọ was attaining in the Yoruba area during the period of its imperial expansion. The evidence suggests that Ọyọ attempts to bring the other major Yoruba kingdoms under its control began in the seventeenth century. Early in that century, there were the unsuccessful Ọyọ invasions of Ijẹṣa and Ekiti country; during the latter half of it, *Alafin* Ajagbo's campaigns in Ẹgbaland and Ijẹbu. The ultimate fruits of Ọyọ military and diplomatic pressure were limited. Most of eastern Yorubaland remained outside the Ọyọ sphere, looking rather to Benin, and while Ọyọ influence was stronger in southern and western Yorubaland, its precise character and extent are difficult to determine. Only the Ẹgba appear to have become in any real sense subjects of Ọyọ, to whom they paid a heavy annual tribute. Some other states—certainly the Ijẹṣa, probably Ila and Ijẹbu, and perhaps Ọtun—acknowledged more loosely the *Alafin*'s seniority of status, while remaining for all practical purposes

---

[136] George, *Historical Notes on the Yoruba Country*, 23–4. According to Moulero, 'Histoire et légende de Chabe', 65–6, Akikanju was king immediately before Ikoṣoni, but George names as Akikanju's successor a Queen called Inẹ Mẹgọ, who is not mentioned in Moulero's account.

[137] There was apparently an unsuccessful revolt in Dahomey during the reign there of Agonglo (1789–1797): cf. below, Ch. 13, pp. 268–9.

[138] Cf. below, Ch. 8, pp. 154–5.

[139] Cf. Le Herissé, *L'Ancien Royaume de Dahomey*, 318.

independent of Ọyọ. Others—Owu, Ketu, and Ṣabẹ—should, on a conservative view of the available evidence, be regarded as allies rather than subjects of Ọyọ. For the Ọyọ, the heritage of Oduduwa remained an aspiration, and possibly a programme, but was never a reality.

CHAPTER 8

Tributaries in the North and West

IN addition to the kingdoms whose rulers traced their origins to Ile Ifẹ, and over whom the *Alafin* claimed authority by virtue of his alleged inheritance of Oduduwa's primacy, there were other states to the north and west of the Ọyọ kingdom which tradition or contemporary report represents as tributaries of Ọyọ. These states form the third category of subjects of Ọyọ distinguished at the beginning of Chapter 6. It should, perhaps, be repeated here that the distinction between the second and third categories of Ọyọ subjects relates principally to the basis upon which Ọyọ rule was justified rather than to the character of that rule. Although states such as Ilẹsa, which conceded only a nominal recognition of the *Alafin*'s dynastic seniority, do constitute a distinct group, with a distinct sort of relationship to Ọyọ, it would be wrong to suppose that there was any essential difference between the character of Ọyọ rule over the Ẹgba and over, for example, the kingdom of Dahomey: the legitimation of Ọyọ rule in the former instance by an appeal to the *Alafin*'s succession to Oduduwa's kingship was evidently secondary, the basis of Ọyọ control in both cases being force. The separate treatment accorded in this study to these two categories of Ọyọ subjects is imposed by the character of the evidence, by the need to examine first the fictitious Ọyọ claim to have ruled over the whole 'family' of kingdoms derived from Ile Ifẹ.

§1. THE NORTHERN NEIGHBOURS OF ỌYỌ: NUPE AND BORGU

To the north, the Ọyọ kingdom had as its neighbours, in the north-east the Nupe (called in Yoruba the *Tapa*), and in the north-west the Bariba of Borgu. During the sixteenth century Ọyọ had suffered invasions by both the Nupe and the Bariba,[1] but the reoccupation of the old capital Ọyọ Ile by *Alafin* Abipa at the beginning of the seventeenth century marked the end of the period during which

---

[1] Cf. above, Ch. 3. For the relations of Ọyọ with Nupe and Borgu, see also R. Law, 'The Ọyọ Kingdom and its Northern Neighbours', *Kano Studies*, new series, 1 (1973), 25–34.

pressure from these northern neighbours had threatened the existence of the Ọyọ kingdom. We have now to examine the sort of relations which developed between Ọyọ and the Nupe and Bariba during the period of Ọyọ power, in the seventeenth and eighteenth centuries.

During this period, the Nupe, earlier divided into several small chieftaincies, were united in a single kingdom, ruled by a king entitled the *Etsu Nupe*. Most of the Nupe lived to the north of the River Niger, and the successive capitals of the Nupe kingdom were also situated in this area.[2] But there was also a Nupe province, centred on the town of Ogudu, on the right bank of the Niger downstream of Jebba.[3] The Bariba, whose territory marched with Ọyọ at the River Moshi, formed a much looser confederacy. They were divided into a number of kingdoms, the most important being Bussa, Nikki, Wawa, and Illo, the king of Bussa exercising a vague suzerainty over the others.[4] The Ọyọ had the most direct dealings with Nikki. The small kingdom of Kaiama, the most southerly of the Bariba states and the immediate neighbour of Ọyọ across the Moshi, was originally a dependency of Nikki.[5]

Johnson's *History* asserts that 'at the time of the greatest prosperity of the [Ọyọ] empire' it included 'portions of the Tapas and Baribas',[6] and Johnson also includes 'the Tapa and Bariba' in a list of the dependencies lost to Ọyọ after the death of *Alafin* Abiọdun in 1789.[7] This claim that 'portions' of Nupe and Borgu were subject to Ọyọ has been accepted by some modern scholars.[8] Morton-Williams, on what evidence does not appear, has even specified the 'portions', stating that 'by the late eighteenth century' Ọyọ controlled in Borgu the eastern kingdoms of Bussa and Wawa and in Nupe the southern town of Ogudu.[9] Others have written of 'Borgu' and 'Nupe', appar-

[2] The capital of Nupe was successively at Gbara, Mokwa, Jima, and Raba.

[3] Elphinstone, *Gazetteer of Ilorin Province*, 24–5. Ogudu was destroyed in the late eighteenth century, and the capital of the province was later established at Tsaragi.

[4] For the political organization of Borgu, see e.g. Clapperton, *Journal of a Second Expedition*, 117; R. and J. Lander, *Journal of an Expedition*, i. 134; Crowder, *Revolt in Bussa*, 23–35.

[5] E. C. Duff, *Gazetteer of Kontagora Province* (London, 1920), 28; R. and J. Lander, *Journal of an Expedition*, i. 134.

[6] Johnson, *History of the Yorubas*, 41; cf. ibid. 179.

[7] Ibid. 187.

[8] e.g. Smith, *Kingdoms of the Yoruba*, 42.

[9] Morton-Williams, 'The Influence of Habitat and Trade on Oyo and Ashanti', 90.

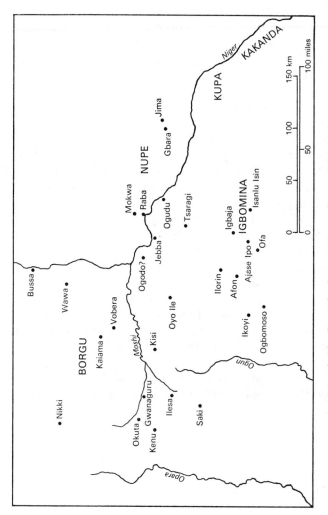

Map 4. The Ọyọ Kingdom and its northern neighbours.

F

ently in their entirety, as subjects of Ọyọ.[10] In fact the evidence in support even of Johnson's more limited claim that Ọyọ ruled 'portions' of Borgu and Nupe is far from decisive.

Johnson's claim does have support from at least one contemporary source, the English trader Robertson, who reported in 1819 that 'It appears, that when the Eyeos commence hostilities against any of their neighbours, the Anagoos . . . and Takpas are compelled to send contingent forces to their support.'[11] The 'Takpas' of this passage are, of course, the Tapa, or Nupe. The name 'Anagoo', or Anago, is usually applied to the western Yoruba, but in this case, since Robertson elsewhere describes Bussa as the capital of 'Anagoo',[12] the reference is apparently to the Bariba. The precise value of Robertson's testimony is, however, questionable. It will be shown below that, whatever the situation earlier, it is unlikely that any of the Bariba or Nupe were subject to Ọyọ in Robertson's time. His statement, if taken seriously, must therefore be supposed to record the conditions of some earlier period. Since Robertson's own informants were probably Ọyọ, his evidence does not provide independent corroboration of the tradition later recorded by Johnson, but merely shows that this tradition was already current in the early nineteenth century.

The suggestion that Ọyọ ever controlled any of the principal kingdoms of Borgu (i.e. Bussa, Nikki, or Wawa) or the central Nupe kingdom should be discounted. It has no support in the recorded traditions of these kingdoms. Bariba tradition does record that the king of Bussa used to exchange presents with the *Alafin* of Ọyọ,[13] and Nupe tradition similarly recalls that the *Etsu Nupe* and the *Alafin* met annually to exchange gifts at the frontier town of Ogudu.[14] But the exchange of gifts was a normal diplomatic courtesy between friendly rulers, and did not necessarily connote the subordination of either party. The silence of Bariba and Nupe tradition over their

---

[10] Ajayi and Smith, *Yoruba Warfare in the Nineteenth Century*, 4; Flint, *Nigeria and Ghana*, 60; Akinjogbin, *Dahomey and its Neighbours*, 81; B. Davidson, *Black Mother* (2nd edn., London, 1970), 201.

[11] Robertson, *Notes on Africa*, 268.

[12] Ibid. 209.

[13] NAK, DOB/HIS/55, T. Hoskyns-Abrahall, 'History of Bussa' (1925), §14; cf. Hermon-Hodge, *Gazetteer of Ilorin Province*, 115, 119.

[14] NAK, MINPROF. 7/4, 279/1909, 'Bida and Oyo', paper sent by the Emir of Bida, encl. to District Officer, Bida, to Resident, Niger Province, 17 Mar. 1928, and 'Oyo and Bida', translation of a statement by the Emir of Bida, encl. to id. to id., 23 Mar. 1928.

alleged subjection to Ọyọ is hardly decisive, since such unpleasant facts are readily suppressed in traditional histories. But even Ọyọ tradition provides no circumstantial details to support the vague claims to authority over Borgu and Nupe. In particular, there is no record of the campaigns which would surely have been necessary in order to bring these large kingdoms under Ọyọ control.[15]

On the other hand, Johnson's more limited claim that Ọyọ controlled 'portions' of Borgu and Nupe seems more acceptable, since it is probable enough that at the height of their power the Ọyọ would have been able to exact tribute from the southernmost areas of these countries. It must be admitted, however, that the evidence which can be cited in support of Johnson is far from satisfactory. In Borgu, it can be suggested that Ọyọ controlled specifically the small kingdom of Kaiama. Clapperton records that the *Alafin* whom he met in 1826 referred to a country to the north of Ọyọ as 'one of his provinces called Yaru', and as 'Yara, in Bamba [*sic*: perhaps an error for Bariba], which was tributary to him'.[16] As Clapperton later realized, the *Alafin* was referring to Kaiama, then ruled by a king called Yaru.[17] Kaiama was certainly *not* tributary to Ọyọ in 1826,[18] and in Borgu Clapperton found that the suggestion that Kaiama or any other Bariba kingdom was subject to Ọyọ was greeted with amusement.[19] But it is possible that the *Alafin* was asserting a claim which had once had some substance. However, the unsupported testimony of an Ọyọ informant is clearly a weak basis for asserting that Kaiama ever paid tribute to Ọyọ.

In the case of Nupe, it seems possible that Ọyọ exacted tribute from those Nupe groups which lived south of the Niger. The Ọyọ expansion into the Igbomina country had apparently involved taking land from the Nupe, for the town of Igbaja is said to have been

[15] Akinjogbin, 'Prelude to the Yoruba Civil Wars', 29, suggests that Nupe became tributary to Ọyọ as a result of *Alafin* Ajiboyede's defeat of the Nupe invasion in the sixteenth century. But this victory, and that of *Alafin* Ọrọmpọtọ over the Bariba in the same period, were defensive, not offensive victories.

[16] Clapperton, *Journal of a Second Expedition*, 44, 46; cf. R. Lander, *Records of Captain Clapperton's Last Expedition*, i. 115.

[17] Clapperton, *Journal of a Second Expedition*, 62: 'Kiama was the name of the province, and Yarro the name of the sultan'; ibid. 73: 'Kiama . . . is governed by a chief whose name [is] Yarro . . . and both city and province are, as frequently happens in Africa, sometimes called after him.'

[18] Cf. ibid. 33, where Clapperton reports being told by Ọyọ informants that Kaiama was 'small, but independent'.

[19] Ibid. 90, describing an interview with the king of Wawa: 'I asked if this country or Borgoo owed any allegiance to Yourriba: he said, none, and laughed

founded by Ọyọ as a base against Nupe raids in the area and on what had been Nupe territory.[20] According to Johnson, the important market town of Ogodo (probably not to be identified with Ogudu), which by the early nineteenth century was apparently part of the Ọyọ kingdom, had likewise originally been a Nupe town.[21] It is likely enough that the Ọyọ also exacted tribute from those Nupe communities which were not dislodged or absorbed, but explicit evidence of this is lacking.[22]

If the extent, and even the existence, of Ọyọ control over the southern Bariba and Nupe is uncertain, it is clear that any such Ọyọ domination had come to an end by the late eighteenth century. By the 1780s, indeed, it was rather the Ọyọ who were falling under the domination of their northern neighbours. In 1783, the Ọyọ were crushingly defeated in an attack on the Bariba kingdom of Kaiama,[23] this campaign perhaps marking the successful revolt of Kaiama against its earlier subjection to Ọyọ. By 1789 Ọyọ was paying tribute to Nupe,[24] and an Ọyọ attempt to throw off this subjection to Nupe was decisively defeated in 1790.[25] These events are best treated in the context of the decline of the Ọyọ empire, and will therefore be discussed in detail in a later chapter.[26]

§2. ỌYỌ EXPANSION IN THE WEST: EARLY STAGES

To the west of the Ọyọ kingdom, beyond its immediate neighbours, the Yoruba kingdoms of Ṣabẹ and Ketu, were the various Ewe-speaking peoples.[27] These were divided into a number of states, the most important of which were those ruled by dynasties which called

---

at the idea. He said he owed allegiance to Boussa, as Kiama, Niki, and Youri did ... that Kiama owed no allegiance to Yourriba, but was a province of Borgoo, subject to the sultan of Borgoo.'

[20] Kẹnyọ, *Founder of the Yoruba Nation*, 51.

[21] Johnson, *History of the Yorubas*, 217.

[22] Bowen, *Central Africa*, 266, states that the *Alafin* was once 'master of ... Kakanda and Kupa', two Nupe sub-groups on the south bank of the Niger east of Ogudu. This seems improbable.

[23] PRO, T.70/1545, L. Abson to R. Miles, 26 Sept. 1783; Duff, *Gazetteer of Kontagora Province*, 28; Hermon-Hodge, *Gazetteer of Ilorin Province*, 144–5.

[24] Norris, *Memoirs of the Reign of Bossa Ahadee*, 139.

[25] Dalzel, *History of Dahomy*, 229.

[26] See below, Ch. 13, pp. 261–6.

[27] The use of the term 'Ewe' to designate this linguistic group is a modernism: the name 'Ewe' properly belongs only to one people in the group, which inhabits the extreme west of the area, straddling the boundary between the modern states of Ghana and Togo.

themselves Aja. The original Aja state was Tado, situated on the River Mono in what is now the Republic of Togo. Princes of the royal dynasty of Tado are said to have migrated eastwards to found the kingdoms of Allada[28] and Hueda (Whydah),[29] while from Allada in turn derived the founders of the kingdom of Dahomey.[30] By the seventeenth century, if not earlier, Allada had eclipsed its parent Tado, and was the most important of the Aja states. The precise extent and character of Allada rule are far from clear,[31] but it appears that Allada was in some sense the overlord of the kingdom of Hueda, and also controlled the small but commercially important coastal ports of Offra and Jakin, to the east of Hueda. By the latter half of the seventeenth century, however, the power of Allada was in decline.[32] There were revolts in the coastal areas, and Hueda became effectively independent of Allada. Hueda, indeed, competed successfully with Allada for control of the increasingly important Atlantic slave trade. The power of Allada was eventually to pass to the northern Aja kingdom of Dahomey, but for most of the seventeenth century Dahomey, although already independent of Allada, was still a state of minor importance. Under the second and third rulers of Dahomey, Wegbaja and Akaba, the kingdom had to fight for its existence against its neighbour to the south-east, the kingdom of Weme, whose forces on one occasion sacked the Dahomian capital at Abomey.[33]

It was into this situation, with power disputed between Allada and Hueda at the coast and between Dahomey and Weme in the hinterland, that the influence of Oyo began to intrude into the Aja country during the seventeenth century. The Aja country, indeed, was to prove the most important, or at least the best-documented, field for the imperialism of Oyo.

[28] Le Herissé, L'Ancien Royaume de Dahomey, 274–6; Dunglas, 'Contribution à l'histoire du Moyen-Dahomey', t.I, 80–3; A. Akindele and C. Aguessy, Contribution à l'étude de l'histoire de l'ancien royaume de Porto-Novo (Dakar, 1953), 20–6.

[29] 'Note historique sur Ouidah par l'administrateur Gavoy (1913)', Études dahoméennes, 13 (1955), 47.

[30] Le Herissé, L'Ancien Royaume de Dahomey, 276–9; Dunglas, 'Contribution à l'histoire du Moyen-Dahomey', t.I, 83–4.

[31] Cf. R. Law, 'The Fall of Allada, 1724—An Ideological Revolution?', JHSN 5.1 (1969), 159–60.

[32] For the decline of Allada and the rise of Dahomey, see Akinjogbin, Dahomey and its Neighbours, Chs. 1–3.

[33] Dunglas, 'Contribution à l'histoire du Moyen-Dahomey', t.I, 96; Le Herissé, L'Ancien Royaume de Dahomey, 292.

Study of the origins of Ọyọ domination over the non-Yoruba peoples to the west is complicated by Ọyọ propaganda, for, as with the Yoruba the Ọyọ appear to have sought to justify their domination of the western peoples by a rewriting of the traditions relating to Oduduwa. The Yoruba refer to the non-Yoruba peoples in the west as 'Popo'.[34] Johnson's account of the dispersal of Oduduwa's children from Ile Ifẹ to found their own kingdoms includes among these children the 'Olupopo, or king of the Popos'.[35] It will be recalled that, in Johnson's account, the other kings descended from Oduduwa acknowledged the primacy of Ọranyan, the first *Alafin*, and paid tribute to him.[36] It does not appear that the *Olupopo* can or should be identified with any historical ruler, and it seems probable that the interpolation of this fictitious ruler into the list of Oduduwa's children represents an attempt by the Ọyọ to rationalize their claim to tribute from the Popo in the eighteenth century: the *Olupopo*'s function, that is, is simply to acquire an obligation to pay tribute to Ọyọ, which could then be 'inherited' by the historical Popo states. However, Bertho has accepted Johnson's account as an authentic tradition, identifying the *Olupopo* as the ruler of Tado, and arguing both that the Tado dynasty derived from Ile Ifẹ and that Tado in consequence paid tribute to Ọyọ.[37] This seems excessively bold. Against Bertho, it can be argued that the identification of the *Olupopo* as the king of Tado is at best speculative; that the derivation of the Tado dynasty from Ile Ifẹ is questionable;[38] and that the claim that Ọyọ received tribute from the time of Ọranyan from all the dynasties descended from Oduduwa is in any case unhistorical. It seems more sensible to see the *Olupopo* story as another instance of Ọyọ imperial propaganda, and to discount it altogether as evidence for the origins of the Ọyọ hegemony in the west.

[34] The term 'Popo' is sometimes applied specifically to the coastal people who inhabit the Badagry-Porto Novo area, who call themselves Egun. But the name seems originally to have had a much wider application, since the European applied it to the ports of Agbanakan and Anecho ('Great Popo' and 'Little Popo' to the west of Hueda. On the origins of the name 'Popo', see also J. Bertho, 'La Parenté des Yoruba aux peuplades de Dahomey et Togo', *Africa*, 19 (1949) 123–4.   [35] Johnson, *History of the Yorubas*, 8.

[36] Cf. above, Ch. 7.

[37] Bertho, 'La Parenté des Yoruba aux peuplades de Dahomey et Togo'.

[38] Tado is sometimes said to have been founded by immigrants from Ketu Bertho, 'La Parenté des Yoruba aux peuplades de Dahomey et Togo', 121, 124 R. Cornevin, *Histoire de Togo* (3rd edn., Paris, 1969), 48. These are likely to have been indigenous peoples displaced from the Ketu area by the Yoruba, rather than Yoruba.

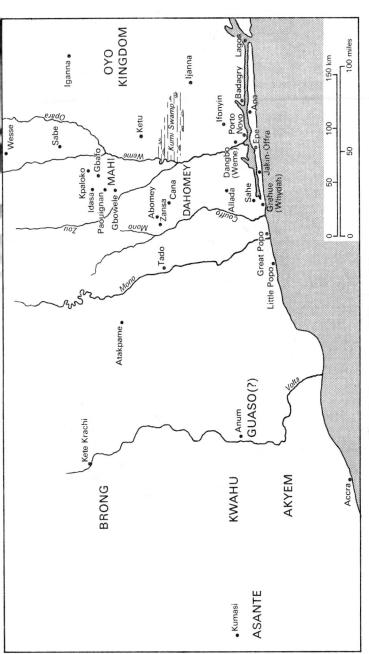

Map 5. The western neighbours of Ọyọ.

Other evidence indicates that it was in the second half of the seventeenth century that Ọyọ power was first felt in the west. This evidence, from Ọyọ tradition, Dahomian tradition, and contemporary European sources, suggests that the three major states in the west—Wemẹ, Dahomey, and Allada—all came under Ọyọ pressure at about the same period. To take first the Ọyọ traditions, the earliest Ọyọ campaign in the west recorded in these is attributed to the reign of *Alafin* Ajagbo, in the latter half of the seventeenth century. Ajagbo is said to have 'destroyed Iwemẹ, in the Popo country',[39] evidently the kingdom of Wemẹ. Unfortunately, nothing seems to be recorded of this campaign in any other source, and the circumstances which led to it and the consequences which may have followed from it both remain obscure.

The traditions of Dahomey also recall clashes with Ọyọ around this time. It has been suggested that Dahomey was founded as a defensive measure against Ọyọ raids in the area, but this view has no support in Dahomian tradition, and should be rejected.[40] Dahomian tradition dates the beginnings of Ọyọ pressure on the peoples of the area to the reigns of the first and second rulers of Dahomey, Dakodonu and Wegbaja, who reigned probably in the second half of the seventeenth century.[41] Wegbaja's successor Akaba is recorded to have defeated an invading army of Yoruba (Nago) at Agrigome, after which he counter-attacked across the River Wemẹ into Yoruba country.[42] The term 'Nago' (or 'Anago') is applied by the Aja to all Yoruba-speakers, but a version of this tradition told to Burton in 1863 identifies the invaders specifically as the Ọyọ: 'Akaba . . · wrested the kingdom from his nephew Abosassa, who, flying to the Oyos of the north, stirred up a useless war.'[43] This account of war, however, is confused. Agbosassa, whose flight to Ọyọ is alleged to have provoked the war, is usually remembered in Dahomian tradition not as the nephew but as the son of Akaba. On his father's death he was passed over for the succession to the throne in favour of Akaba's brother Agaja. He then left Dahomey and established a kingdom of his own at Wesse, north of Ṣabẹ.[44] The

[39] Johnson, *History of the Yorubas*, 169.

[40] Davidson, *Black Mother*, 211; R. Oliver and J. D. Fage, *A Short History of Africa* (3rd edn., London, 1970), 123: refuted by Akinjogbin, *Dahomey and its Neighbours*, 24.

[41] Le Herissé, *L'Ancien Royaume de Dahomey*, 318.

[42] Ibid. 291–2.   [43] Burton, *Mission to Gelele*, ii. 381.

[44] A. Coissy, 'Un Règne de femme dans l'Ancien Royaume d'Abomey',

king who 'wrested the kingdom from his nephew Abosassa' was therefore not Akaba, but Agaja, and the disputed succession has been incorrectly transferred to the earlier reign. Agbosassa may possibly have appealed to Ọyọ in connection with the Ọyọ invasions of Dahomey in the 1720s, though no traditional or contemporary source records that he did so. The reign of Akaba is conventionally dated to *c*. 1680–1708, but his death should more probably be placed in *c*. 1716, and his accession perhaps as late as *c*. 1697.[45] Akaba's war against Ọyọ may therefore belong to the early eighteenth century rather than the late seventeenth century.

There remain the contemporary European sources, which record warfare between Ọyọ and Allada in the later seventeenth century. An account published by de Clodoré in 1671, which is based upon information obtained from an ambassador of the king of Allada who visited France in 1670, reports that Allada was at this period frequently at war with Ọyọ.[46] Barbot, a French trader who visited the Allada area in 1682, likewise reports finding Ọyọ slaves on sale at the coast, and comments that the Ọyọ were 'irreconcilable enemies' of the Allada:[47] this presumably means that the slaves were captives

---

Études dahoméennes, 2 (1949), 5–8; Dunglas, 'Contribution à l'histoire du Moyen-Dahomey', t.I, 99–100.

[45] The received chronology of the kings of Dahomey goes back to Norris, *Memoirs of the Reign of Bossa Ahadee* (1789), who dated Dakodonu to *c*. 1620–50, Wegbaja to 1650–80, Akaba to 1680–1708, and Agaja to 1708–32. It is not known how Norris calculated these dates: presumably by reckoning through a series of remembered or estimated regnal lengths back from 1774, the known date of the death of Agaja's successor Tegbesu. However, it is now known that Agaja in fact died not in 1732, but in 1740: Akinjogbin, *Dahomey and its Neighbours*, 91; Verger, *Flux et Reflux de la Traite des Nègres*, 171–2. If Norris nevertheless correctly recorded Agaja's reign as lasting for twenty-four years, his accession and Akaba's death will have fallen in *c*. 1716 rather than in 1708. The twenty-eight years credited by Norris to the reign of Akaba may be too long: Dalzel, *History of Dahomy*, 7, states that Agaja was aged only nineteen at his accession, and as Agaja was a son of Akaba's predecessor Wegbaja this would make it impossible for Akaba to have reigned for more than about nineteen years, bringing his accession forward from *c*. 1680 to *c*. 1697 or later.

[46] de Clodoré, *Relation de ce qui s'est passé dans les Isles et Terre-ferme de l'Amérique*, iii. 558. In the account of the Allada embassy to France in 1670 given by J.-B. Labat, *Voyage du Chevalier des Marchais* (Paris, 1730), ii. 340, it is stated that the Allada ambassador claimed to have undertaken diplomatic missions to Ọyọ, but no such statement is made in the original account published by de Clodoré.

[47] Barbot, 'Description des côtes d'Affrique', 3e Partie, 136; cf. the published version of this work, J. Barbot, *A Description of the Coasts of North and South Guinea* (London, 1732), 327.

taken in war by the Allada, but it is likely that Barbot's comment is
merely an echo of the earlier account of de Clodoré rather than an
independent report of warfare between Ọyọ and Allada. There is no
indication as to where this fighting between Ọyọ and Allada was
taking place: possibly in Anago or Wemẹ country to the east of
Allada. It has sometimes been suggested, on the basis of a passage
in the published version of Barbot's journal, that the Ọyọ in 1682
actually invaded and overran the Allada kingdom, but the relevant
passage appears not to have been based upon Barbot's own observations in 1682, but to have been interpolated from Bosman's
account of a later invasion of Allada, in 1698.[48] Bosman records
that some disaffected subjects of the king of Allada had complained
of his misgovernment to the ruler of a powerful kingdom in the
interior. The interior ruler then sent an embassy to remonstrate
with the king of Allada, who responded by murdering his ambassadors. The king of the interior state thereupon dispatched a large
army of cavalry which, in alliance with the people of Hueda, proceeded to overrun and ravage the Allada kingdom:

> . . . the Slaughter was prodigious great and . . . the General of this Great
> Army, contenting himself therewith, returned home, expecting to be very
> well received by his Master, but found himself Mistaken: For the King
> as a Reward of his Heroick Expedition, caused him to be Hanged on a
> Tree; because according to his Order he did not bring the Person of the
> King of *Great Ardra*, along with him, on whom and not his Subjects he
> aimed his Revenge.[49]

Bosman does not name the invaders, but their use of cavalry makes it
probable that they were the Ọyọ, and this identification was made
by commentators in the eighteenth century.[50]

It does not appear that these attacks on Wemẹ, Dahomey, and
Allada succeeded in bringing any of these western kingdoms under
Ọyọ rule. It has sometimes been suggested that Allada became
tributary to Ọyọ, either before or as a result of the invasion of

---

[48] Akinjogbin, *Dahomey and its Neighbours*, 36; Smith, *Kingdoms of the
Yoruba*, 42; Fage, *History of West Africa*, 102: following Barbot, *Description of
the Coasts of North and South Guinea*, 351–2. The relevant passage is borrowed
by Barbot from Bosman, *New and Accurate Description of the Coast of Guinea*,
396–8: there is no corresponding passage in Barbot's original (1688) manuscript,
'Description des côtes d'Affrique'.

[49] Bosman, *New and Accurate Description of the Coast of Guinea*, 396–8.

[50] Cf. Barbot, *Description of the Coasts of North and South Guinea*, 352;
Dalzel, *History of Dahomy*, 13.

1698.[51] On this view, the tribute later paid to Ọyọ by Dahomey is seen as a continuation of the tribute paid earlier by Allada.[52] The basis for this suggestion appears to be, first, the *Alafin*'s claim in 1698 to be the protector of the king of Allada's subjects against his misgovernment, and second, the fact that later, in the 1720s, the king of Allada appealed to Ọyọ for assistance when attacked by Dahomey. But these incidents hardly constitute decisive, or even strong, evidence for an Ọyọ overlordship over Allada. The *Alafin*'s right to interfere in Allada was clearly not accepted by its king in 1698, and the *Alafin*'s intervention should be seen merely as an attempt to exploit disaffection within the declining Allada kingdom. Bosman's account can reasonably be interpreted as recording the beginning of an Ọyọ attempt to establish control over Allada, but even the invasion of 1698 did not represent an Ọyọ conquest of Allada: on Bosman's account, it was no more than a punitive raid, which the *Alafin* himself judged to be a failure. As for the appeal of Allada (and similar appeals from Wemẹ and Hueda) for Ọyọ aid in the 1720s, there is no need to invoke an Ọyọ overlordship to explain these, since the victims of Dahomian aggression would naturally turn to Ọyọ, as a major power capable, as the invasion of 1698 had demonstrated, of effective intervention in the area. There is, in fact, no compelling evidence that Ọyọ rule was established on any formal basis over any part of the 'Popo' country before the eighteenth century.

§3. THE CONQUEST OF DAHOMEY (1726–1748)

The political situation in the Aja country was transformed in the early eighteenth century by the southward expansion of Dahomey. At about the time of king Akaba's death (*c.* 1716?), the Dahomians finally shattered the power of their old rivals the Wemẹ, inflicting a crushing defeat on the Wemẹ army in which the king of Wemẹ, Yahaze Kpolu, was killed. The Wemẹ kingdom was overthrown, and its royal family sought safety in withdrawal down the River Wemẹ.[53] Akaba's successor Agaja proceeded to the conquest of the coastal Aja states. An opportunity for intervention in Allada was provided by a disputed succession to the Allada throne. The defeated

[51] Akinjogbin, *Dahomey and its Neighbours*, 36, 81; Fage, *History of West Africa*, 102; Davidson, *Africa in History*, 217.

[52] Fage, *History of West Africa*, 104.

[53] E. Dunglas, 'Adjohon: étude historique', *Études dahoméennes*, new series, 7 (1966), 64–6; id., 'Contribution à l'histoire du Moyen-Dahomey', t.I, 97–9.

claimant, called in contemporary sources 'Hussar' or 'Cossa', appealed for aid to Agaja, and in March 1724 Dahomian forces attacked and sacked the capital of Allada, killing its king.[54] Initially Agaja appears to have set up Cossa as puppet king of Allada, but six months later he expelled Cossa and annexed Allada to Dahomey.[55] Jakin, the port of Allada, became tributary to Dahomey.[56] In February 1727 the Dahomians invaded the kingdom of Hueda, destroying its capital Sahe and securing control of its port at Grehue. The king of Hueda, Huffon, and many of his subjects took refuge in the lagoon area to the west of Grehue.[57] The process of conquest was completed when Jakin, having plotted rebellion, was destroyed by the Dahomians in 1732.[58] By these operations Agaja had established the eastern boundary of the Dahomian kingdom along the River Weme.

But at the very moment of its birth, the enlarged Dahomey kingdom of Agaja was attacked by the Oyo, and in 1730 became tributary to Oyo. The motives behind this Oyo intervention can only be surmised. The rulers of Oyo may simply have grasped the opportunity presented by the local conflicts in the south-west to strengthen their influence in the area. There may, however, have been a more specific interest. Oyo was by this time involved in the export of slaves for sale to the European traders who operated at the ports of Grehue and Jakin. The Dahomian conquest of the coast threatened the commercial interests of Oyo, since Dahomian military operations disrupted the trade routes to the coastal ports. It is also possible that Agaja sought to bring the slave trade under closer control than the kings of Allada and Hueda had operated. It may well be, therefore, that the *Alafin* intervened in order to keep open the slave-trade ports for the Oyo traders.[59]

The conquest of Dahomey is recorded in Oyo tradition, which attributes it to the reign of *Alafin* Ojigi.[60] The campaigns can be

[54] Akinjogbin, *Dahomey and its Neighbours*, 64–6.

[55] AN, C.6/25, Pruneau and Guestard, 'Mémoire pour servir à l'intelligence du commerce de Juda', 18 Mar. 1750.

[56] W. Snelgrave, *A New Account of Some Parts of Guinea* (London, 1734), 20.

[57] Akinjogbin, *Dahomey and its Neighbours*, 70–1.

[58] Ibid. 98–9.

[59] Cf. below, Ch. 10, pp. 220–1.

[60] Johnson, *History of the Yorubas*, 174. Johnson states that the Oyo invaded Dahomey three times, but the contemporary sources attest four Oyo invasions between 1726 and 1730. Dahomian tradition appears to recall only a single invasion: cf. Le Herissé, *L'Ancien Royaume de Dahomey*, 318.

followed in some detail in the contemporary sources, which include both the unpublished records of the European forts on the coast and the published account of the English trader William Snelgrave, who visited the area in 1727 and 1730.[61] The immediate occasion of the Oyǫ intervention was provided, as Snelgrave records, by appeals for aid from 'several fugitive Princes, whose Fathers the King of *Dahome* had conquered and beheaded'.[62] Among the victims of Dahomian aggression who sought assistance from Oyǫ were Cossa, the dispossessed king of Allada,[63] and the exiled princes of Wemę.[64]

According to a report by the Governor of the Portuguese fort at Grehue, the Oyǫ invaded Dahomey in 1726 and defeated Agaja's forces with great slaughter. Agaja then took refuge in bush country, and returned only after the Oyǫ had withdrawn home.[65] The account of this campaign given to Snelgrave in 1727 claims that the Oyǫ were in fact beaten off after a fierce battle, but this is no doubt merely Dahomian propaganda.[66] Snelgrave's account does show, however, that the Oyǫ owed their military superiority over the Dahomians primarily to their use of cavalry. Soon after the departure of the Oyǫ, the Dahomians succeeded in defeating and killing Cossa, the ex-king of Allada.[67] Despite this success, Agaja, fearful of a second Oyǫ invasion, sent gifts to the *Alafin* in an attempt to make peace.[68] The Oyǫ, for their part, perhaps felt that the death of Cossa had destroyed their original purpose in the war. At any rate,

[61] Cf. also the reconstruction of these wars by Akinjogbin, *Dahomey and its Neighbours*, 82–92.   [62] Snelgrave, *New Account of Some Parts of Guinea*, 56.
[63] AN, C.6/25, Pruneau and Guestard, 'Mémoire pour servir à l'intelligence du commerce de Juda', 18 Mar. 1750. This account states that Cossa actually went to Oyǫ, but a contemporary report indicates that he was in the Hueda area at the time of the Oyǫ invasion in 1726: APB, O.R. 20, doc.61, Francisco Pereyra Mendes to Viceroy of Brazil, 22 May 1726, quoted in Verger, *Flux et Reflux de la Traite des Nègres*, 144–5.
[64] Wemę tradition recalls that one of the sons of Yahaze Kpolu, the Wemę king killed by the Dahomians, went to Oyǫ: Dunglas, 'Adjohon: étude historique', 65–6; id., 'Contribution à l'histoire du Moyen-Dahomey', t.I, 96–9; cf. Snelgrave, *New Account of Some Parts of Guinea*, 120, refers to an appeal from princes of Wemę in connection with a later Oyǫ invasion of Dahomey, in 1729.
[65] APB, O.R. 20, doc. 61, Francisco Pereyra Mendes to Viceroy of Brazil, 22 May 1726, quoted in Verger, *Flux et Reflux de la Traite des Nègres*, 144–5.
[66] Snelgrave, *New Account of Some Parts of Guinea*, 56–8; cf. Akinjogbin, *Dahomey and its Neighbours*, 82, n.3. Snelgrave's informant was a 'mulatto Portuguese gentleman' who belonged to Agaja's court.
[67] AN, C.6/25, Pruneau and Guestard, 'Mémoire pour servir à l'intelligence du commerce de Juda', 18 Mar. 1750.
[68] Snelgrave, *New Account of Some Parts of Guinea*, 58.

it appears that a treaty was made, whereby Agaja kept possession of Allada but himself became tributary to Ọyọ.[69]

The peace was of short duration, being broken in consequence of the Dahomian conquest of Hueda in February 1727. Huffon, the expelled king of Hueda, now added his voice to those appealing for Ọyọ aid against Dahomey.[70] The Hueda had a claim upon the gratitude of Ọyọ, for their support against Allada in 1698. In any case, the Ọyọ may have felt that Agaja was becoming too powerful. In the next dry season, in March 1728, an Ọyọ army invaded Dahomey.[71] Agaja on this occasion declined to offer battle, and retired southwards into Hueda.[72] The Ọyọ, having ravaged the country, returned home, whereupon Agaja reoccupied his kingdom.[73] Next year, around May 1729, the Ọyọ again invaded Dahomey. Agaja again refused battle, and withdrew for safety across a river— probably the Mono, a tributary of the Couffo, north-west of Abomey. The Ọyọ attempted to frustrate Agaja's tactics by remaining in possession of the country through the rainy season, but after two months, around July, difficulties of supply compelled them to withdraw once more.[74]

In January 1730 the Ọyọ invaded Dahomey for the fourth time.[75]

[69] AN, C.6/25, Pruneau and Guestard, 'Mémoire pour servir à l'intelligence du commerce de Juda', 18 Mar. 1750. Akinjogbin, Dahomey and its Neighbours, 83, places Agaja's negotiations with the Ọyọ immediately after his conquest of Hueda in February 1727, but the account of Pruneau and Guestard indicates that they took place before the conquest of Hueda, and this makes better sense of the course of events.

[70] AN, C.6/25, Pruneau and Guestard, 'Mémoire pour servir à l'intelligence du commerce de Juda', 18 Mar. 1750; cf. Snelgrave, New Account of Some Parts of Guinea, 120.

[71] AN, C.6/25, du Petitval to Compagnie des Indes, 4 Oct. 1728; cf. ARA, NBKG. 94, Elmina Journal, entries for 19 Feb. and 23 Mar. 1728, in van Dantzig, Dutch Documents Relating to the Gold Coast and the Slave Coast, 153–4.

[72] APB, O.R. 23, f. 40, Francisco Pereyra Mendes to Viceroy of Brazil, 5 April 1728, quoted in Verger, Flux et Reflux de la Traite des Nègres, 146; cf. Snelgrave, New Account of Some Parts of Guinea, 58–9, was told in 1727 of Agaja's intention to refuse battle and withdraw to the coast in the event of a further Ọyọ invasion.

[73] AN, C.6/25, Pruneau and Guestard, 'Mémoire pour servir à l'intelligence du commerce de Juda', 18 Mar. 1750.

[74] APB, O.R. 24, f. 158, Viceroy of Brazil to King of Portugal, 28 July 1729, quoted in Verger, Flux et Reflux de la Traite des Nègres, 149; cf. the account of this campaign heard at Jakin in 1730 by Snelgrave, New Account of Some Parts of Guinea, 120–2. For the identity of the river across which Agaja sought refuge, cf. Le Herissé, L'Ancien Royaume de Dahomey, 318.

[75] PRO, T.70/1466, 'Whydah Diary', entries for 3 Jan., 9 Jan., and 21 Feb. 1730, in Copybook of Diaries from Cape Coast Castle.

By now the repeated devastations of his country had made Agaja anxious for peace. The Ọyọ, for their part, though able to dominate the country whenever they invaded it, had failed to establish any permanent control over it. In these circumstances it was possible for a compromise peace to be arranged. Agaja opened negotiations with the Ọyọ forces, enlisting as mediator the Governor of the Portuguese fort at Grehue.[76] Dahomian tradition records that he also employed the Yoruba inhabitants of Cana, a town in the Dahomian kingdom, as intermediaries.[77] Agaja's approaches were successful. By a gift of 600 slaves, the Ọyọ army was induced to withdraw from Dahomey.[78] Agaja followed this by dispatching ambassadors, with rich presents and 'one of his handsomest Daughters', to Ọyọ. These ambassadors, according to Snelgrave,

> were civilly received, and had the good fortune to succeed in their Negotiations. For they so gained some of the great Men about the King, by presenting them with large pieces of *Coral* (which the *J-oes* [Ọyọ] esteem above all things) that by their means an advantageous Peace was obtained for their Master.

The *Alafin* reciprocated Agaja's gesture by sending one of his own daughters to be married to Agaja.[79] Dahomian tradition indicates that Ọyọ also received hostages from Dahomey at this time, for Agaja's son Avisu is said to have spent some time as a hostage at Ọyọ.[80] No source specifies the terms of the 1730 treaty: presumably, as under that of 1726–7, Agaja retained his conquests but undertook to pay tribute to Ọyọ.

It is unclear for how long the peace of 1730 endured. In the coastal Aja area, hopes of Ọyọ intervention against Dahomey persisted for some years after 1730,[81] but this may have been merely wishful thinking. There is, however, some suggestion that Ọyọ and

[76] APB, O.R. 26, f. 140, Viceroy of Brazil to King of Portugal, 10 July 1730, quoted in Verger, *Flux et Reflux de la Traite des Nègres*, 150.

[77] Dunglas, 'Contribution à l'histoire du Moyen-Dahomey', t.I, 146.

[78] ADLA, C.739, Mallet de la Mine to du Premenil, 8 Jan. 1732.

[79] Snelgrave, *New Account of Some Parts of Guinea*, 135.

[80] Dunglas, 'Contribution à l'histoire du Moyen-Dahomey', t.I, 146–7.

[81] APB, O.R. 27, f. 129, Joao Basilio to Viceroy of Brazil, 20 May 1731, encl. to Viceroy of Brazil to King of Portugal, 17 July 1731, quoted in Verger, *Flux et Reflux de la Traite des Nègres*, 153; AHU, Sao Thome caixa 4, Joao Basilio to Antonio Pinto Carneyro, 8 Sept. 1732, quoted ibid. 155; ARA, NBKG. 99, Elmina Journal, entry for 6 Dec. 1733, in van Dantzig, *Dutch Documents Relating to the Gold Coast and the Slave Coast*, 202–3. In 1734/5 there were even rumours that the Ọyọ had actually invaded Dahomey: ARA, WIC. 110, From to Pranger, 10 Dec. 1734, and id. to id., 4 Feb. 1735, in van Dantzig, *Dutch Documents*, 214.

Dahomey were already fighting again in 1731. In that year, Agaja sent forces to raid the territory of the Mahi, to the north-east of Dahomey, through which the Qyǫ had presumably invaded Dahomey.[82] Snelgrave's account of this war curiously names the victims of Agaja's attack not as the Mahi but as the 'Yahoos', i.e. the Qyǫ.[83] This may be merely a confusion, but it is possible that the Qyǫ were in fact involved as allies of the Mahi. A French trader, writing in 1732, recalls that Agaja, having persuaded the Qyǫ forces to withdraw from Dahomey (presumably in 1730), had then found himself attacked by the Mahi. The Qyǫ reappeared in support of the Mahi, and the Dahomians were defeated.[84] This account might refer in its entirety to the events of 1730, before the conclusion of a definitive peace in that year.[85] But it might also allude to Qyǫ participation in the war of 1731.

However, it does not appear that there was a complete breach between Qyǫ and Dahomey. The maintenance of peaceful relations is attested by an incident recorded in Dahomian tradition, which must be assigned to the 1730s. One of Agaja's wives, who had charge of the Dahomian royal treasury, is said to have sent large pieces of coral to Qyǫ as a bribe to secure support for the succession to the Dahomian throne of her son, Aghidisu. The Qyǫ responded by sending messengers to Agaja to inform him that they desired Aghidisu to be designated as his successor. However, the intrigue was discovered, and Agaja had Aghidisu's mother imprisoned.[86] It is not indicated how the Qyǫ reacted to Agaja's rejection of their representations.

At any rate, open warfare between Qyǫ and Dahomey was resumed in the late 1730s. According to Norris, whose account was written in 1773, an Qyǫ army again invaded Dahomey in 1738. The Dahomian forces were defeated before Abomey, and the Qyǫ sacked Abomey, Cana, and Zansa before retiring. The Qyǫ commander was nevertheless 'disgraced' on his return, for failing to capture Agaja himself.[87] Akinjogbin has shown that this invasion must in fact have occurred

---

[82] Akinjogbin, *Dahomey and its Neighbours*, 98–9.

[83] Snelgrave, *New Account of Some Parts of Guinea*, 148.

[84] ADLA, C. 739, Mallet de la Mine to du Premenil, 8 Jan. 1732.

[85] Cf. Akinjogbin, *Dahomey and its Neighbours*, 89.

[86] Le Herissé, *L'Ancien Royaume de Dahomey*, 299–300.

[87] Norris, *Memoirs of the Reign of Bossa Ahadee*, 12–15. For the date of writing, cf. ibid. 1: Norris probably obtained much of his information on his visit to Abomey in 1772.

in 1739.[88] The reason for the renewal of the war by the Ọyọ is not indicated. The Ọyọ invasion may have been a reaction to the continued aggressions of Agaja in the 1730s, and perhaps particularly to a Dahomian raid east of the River Wemẹ, against Badagry, in 1737.[89] This must remain a speculation. Rather better supported by evidence is the suggestion that Agaja had ceased to pay tribute to Ọyọ. Norris, describing the negotiations to end the war in the 1740s, states that the Ọyọ 'claimed, in consequence of an old treaty, an annual tribute; the payment of which had been omitted in the prosperous days of *Trudo* [Agaja]. These arrears were considerable, and fresh demands were also added, on account of the conquest of *Whydah*.'[90] The treaty referred to is presumably that of 1730, though Norris is confused here, since the conquest of Hueda in fact preceded the treaty.[91] This explanation of the war is also supported by the testimony of Pruneau de Pommegorge, in a work published in 1789. Pruneau observes:

Le peuple dahomet . . . a plusieurs fois été obligé, dans le tems même de leur plus grande prosperité, de fuir de son pays pendant trente ou quarante jours, lorsque son roi ne pouvoit payer le tribut annuel à un autre roi beaucoup plus puissant qui lui, qui se nomme le roi des *ayeots*.[92]

Since Pruneau was active on the coast in the 1750s and early 1760s, this is probably to be understood as an allusion to the Ọyọ invasions of Dahomey after 1739.

In 1740 Agaja, the king of Dahomey, died.[93] There followed a disputed succession to the Dahomian throne. The ultimate victor was Avisu, the son of Agaja who had earlier lived at Ọyọ as a hostage. When, and under what circumstances, he had left Ọyọ is not recorded. At any rate, he now became king under the name

[88] Akinjogbin, *Dahomey and its Neighbours*, 107, n.2: Gregory, the Governor of the British fort at Whydah, whom Norris represents as attendant upon Agaja at the time of the invasion, did not arrive on the coast until March or April 1739.
[89] Akinjogbin, *Dahomey and its Neighbours*, 107. Akinjogbin suggests that the 1730 treaty had forbidden Dahomian operations east of the River Wemẹ, but there is no direct evidence for this.
[90] Norris, *Memoirs of the Reign of Bossa Ahadee*, 16.
[91] Unless the reference is to the original treaty made in 1726/7. Akinjogbin, *Dahomey and its Neighbours*, 82, n.2, suggests that the 'old treaty' may be one made between Ọyọ and Allada in the late seventeenth century.
[92] Pruneau de Pommegorge, *Description de la Nigritie* (Paris, 1789), 235.
[93] For the date, see Akinjogbin, *Dahomey and its Neighbours*, 91; Verger, *Flux et Reflux de la Traite des Nègres*, 171–2.

Tegbesu. An unsuccessful claimant to the throne was Aghidisu, earlier the choice of the Ǫyǫ for the succession,[94] and there may have been others.[95] It is not clear whether the Ǫyǫ played any role in these disputes, or if they did, whether they would have seen Avisu or Aghidisu as their favoured candidate. Anyway, the succession of Tegbesu did not bring to an end the war between Ǫyǫ and Dahomey. According to Norris, after the invasion of 1738 (actually, of 1739) the Ǫyǫ invaded Dahomey every year until peace was made in 1747 (in fact, in 1748), the Dahomians on each occasion refusing battle and retiring into the bush.[96] The contemporary records, however, attest only one Ǫyǫ invasion of Dahomey between 1739 and 1748, in 1742.[97] While it would be unwise, given the fragmentary character of the sources, to press negative evidence of this sort, Akinjogbin may be right in rejecting the assertion of annual Ǫyǫ invasions.[98] A final Ǫyǫ invasion of Dahomey was reported at the coast in 1748,[99] but by June of that year Tegbesu had succeeded in making peace with Ǫyǫ, and the payment of tribute by Dahomey was resumed.[100] Dahomey then remained tributary to Ǫyǫ for over seventy years, until a successful revolt in 1823.

The peace of 1748 can be taken to represent the definitive conquest of Dahomey by Ǫyǫ. Thereafter, as the *Alafin* warned Tegbesu's successor Kpengla in the 1770s or 1780s, the king of Dahomey 'held his dominions no longer than whilst he regularly paid his tribute;

---

[94] Le Herissé, *L'Ancien Royaume de Dahomey*, 299–300.

[95] Norris, *Memoirs of the Reign of Bossa Ahadee*, 5–6, records an unsuccessful claim to the throne by an elder brother of Tegbesu called 'Zingah'; Dunglas, 'Contribution à l'histoire du Moyen-Dahomey', t.I, 166–7, has a similar story about a brother called So-Amamu: it is not clear whether Aghidisu, Zingah, and So-Amamu were one, two, or three individuals.

[96] Norris, *Memoirs of the Reign of Bossa Ahadee*, 15–16.

[97] ARA, NBKJ. 106, Elmina Journal, entry for 23 May 1742, in Van Dantzig, *Dutch Documents Relating to the Gold Coast and the Slave Coast*, 248; cf. AN, C.6/25, Levet to Compagnie des Indes, 20 Aug. 1743. The possibility of an Ǫyǫ invasion is also alluded to in AN, C.6/25, Levet to Compagnie des Indes, 31 Jan. 1744.

[98] Akinjogbin, *Dahomey and its Neighbours*, 111. But Akinjogbin's assertion (ibid. 123) that Dahomey paid tribute to Ǫyǫ in 1746 seems unwarranted: PRO, T.70/704, 'Sundry Accounts for William's Fort Whydah, 1 Jan. to 30 June 1746', in Cape Coast Journal, Nov.–Dec. 1746, which Akinjogbin cites, records only that the European forts at Whydah sent gifts to the king of Dahomey to assist him 'to defray some Customs he was to make'.

[99] PRO, T.70/424A, 'Sundry Accounts for William's Fort Whydah, 1 Jan. to 30 June 1748', in Cape Coast Journal, Sept.–Oct. 1748.

[100] ibid.; cf. Norris, *Memoirs of the Reign of Bossa Ahadee*, 16, who incorrectly dates the peace to 1747.

and when he neglected that, Dahomy belongs to Eyeo.'[101] The annual tribute, known in Dahomey as the *agban* or 'load',[102] was very considerable. According to the contemporary testimony of Dalzel, it consisted of 'cowries and merchandise',[103] and it appears from a story which he relates that the 'merchandise' included coral.[104] Later sources add further details. The missionary Dawson, who visited Dahomey in 1861, was told that the tribute had consisted of imported textiles—silk damask and cotton shirting.[105] Four slightly different detailed accounts of the content of the tribute have been recorded from traditional sources: Le Herissé, from Dahomian tradition, states that it consisted of 40 men, 40 women, 40 muskets, 400 loads ('charges') of cowries, and coral;[106] Dunglas, also from Dahomian tradition, gives 41 muskets, 41 barrels of gunpowder, 41 bales each of 41 pieces of cloth, 41 baskets each containing 41 strings of beads or coral, 41 rams, 41 goats, 41 cocks, and 41 hens;[107] Bertho, from unspecified sources, presumably Dahomian, gives 41 men, 41 women, 41 muskets, red beads, and 400 sacks ('sacs') of cowries;[108] and Biobaku, from Ọyọ tradition, gives 41 boys, 41 girls, and one large pitcher each of brown, green, and assorted coral beads.[109] It is explained that the number forty-one was a 'royal' number, in which presents made by kings were always reckoned in Dahomey.[110] If the reference to 400 'loads' or 'sacks' of cowries alludes to the standard 'bag' (*oke*) of 20,000 cowries, this would be 8,000,000 cowries, equivalent in value to about 4,000 dollars.[111]

According to Norris, the tribute was 'paid annually at *Calmina*

[101] Dalzel, *History of Dahomy*, 208.

[102] Dunglas, 'Contribution à l'histoire du Moyen-Dahomey', t.I, 146.

[103] Dalzel, *History of Dahomy*, xii.   [104] Ibid. 209.

[105] CMS, CA2/016, Dawson to F. Fitzgerald, 30 Nov. 1861 (extract), encl. to C. Chapman to H. Venn, 20 Aug. 1864.

[106] Le Herissé, *L'Ancien Royaume de Dahomey*, 319.

[107] Dunglas, 'Contribution à l'histoire du Moyen-Dahomey', t.I, 146.

[108] Bertho, 'La Parenté des Yoruba aux peuplades de Dahomey et Togo', 126: strictly, Bertho gives this as the tribute supposedly paid by Tado in 'about 1720'.

[109] S. O. Biobaku, 'The Egba State and its Neighbours, 1842–1872' (Ph.D. Thesis, University of London, 1951), 5, n.20.

[110] Dunglas, 'Contribution à l'histoire du Moyen-Dahomey', t.I, 146.

[111] But if so, the reference may be anachronistic, since other evidence suggests that the 'bag' became a unit of cowry enumeration only in the nineteenth century: M. Johnson, 'The Cowrie Currencies of West Africa', Part 1, *JAH* 11 (1970), 44. The earliest contemporary reference to the *oke* of cowries appears to be that in M. d'Avezac-Maçaya, *Notice sur le pays et le peuple des Yébous en Afrique* (Paris, 1845), 78.

[Cana], in the month of November',[112] i.e. at the beginning of the dry season, no doubt so that the Ọyọ could at once launch a punitive expedition if payment was not forthcoming. Pruneau de Pommegorge and Dalzel refer to Ọyọ 'ambassadors' or 'messengers' who came to Dahomey to collect the tribute.[113] These were probably the *Alafin*'s *ilari*. It appears that they merely supervised the payment of the tribute, for according to Dahomian tradition the actual carriage of the tribute to Ọyọ was the responsibility of a Dahomian chief with the title *Agbangan* (Chief of the *Agban*), a post created especially for this task by Agaja, and conferred by him on a Dahomian who had connections at Ọyọ.[114]

It seems clear that Dahomey normally paid to Ọyọ only this fixed annual tribute. A claim by the *Alafin* whom Clapperton met in 1826 that Dahomey, together with the coastal ports of Badagry and Porto Novo, 'paid custom for every ship that anchored there',[115] has no support from any other source, and should be rejected. There were, however, certain additional irregular impositions over and above the annual tribute. It seems likely that the kings of Dahomey were required, or thought it advisable, to send gifts to Ọyọ whenever a new *Alafin* was installed. There is no direct evidence for this, but it is suggestive that in 1774 king Kpengla of Dahomey sent an 'embassy of congratulation' to *Alafin* Abiọdun after his successful *coup d'état* against *Baṣọrun* Gaha.[116] It also appears that Dahomey from time to time suffered arbitrary exactions from Ọyọ. Dalzel records that under king Kpengla (1774–89) the Ọyọ messengers sent to collect the annual tribute habitually demanded at the same time a share of the booty taken by the Dahomians in their campaigns: 'it had been usual for them, on the eve of the return of the Dahomans from any victory, to covet every thing they saw in Dahomy that was curious or valuable.'[117]

[112] Norris, *Memoirs of the Reign of Bossa Ahadee*, 16; for the payment of the tribute at Cana, cf. CMS, CA2/016, Dawson to F. Fitzgerald, 30 Nov. 1861 (extract), encl. to C. Chapman to H. Venn, 20 Aug. 1864.

[113] Pruneau de Pommegorge, *Description de la Nigritie*, 235; Dalzel, *History of Dahomy*, 175, 205, 208–9.

[114] Dunglas, 'Contribution à l'histoire du Moyen-Dahomey', t.I, 146.

[115] Clapperton, *Journal of a Second Expedition*, 39.

[116] Dalzel, *History of Dahomy*, 157; cf. Akinjogbin, *Dahomey and its Neighbours*, 125. Such embassies did not necessarily connote subjection—Kpengla is also recorded to have sent an embassy to congratulate Osei Kwame of Asante on his accession (in 1777): Dupuis, *Journal of a Residence in Ashantee*, 244.

[117] Dalzel, *History of Dahomy*, 205; for examples, cf. ibid. 187 (in 1784), 205 (in 1788).

Dalzel also records that when the *Mehu*, one of the principal Dahomian chiefs, died in 1779, the Ọyọ messengers demanded a hundred of his wives for the *Alafin*. These were duly handed over, but the *Alafin* then sent a further demand, for the remainder of the *Mehu*'s wives. Kpengla eventually supplied war captives as substitutes for these women.[118] Akinjogbin generalizes from this incident: 'The kings of Ọyọ became the heirs of all the most important chiefs in Dahomey, from the king downwards.'[119] But this seems unwarranted: the very fact that so much is made of the incident in our source suggests rather that it was exceptional.

Apart from these financial exactions, it does not appear that Ọyọ rule over Dahomey amounted to very much in practice. It is true that Ọyọ occasionally interfered in both the external and the internal affairs of the kingdom. Akinjogbin has listed the 'rights' of interference in Dahomey which he suggests the *Alafin* gained by the treaty of 1748. With regard to the external affairs of Dahomey, he states: 'Ọyọ could ask Dahomey to send contingents to any military expedition that it might wish to make, or could commission Dahomey to fight such wars under, or without, Ọyọ officers. It could also prevent Dahomey from undertaking any war.'[120] But this generalized account is probably misleading. While instances of all these forms of interference can be documented from the reign of Kpengla, our source for these incidents (Dalzel's *History of Dahomy*) hardly gives the impression of any regularized or formally acknowledged arrangement.[121] It seems improbable that any such 'rights' were specified in the treaty of 1748. The degree to which the *Alafin* interfered in Dahomian foreign policy was probably limited less by reference to any formal agreement than by what he felt he could at any time get away with.

Ọyọ interest in the internal affairs of Dahomey seems to have been equally fitful. There is no indication that the attempt to influence the succession to the Dahomian throne made in the 1730s was ever

[118] Ibid. 175–6. Dalzel places this incident in 1781, but the death of the *Mehu* was reported at Whydah in 1779: PRO, T.70/1162, Day Book, William's Fort Whydah, entry for 27 Jan. 1779; cf. Akinjogbin, *Dahomey and its Neighbours*, 162 and n.3.

[119] Akinjogbin, *Dahomey and its Neighbours*, 125. The background to this incident is that under Dahomian law, when a lineage head died his property was delivered to the king, who normally returned most of it to the dead man's successor: Le Herissé, *L'Ancien Royaume de Dahomey*, 84–5.

[120] Akinjogbin, *Dahomey and its Neighbours*, 124–5.

[121] For Dahomian operations under Ọyọ military advisers, see Dalzel, *History*

repeated after 1748. Akinjogbin asserts that 'Ọyọ . . . made laws for
Dahomey, though we shall never know how many', citing as an
example a law prohibiting the wearing of silk damask at Cana.[122]
This rests upon the testimony of the missionary Dawson, who in 1861
witnessed at Cana a ceremony commemorating the revolt of
Dahomey against Ọyọ (in 1823), which involved the sacrifice of
twelve Ọyọ representing the messengers who had formerly collected
the tribute at Cana. The Dahomian king, Glele, made a speech to
the victims, in which he stated that 'their ancestors would not allow
silk damasks to be worn in Kanna'.[123] Such a sumptuary restriction
would be in keeping with Yoruba custom, whereby the wearing of
the most expensive cloths was often restricted to the *ọba*, and would
have served to indicate that the Dahomian king was inferior in status
to the *Alafin*. But Glele's words could equally be a rhetorical way of
saying that the Ọyọ demands for tribute in the form of silk damask
left none to be worn in Cana. Akinjogbin also states that 'Generally
no Dahoman law bound any Ọyọ citizen in Dahomey.'[124] This
suggestion of extra-territorial rights presumably rests upon an
incident when Kpengla expelled all foreigners from Dahomey, but
made an exception of the Ọyọ.[125] But Kpengla could surely have
seen the advisability of exempting the Ọyọ from this decree without
being constrained to do so by any formal obligation. It appears, in
fact, that Dahomey was left virtually autonomous after the peace of
1748.

The principal mechanism by which the *Alafin* enforced compliance
with his demands on Dahomey was the threat, and on occasions the
actuality, of an Ọyọ invasion of Dahomey. Presumably after 1748,
as in the 1730s, the Ọyọ also took hostages from Dahomey, though
there is no direct evidence for this. It does not appear that there
was any imposition of resident Ọyọ agents in Dahomey, corresponding to the *ajẹlẹ* of the Ọyọ kingdom. Argyle refers to Ọyọ ambassadors being 'established' in Dahomey,[126] but the passages of Dalzel's
History which he cites clearly refer to the messengers sent from Ọyọ

---

of Dahomy, 182–3; for Dahomian operations at the request of Ọyọ, ibid. 192;
for Ọyọ restrictions on Dahomian operations, ibid., 193–6.
   [122] Akinjogbin, *Dahomey and its Neighbours*, 124.
   [123] CMS, CA2/016, Dawson to F. Fitzgerald, 30 Nov. 1861 (extract), encl.
to C. Chapman to H. Venn, 20 Aug. 1864.
   [124] Akinjogbin, *Dahomey and its Neighbours*, 124.
   [125] Dalzel, *History of Dahomy*, 213.
   [126] W. J. Argyle, *The Fon of Dahomey* (Oxford, 1966), 25.

to collect the annual tribute, and not to permanently resident officials.[127] There is, however, some evidence suggesting some sort of resident Ọyọ representatives in Dahomey. Burton, who visited Dahomey in 1863, asserts that the town of Cana was an Ọyọ colony, and that in the revolt of 1823 king Gezo of Dahomey attacked and defeated the Ọyọ inhabitants of Cana.[128] Skertchly, who seems to have based his account on Burton but may have acquired additional information on his own visit to Dahomey in 1871, even speaks of an 'Eyeo garrison' at Cana.[129] This assertion that there was an Ọyọ garrison at Cana has recently been accepted by Ross. Since no such garrison is mentioned by the very detailed contemporary sources of the eighteenth century, Ross concludes that this garrison was not installed until the reign in Dahomey of Adandozan (1797–1818).[130] This is very doubtful. That there were Yoruba settlers in Cana is confirmed by Dahomian tradition, but the origins of this colony antedated the period of Ọyọ domination.[131] Dahomian tradition alleges that the Yoruba inhabitants of Cana collaborated with the Ọyọ in their invasions of Dahomey,[132] and it is likely enough that Gezo attacked them when he revolted. However, the accounts of Burton and Skertchly of a great battle at Cana are probably due to a misunderstanding. They believed that the annual commemorative sacrifice at Cana, of which they also heard, recalled a battle at Cana, whereas in fact it commemorated Gezo's murder of the Ọyọ messengers sent to demand the tribute.[133]

§4. THE FAR WEST: ASANTE, TADO, AND ACCRA

The establishment of Ọyọ domination over Dahomey in 1748 opened the way for Ọyọ expansion further west. The main power to the west of Dahomey, beyond the River Volta, had been since the late

---

[127] Dalzel, *History of Dahomy*, 175, 205.

[128] Burton, *Mission to Gelele*, i. 198–9; cf. ibid. ii. 406.

[129] J. A. Skertchly, *Dahomey As It Is* (London, 1874), 118–19.

[130] D. A. Ross, 'The Autonomous Kingdom of Dahomey, 1818–94' (Ph.D. Thesis, University of London, 1967), 25–6.

[131] Cf. Le Herissé, *L'Ancien Royaume de Dahomey*, 318; Dunglas, 'Contribution à l'histoire du Moyen-Dahomey', t.I, 146. The suggestion of Akinjogbin, *Dahomey and its Neighbours*, 86, n.3, that the Yoruba settlement at Cana originated during the Ọyọ invasion of Dahomey in 1729 seems implausible.

[132] Le Herissé, *L'Ancien Royaume de Dahomey*, 318.

[133] This is clear from the account in CMS, CA2/016, Dawson to F. Fitzgerald, 30 Nov. 1861 (extract), encl. to C. Chapman to H. Venn, 20 Aug. 1864.

seventeenth century the kingdom of Asante (Ashanti).[134] Johnson in three passages of his *History* makes the surprising claim that Asante, or 'parts' of it, was tributary to Ọyọ.[135] In one passage, he associates this supposed subjection of Asante to Ọyọ with the legendary conquests of *Alafin* Ọranyan.[136] One is tempted to dismiss these claims as due to the excesses of patriotic fancy, but while Ọranyan's involvement may be discounted, there is evidence suggesting that Johnson's claim may have a historical basis, in a defeat of an Asante army by the Ọyọ.

In 1764 it was reported from Cape Coast Castle on the Gold Coast, in explanation of delays in establishing direct trade between Asante and the coast, that

The Ashantees have met with a very considerable loss lately. . . . The affair is one of their Caboceers called Odanquah having made an incursion into the Io country which is behind Whydah, he & all his people to the number of 10 or 1200 Men fell into an Ambuscade & where [sic] killed or made Slaves of.[137]

This war appears to be recalled also in Asante tradition. Dupuis, who visited Kumasi, the capital of Asante, in 1820, was told that under Kusi Obodum of Asante (1750–64) the king of Dahomey incited a revolt in Kwahu and Akyem, the eastern provinces of Asante, and among the Brong to the north. The Asante, having crushed these revolts, crossed the River Volta and ravaged the territory of 'Gouaso', a tributary of Dahomey, but were attacked and defeated by the Dahomians.[138] There is also a tradition, recorded in the 1920s, which recalls the death of Dankwa, the chief of Juaben (one of the component states of the Asante confederacy), who can be identified with the 'Odanquah' of the contemporary report, in a war against a country called 'Apo': this last name seems not to occur in any other source, but it is stated that the army of 'Apo' included female soldiers, suggesting identification with Dahomey, which was notorious for employing regiments of female soldiers drawn from

[134] For Asante, see J. K. Fynn, *Asante and its Neighbours 1700–1807* (London, 1971); I. Wilks, *Asante in the Nineteenth Century* (Cambridge, 1975).

[135] Johnson, *History of the Yorubas*, 15, 41, 179.

[136] Ibid. 15.

[137] PRO, T.70/31, W. Mutter to Committee, 27 May 1764; cf. Akinjogbin, *Dahomey and its Neighbours*, 124; Fynn, *Asante and its Neighbours*, 96–7; Wilks, *Asante in the Nineteenth Century*, 320–1.

[138] Dupuis, *Journal of a Residence in Ashantee*, 237–9.

among the king's wives.[139] The contradiction between the contemporary account, which names the enemies of Asante in this war
as the Ọyọ, and the traditions, which implicate the Dahomians, is
hardly surprising, since the fact that Dahomey was tributary to Ọyọ
at this period would encourage confusion between the two states.
The contemporary account should probably be preferred, since
Dahomey was better known than Ọyọ to the Asante, and the sub-
stitution of a familiar for an unfamiliar name in later tradition
would be readily intelligible. It is quite possible, however, that the
campaign of 1764 was in fact a joint operation by the Ọyọ and the
Dahomians. The location of the battle at which the Asante were
defeated is uncertain, since the 'Gouaso' of Dupuis's account defies
precise identification. Bowdich describes 'Guasoo' [*sic*] as 'the
southern district or province of Inta [Gonja]', which would presumably place it in the Kete Krachi area,[140] but a German traveller
in 1887 described a 'Guaso' [*sic*] located more plausibly on the left
bank of the Volta below Anum.[141]

The operation of Ọyọ forces close to the River Volta, some 300
miles or more from the Ọyọ capital, is a surprising episode, but the
circumstances which led to the commitment of these forces so far
west are obscure. Akinjogbin suggests that under the treaty of 1748
between Ọyọ and Dahomey, Ọyọ forces were stationed permanently
in the Atakpame area for the defence of Dahomey.[142] This seems
unlikely, though it is probable that the 1764 campaign was undertaken in co-operation with the Dahomians. It is more likely that the
intentions of the Ọyọ were aggressive, as Dupuis's account of the
incitement of revolts among the dependencies of Asante implies.
However, if the Ọyọ were seeking to extend their empire westwards,
it does not appear that they succeeded. There is certainly no reason
to take seriously Johnson's claim that Asante became tributary to
Ọyọ. It seems, indeed, that after the war of 1764 Ọyọ and Dahomey
adopted a policy of friendship towards Asante. Dupuis records that
when a new king came to the throne in Dahomey (i.e. Kpengla, in
1774), he sent an embassy to Asante to announce his accession, and

[139] R. S. Rattray, *Ashanti Law and Constitution* (London, 1929), 221.

[140] Bowdich, *Mission from Cape Coast to Ashantee*, 176.

[141] P. Hall, 'Bericht über die Reisen nach Nkónya und Boem', *Mitteilungen
der Geographischen Gesellschaft*, 8 (1889), 110: my thanks are due for this
reference to Marion Johnson. It is not clear on what grounds Akinjogbin, *Dahomey
and its Neighbours*, 124, places the battle in the Atakpame area.

[142] Akinjogbin, *Dahomey and its Neighbours*, 124.

that at the accession in Asante of Osei Kwame in 1777 the Dahomian king sent an embassy to congratulate him.[143] According to Dupuis's informants, the Dahomians made these conciliatory gestures on the advice of the ruler of 'Dogho', or 'Zogho', a powerful state to which Dahomey was tributary.[144] 'Dogho' appears to represent the western Bariba kingdom of Djougou,[145] but throughout Dupuis's account it is consistently confused with Ǫyǫ,[146] which must be the state involved in these transactions. It would appear, therefore, that any expansionist ambitions the Ǫyǫ may have had with regard to Asante were abandoned in the 1770s. The Asante, however, seem to have retained a fear of Ǫyǫ power long after the war of 1764. In the early nineteenth century, Robertson found that the Asante spoke with dislike of the Ǫyǫ, 'and relate some of their barbarities on their marauding excursions with horror.'[147]

We should probably associate with the campaign of 1764 a story that the Ǫyǫ once conquered Tado, the westernmost (and most ancient) of the Aja kingdoms. This story comes from Tado tradition. During the reign at Tado of Aza, the Ǫyǫ are said to have attacked and conquered Tado. Aza's brother, Efin, was taken as a hostage to Ǫyǫ, where a son called Togbe Ani was born to him. Togbe Ani later escaped to Tado, where he was made king.[148] The tale of the royal hostage who returns to succeed to the throne is, no doubt, a traditional stereotype, such as might be employed to conceal a change of dynasty.[149] But the story may nevertheless preserve an authentic tradition of an Ǫyǫ conquest, or at least defeat, of Tado. The date at which Aza and Togbe Ani reigned is unclear, but Tado tradition

---

[143] Dupuis, *Journal of a Residence in Ashantee*, 243, 244.

[144] Ibid, 243 n.

[145] This is clear from the itineraries given ibid. ciii, cxxv, cxxx; cf. Bowdich, *Mission from Cape Coast to Ashantee*, 208.

[146] In one passage there is what seems to be an attempt to unravel this confusion, in a statement that Ǫyǫ is situated south of 'Zogho' and is tributary to it, and collects tribute from Dahomey on behalf of 'Zogho': Dupuis, *Journal of a Residence in Ashantee*, xlvi–xlvii.

[147] Robertson, *Notes on Africa*, 282. Robertson also reports (ibid. 181), on the authority of the Dahomians, that the Ǫyǫ 'sometimes' paid tribute to Asante: this seems improbable.

[148] Personal communication from M. Christian Merlo, reporting oral evidence collected in the Tado area in 1933.

[149] For a close parallel, cf. the case of the replacement of the *Za* dynasty by the *Sī* dynasty in Songhai. One tradition claims that the first *Sī* was a nephew of one of the last *Za* who was taken as a hostage to Mali and escaped and returned to Songhai, but another indicates that he was a Malinke and unrelated to the *Za* dynasty: 'Abd al-Raḥman al-Sa'dī, *Ta'rīkh al-Sudān* (trans. O. Houdas,

locates them in remote antiquity.[150] Since all other evidence indicates that Ọyọ power was not felt in the west before the later seventeenth century, it must be supposed that the Ọyọ defeat of Tado, if it is historical, has become chronologically displaced in Tado tradition, and in reality belongs to a later period. Since the 1764 campaign against Asante is the only recorded occasion on which Ọyọ forces operated so far west, it is at least an economical solution to suppose that the attack on Tado was part of the campaign of that year.

If there appears to be some historical basis for Johnson's claim that Asante was subject to Ọyọ, it is more difficult to find any justification for his inclusion among the dependencies of Ọyọ of the coastal Ga kingdom of Accra (which itself became tributary to Asante in 1742).[151] Johnson does, indeed, explain that 'the Gas say that their ancestors came from Ile Ifẹ',[152] but no such tradition has been recorded by any other writer. However, certain sources, of which Johnson may have been aware, suggest a traditional connection between Accra and Benin, which was in turn connected with Ile Ifẹ.[153] Possibly Johnson misunderstood or reinterpreted this tradition. At any rate, there is no reason whatever to suppose that Accra ever paid tribute to Ọyọ.

§5. THE CONSOLIDATION OF ỌYỌ POWER IN THE WEST (1774–1789)

As far as the evidence goes, after the peace of 1748 the subjection of Dahomey to Ọyọ was not again called into question until after the death of Tegbesu in 1774.[154] The death of Tegbesu and the accession of Kpengla in Dahomey in May 1774 roughly coincided with the

---

Paris, 1900), 9–12; Mahmūd Ka'ti, *Ta'rīkh al-Fattāsh* (trans. O. Houdas and M. Delafosse, Paris, 1913), 333–4. More information is needed on Togbe Ani and Aza: Cornevin, *Histoire du Togo*, 72, describes Togbe Ani as the 'founder' of Tado, which might support the suggestion that he founded a new dynasty' 'Aza' appears to be an eponym of the Azanu, a clan or people sometimes confused with the Ajanu or Aja, but possibly representing the indigenous population conquered by the immigrant Aja from the east.

[150] M. Christian Merlo, in a personal communication, suggests the sixteenth century.

[151] Johnson, *History of the Yorubas*, 15, 179.

[152] Ibid. 15.

[153] C. C. Reindorf, *History of the Gold Coast and Asante* (Basel, 1895), 3–9.

[154] There were fears of an Ọyọ invasion of Dahomey in 1754, when Tegbesu had been falsely reported dead: AN, C.6/25, Guestard to Compagnie des Indes, 10 July 1754. Otherwise, there is no suggestion of tension between Ọyọ and Dahomey between the 1740s and the 1770s.

coup d'état by which *Alafin* Abiọdun recovered effective power from *Basọrun* Gaha in Qyọ,[155] and the two kings, Kpengla and Abiọdun, also died within a few days of one another, in April 1789.[156] The relations between Qyọ and Dahomey during the reigns of Kpengla and Abiọdun are extensively documented from contemporary sources, including Dalzel's *History of Dahomy*, published in 1793.[157] It appears that Dahomey was becoming increasingly restive against its subjection to Qyọ. In 1775 Kpengla publicly announced his intention to liberate Dahomey from Qyọ,[158] but in practice these brave words did not amount to much. On one occasion Kpengla attempted to evade the payment of coral as part of the tribute to Qyọ on the plea that none was obtainable from the European traders: when his trick was discovered, he received a stern warning from *Alafin* Abiọdun.[159] On two other occasions Kpengla is recorded to have successfully evaded the extortion by Qyọ, over and above the regular tribute, of booty taken in Dahomian campaigns.[160] The tension between Qyọ and Dahomey became most evident, however, in competition for influence in the coastal Egun area.[161]

The expansion of Dahomey under Agaja had left the small Egun states, to the east of the River Wemẹ, independent. Before Agaja's conquests, the main states in the area appear to have been two small kingdoms situated on the southern shore of the lagoon, Epe in the west and Apa to the east.[162] These states seem to have been subject to Allada.[163] During the 1720s and 1730s, other states were established in the area by groups of refugees displaced by the Dahomian

[155] Dalzel, *History of Dahomy*, 156–7.

[156] AN, C.6/26, Gourg to Ministre de Marine, 8 June 1789.

[157] Dalzel's source for the history of this period was Lionel Abson, Governor of the British fort at Whydah in 1770–1803.

[158] AN, C.6/27 bis, Chenevert and Bullet, 'Reflexions sur Juda', 1776, cited by Akinjogbin, *Dahomey and its Neighbours*, 154 and n. 3: this document has apparently been lost, and can no longer be located in the Archives Nationales.

[159] Dalzel, *History of Dahomy*, 208–9.

[160] Ibid. 187, 205.

[161] The use of the term 'Egun' in this context may be anachronistic: there is no record of the use of the name earlier than d'Avezac-Maçaya, *Notice sur le pays et le peuple des Yébous*, 26, 58.

[162] The difficulty of distinguishing in the sources between references to Epe (often called 'Apee') and Apa complicates interpretation of Egun history in this period: Epe and Apa are, however, clearly distinguished in ARA, NBKG. 94, Elmina Journal, entry for 8 May 1727, in Van Dantzig, *Dutch Documents Relating the Gold Coast and the Slave Coast*, 148.

[163] Apa is called a 'province' of Allada in AN, C.6/25, du Colombier to Compagnie des Indes, 16 Apr. 1715.

conquests. A section of the royal family of Allada founded a new kingdom, also called Allada but more often known by the European name of Porto Novo,[164] on the northern shore of the lagoon.[165] Similarly, after the death of Yahaze Kpolu, king of Wemẹ, in battle against the Dahomians, some of his sons took their followers southwards and established a new Wemẹ kingdom, with its capital at Dangbo, in the hinterland of Porto Novo.[166] A third new state emerged at Badagry (Agbadagiri), on the northern shore of the lagoon between Porto Novo and Apa. Originally a farming hamlet of Apa, Badagry was occupied in about 1736 by a Dutch slave trader, and quickly developed into a larger and more important town than Apa itself. Its population was made up mainly of refugees from the kingdoms of Hueda and Wemẹ, its principal chief, the *Akran*, deriving from Hueda.[167]

As might be expected from their origins, the Egun states tended to take up an attitude of hostility towards the Dahomians. For example,

---

[164] Strictly, 'Porto Novo' was the name of the kingdom's sea-port, to the south of the lagoon, but it was commonly applied to the kingdom as a whole: in the present work, in order to avoid confusion with the old kingdom of Allada destroyed in the 1720s, the name Porto Novo will be used throughout.

[165] Most sources place the foundation of Porto Novo earlier than this. Some versions make the foundation of Porto Novo contemporary with that of Dahomey, i.e. probably in the first half of the seventeenth century: Le Herissé, *L'Ancien Royaume de Dahomey*, 277; E. Dunglas, 'Origine du royaume de Porto-Novo', *Études dahoméennes*, new series, 9–10 (1967), 29; id., 'Contribution à l'histoire du Moyen-Dahomey', t.I, 83–4. Another places the foundation of Porto Novo in c. 1688: Akindele and Aguessy, *Contribution à l'étude de l'histoire de l'ancien royaume de Porto-Novo*, 67. But another tradition asserts that Porto Novo was founded by a section of the royal family of old Allada after its destruction in 1724, and this seems more probable: E. Foa, *Le Dahomey* (Paris, 1895), 37–8; cf. Akinjogbin, *Dahomey and its Neighbours*, 91 and n.5.

[166] Dunglas, 'Adjohon: étude historique', 65–6; id., 'Contribution à l'histoire du Moyen-Dahomey', t.I, 96–9.

[167] For the origins of Badagry, see T. O. Avoseh, *A Short History of Badagry* (Lagos, 1938), 8–13; C. W. Newbury, *The Western Slave Coast and its Rulers* (Oxford, 1961), 30. Badagry tradition tells of a Portuguese slave-trader called 'Huntokonu', who came to Apa from the west at the time of the Dahomian conquest of the coast, left Apa to occupy Badagry, and was murdered at Badagry by a Hueda prince. The contemporary Dutch records show that 'Huntokonu' is to be identified with the *Dutch* factor Hertogh, who left Jakin at its destruction by the Dahomians in 1732 to settle at Apa, left Apa for Badagry in 1736, and was murdered at Badagry by a Hueda prince in 1738: see esp. ARA, WIC. 138, Hertogh to Pranger, 16 Apr. 1732; WIC. 110, des Bordes to Assembly of Ten, 31 May 1736; and WIC. 111, Jan Bronssema to Assembly of Ten, 31 July 1738: in van Dantzig, *Dutch Documents Relating to the Gold Coast and the Slave Coast*, 175, 215, 229.

Wemẹ in 1731 harboured an exiled Dahomian prince,[168] and both
Wemẹ and Apa supported the rebellious intrigues of Jakin before
1732.[169] The Egun ports also emerged from the 1730s as rivals to
the Dahomian port of Whydah (Grehue) in the Atlantic slave trade.
Dahomey responded by military pressure, attacking Badagry in
1737[170] and Epe in 1747.[171] Whether Ọyọ was politically involved
in the Egun area so early is much less clear. Akinjogbin has suggested
that the treaty of 1730 between Ọyọ and Dahomey formally guaranteed the Egun states against Dahomey by forbidding Dahomian
expansion east of the River Wemẹ, and that the kingdoms of Wemẹ
and Porto Novo at least became tributary to Ọyọ at the same time.[172]
But the grounds for this view are purely presumptive. There is no
direct evidence that Ọyọ was politically involved in the Egun area
before the 1770s. This seems an equally plausible date for the
beginnings of Ọyọ influence in the area, which could then be linked
to the activities of *Alafin* Abiọdun in colonizing the southern
Ẹgbado area, to the north-east of the Egun country.[173]

The immediate precipitant of Ọyọ intervention in the Egun area
was probably the determination of Kpengla, who came to the
Dahomian throne in 1774, to arrest the diversion of trade away from
his own port at Whydah to the Egun ports by military action against
the latter.[174] At any rate, soon after Kpengla's accession, we find
Alafin Abiọdun extending his 'protection' to Porto Novo and
Badagry. In 1777 a French observer noted of these two states: 'les
Ayots, très puissants, les protègent, et la traite par là est très con-
sidérable.'[175] In 1780 another French observer similarly drew
attention to the flourishing commerce of Porto Novo, and explained
that the king of Ọyọ 'regards the country as his own.'[176] These vague
statements do not permit us to determine the precise character of
Ọyọ relations with Porto Novo and Badagry. Nor is it clear whether a
similar 'protection' was being extended to the other Egun states,
though a little later we learn that Wemẹ also was 'on a friendly

[168] Snelgrave, *New Account of Some Parts of Guinea*, 148.
[169] Ibid. 83, 84, 91, 149, 151.
[170] Akinjogbin, *Dahomey and its Neighbours*, 107.
[171] Ibid. 128.
[172] Ibid. 91–2.
[173] Cf. above, Ch. 6, pp. 93–5.
[174] For Kpengla's policy, see Dalzel, *History of Dahomy*, 166.
[175] AN, C.6/26, Baud-Duchiron, 'Mémoire pour servir à faire de nouveaux
établissemens à la Côte de Guinée', 23 July 1777.
[176] AN, C.6/26, Ollivier de Montaguère to Ministre de Marine, 30 Dec. 1780.

footing' with Ọyọ, making the Dahomians reluctant to attack it.[177]

The Ọyọ policy of protecting both Porto Novo and Badagry broke down in 1781, when war broke out between these two states. Other states in the lagoon area were drawn into the conflict, Epe supporting Porto Novo and the Yoruba kingdom of Lagos, to the east of the Egun country, supporting Badagry.[178] This situation created a serious threat to the interests of Ọyọ, since the dissensions of the Egun states might be exploited by Kpengla of Dahomey to establish his control over the area. At the outbreak of the war in 1781, the *Alafin* of Ọyọ was reported to 'support' Porto Novo, and his active intervention was anticipated.[179] What *Alafin* Abiọdun eventually decided to do, however, was rather to authorize Dahomian intervention in the interests of Ọyọ. Abiọdun's plan, it appears from Dalzel's account, was to concentrate the slave trade under his own control at Porto Novo. The support of Kpengla was secured by giving him to understand that slaves brought to Porto Novo would be sent by canoe to be sold at the Dahomian port of Whydah. Kpengla was then encouraged to assist Porto Novo in eliminating the other Egun states.[180]

In 1782 the town of Epe, which had repudiated its earlier alliance with Porto Novo, was attacked and destroyed by forces from Dahomey and Porto Novo.[181] In 1783 the Dahomians and Porto Novians attacked Badagry, but were repulsed.[182] In 1784, therefore, a more substantial expedition against Badagry was organized, now with the active participation of the Ọyọ. The support of Lagos (earlier an ally of Badagry) was secured, and auxiliary troops from the Mahi and 'Nago' (Yoruba) accompanied the Dahomian army, while 'Kossu, a Nago chief, belonging to Eyeo' supplied provisions. Moreover, Ọyọ 'messengers' (*ilari*?) accompanied the army, and appear to have been in effective command. As Dalzel observes, 'The operations of the Dahomian army were directed by the Eyeo messengers, who had conducted them hither; and nothing of importance was undertaken without their concurrence.' Badagry

---

[177] Dalzel, *History of Dahomy*, 170 (an incident in 1782).
[178] AN, C.6/26, Ollivier de Montaguère to Ministre de Marine, 24 Nov. 1781.
[179] Ibid.
[180] Dalzel, *History of Dahomy*, 206–7.
[181] Ibid. 167–70. Dalzel dates the fall of Epe to 1778: the correct date is shown by PRO, T.70/1545, L. Abson to R. Miles, 14 Dec. 1782; T.70/1162, Day Book, William's Fort Whydah, entry for 25 Dec. 1782.
[182] Dalzel, *History of Dahomy*, 179–82.

was taken, and, in accordance with an agreement made beforehand, the prisoners captured in the campaign were sent to Ọyọ. *Alafin* Abiọdun was nevertheless dissatisfied, and was reported to have dispatched a force south to intercept the Dahomian army on its way home, 'and bring the Dahomans, with all their plunder, to Eyeo.' Kpengla, however, apprised of the plan, instructed his generals to dismiss the Ọyọ messengers and return home by a different route.[183] It does not appear that this incident caused a lasting breach between Ọyọ and Dahomey. Indeed, according to Dahomian tradition, the *Alafin* reduced by half the tribute due to Ọyọ in gratitude for the assistance of the Dahomians against Badagry.[184]

The destruction of Epe and Badagry was soon followed by that of Wemẹ. Earlier, as has been seen, Wemẹ had enjoyed the friendship of Ọyọ, but in 1786 some Ọyọ traders on their way to the coast were waylaid and robbed by a party from Wemẹ. *Alafin* Abiọdun therefore requested Kpengla to 'chastise' Wemẹ for him, explaining that 'it was too far for him to send an army for that purpose.' The Dahomians accordingly proceeded to invest and destroy the Wemẹ capital.[185] This, however, was the limit of Kpengla's successes. Instead of trade being redirected to Whydah, Kpengla found that it had become concentrated at Porto Novo. Angry at this turn of events, he petitioned *Alafin* Abiọdun for permission to attack Porto Novo also, but Abiọdun would permit no more than that Kpengla might 'repel any insult' he received from the king of Porto Novo.[186] Interpreting this permission broadly, Kpengla in 1787 sent forces to raid the beach at Porto Novo. Abiọdun, furious, dispatched a message to Kpengla, 'forbidding him ever to think of a hostile visit to Ardrah [Allada, i.e. Porto Novo] in the future, and telling him, "that *Ardrah was Eyeo's callabash, out of which nobody should be permited to eat but himself*".' Kpengla sought to pacify Abiọdun by sending to Ọyọ a share of the booty taken by his troops at Porto Novo.[187] However, Kpengla clearly realized that he had gone too

---

[183] Ibid. 182–7. The involvement of the Ọyọ in this campaign is presumably the basis for the tradition recorded by Johnson, *History of the Yorubas*, 187, that *Alafin* Abiọdun waged war 'against the Popos every other year', unless this alludes to otherwise undocumented operations, perhaps in connection with the Ọyọ colonization of Ẹgbado.

[184] Le Herissé, *L'Ancien Royaume de Dahomey*, 319. The original rate was reimposed under Kpengla's successor Agonglo (1789–97).

[185] Dalzel, *History of Dahomy*, 192.   [186] Ibid. 191, 193.

[187] Ibid. 193–6. Dalzel dates this raid to 1786, but the correct date is 1787:

far. In 1788, when an Ọyọ army was operating in the neighbouring country of the Mahi, there was a panic in Dahomey that Abiọdun had sent the army to invade Dahomey in revenge for the raid on Porto Novo.[188] Abiọdun, for his part, was apparently prepared for such action should Kpengla again transgress. In 1789, on a false rumour that Kpengla was again about to send forces against Porto Novo, the king of Porto Novo appealed to Ọyọ, and Abiọdun is said to have promised to invade Dahomey if any attack on Porto Novo took place.[189]

The episode of the Dahomian raid on Porto Novo in 1787 serves to illustrate the fragile basis of Ọyọ power in the Egun area. As Abiọdun had virtually admitted in 1786, in asking Kpengla to attack Wemẹ for him, the Egun area was too remote from the centre of Ọyọ for a major Ọyọ military presence to be maintained there. There was therefore little that Ọyọ could do directly to counter Dahomian military moves against Porto Novo. The only sanction which Ọyọ possessed was the threat of an invasion of Dahomey itself. While this threat could be very effective in bringing Dahomey to heel, an invasion of Dahomey would be a major operation and the threat could not be made lightly. The Dahomians therefore had in practice considerable freedom to act against the interests of Ọyọ in the Ẹgun area, provided that they did not go so far as to provoke the Ọyọ into considering seriously an expedition against Dahomey.

By the end of Abiọdun's reign, if not already in the 1770s, Porto Novo was purchasing its protection from Ọyọ by lavish presents to the *Alafin*. As Dalzel observes,

[Kpengla] . . . left no method untried to set Eyeo against [Porto Novo], but they were too rich, and constantly defeated Dahomy's design, by heaping a profusion of presents on the King of Eyeo . . . the richest European commodities were continually passing from thence, to be presented to the King of Eyeo.[190]

Later sources, indeed, describe Porto Novo as being tributary to Ọyọ.[191] It is doubtful whether this represents a change in the status

cf. AN, C.6/26, King and Chiefs of Ardres (Porto Novo), 'Avis et Certificat à tous MM. Négocians et Armateurs dans la Ville de la Rochelle', 25 Sept. 1787.
    [188] Dalzel, *History of Dahomy*, 196; cf. Norris, *Memoirs of the Reign of Bossa Ahadee*, 139. For rumours at Porto Novo that the Ọyọ were about to invade Dahomey, cf. AN, C.6/26, Gourg to Ministre de Marine, 24 Jan. 1788.
    [189] AN, C.6/26, Gourg to Ministre de Marine, 28 Feb. 1789.
    [190] Dalzel, *History of Dahomy*, 207.
    [191] Adams, *Remarks on the Country Extending from Cape Palmas*, 79; Clapperton, *Journal of a Second Expedition*, 56.

G

of Porto Novo: presumably the same payments might be described as 'tribute' or 'presents', according to the point of view of the informant. As noted earlier, the *Alafin* in 1826 claimed that Porto Novo, together with Dahomey and Badagry, 'paid custom for every ship that anchored there', but this is unlikely.[192] The suggestion in some modern accounts that *Alafin* Abiọdun posted his *Arẹ Ọna Kakamfo*, or senior military chief, in the Porto Novo area, is also without foundation.[193]

The relationship of Badagry to the Ọyọ empire after 1784 is unclear. After its destruction in that year, Badagry was soon reoccupied, by Zinsu, a renegade chief of Badagry who had aided the Dahomians in their attacks on the town.[194] During the 1780s and 1790s Badagry suffered further attacks from Dahomey and Lagos,[195] and according to some accounts became tributary to Lagos.[196] Whether Badagry also paid tribute to Ọyọ during this period is uncertain. Current tradition at Badagry denies that the town ever paid tribute to Ọyọ,[197] but contemporary evidence suggests that Badagry was paying tribute to Ọyọ in the 1820s.[198]

Besides consolidating Ọyọ influence over the Egun area in the south, *Alafin* Abiọdun appears also to have extended formal Ọyọ rule over the Mahi, to the north-east of Dahomey. The Mahi formed a loose confederacy, comprising a large number of small chieftaincies.[199] Ọyọ influence in the Mahi area certainly long antedates the reign of Abiọdun: indeed, one of the Mahi towns, Gbafo, is

[192] Clapperton, *Journal of a Second Expedition*, 39.

[193] Morton-Williams, 'The Ọyọ Yoruba and the Atlantic Trade', 41; Fọlayan, 'Egbado to 1832', 24. Ọyabi, the *Arẹ Ọna Kakamfo* who assisted *Alafin* Abiọdun against *Baṣọrun* Gaha in 1774 was from the town of Ajaṣẹ: Johnson, *History of the Yorubas*, 183–5. The name Ajaṣẹ is regularly applied by the Yoruba to Porto Novo, but Ọyabi's Ajaṣẹ was a quite different place, in the Ẹkun Osi province of the Ọyọ kingdom.

[194] Dalzel, *History of Dahomy*, 197, n. According to Dalzel, 'Sessu' (Zinsu) was an exile from Porto Novo who had settled at Badagry, but Badagry tradition, as represented by Avoseh, *Short History of Badagry*, 15, legitimates his usurpation of power in Badagry by making him a nephew of a previous *Akran* (senior chief) of Badagry.   [195] Akinjogbin, *Dahomey and its Neighbours*, 167, 181.

[196] R. and J. Lander, *Journal of an Expedition*, i. 47–8, state that Badagry was tributary to Lagos before the arrival there (in *c.* 1821) of Adele, the exiled king of Lagos; cf. PRO, CO.147/1, H. S. Freeman to Lord Newcastle, 9 Oct. 1862.

[197] Oral evidence, from T. O. Avoseh, a local historian of Badagry.

[198] PRO. C.O.2/15, H. Clapperton, 'Journal of the African Mission from Badagry to Jennah', entry for 6 Dec. 1825; cf. Clapperton, *Journal of an Expedition*, 39, 56.

[199] Norris, *Memoirs of the Reign of Bossa Ahadee*, 17; for the Mahi, see also R. Cornevin, *Histoire du Dahomey* (Paris, 1962), 139–42.

said to have been founded by colonists from Ọyọ,[200] and there is a similar tradition about the Yoruba town of Idaṣa, to the north of Mahi country proper.[201] Friendly relations between Ọyọ and the Mahi are presupposed by the Ọyọ invasions of Dahomey from the seventeenth century onwards, since these must have been launched through Mahi territory. Co-operation between Ọyọ and the Mahi is first explicitly attested, however, only for 1730 or 1731, when the two peoples fought in alliance against the Dahomians.[202] Mahi auxiliaries are also reported to have taken part in the siege of Badagry in 1784.[203] It does not appear, however, that the Mahi were brought under formal Ọyọ rule before the late 1780s. Certainly, the Dahomians were able to fight a series of wars against the Mahi between the 1730s and the 1770s without provoking any reaction from Ọyọ.[204] The earliest evidence for Ọyọ rule over the Mahi is an observation by a French trader in 1788 that 'les Mahis . . . sont ennemis des Dahomets et ont secoué le joug des Ayaux.'[205] This should probably be related to an Ọyọ invasion of the Mahi country during the dry season of 1787-8, which is graphically recorded by Norris:

The *Eyoes* are even now engaged in hostilities against the *Mahees*, with the usual fury of savages. At the commencement of the last periodical rains (in May 1788), they had ravaged no less than fourteen districts; and, burning and destroying multitudes of towns and villages, continued their progress with such devastation and horror, that the tyrant of *Dahomy* was not without apprehensions for his own safety.[206]

We can accept 1788 as the date of the Ọyọ conquest of the Mahi. What Ọyọ rule over the Mahi involved is not made clear in these accounts. However, Clapperton later described the Mahi as

[200] Cornevin, *Histoire du Dahomey*, 142.

[201] Ibid. 157; YHRS, H. U. Beier, 'Notes on Dassa Zoume, A Yoruba Kingdom in French Dahomey', n.d. Later, however, Idaṣa accepted the rule of a dynasty of Ẹgba origin, in return for protection against Dahomian raids.

[202] ADLA, C.739, Mallet de la Mine to du Premenil, 8 Jan. 1732; cf. above, p. 162.   [203] Dalzel, *History of Dahomy*, 182.

[204] Norris, *Memoirs of the Reign of Bossa Ahadee*, 17–24, records two major wars under Tegbesu, the first culminating in a siege of 'Boagry' (Gbowele) in 1752 and the second beginning in 1764 and ending in a compromise peace in 1772. Later, Kpengla sent forces to raid the Mahi country in 1778: Akinjogbin, *Dahomey and its Neighbours*, 155.

[205] P. Labarthe, *Voyage à la côte de Guinée* (Paris, 1803), 104, quoting the account of D. Bonnaventure (1788).

[206] Norris, *Memoirs of the Reign of Bossa Ahadee*, 138–9; cf. Dalzel, *History of Dahomy*, 196.

'tributary' to Ọyọ,[207] and Robertson reported that the Mahi were obliged to supply forces to serve with the Ọyọ army.[208]

§6. CONCLUSION

It may well be that the third category of Ọyọ subjects has been treated at disproportionate length in comparison with the other two categories. This disparity is due to the state of the evidence, whose unevenness makes it impossible to preserve true proportion and perspective while exploring each aspect of Ọyọ history as fully as the available evidence permits. The tributaries of Ọyọ were not, it would appear, as numerous as its traditions claim. In the north the Ọyọ may at times have controlled the southernmost areas of Borgu and Nupe, perhaps specifically the Bariba kingdom of Kaiama and the Nupe communities to the south of the Niger, but the evidence for this is poor, and any Ọyọ domination of these areas had certainly been brought to an end by the close of the 1780s. In the west Ọyọ military power was asserted by a series of invasions, beginning probably in the latter half of the seventeenth century. In the 1760s Ọyọ operations appear to have extended as far west as the River Volta, but it is improbable that Ọyọ rule on any formal basis was ever established in this remote area. The earliest and most important dependency of Ọyọ in the west was the kingdom of Dahomey, which was compelled to pay tribute by a series of wars fought between 1726 and 1748. Under *Alafin* Abiọdun (1774–89) the Egun states of Porto Novo and (perhaps) Badagry, and the Mahi, were also made tributary to Ọyọ.

[207] Clapperton, *Journal of a Second Expedition*, 56.
[208] Robertson, *Notes on Africa*, 268.

CHAPTER 9

The Army

THE power of Ọyọ, as of any state, depended in the last resort upon its military forces, and control of these was also crucial to the balance of power between the rival elements within the Ọyọ state. In order fully to understand both the successful expansion of the Ọyọ empire in the seventeenth and eighteenth centuries, and the course of the internal struggle for power in Ọyọ in the eighteenth century, it is therefore necessary to examine in some detail the armament and organization of the military forces of Ọyọ.

§1. ARMAMENT

Ellis reports that before the general adoption of European firearms in Yorubaland in the nineteenth century, a Yoruba army normally consisted of three divisions: the cavalry (ẹlẹṣin), the archers (ọlọfa), and the 'foot-soldiers' (ẹlẹsẹ), these last forming 'the bulk of the army' and being armed with spears, swords, and axes.[1] His inform-ants certainly meant to refer to Ọyọ, which was the only Yoruba state to employ cavalry on a large scale. Of the three divisions, while the 'foot-soldiers' may well have formed 'the bulk of the army' numerically, it is clear that the cavalry and archers formed its real strength. Both cavalry and archers would require intensive training, and probably these categories of troops were represented by the specialist war-chiefs and their retainers, while the ẹlẹsẹ comprised the rest of the free adult male population, who were not specialist soldiers but might still be required to serve in major campaigns.

It is the Ọyọ cavalry of which we hear most, both in the traditional and in the contemporary sources.[2] As has been seen in an earlier chapter, the earliest instance of the use of cavalry recalled in Ọyọ tradition relates to the reign of *Alafin* Ọrọmpọtọ in the sixteenth century,[3] and it is probable that the Ọyọ adopted the use of cavalry from their northern neighbours, the Nupe and Bariba, during the

[1] Ellis, *Yoruba-Speaking Peoples*, 172–3.
[2] For the Ọyọ cavalry, see further Law, 'A West African Cavalry State'.
[3] Johnson, *History of the Yorubas*, 161.

period following the Nupe sack of Ọyọ Ile at the beginning of the sixteenth century.[4] Later, there is evidence that the Ọyọ employed cavalry in their unsuccessful attempt to conquer eastern Yorubaland around the beginning of the seventeenth century,[5] while contemporary European sources attest the use of cavalry in the Ọyọ invasions of Allada in 1698[6] and of Dahomey in the 1720s.[7] Cavalry probably continued to pay an important role in the Ọyọ army throughout the eighteenth century, though we have no record of the use of cavalry in specific campaigns.[8] By the time Clapperton and the Landers visited Ọyọ in 1826–30, however, it appears that the kingdom no longer possessed a powerful cavalry force.[9]

The horses used by the Ọyọ cavalry were imported from the countries to the north. The incidence of the tsetse fly, the vector of trypanosomiasis, over most of Yorubaland makes it difficult to maintain horses in health, and uneconomic to attempt local breeding. There are tsetse-free areas in northern Yorubaland, in the heart of the Ọyọ kingdom,[10] where horses can be bred, but horse-breeding seems never to have been practised there on a large scale.[11] In any

[4] Cf. above, Ch. 3, p. 43.

[5] YHRS, I. A. Akinjogbin, 'Report on Idanre History', n.d.; Dapper, *Naukeurige Beschrijvinge der Afrikaensche Gewesten,* 505; cf. above, Ch. 7, pp. 129–30.

[6] Bosman, *New and Accurate Description of the Coast of Guinea,* 397.

[7] Snelgrave, *New Account of Some Parts of Guinea,* 55–7, 121–2; ARA, NBKG. 94, Elmina Journal, entry for 23 Mar. 1728, in Van Dantzig, *Dutch Documents Relating to the Gold Coast and the Slave Coast,* 154.

[8] Later writers refer to the cavalry of Ọyọ in general terms: e.g. Adams, *Remarks on the Country Extending from Cape Palmas,* 92; Robertson, *Notes on Africa,* 208; cf. the tall story reported by Pruneau de Pommegorge, *Description de la Nigritie,* 235–6, that the Ọyọ put their war captives to death by dragging them from the tails of their horses. The description of the Ọyọ cavalry in Dalzel, *History of Dahomy,* 12, merely echoes Snelgrave. The account of the Ọyọ-Dahomey war of 1739–48 in Norris, *Memoirs of the Reign of Bossa Ahadee,* 12–16, does not refer to the use of cavalry.

[9] A force of 200 cavalry escorted Clapperton and Richard Lander into Ọyọ in 1826: R. Lander, *Records of Captain Clapperton's Last Expedition,* i. 103. Clapperton was unimpressed with its quality: Clapperton, *Journal of a Second Expedition,* 34. In any case, this force appears to have represented something like the total cavalry strength of the capital at this time: cf. the estimate of R. and J. Lander, *Journal of an Expedition,* i. 190, that in 1830 there were under 300 horses in the Ọyọ capital; the scarcity of horses in the Ọyọ kingdom was also noted by Clapperton, *Journal of a Second Expedition,* 56.

[10] The tsetse-free areas may, indeed, have been more extensive during the imperial period, before the depopulation of the northern Ọyọ area by the civil wars of the nineteenth century, and the consequent spread of secondary bush, which favours the expansion of tsetse.

[11] Oral evidence, from the *Kudefu* and the *Olokun Ẹṣin* of Ọyọ.

case, the horses bred locally were unsuitable for use as cavalry mounts, being too small and weak to carry a heavy rider at speed over large distances. Snelgrave in 1727 noted the contrast between the diminutive horses, 'but little bigger than our Asses', obtainable at the coast, and the larger horses, 'about thirteen Hands high', used by the Ọyọ cavalry.[12] Later European travellers in Ọyọ, Borgu, and Nupe similarly distinguish between a breed of 'ponies' and a breed of larger horses, and add that the ponies were indigenous to the area, the larger horses imports from Bornu.[13] The distinction between the two breeds is also acknowledged in local terminology, the ponies being called in Yoruba *kùùrú*, the larger breed *baarú*.[14]

Horses had not only to be imported, they had to be continually replaced by fresh imports, since the mortality of horses from trypanosomiasis was high. Horses taken from the tsetse-free areas in the north of the kingdom south towards the coast died quickly.[15] The danger of infection with trypanosomiasis was especially great during the rainy season, when the tsetse flies dispersed more widely over the countryside. This danger was no doubt the reason for the reluctance of the Ọyọ cavalry to campaign during the rains, noted by Snelgrave.[16]

The importation of horses from the north was an expensive business. Robertson reports that good Ọyọ horses could be bought at the coast for between £10 and £15,[17] while Clapperton gives the price of a horse at the Ọyọ capital in 1826 as between 80,000 and 120,000 cowries, or about twice the price of a slave.[18] The Landers in 1830 report buying two horses, at Badagry and Ijanna, for $80 and $34.[19] These prices are all broadly consistent, given the equivalence

---

[12] Snelgrave, *New Account of Some Parts of Guinea*, 26, 55; cf. Robertson, *Notes on Africa*, 207–8, 284–5, describes the Ọyọ horses as resembling Welsh ponies, the largest being of 13 or 14 hands' height.

[13] Clapperton, *Journal of a Second Expedition*, 74, 93; R. Lander, *Records of Captain Clapperton's Last Expedition*, i. 140 and ii. 13; M. Laird and R. A. K. Oldfield, *Narrative of an Expedition into the Interior of Africa* (London, 1837), ii. 88.

[14] Cf. Abraham, *Dictionary of Modern Yoruba*, s.v. *baarú, kùùrú*.

[15] As noted by Robertson, *Notes on Africa*, 208.

[16] Snelgrave, *New Account of Some Parts of Guinea*, 121–2.

[17] Robertson, *Notes on Africa*, 284.

[18] Clapperton, *Journal of a Second Expedition*, 59.

[19] R. and J. Lander, *Journal of an Expedition*, i. 67, 90: this published account actually gives the price of the second horse as $30, but the manuscript journal of Richard Lander (Wellcome Historical Medical Library, MS. 1659, p. 8) gives $34.

of £1 to 8,000 cowries and of $1 to 2,000 cowries.[20] These prices appear to relate to the smaller horses: other evidence suggests that the larger imports from Bornu were very much more expensive.[21] Horses were also expensive to maintain. They were normally kept in stables in the compounds of their owners in the towns, and food (grass and guinea-corn) had to be brought to them from the rural areas. This involved a substantial commitment of labour. The labour for feeding horses was normally supplied by slaves, and slaves of northern origin, such as Hausa and Nupe, seem to have been preferred for this work, as being more experienced in the care of horses.[22] The feeding of horses also presented considerable problems on campaigns.[23] The *Olokun Ẹṣin*, the official in charge of the royal stables at Ọyọ, together with his subordinate slaves, normally accompanied the army on long expeditions, to organize the collection of fodder for the horses.[24]

The Ọyọ cavalry have been described as 'mounted archers',[25] but this is probably inaccurate. The use of mounted archers was extremely uncommon in West Africa,[26] cavalry being normally armed with spears and swords, although regularly accompanied by archers on foot. That this was also true of Ọyọ is indicated by Clapperton's account of the force which escorted him into the Ọyọ capital in 1826, which clearly distinguishes between the cavalry, who were armed with 'two or three long spears', and the archers, who went on foot.[27] However, Snelgrave's account of the Ọyọ invasion of Dahomey in

[20] For these equivalences, cf. Robertson, *Notes on Africa*, 274–5; Clapperton, *Journal of a Second Expedition*, 59.

[21] In the 1850s, it is reported that a pony cost between $10 and $100 (a price comparable to those given by Robertson, Clapperton, and the Landers), but a horse of 'Arab' breed such as were used by the cavalry of Ilọrin cost between $300 and $500: Clarke, *Travels and Discoveries in Yorubaland*, 229.

[22] Oral evidence, from the *Kudẹfu* of Ọyọ; cf. Webster and Boahen, *West Africa since 1800*, 73; Ajayi, 'Aftermath of the Fall of Old Ọyọ', 143.

[23] As noted by Snelgrave, *New Account of Some Parts of Guinea*, 121–2.

[24] Oral evidence, from the *Olokun Ẹṣin* of Ọyọ.

[25] P. Morton-Williams, 'The Fulani Penetration into Nupe and Yoruba in the Nineteenth Century', in I. M. Lewis (ed.), *History and Social Anthropology* (London, 1968), 1; cf. id., 'The Influence of Habitat and Trade on Oyo and Ashanti', 91.

[26] As noted by H. Barth, *Travels and Discoveries in North and Central Africa* (centenary edn., London, 1965), i. 581.

[27] Clapperton, *Journal of a Second Expedition*, 34; cf. R. Lander, *Records of Captain Clapperton's Last Expedition*, i. 103. The Landers in 1830 were similarly escorted at one point by 'a horseman, armed with a sword and a spear' and 'four foot-soldiers, who were equipped with bows and arrows': R. and J. Lander, *Journal of an Expedition*, i. 154.

1726 asserts that the cavalry were armed, comprehensively, with 'Bows and Arrows, Javelins, and Cutting Swords',[28] and the use of bows and arrows by the Ọyọ cavalry, as well as by the infantry, is also reported by Robertson.[29] It is conceivable that on expeditions to distant areas in the south-west, the Ọyọ archers were mounted for more rapid mobility, but fought on foot,[30] but perhaps it is as likely that the accounts of Snelgrave and Robertson, which are both based on hearsay, are confused. Certainly, the normal weapon of the Ọyọ cavalry was the spear: both the thrusting-spear, or lance (ọkọ), and the throwing-spear, or javelin (ẹṣin), seem to have been used.[31]

Bosman and Snelgrave assert that the forces that invaded Allada in 1698 and Dahomey in the 1720s consisted entirely of cavalry.[32] Whether or not this is true, it seems clear that cavalry normally operated in combination with infantry. Of the infantry forces, as has already been indicated, the archers were the most important. Robertson reports that the Ọyọ were 'very expert' in the use of bows and arrows,[33] while Richard Lander similarly observes that the Ọyọ 'have the reputation of being the best bowmen in Africa'.[34] Clapperton in 1826 was also very impressed with the quality of the Ọyọ archers: 'These men always appeared to me to be the best troops in this country [Ọyọ] and Soudan [i.e. Hausaland], from their lightness and activity.'[35] Skill in archery presupposes regular training, and Richard Lander witnessed the assiduous target practice of the young men at Ọyọ.[36] The efficacy of Ọyọ archery should not, however, be exaggerated. The Yoruba archer used a simple bow and normally fletchless arrows,[37] and his effective range was limited. Richard Lander's statement that the Ọyọ archers could regularly hit a target at a distance of 'upwards of a hundred yards' must be an exaggeration:[38] other evidence suggests an effective range of about sixty yards.[39] The arrows were regularly treated with poison.[40]

[28] Snelgrave, *New Account of Some Parts of Guinea*, 56.
[29] Robertson, *Notes on Africa*, 208.
[30] Cf. R. Smith, 'Yoruba Armament', *JAH* 8 (1967), 96.   [31] Ibid. 95.
[32] Bosman, *New and Accurate Description of the Coast of Guinea*, 397; Snelgrave, *New Account of Some Parts of Guinea*, 56, 121.
[33] Robertson, *Notes on Africa*, 208.
[34] R. Lander, *Records of Captain Clapperton's Last Expedition*, ii. 222.
[35] Clapperton, *Journal of a Second Expedition*, 34.
[36] R. Lander, *Records of Captain Clapperton's Last Expedition*, ii. 222.
[37] Smith, 'Yoruba Armament', 96–8.
[38] R. Lander, *Records of Captain Clapperton's Last Expedition*, ii. 222.
[39] Smith, 'Yoruba Armament', 96.
[40] Robertson, *Notes on Africa*, 269, 282; Smith, 'Yoruba Armament', 95, 97.

It has sometimes been suggested that the armies of Ọyọ made use of imported European firearms.[41] In fact, the use of firearms was negligible. Firearms had been adopted by the peoples nearer the coast, who were in direct contact with the European traders, during the latter half of the seventeenth century,[42] and the Ọyọ became acquainted with the new weapons when they began to expand in this direction. In 1726, it is reported, the Ọyọ cavalry had difficulty in mounting a charge against the Dahomian army because their horses were frightened by the unfamiliar sound of the Dahomians' muskets.[43] Their possession of firearms, however, did not prevent the conquest of Dahomey by Ọyọ, a fact which should prompt doubts about the efficacy of the muskets obtainable through the Atlantic trade. The Ọyọ, however, were sufficiently impressed with the new weapons to include muskets and gunpowder in the tribute exacted from Dahomey after 1730.[44] No doubt, they also began to acquire firearms through trade: Dalzel observes that in Dahomey, foreigners were prohibited from purchasing muskets and powder, and that this was one of the reasons why the 'Nago' (Yoruba) traders preferred to take their slaves to ports further east which were outside Dahomian control, such as Porto Novo.[45] But the Ọyọ did not make effective use of the muskets which they acquired. Richard Lander in 1827 found that 'quantities of muskets' were being imported, but that the Ọyọ did not understand how to use them effectively in battle.[46] Possibly the Ọyọ valued muskets more for firing on ceremonial occasions than for use in war.[47] According to tradition, the first effective use of firearms in Yorubaland was by the Ijẹbu, who used them to inflict a shattering defeat on the Owu in c. 1817.[48] The use of

---

The poison was usually of vegetable origin, but R. and J. Lander, *Journal of an Expedition*, i. 162, refer to the use of snake venom.

[41] Davidson, *Black Mother*, 201; L. H. Gann and P. Duignan, *Africa and the World* (San Francisco, 1972), 350.

[42] Cf. R. A. Kea, 'Firearms and Warfare on the Gold and Slave Coasts from the Sixteenth to the Nineteenth Centuries', *JAH* 12 (1971), 185–213.

[43] Snelgrave, *New Account of Some Parts of Guinea*, 56.

[44] Le Herissé, *L'Ancien Royaume de Dahomey*, 319; Dunglas, 'Contribution à l'histoire du Moyen-Dahomey', t.I, 146; Bertho, 'La Parenté des Yoruba aux peuplades de Dahomey at Togo', 126. Cf. the tribute of Ilaṣe, in the Anago area of the Ọyọ kingdom proper, included gunpowder and flints: Thomas, 'Historical Survey of the Towns of Ilaro, Ilobi, Ajilete, and Ilashe', 106.

[45] Dalzel, *History of Dahomy*, 214.

[46] R. Lander, *Records of Captain Clapperton's Last Expedition*, ii. 222.

[47] Clapperton, *Journal of a Second Expedition*, 49, notes that 'a rich man has guns fired' at his funeral.   [48] Johnson, *History of the Yorubas*, 208, 210.

firearms was only beginning to play an important part in warfare in the interior when Ọyọ collapsed in the 1830s.

§2. ORGANIZATION

In dealing with the organization of the Ọyọ army, it is convenient to consider separately the army of the capital and the forces supplied by the subordinate towns of the Ọyọ kingdom.

Reconstruction of the organization of the armed forces of the capital is hampered by the fact that the metropolitan army was considerably reorganized when the capital was transferred from Ọyọ Ile to New Ọyọ in the 1830s. The principal feature of this reorganization seems to have been an expansion of the role of the *Alafin*'s palace slaves, at the expense of the free chiefs of the capital.[49] What is clear is that the principal war-chiefs of the capital were the seventy *Ẹsọ*, divided into sixteen senior and fifty-four junior titles.[50] The *Ẹsọ* titles were not hereditary, but were conferred individually on merit:[51] this was no doubt a concession to the demands of military efficiency. The precise functions of the *Ẹsọ* are a matter of dispute. Biobaku has described them as a 'praetorian guard', i.e. a royal bodyguard,[52] but this is misleading. It appears that the *Ẹsọ* served rather as the officers of the main field army. It may be that specific responsibilities attached to each of the *Ẹsọ* titles, as is suggested by Johnson's explanation of the *Ẹsọ* title of *Gbọnka* as 'leader of the van'.[53] Each of the *Ẹsọ* brought to the army his own band of troops, recruited from his personal retainers.[54] The *Ẹsọ* and their retainers provided a core of specialist soldiers, and it was probably they who served as the cavalry and archers, highly trained soldiers in whom the power of the Ọyọ army primarily rested. Many of the retainers of the Ọyọ war-chiefs were slaves, and for service as cavalry slaves of northern origin were often employed.[55] The *Ẹsọ* did not normally go to war

---

[49] Personal communication from S. O. Babayẹmi, who is engaged in research on the history of New Ọyọ in the pre-colonial period.

[50] Johnson, *History of the Yorubas*, 73.

[51] Ibid. 70, 73. At New Ọyọ, the surviving *Ẹsọ* titles have tended to become hereditary: cf. Simpson, 'Intelligence Report on the Oyo Division', §§54–5.

[52] Biobaku, *The Egba and their Neighbours*, 2.

[53] Johnson, *History of the Yorubas*, 162.

[54] Oral evidence, from the *Kudẹfu* and other palace officials at Ọyọ; cf. Morton-Williams, 'The Influence of Habitat and trade on Oyo and Ashanti', 91.

[55] Oral evidence, from the *Kudẹfu* of Ọyọ; cf. Clapperton, *Journal of a Second Expedition*, 2–3, records meeting an Ọyọ war-chief whose two mounted retainers were both Muslims from Bornu.

in their full strength, it being conventional to send only thirty-five at any time on a campaign, leaving the other thirty-five to defend the capital.[56]

While it is clear that the *Ęşo* provided the main strength of the metropolitan army, it is less clear under whose authority the *Ęşo* served. Johnson describes them as being subordinate to the *Qyǫ Mesi*, each of whom commanded ten of the *Ęşo*,[57] and Morton-Williams adds that the *Qyǫ Mesi* were responsible for nominating candidates for *Ęşo* titles, to be approved by the *Alafin*.[58] However, Simpson asserts that only thirty of the *Ęşo* came under the *Qyǫ Mesi*, the other forty being subordinate to the *Alafin*'s palace eunuchs.[59] Probably Johnson and Morton-Williams record the arrangement which held during the imperial period, while Simpson describes the new arrangement after the reorganization at New Qyǫ.

In addition to the *Ęşo*, who came under the immediate authority of the *Qyǫ Mesi*, the *Alafin* had a smaller force of specialist soldiers under his own direct control, recruited from his palace slaves. Johnson records that certain of the senior *ilari* formed a royal bodyguard.[60] This was no doubt an ancient institution. There was also, at any rate at New Qyǫ, a group of palace officials who served as regular war-chiefs, notably the *Sarunmi* and the *Arę Agǫ*,[61] while the *Osi Iwęfa*, one of the senior palace eunuchs, also had military duties.[62] The development of the *Alafin*'s private army probably dates mainly from the post-imperial period, but the process had certainly begun in the later years of the empire. We have the evidence of Clapperton that Ebo, the 'chief eunuch' (*Osi Iwęfa?*) at Qyǫ in 1826–30, was 'well-skilled as a war captain'.[63]

In early times the *Alafin* himself had led the Qyǫ army in battle. An early *Alafin*, Oluodo, is said to have been drowned in the River Niger while campaigning against the Nupe,[64] and *Alafin* Ajiboyede

[56] This convention allegedly dated from the Nupe sack of Qyǫ Ile under *Alafin* Onigbogi, when the capture of the city is said to have been facilitated by the absence of the whole Qyǫ army on a campaign: Johnson, *History of the Yorubas*, 159.

[57] Ibid. 73.

[58] Morton-Williams, 'The Yoruba Kingdom of Oyo', 57.

[59] Simpson, 'Intelligence Report on the Oyo Division', §§54–5.

[60] Johnson, *History of the Yorubas*, 62.

[61] Oral evidence, from the *Arę Agǫ* of Qyǫ.

[62] Johnson, *History of the Yorubas*, 59; oral evidence, from the *Kudęfu* and other palace officials at Qyǫ.

[63] Clapperton, *Journal of a Second Expedition*, 52.

[64] Smith, 'The Alafin in Exile', 74, n.52.

only narrowly escaped death in battle against the Nupe during the sixteenth century.[65] During the imperial period, however, the practice of personal command by the *Alafin* appears to have lapsed:[66] the reason for this was no doubt precisely the danger illustrated by the cases of Oluodo and Ajiboyede.[67] In the absence of the *Alafin*, command of the metropolitan army appears to have devolved upon the *Basorun*, the head of the *Oyo Mesi*. It is the *Basorun* who appears most frequently in Johnson's narrative as the commander of the Oyo army,[68] and his military role is confirmed by a contemporary report that the *Alafin* in 1779 threatened to send 'the Eyeo general *Banchenoo* [*Basorun*]' against Dahomey.[69] At New Oyo, command of the army was often entrusted to the *Osi Iwefa* rather than to the *Basorun*,[70] but it is unclear whether this practice had developed before the fall of the Oyo empire in the 1830s.

In addition to the military forces of the capital, the Oyo army also included a substantial provincial contingent. As has been noted in an earlier chapter, one of the obligations of the subordinate towns of the Oyo kingdom was to supply forces on demand for the Oyo army.[71] These provincial troops served under the immediate command of the *oba* and *bale* of their own towns, or of war-chiefs appointed by them. Beyond this, it appears that the principal rulers of the various *ekun* (provinces) of the Oyo kingdom, such as the *Onikoyi* of Ikoyi in the Ekun Osi, the *Okere* of Saki in the Ekun Otun, and the *Sabiganna* of Iganna in the Ekun Onko, each commanded the forces from the towns within his own *ekun*.[72] The *Onikoyi* of Ikoyi, as the senior provincial ruler, was regarded as the commander-in-chief of the provincial army, though it is not clear

[65] Johnson, *History of the Yorubas*, 162–3.

[66] In the last years of the empire, when the *Alafin* was at odds with his senior chiefs, the practice of personal command by the *Alafin* was revived by *Alafin* Maku (c. 1796) and *Alafin* Oluewu (c. 1834–6): Johnson, *History of the Yorubas*, 196, 262–7. However, after the death of Oluewu in battle, it was formally decided that the *Alafin* should no longer go to war in person: ibid. 282.

[67] For a parallel development at Benin in the seventeenth century, cf. Egharevba, *Short History of Benin*, 34.

[68] Johnson, *History of the Yorubas*, 159, 169, 174, 191–2.

[69] Dalzel, *History of Dahomy*, 175.

[70] Oral evidence, from the *Kudefu* and other palace officials at Oyo; Johnson, *History of the Yorubas*, 59. The *Osi Iwefa* is recorded, e.g., to have commanded the Oyo forces sent to assist Ketu against the Dahomians in 1884: CMS, G.3, A2/1886, A. F. Foster, Journal, 8 Feb. 1884.

[71] Cf. above Ch. 6, p. 100.

[72] Oral evidence, from Chief S. Ojo, the *Bada* of Saki, and from the *Sabiganna* and Chiefs of Iganna.

whether this involved an effective over-all operational command.[73]

During the imperial period, a new command structure was super-imposed on this, with the institution of the title of *Arẹ Ọna Kakamfo*, whose holder was always resident in one of the provincial towns. The functions of the *Arẹ Ọna Kakamfo* have sometimes been misunder-stood. Biobaku suggests that he was appointed as the ruler of a semi-independent 'palatinate' in a frontier area where enemy pressure was especially great.[74] In fact, he appears to have served as the commander-in-chief of the provincial forces. The title *Arẹ Ọna Kakamfo* means 'Chief of the *Ọna Kakamfo*', or 'Chief of the Chiefs of the *Kakamfo*',[75] and the term *Kakamfo*, according to some inform-ants, was used of the provincial *ọba* who served as the heads of the *ẹkun* of the kingdom, such as the *Onikoyi*, the *Okẹrẹ*, and the *Ṣabiganna*.[76] It is at any rate clear that the forces of the provincial towns came under the command of the *Arẹ Ọna Kakamfo*.[77] This arrangement possibly created tension with the *Onikoyi* and the other senior provincial *ọba*. Johnson in an interesting passage states:

In time of war, the Balẹ [of a provincial town] appoints the Jaguna [war-chief] to go with the [Arẹ Ọna] Kakamfo to any expedition to which the Alafin appoints the latter; but if . . . he appoints the Onikoyi, all the other vassal kings, and the Balẹs of every town were bound to go with him.[78]

This suggests that the *Onikoyi* and the other provincial rulers were excused from personal participation in campaigns where the *Arẹ Ọna Kakamfo* exercised the command, an arrangement readily intelligible as an attempt to minimize disputes and resentments over relative status. However, it does appear that on some occasions the *Arẹ Ọna Kakamfo* and the *Onikoyi* served together with the Ọyọ army.[79]

Like the *Ẹṣọ* titles in the capital, the title of *Arẹ Ọna Kakamfo* was

[73] Oral evidence, from the *Kudẹfu* and other palace officials at Ọyọ; cf. Morton-Williams, 'Fulani Penetration into Nupe and Yoruba', 10.

[74] Biobaku, *The Egba and their Neighbours*, 12; cf. Morton-Williams, 'The Yoruba Kingdom of Oyo', 57.

[75] Cf. Hethersett, in *Iwe Kika Ẹkẹrin*, 72, describes the *Arẹ Ọna Kakamfo* as commanding twelve *Ọna Kakamfo*.

[76] Oral evidence, from the *Ṣabiganna* and Chiefs of Iganna; cf. Ellis, *Yoruba-Speaking Peoples*, 173, glosses *Kakamfo* as 'leader of a local contingent'.

[77] Oral evidence, from Chief S. Ojo of Ṣaki and the *Ṣabiganna* and Chiefs of Iganna.

[78] Johnson, *History of the Yorubas*, 77.

[79] Ibid. 192, 203–4.

non-hereditary, being filled by appointment by the *Alafin*. It has sometimes been stated that the *Arẹ Ọna Kakamfo* was appointed by the *Alafin* from among the *ilari* of the palace,[80] but this seems to be incorrect. The *Arẹ Ọna Kakamfo* is certainly regularly described by informants as *ẹru Alafin*, 'a slave of the *Alafin*', but this apparently alludes to the fact that at his installation his head was shaved and treated with charms as was done with the *ilari*.[81] The purpose of this was no doubt to assimilate the *Arẹ Ọna Kakamfo* in status to the *ilari*, in order to emphasize and secure his allegiance to the *Alafin*. The view that the *Arẹ Ọna Kakamfo* was appointed from among the *Ẹsọ* of the capital,[82] which seems to derive from an admittedly curious statement of Johnson that he 'stands at the head of the Ẹsọs',[83] is also incorrect. In all known instances, the title was conferred upon a man who was already the ruler of a provincial town.[84]

The title of *Arẹ Ọna Kakamfo* was first conferred by *Alafin* Ajagbo, in the latter half of the seventeenth century.[85] Johnson gives a list of holders of the title, but this appears to be incomplete, for two additional names are supplied by another source.[86] The first two holders of the title, Kokoro Gangan and Ọyatọpe, are both said to have resided at Iwoye, probably the town of this name in the Ibọlọ province, north-west of Ẹdẹ.[87] Subsequently, the title was held by Jogioro of Ogbomọsọ (in the Ẹkun Osi), and by Olangbin of Jabata

[80] Crowder, *Story of Nigeria*, 58; Morton-Williams, 'Fulani Penetration into Nupe and Yoruba', 10.

[81] Johnson, *History of the Yorubas*, 74.

[82] Smith, *Kingdoms of the Yoruba*, 121.

[83] Johnson, *History of the Yorubas*, 74; cf. Hethersett, in *Iwe Kika Ẹkẹrin*, 63, writes of the *Arẹ Ọna Kakamfo* commanding twelve *Ẹsọ*. Probably the term *Ẹsọ* is being used here in the general sense of 'warrior', rather than with specific reference to the 70 *Ẹsọ* of the capital.

[84] Ojo, *Iwe Itan Ṣaki*, 44, claims that *Alafin* Oluewu in *c.* 1834 offered the title of *Arẹ Ọna Kakamfo* to Alausa, the *Bada* of Ṣaki, who was not the ruler of his town but one of its war-chiefs, but that Alausa declined the honour: since Chief Ojo is here dealing with his own ancestor, the story should be treated with some reserve.

[85] Johnson, *History of the Yorubas*, 74, 169.

[86] Ibid. 75. According to this list, Ọyabi (d. *c.* 1776) was only the third holder of the title, but Oyerinde, *Iwe Itan Ogbomọsọ*, 18, supplies two additional names (Jogioro and Olangbin) which have to be inserted immediately before Ọyabi: other names may also have been omitted.

[87] Oral evidence, from Chief Ojo of Ṣaki. But informants at this Iwoye disclaimed any knowledge of Kokoro Gangan or Ọyatọpe, or of any *Arẹ Ọna Kakamfo* resident in the town: Oral evidence, from the *Oluwoye* and Chiefs of Iwoye.

(a town in the Epo province, near the site of modern Ọyọ). Olangbin was compelled to commit suicide by *Alafin* Abiọdun, who replaced him with Ọyabi of Ajaṣẹ (in the Ẹkun Osi, north-east of Ogbomọṣọ[88]). This was evidently before 1774, when Ọyabi as *Arẹ Ọna Kakamfo* assisted Abiọdun in the overthrow of *Baṣọrun* Gaha.[89] Ọyabi is said to have died two years after the fall of Gaha, i.e. in *c.* 1776.[90] He was followed as *Arẹ Ọna Kakamfo* by two further chiefs of Jabata, Adeta and Oku, and they by Afọnja of Ilọrin (another Ẹkun Osi town). Afọnja was probably appointed to the title by Abiọdun shortly before the latter's death in 1789.[91] The last regularly appointed *Arẹ Ọna Kakamfo* of the empire, who received the title after Afọnja's death in the 1820s, was Toyejẹ of Ogbomọṣọ.[92] All the holders of the title were from towns in the eastern provinces of the kingdom (Ẹkun Osi, Ibọlọ, and Epo), but the reason for this is not known.[93] It also appears that, with the possible exception of the first two incumbents, the title was always given to a provincial ruler with the inferior status of a *balẹ* rather than to a provincial *ọba*.[94] This probably represents a deliberate effort to keep high military command and high civil status separate, so as to prevent an undue concentration of power. It may also be noted here that Richard Lander claims that the *Alafin* in 1827 offered him the post of 'great war-chief, or generalissimo of his forces', meaning presumably that of *Arẹ Ọna Kakamfo*.[95]

The *Arẹ Ọna Kakamfo* had under him two subordinate chiefs, the *Ọtun Kakamfo* and the *Osi Kakamfo*, commanders respectively of the right and left wings in battle, the former being considered the senior.

[88] Ọyabi's town was not Porto Novo (called Ajaṣẹ by the Yoruba), as suggested by Morton-Williams, 'The Ọyọ Yoruba and the Atlantic Trade', 42; followed by Fọlayan, 'Ẹgbado to 1832', 24. Nor was it Ajaṣẹ Ipo in the Igbomina province of the Ọyọ kingdom, as the present writer once suggested: cf. Smith, *Kingdoms of the Yoruba*, 194, n.30.

[89] Cf. Johnson, *History of the Yorubas*, 183–5.

[90] Ibid. 186.

[91] Ojo, *Short History of Ilorin*, 10.

[92] Johnson, *History of the Yorubas*, 201. There were also, during the last years of the empire, some dissident provincial rulers who assumed the title of *Arẹ Ọna Kakamfo* without authorization by the *Alafin*: notably Ẹdun of Gbogun and Ojo Amepo of Akesẹ.

[93] However, one story claims that the title was once offered to a chief of Ṣaki, in the Ẹkun Ọtun: Ojo, *Iwe Itan Ṣaki*, 44.

[94] If the Iwoye of the first two *Arẹ Ọna Kakamfo* is to be identified with the Iwoye north-west of Ẹdẹ, this is nowadays ruled by an *ọba*, the *Oluwoye*: though it is possible that its ruler has been upgraded in status since the seventeenth century.

[95] R. Lander, *Records of Captain Clapperton's Last Expedition*, ii. 224.

It seems to have been usual for the *Ǫtun Kakamfo* to be promoted to succeed the *Arę Ǫna Kakamfo* on the latter's death. Ǫyabi of Ajașę was *Ǫtun Kakamfo* to Olangbin of Jabata before succeeding him,[96] and Toyeję of Ogbomǫșǫ had similarly served as *Ǫtun Kakamfo* under Afǫnja of Ilǫrin.[97] Afǫnja had as his *Osi Kakamfo* another chief of Jabata, called Fagbohun.[98]

It is difficult to determine the relative importance of the metropolitan and provincial forces in the Ǫyǫ army. The capital could no doubt produce more troops than any other town in the kingdom, but the combined strength of the provincial towns must have been substantially greater than that of the capital. However, it may be that the provincial towns, unlike the capital, were not strong in cavalry. Oral evidence from the provincial towns suggests that, although their chiefs regularly went to war on horseback, they did not supply large numbers of mounted warriors.[99] The cavalry which formed the principal strength of the Ǫyǫ army seems therefore to have been drawn mainly from the metropolitan army, principally the seventy *Ęșǫ* and their retainers.

In addition to the forces of the capital and the provincial towns of the Ǫyǫ kingdom, the Ǫyǫ could also draw military forces from their tributaries outside the kingdom proper. It does not appear that this was done on any regular or organized basis. Robertson observes that certain tributaries of Ǫyǫ, including the Mahi, were 'compelled to send contingent forces' to serve in the wars of the Ǫyǫ,[100] which seems to imply a general obligation, but other evidence suggests that military assistance was demanded from these peripheral tributaries only exceptionally and on an *ad hoc* basis. The Dahomians, for example, undertook a campaign against Badagry in 1784, in agreement with Ǫyǫ and under the supervision of *ilari* from Ǫyǫ,[101] and a campaign against Wemę in 1786, at the request of the *Alafin*.[102]

It is difficult to estimate the size of the Ǫyǫ armies. Norris reports a picturesque story:

[96] Oyerinde, *Iwe Itan Ogbomǫșǫ*, 18, 58.
[97] Johnson, *History of the Yorubas*, 197, 201.
[98] Ibid. 198.
[99] Oral evidence, from Chief S. Ojo of Șaki, the *Șabiganna* and Chiefs of Iganna, the *Oniwere* and Chiefs of Iwere, the *Oluwoye* and Chiefs of Iwoye, and D. A. Adeniji of Iwo.
[100] Robertson, *Notes on Africa*, 268.
[101] Dalzel, *History of Dahomy*, 182–7.
[102] Ibid. 192.

The *Dahomeans*, to give an idea of the strength of an *Eyoe* army, assert, that when they go to war, the general spreads the hide of a buffalo before the door of his tent, and pitches a spear on each side of it; between which the soldiers march until the multitude, which pass over the hide, have worn a hole through it; as soon as this happens, he presumes that his forces are numerous enough to take the field.[103]

This tale is of no value whatever, being no more than a traditional stereotype.[104] Where contemporary sources give precise figures for the strength of Ọyọ armies, these hardly inspire greater confidence. Bosman claims that the army which invaded Allada in 1698 numred, together with allies from Hueda, no less than 1,000,000.[105] Later, the figure of 100,000 appears to have been current as a conventional estimate of the size of an Ọyọ army.[106] Such figures provide no information about the reality. Clapperton in 1826 is more sober: 'The military force consists of the caboceers and their own immediate retainers, which, allowing one hundred and fifty to each, will not give such immense armies as we have sometimes heard stated; that of Yourriba is perhaps as numerous as any of the kingdoms of Africa.'[107] It is not altogether clear whether this refers to the provincial or to the metropolitan army, or to both: Clapperton uses the term 'caboceer' both of the provincial rulers (many of whom were gathering at Ọyọ during Clapperton's visit, probably for the Bẹrẹ festival[108]) and of the chiefs of the capital. If the figure of 150 retainers is applicable to the seventy Ẹsọ of the capital, this would give a strength for the metropolitan army of about 10,000, a high but perhaps not impossible figure.[109] The oral traditions provide little information on the size of Ọyọ armies, but the statement in

---

[103] Norris, *Memoirs of the Reign of Bossa Ahadee*, 12; repeated by Dalzel, *History of Dahomy*, 71–2. Cf. the story that for the war against Nupe in 1790, the *Alafin* 'ordered the buffalo's hide to be twice trodden': Dalzel, *History*, 229.

[104] The same story is reported, at about the same time, of the army of Bornu: S. Lucas, in *Proceedings of the Association for Promoting the Discovery of the Interior Parts of Africa* (London, 1810), i. 154–5.

[105] Bosman, *New and Accurate Description of the Coast of Guinea*, 397.

[106] This figure is given, apparently independently, by Pruneau de Pommegorge, *Description de la Nigritie*, 235; Adams, *Remarks on the Country Extending from Cape Palmas*, 92; F. Forbes, *Dahomey and the Dahomans* (London, 1851), ii. 87.

[107] Clapperton, *Journal of a Second Expedition*, 57.

[108] Cf. ibid. 47.

[109] The plausibility of this figure depends upon an unknown, namely the total population of the city of Ọyọ: if the latter was much more than, say, 60,000, a total strength for the metropolitan army of well over 10,000 would be quite conceivable, but the Ẹsọ and their retainers should represent only a minority of this total strength.

Dahomian tradition that the Ọyọ army defeated when Dahomey finally revolted against Ọyọ in 1823 numbered 4,000 men seems moderate enough to be worthy of credence.[110]

It will have been seen from the above discussion of the organization of the Ọyọ army that the Ọyọ disposed of no permanent standing force of soldiers. Even the specialist warriors such as the *Ẹsọ* and the military *ilari* in the capital served on a part-time basis, and would normally expect to return to their homes once a campaign was concluded. It was therefore impracticable to arrange the continuous garrisoning of disaffected areas or threatened frontiers. The solution adopted for this problem, it appears, was the foundation of military colonies. The town of Ẹdẹ, for example, is said to have been founded by an *Ẹsọ* sent from the capital to check Ijẹsa raids in the area,[111] and the town of Igbaja was similarly founded as a base against Nupe raids in the Igbomina province of the Ọyọ kingdom.[112]

A final aspect of the organization of the Ọyọ army which merits notice was the very severe punishment of military failure. European sources record that the general who commanded the invasion of Allada in 1698 was hanged on his return to Ọyọ, for failing to capture the king of Allada,[113] and that the commander of the invasion of Dahomey in 1739 was 'disgraced' for failing to capture the king of Dahomey.[114] The traditions assert that the *Arẹ Ọna Kakamfo* was required to commit suicide if he was not victorious in any campaign within three months.[115] As will be seen in a later chapter, *Alafin* Awolẹ in *c.* 1796 attempted to exploit this convention in order to eliminate his *Arẹ Ọna Kakamfo*, Afọnja of Ilọrin, by ordering him to attack a reputedly impregnable town.[116]

§3. MILITARY FACTORS IN ỌYỌ EXPANSION

The successful expansion of the Ọyọ empire in the seventeenth and eighteenth centuries clearly depended upon the ability of its armies to defeat its enemies in battle. It is not easy, however, to explain the military superiority of Ọyọ over its neighbours in this period. Ọyọ military power doubtless benefited from the creation of a semi-professional force of specialist soldiers (the *Ẹsọ* and their retainers),

[110] Le Herissé, *L'Ancien Royaume de Dahomey*, 321.
[111] Johnson, *History of the Yorubas*, 156.
[112] Kẹnyọ, *Founder of the Yoruba Nation*, 51.
[113] Bosman, *New and Accurate Description of the Coast of Guinea*, 397–8.
[114] Norris, *Memoirs of the Reign of Bossa Ahadee*, 15.
[115] Johnson, *History of the Yorubas*, 74.
[116] Ibid. 191: cf. below, Ch. 12, pp. 249–50.

but the development of such forces was far from being peculiar to
Ọyọ, and was, indeed, taken rather further in some other states,
notably Dahomey.[117] The dominance of Ọyọ was probably related
less to the organization than to the armament of its forces, and in
particular to their use of cavalry.

It has often been suggested that the remarkable recovery of Ọyọ
power after the Nupe conquest in the sixteenth century was due to the
introduction of cavalry, which placed the Ọyọ on terms of equality
with their cavalry-using northern neighbours, the Nupe and Bariba.[118] Equally, the possession of cavalry gave the Ọyọ a substantial
military advantage when they began their imperial expansion against
the horseless peoples further south. That it was the use of cavalry
that enabled the Ọyọ to dominate these southern areas is suggested,
above all, by Snelgrave's account of the Ọyọ invasions of Dahomey
in the 1720s.[119] Snelgrave's account, however, also serves to illustrate
the limitations of cavalry power: Ọyọ operations against Dahomey
were restricted to brief raids, as the cavalry could not operate during
the rainy season (presumably because of the danger from trypanosomiasis) and were hampered by the problem of securing fodder for
the horses. Consequently, although they could overrun the country
and defeat any Dahomian army which stood and fought, they could
not effect a complete and permanent conquest, so that in the end
Dahomey had to be left autonomous and tributary.

There were other limitations to the effectiveness of cavalry.
Mounted troops were primarily useful in open savanna country, in
which alone they could deploy for an effective massed charge. In the
savanna, indeed, cavalry had a decisive advantage over unmounted
troops, as a Yoruba proverb attests:

> A ki i ba onwẹ jagun odo,
> Tani i ba ẹlẹsin jagun papa?
>
> One cannot beat a warrior who is a swimmer in a river,
> Who shall beat a warrior who is a horseman in a plain?[120]

The Ọyọ were therefore able to build up a large kingdom in the
northern, savanna area of Yorubaland. The success of Ọyọ expansion

[117] For the existence of a standing army in Dahomey in the eighteenth century,
see esp. Pruneau de Pommegorge, *Description de la Nigritie*, 164; Dalzel, *History
of Dahomy*, x; Snelgrave, *New Account of Some Parts of Guinea*, 78.

[118] Cf. above, Ch. 3, p. 43.

[119] Snelgrave, *New Account of Some Parts of Guinea*, 55–7, 121–2.

[120] Personal communication from Robert Smith, reporting oral evidence from
D. A. Adeniji of Iwo.

towards the south-west was also a function of the terrain, since in this direction the savanna extends all the way to the coast. As Snelgrave observed, the effectiveness of the Ọyọ cavalry in Dahomey was due to 'the Country being open and without Inclosures'.[121] On the other hand, Ọyọ expansion towards the south-east brought their cavalry into less congenial terrain—thick forest—and this doubtless explains the failure of the Ọyọ to establish their power here. Johnson, it will be recalled, attributes the defeat of the Ọyọ in Ijẹṣaland to their unfamiliarity with 'bush fighting'.[122]

Purely technical military factors thus go some way to explain both the successes and the limitations of Ọyọ power. They do not, however, quite explain everything, since the Ọyọ were also able to dominate the forest country of the Ẹgba and Ẹgbado and the hilly country of the Mahi, none of which was good cavalry country. For the success of Ọyọ expansion in these areas, other explanations have to be sought. In Ẹgba and Mahi country, perhaps, the task of the Ọyọ was facilitated by the political fragmentation of these peoples (and in Mahi, also by the desire of the local people for protection against Dahomey), while Ẹgbado appears to have been a sparsely populated area which was for the most part colonized rather than conquered by the Ọyọ.[123]

§4. THE ARMY IN THE INTERNAL POLITICS OF ỌYỌ

During the eighteenth century there was a protracted struggle for power within the Ọyọ capital between the *Alafin* and his principal chiefs, headed by the *Baṣọrun*, which culminated in the usurpation of effective power by *Baṣọrun* Gaha in 1754–74.[124] It is probable that control of the armed forces of the Ọyọ kingdom played a crucial part in determining the course and outcome of these troubles.

As has been seen above, the main military forces of the capital itself (the *Ẹsọ* and their retainers) came under the immediate authority of the *Baṣọrun* and the other *Ọyọ Mesi*. This control of the principal strength of the metropolitan army, it may be suggested, helps to explain the success of the *Ọyọ Mesi* throughout the eighteenth century in compelling unpopular *Alafin* to commit suicide, since in the last resort the *Ọyọ Mesi* could enforce their will by force of arms. It is recorded that when one *Alafin*, Karan, attempted to refuse a

---

[121] Snelgrave, *New Account of Some Parts of Guinea*, 56.
[122] Johnson, *History of the Yorubas*, 168.
[123] Cf. above, Ch. 6, pp. 92–5. [124] Cf. above, Ch. 5, pp. 76–82.

demand for his suicide, the Ọyọ army stormed the palace and killed
him.[125] It is also likely that *Başọrun* Gaha depended upon the
support of the *Ẹşọ* during his period of power between 1754 and
1774. It is at any rate suggestive that when *Alafin* Abiọdun, after
overthrowing Gaha in 1774, carried out a purge of Gaha's supporters,
he found it necessary to include in the massacre the *Ẹsiẹlẹ*, the
Sakin, and the *Sahadọwẹ*—three of the senior *Ẹşọ*.[126]

The *Alafin* was in a weak position *vis-à-vis* the *Ọyọ Mesi*, since he
controlled no military force in the capital comparable to the *Ẹşọ*.
He did have a bodyguard of *ilari*, and may have sought to expand
the military importance of his palace slaves, increasing the military
role of the *Osi Iwefa* and other palace officials. There is also a
curious story that *Alafin* Abiọdun created the title of *Agunpopo* for
one of his sons, to serve as the commander of a bodyguard of 4,000
'Popo' (Egun) soldiers in the capital.[127] This would be intelligible
as a move by the *Alafin* to redress the balance of military power to
his own advantage, but the story is of doubtful authenticity: the
Agunpopo's function today is to mix medicines for the *Alafin*'s wives,
and the title *Agunpopo* appears to mean 'Mixer'.[128] It is, at any rate,
clear that the balance of military power inside the capital lay in
favour of the *Ọyọ Mesi*.

The apparent inability of the *Alafin* to create a large military force
under his personal control, which would both overawe the *Ọyọ Mesi*
and decrease the *Alafin*'s dependence upon them, clearly calls for
some explanation. The explanation may be related to the importance
of cavalry in the Ọyọ army. Goody has argued that cavalry armies,
in West African conditions, were difficult to bring under centralized
royal control, because of the enormous expense involved in the
purchase and maintenance of horses. Royal revenues were not
adequate to finance a large cavalry force, so that cavalry armies had
to be raised through an estate of self-financing nobles.[129] This
argument, however, needs some qualification. Oral evidence suggests
that the *Alafin* had no difficulty in mobilizing the resources required
for the purchase of large numbers of horses: it is claimed that he
supplied horses not only to his kinsmen and palace slaves, but also

[125] Johnson, *History of the Yorubas*, 170.   [126] Ibid. 186.   [127] Ibid. 186–7.
[128] The present writer was unable to obtain confirmation or denial of Johnson's
story from members of the *Agunpopo* lineage in 1969, since the title was vacant
and they were therefore reluctant to tell the traditions relating to it.
[129] J. Goody, *Technology, Tradition and the State in Africa* (London, 1971),
50–3.

to the *Ọyọ Mesi* and the *Ẹṣọ*, although these latter chiefs could and
did also buy horses for themselves.[130] The fact that the *Alafin* distributed many of the horses he purchased to the chiefs rather than
using them to build up the strength of his private army may, however,
indicate that he had difficulty in meeting the high cost of *maintaining*
large numbers of horses. In this case, the constraint on military
centralization may have been, not the high cost of purchasing
horses, but the large numbers of slaves needed to organize the
feeding of them.[131]

The *Alafin* might, however, offset the military power of the *Ọyọ
Mesi* in the capital by relying upon the forces supplied by the
provincial towns of the Ọyọ kingdom. These owed their immediate
allegiance to the *Alafin* rather than to the *Ọyọ Mesi*, since the
commander-in-chief of the provincial forces, the *Arẹ Ọna Kakamfo*,
was an appointee of the *Alafin* and in status an *ilari*. Indeed, the
creation of the title of *Arẹ Ọna Kakamfo* by *Alafin* Ajagbo in the
latter half of the seventeenth century should probably be seen as a
deliberate attempt to create a command structure for the provincial
forces which would be under the *Alafin*'s control and independent of
the *Ọyọ Mesi*. There seems to have been a convention forbidding the
Arẹ Ọna Kakamfo to visit the capital.[132] Johnson supposes that this
was intended to avoid the danger of a clash between the *Alafin* and
the *Arẹ Ọna Kakamfo*, but it seems more likely that it was devised in
the interests of the *Ọyọ Mesi*, to prevent the *Arẹ Ọna Kakamfo* from
intervening in the politics of capital in support of the *Alafin*. Certainly
this view is supported by the events of 1774. *Alafin* Abiọdun first
secured his control of the provincial army by compelling the existing
Arẹ Ọna Kakamfo, Olangbin of Jabata, who was a personal enemy
of his, to commit suicide, and replacing him by Ọyabi of Ajaṣẹ.[133]
He then organized a *coup d'état* in which Ọyabi led the provincial
forces against the capital and joined with Abiọdun in suppressing
Gaha.[134] In this way the provincial forces were called in to restore
the *Alafin*'s authority in the capital. In the long run, however, as will
be argued later, this established an unhealthy precedent which did
much to destroy the internal stability of the Ọyọ kingdom.

---

[130] Oral evidence, from the *Kudefu* of Ọyọ.

[131] Cf. Law, 'A West African Cavalry State', 12–13.

[132] Johnson, *History of the Yorubas*, 74; Morton-Williams, 'The Yoruba
Kingdom of Oyo', 57.   [133] Oyerinde, *Iwe Itan Ogbomọṣọ*, 18, 58.

[134] Johnson, *History of the Yorubas*, 183–5; Hethersett, in *Iwe Kika Ẹkẹrin*,
63.

CHAPTER 10

The Economics of Empire

THE economic, no less than the military, basis of Ọyọ power requires examination before any general interpretation of the rise of the Ọyọ empire can be attempted. In this chapter, an attempt is made to reconstruct the economic activities of the inhabitants of the Ọyọ empire, and to suggest the precise ways in which the power of Ọyọ was related to its economic organization. First, an impressionistic description is offered of the domestic economy of the Ọyọ kingdom. This is followed by a detailed consideration of the involvement of Ọyọ in long-distance trade, particularly in the Atlantic slave trade. And finally, attention is directed to the major sources of revenue of the Ọyọ state, and to the part played by economic considerations in the formation of national policy.

§1. THE DOMESTIC ECONOMY: PRODUCTION

There is much less contemporary evidence for the character of the domestic economy of Ọyọ than for its involvement in the business of long-distance trade, and reconstruction of the former has to depend to a large extent upon extrapolation backwards from the better-documented conditions of the middle and later nineteenth century, and in some contexts even of the twentieth century. It is nevertheless possible to describe the general character of the Ọyọ economy with some confidence.

The great majority of Ọyọ were undoubtedly engaged in agri-culture, and more specifically in the cultivation of foodstuffs.[1] In the northern areas of the Ọyọ kingdom, in the savanna, the main crops were cereals, especially millet and maize. In the southern, forest areas, the principal crops were roots, especially yams and cassava. Tree crops, of which the most important were the oil palm, the kola nut, pepper, and plantains, were also cultivated mainly in the south. Some important crops, including maize and cassava, are known to

---

[1] For agriculture in Yorubaland, see Ojo, *Yoruba Culture*, Ch. 3. Information on the crops cultivated in the Ọyọ kingdom can also be gleaned from Clapperton, *Journal of a Second Expedition, passim.*

have been introduced into Africa from the Americas by the Portuguese, and would not have been available to the Yoruba before, at earliest, the sixteenth century. Soil fertility was preserved by a system of rotation, plots of land being alternately cultivated for a few years and left fallow. Farmers made use of the hoe, but no form of plough was used. The ownership of land was vested in the lineage (*idile*), but the working of the land was carried on by the individual 'households' (comprising a man, his wives, children, and slaves) which made up the *idile*. The large-scale labour required seasonally for agricultural work might be obtained from kinsmen, but voluntary co-operation work groups (*aro*), which drew their membership from different lineages, were also important.

Animal husbandry was of less importance. Sheep and goats were commonly raised, but the incidence of the tsetse fly over much of Yorubaland limited the possibilities of rearing cattle. In the northern areas of the Ọyọ kingdom, however, there were numerous groups of immigrant Fulani pastoralists, who lived on peaceful terms with the Ọyọ towns, to which they traded their produce, such as milk, butter, and cheese.[2] Some Ọyọ owned their own cattle, employing slaves of northern (especially Hausa) origin to tend them.[3] Another supplement to agriculture, important as a source of meat, was hunting.[4]

In addition to food production, many Ọyọ were engaged in producing manufactured goods. There was, first, the manufacture of the necessary articles of everyday use. Iron tools and weapons were manufactured locally, and the excellent quality of Ọyọ blacksmithing was remarked upon by Adams, in the late eighteenth century.[5] Iron was smelted locally,[6] but the Ọyọ blacksmiths probably also made much use of European iron, imported in the form of iron bars.[7] Clay pottery was also made locally. The potters of modern Ilọrin, whose wares have enjoyed a considerable reputation, claim to have originated from Ọyọ Ile,[8] and the site of Ọyọ Ile has

[2] Clapperton, *Journal of a Second Expedition*, 26, 27, 28, 31; R. and J. Lander, *Journal of an Expedition*, i. 126–7, 130, 135, 142–3, 146, 203, 207–8.

[3] Johnson, *History of the Yorubas*, 123, 193.

[4] For hunting in Yorubaland, see Ojo, *Yoruba Culture*, Ch. 2.

[5] Adams, *Remarks on the Country Extending from Cape Palmas*, 94.

[6] There is no direct evidence for the imperial period, but for local iron-smelting in the nineteenth century, cf. Campbell, *Pilgrimage to My Motherland*, 44–5, 94; Johnson, *History of the Yorubas*, 119–20.

[7] For the importation of iron bars into the Slave Coast area, cf. Adams, *Remarks on the Country Extending from Cape Palmas*, 238.

[8] Hermon-Hodge, *Gazetteer of Ilorin Province*, 281.

yielded much pottery similar to that of Ilọrin, the similarity extending in some cases even to the identity of the potters' marks.[9]

Also of considerable importance was the manufacture of cotton cloth. The earliest unequivocal references to cloth made in Ọyọ date only from the late eighteenth century,[10] but the industry was certainly much older. Ọyọ cloth was of high quality: in the opinion of the European trader Adams, 'The cloth manufactured in Hio is superior, both for variety of pattern, colour, and dimensions, to any made in the neighbouring countries.'[11] Two distinct techniques of weaving were practised: men weaving on upright looms producing narrow (c. 6 inches) strips of cloth, and women using horizontal looms which produced broader (c. 18 inches) strips.[12] The city of Ọyọ Ile was an important centre of cloth production.[13] The weavers there seem to have been mainly men, using the upright loom: they are said to have been largely Muslims, possibly reflecting the introduction of this technique of weaving from the north.[14] Another important cloth-producing centre in the Ọyọ kingdom was Ijanna, in the Ẹgbado province.[15] In recent times, the town of Isẹyin has been an important centre for the manufacture of cloth, but the Isẹyin cloth industry seems to have been founded only during the nineteenth century, by refugees from Ọyọ Ile.[16] Outside the Ọyọ kingdom, important cloth-producing centres were the Igbomina town of Ila[17] and the southern Yoruba kingdom of Ijẹbu.[18] Ila specialized in the production of broadcloth, woven on the female horizontal loom, and the technique of 'female' weaving is said to have been introduced into the Ọyọ kingdom from this town.[19] The cotton used in the manufacture of Ọyọ cloth was cultivated locally.[20] For the more expensive cloths

[9] Willett, 'Investigations at Old Oyo', 76.

[10] Norris, Memoirs of the Reign of Bossa Ahadee, 87, 125, 138; Adams, Remarks on the Country Extending from Cape Palmas, 89, 173.

[11] Adams, Remarks on the Country Extending from Cape Palmas, 89.

[12] Johnson, History of the Yorubas, 110, 119, 124; cf. Clarke, Travels and Explorations in Yorubaland, 272–3.

[13] Clapperton, Journal of a Second Expedition, 57.

[14] Bray, 'The Organization of Traditional Weaving in Iseyin', 271.

[15] Clapperton, Journal of a Second Expedition, 14–16; R. and J. Lander, Journal of an Expedition, i. 90–1.

[16] Cf. Bray, 'The Organization of Traditional Weaving in Iseyin', 271.

[17] There is no contemporary evidence for textile production at Ila before the 1850s: Clarke, Travels and Discoveries in Yorubaland, 152.

[18] Adams, Remarks on the Country Extending from Cape Palmas, 108; Robertson, Notes on Africa, 301.

[19] Johnson, History of the Yorubas, 110.

[20] Norris, Memoirs of the Reign of Bossa Ahadee, 138; Clapperton, Journal

some use was also made of silk, which was imported from the north, ultimately from across the Sahara.[21] Indigo, the most commonly used dye, was also cultivated locally.[22] Richard Lander estimated that at Ọyọ Ile between 500 and 600 acres were devoted to indigo cultivation.[23]

Other crafts were practised on a more limited scale. The city of Ọyọ seems to have been a minor centre for the manufacture of jasper beads. At any rate, the bead-makers of modern Ilọrin assert that their ancestors were refugees from Ọyọ Ile,[24] and jasper beads (though no direct evidence of their manufacture) have been found at Ọyọ Ile.[25] The Ilọrin bead-makers import their jasper from the Upper Volta area.[26] The manufacture of leather articles, such as umbrellas, was probably also carried on at Ọyọ Ile: at modern Ọyọ there is a lineage which manufactures leather articles for the *Alafin*, and claims to be descended from ancestors who fulfilled the same function at Ọyọ Ile.[27]

Craft production was normally carried on on a household basis, and the practice of crafts tended to be hereditary. Craft guilds (*ẹgbẹ*) also existed, to which all the practitioners of a craft in a town were obliged to belong. These guilds regulated standards, prices, and other matters of general interest.[28]

One feature of the productive system of Ọyọ which calls for extended comment is the use of slaves. By the end of the imperial period, it appears that the slave population was very considerable, though the estimate of the Landers in 1830 that two-thirds of the

---

of a Second Expedition, 57 and *passim*; R. and J. Lander, *Journal of an Expedition*, i. 90–1, etc.

[21] R. and J. Lander, *Journal of an Expedition*, i. 90–1; cf. Clapperton, *Journal of a Second Expedition*, 137.

[22] Adams, *Remarks on the Country Extending from Cape Palmas*, 173.

[23] R. Lander, *Records of Captain Clapperton's Last Expedition*, ii. 211.

[24] NAK, ILORPROF. 4, 900/1912, G. J. Lethem, 'Reassessment Report, Ilorin Town' (1912), §28; J. D. Clarke, 'Ilorin Stone Bead Making', *Nigeria Magazine*, 14 (1938), 156–7.

[25] Willett, 'Investigations at Old Oyo', 74; cf. Clapperton, *Journal of a Second Expedition*, 27, refers to Fulani women in the Ọyọ kingdom wearing 'coarse jasper beads, made in the country'.

[26] NAK, ILORPROF. 4, 900/1912, G. J. Lethem, 'Reassessment Report, Ilorin Town' (1912), §29.

[27] C. B. Dodwell, 'The Tim-Tim Makers of Oyo', *Nigeria Magazine*, 42 (1953), 126–31.

[28] P. C. Lloyd, 'Craft Organization in Yoruba Towns', *Africa*, 23 (1953), 30–44.

population of the Qyǫ capital were slaves[29] is perhaps an exaggeration. Many of the slaves were of northern, mainly Hausa, origin, and there was a serious revolt of the Hausa slaves in the Qyǫ kingdom in 1817.[30] Some slaves, such as the *Alafin*'s palace slaves, were employed in administrative and military roles, but it seems clear that most were used for productive purposes. In some instances slavery was a means of recruiting scarce technical skills, foreign slaves being used in jobs for which local people were not qualified, as, for example, Hausa slaves were employed to tend cattle, and to practise rope-making and barbing.[31] However, many slaves were employed merely to supplement free labour in agricultural production.[32] Even in agriculture, non-Yoruba slaves might be preferred, since there was less danger of successful escape with foreign slaves than with slaves whose homeland was nearby.[33]

It is customary to stress the benign character of domestic slavery in Yorubaland, and it is certainly the case that slaves were commonly integrated into the household, of which they formed only marginally disprivileged members, and might ultimately intermarry with the free members of the lineage.[34] However, the slave revolt of 1817 indicates that alongside this benign patriarchal form of slavery, a more exploitative form had developed. The stimulus towards this development is far from clear. In the case of the Upper Guinea coast, Rodney has argued that the growth of domestic slavery was a consequence of the Atlantic slave trade, a portion of the slaves obtained for sale to the Europeans being retained for local use by the African rulers.[35] But while the Atlantic slave trade doubtless affected African attitudes towards slaves, the expansion of slavery

[29] R. and J. Lander, *Journal of an Expedition*, i. 194.

[30] Cf. below, Ch. 12, pp. 246–7, 258.

[31] Johnson, *History of the Yorubas*, 123, 193.

[32] There is little direct evidence for the imperial period, but R. and J. Lander, *Journal of an Expedition*, i. 105, record finding the chief of 'Chow' in northern Egbado 'engaged in supervising the slaves at his corn and yam plantations'.

[33] Cf. the episode recorded by Mungo Park in the Gambia area, when a man was anxious to dispose of a slave from Futa Djallon, since 'as that country was at no great distance, he could not safely employ him in the labours of the field, lest he should effect his escape': M. Park, *Travels in Africa* (ed. by R. Miller, London, 1954), 267.

[34] For Yoruba slavery, see esp. Oroge, 'The Institution of Slavery in Yorubaland'; Fadipę, *The Sociology of the Yoruba*, 180–9.

[35] W. Rodney, 'African Slavery and Other Forms of Social Oppression on the Upper Guinea Coast in the Context of the Atlantic Slave-Trade', *JAH* 7 (1966), 431–43.

can only be explained in terms of expanding opportunities for their profitable employment. The suggestion of Fage, that the growth of slavery was a consequence of the general expansion of trade, and not solely of the slave trade, in West Africa seems therefore more plausible.[36] It should be stressed, however, that in Ọyọ at least few slaves were directly employed in the production of commodities for trade, since the crops grown by slaves (except perhaps cotton) did not enjoy a rapidly expanding market during the imperial period.[37] More commonly, it appears, slaves were employed in the production of foodstuffs, to maintain the large non-productive households of chiefs and their retainers.

§2. THE DOMESTIC ECONOMY: TRADE

It is by now something of a commonplace to point out that the conventional picture of a 'subsistence economy', in which each household produced its own requirements, has little application in pre-colonial West Africa.[38] Trade was certainly an important aspect of the domestic economy of Ọyọ. Craft production was normally carried on on a specialized basis by a few households in each community, so that the majority of households had to obtain their manufactured goods by purchase. Many of the inhabitants of the urban centres also obtained their food by purchase, often in already cooked form.[39] Households engaged in craft production seem to have purchased not only their food, but also their raw materials: weaving households, for example, did not produce their own cotton thread, but purchased it from others.[40] In consequence, all towns of any importance had flourishing markets, dealing in foodstuffs, raw materials, and manufactures.[41]

Trade over substantial distances, between towns and regions of the

[36] J. D. Fage, 'Slavery and the Slave Trade in the Context of West African History', *JAH* 10 (1969), 393–404.

[37] This changed in the nineteenth century, after the fall of the Ọyọ empire, with the growth of an export trade in palm oil, which could be harvested and processed by slave labour: cf. A. G. Hopkins, 'Economic Imperialism in West Africa: Lagos 1880–92', *Economic History Review*, 21 (1968), 587–8.

[38] See esp. A. G. Hopkins, *An Economic History of West Africa* (London, 1973), Ch. 2.

[39] Cf. S. Goddard, 'Town-Farm Relationships in Yorubaland: A Case Study from Oyo', *Africa*, 35 (1965), 27.   [40] Johnson, *History of the Yorubas*, 124.

[41] For descriptions of the markets in the Ọyọ capital, see Clapperton, *Journal of a Second Expedition*, 59; R. and J. Lander, *Journal of an Expedition*, i. 179. For markets in other Ọyọ towns, cf. R. and J. Lander, *Journal of an Expedition*, i. 108, 165.

Ọyọ kingdom and between Ọyọ and its neighbours, was inhibited by difficulties of transport. Wheeled transport was not known, and beasts of burden, owing to the danger from the tsetse fly, very rare.[42] The horse, so important for military purposes, was not used to transport goods. On the rivers and along the coastal lagoons, canoe transport could be employed:[43] for example, Clapperton and the Landers in 1825 and 1830 were able to travel by canoe from Badagry a short distance up the River Yewa.[44] But the possibilities of such river transport were limited. Transport was therefore effected mainly by human porters, the goods being carried on the head.[45] At least some Ọyọ traders employed slaves as porters.[46] Slaves destined for sale abroad had normally to make the entire journey to the coast on foot.[47] The slow movement of numerous traders, porters, and slaves overland posed considerable logistical problems, and towns on important trade-routes developed their food production in order to supply the trading caravans.[48] In these conditions the cost of transport was high, and precluded the possibility of substantial trade over long distances in basic foodstuffs and other commodities of great bulk and low value. Luxury foodstuffs and manufactured goods of high quality could, however, be profitably traded over considerable distances. Ọyọ cloth, for example, was taken to Dahomey[49] and to Porto Novo.[50] Kola nuts were imported from the forest areas of Yorubaland, especially from the Ijẹṣa kingdom, to the savanna.[51] Salt, extracted from sea-water at the coast, and camwood (powdered

[42] Cf. when the Landers met a party of Nupe traders on their way to Gonja with donkeys loaded with natron in the extreme north of the Ọyọ kingdom, they observed that 'these asses were the first beasts we had observed employed in carrying burdens': R. and J. Lander, *Journal of an Expedition*, i. 152–3.

[43] For canoe transport in Yorubaland, cf. R. Smith, 'The Canoe in West African History', *JAH* 11 (1970), 522–5.

[44] Clapperton, *Journal of a Second Expedition*, 1; R. and J. Lander, *Journal of an Expedition*, i. 55, 58, 71.

[45] R. and J. Lander, *Journal of an Expedition*, i. 93, 153.

[46] Ibid. i. 112–13.

[47] Adams, *Remarks on the Country Extending from Cape Palmas*, 221–2.

[48] R. and J. Lander, *Journal of an Expedition*, i. 202, note that at Gbọngbọn, a northern Ọyọ town on the trade-route between Gonja and Hausaland, 'a vast quantity of land' was planted with corn and yams to supply traders.

[49] Norris, *Memoirs of the Reign of Bossa Ahadee*, 87, 125.

[50] Adams, *Remarks on the Country Extending from Cape Palmas*, 89. The sale of Ọyọ cloth at the coast is also mentioned by Clapperton, *Journal of a Second Expedition*, 57; R. and J. Lander, *Journal of an Expedition*, i. 110.

[51] There is no direct evidence from the imperial period, but for the Ijẹṣa kola trade later in the nineteenth century, see e.g. Clarke, *Travels and Explorations in Yorubaland*, 138, 263.

for use as a medicinal ointment) from Benin were taken to Ọyọ, and even beyond into Nupe.[52]

Local trade was facilitated by the use as currency of the cowry shell (*cypraea moneta*), which was imported ultimately from the Maldive Islands in the Indian Ocean.[53] The date at which the Ọyọ adopted this currency is uncertain. The use of cowries in Ọyọ is first attested in a contemporary source only in the 1780s.[54] Cowries were brought into West Africa by two routes: they were imported overland across the Sahara from as early as the eleventh century, and by sea by European traders from the sixteenth century.[55] In the late eighteenth century, the cowries in use in Ọyọ were imported from the coast.[56] If this was always the source from which the Ọyọ obtained their cowries, they would probably have obtained them first, through the Dahomey area, during the seventeenth century.[57] It is to be noted, however, that two distinct systems of cowry enumeration were used in Yorubaland. One system, based on a 'string' of 40 cowries and a 'head' of 50 strings (2,000 cowries), was certainly derived from the coast, but the other, based on units of 20, 200, and 2,000 cowries, has affinities with systems in use in the interior of West Africa, in Hausaland and at Kong, an important trading centre of the Mande, north-west of Asante.[58] The existence of this alternative system of enumeration suggests the possibility that the Ọyọ had adopted the cowry currency from their northern neighbours before they gained access to supplies of cowries from the coast in the seventeenth century. The traditions of Kano in Hausaland indicate that cowries reached there only during the eighteenth century, probably from Ọyọ,[59] so that introduction into Ọyọ from the north-west rather than from the north-east would have to be assumed.

Cowry shells were units of very low value: Clapperton in 1826

---

[52] For trade in salt, see e.g. Clapperton, *Journal of a Second Expedition*, 122, 136; for camwood, ibid. 46, 136.

[53] The large-scale importation of East African cowries (*cypraea anulus*) from Zanzibar into West Africa did not begin until the 1840s: Johnson, 'The Cowrie Currencies of West Africa', Part 1, 23.

[54] The earliest reference is by D. Bonnaventure (1788), in Labarthe, *Voyage à la côte de Guinée*, 104.

[55] Johnson, 'The Cowrie Currencies of West Africa', Part 1, 33–4.

[56] Adams, *Remarks on the Country Extending from Cape Palmas*, 204.

[57] Cf. Johnson, 'The Cowrie Currencies of West Africa', Part 1, 34–5.

[58] Ibid. 27, 41.

[59] See the 'Kano Chronicle', in Palmer, *Sudanese Memoirs*, iii. 123; M. Hiskett, 'Materials Relating to the Cowry Currency of the Western Sudan', Part 2, *Bulletin of S.O.A.S.*, 29 (1966), 355–8.

gives 2,000 cowries as the equivalent of one Spanish dollar.[60] Their use was therefore limited by their physical bulk. It appears that they were normally employed only in small-scale transactions, while traders dealing in large quantities of goods operated by barter.[61] Cowries were therefore primarily a lubricant of local exchange, in the urban markets. The existence of the cowry currency, however, facilitated barter transactions also, by providing a unit of account in terms of which goods could be valued.[62] Being imperishable, cowries also provided a convenient means of storing wealth.[63]

Petty trade, in foodstuffs and other articles of small value, was largely in the hands of women.[64] Women traders might travel considerable distances: Clapperton, for example, found women from Ọyọ trading at Kulfo in northern Nupe.[65] But large-scale trade over long distances must have been largely a male preserve. This is especially true of the slave trade, which involved the escorting of large parties of slaves under armed guard.[66] In some other Yoruba states, trade in commodities of foreign origin was controlled by guilds of male traders: such were the *Parakoyi*, among the Ẹgba;[67] the *Ipanpa*, whose head was entitled the *Parakoyi*, in Ifẹ;[68] and the *Alarubọ*, also headed by a *Parakoyi*, in later Ibadan.[69] It does not appear that any similar traders' guild existed in Ọyọ. The title of *Parakoyi* existed in Ọyọ, but its holder was the head of the Muslim ward of the city, and had no commercial functions.[70]

[60] Clapperton, *Journal of a Second Expedition*, 59; cf. Robertson, *Notes on Africa*, 274–5. But R. Lander, in Clapperton, *Journal of a Second Expedition*, 323, observes that 4,000 cowries were 'little more than a dollar', implying perhaps an exchange rate of 3,000 cowries to the dollar: cf. Johnson, 'The Cowrie Currencies of West Africa', Part 2, 336 and n.31.

[61] Johnson, *History of the Yorubas*, 118; cf. Clapperton, *Journal of a Second Expedition*, 136.

[62] Cf. Johnson, 'The Cowrie Currencies of West Africa', Part 1, 46–7.

[63] The 'chief eunuch' Ebo in 1827 had 'a small apartment in his house filled with cowries': R. Lander, *Records of Captain Clapperton's Last Expedition*, ii. 203–4.

[64] Cf. Clapperton, *Journal of a Second Expedition*, 136; R. and J. Lander, *Journal of an Expedition*, i. 108.

[65] Clapperton, *Journal of a Second Expedition*, 136, 138.

[66] For slave caravans, see Clapperton, *Journal of a Second Expedition*, 33; R. Lander, *Records of Captain Clapperton's Last Expedition*, i. 100–1; R. and J. Lander, *Journal of an Expedition*, i. 119.

[67] Biobaku, *The Egba and their Neighbours*, 6.

[68] Bascom, *The Yoruba of Southwestern Nigeria*, 26.

[69] B. Awẹ, 'Militarism and Economic Development in Nineteenth Century Yoruba Country: The Ibadan Example', *JAH* 14 (1973), 73.

[70] Oral evidence, from the *Parakoyi* of Ọyọ.

§3. LONG-DISTANCE TRADE: THE NORTHERN TRADE

In the seventeenth century, as will be seen below, Ọyọ became involved on a large scale in supplying slaves for sale to the European traders at the coast. Ọyọ had certainly been involved in substantial long-distance trade earlier than this, with other countries in the interior of West Africa, but unfortunately little is known of the northern trade of Ọyọ. We have little information on the commercial links of Ọyọ with its northern neighbours before the early nineteenth century, by which time the pattern of trading had been considerably modified by the involvement of Ọyọ in the Atlantic slave trade. Our assessment of the significance of this early northern trade must therefore remain somewhat speculative.

Certainly, by the end of the imperial period, trade with the north was very substantial. The principal market for this northern trade is said by tradition to have been at a town called Ogodo, on the frontier with Nupe to the north-east of Ọyọ Ile. According to Johnson, Ogodo was

a market town, at the confluence of the river Niger, where the Yorubas and Tapas [Nupe] met for an exchange of merchandise. Ogodo was originally a Tapa town, but subsequently the Yoruba population predominated, nearly all the children of influential Ọyọ chiefs resided there permanently for the purpose of trade.[71]

It has been suggested that Ogodo should be identified with Ogudu, the capital of the Nupe province on the south bank of the Niger, but this is uncertain.[72] European sources in the early nineteenth century locate the main market for trade between Ọyọ and the north at a town called Raka, situated apparently within the Ọyọ kingdom, north-east of Ọyọ Ile and close to the River Niger.[73] 'Raka' was apparently the Hausa name for the town, since Clapperton observes that 'the Yourriba name of Rakah is Saguda'.[74] It may be that at some date the main centre of trade between Ọyọ and Nupe had been

---

[71] Johnson, *History of the Yorubas*, 217.

[72] Smith, *Kingdoms of the Yoruba*, 204, n.32; cf. Law, 'The Ọyọ Kingdom and its Northern Neighbours', 30.

[73] Raka is first mentioned in 1817: Bowdich, *Mission from Cape Coast to Ashantee*, 202, 485, 487. For later references, see e.g. Denham and Clapperton, *Narrative of Travels and Discoveries*, Clapperton's Narrative, 42, 87; Clapperton, *Journal of a Second Expedition*, 45, 46, 60, 63; PRO, FO. 2/31, W. B. Baikie to Lord Malmesbury, 4 Mar. 1859; PRO, FO. 97/434, map encl. to W. B. Baikie to Lord Russell, 5 Feb. 1862.

[74] Clapperton, *Journal of a Second Expedition*, 60.

H

transferred from Ogodo to Raka. If Ogodo is to be identified with
Ogudu, this might have occurred in the late eighteenth century,
when Ogudu is said to have been destroyed in a Nupe civil war, after
which the capital of the Nupe province was transferred to Tsaragi.[75]
However, it seems possible that Ogodo and Raka are in fact identical.[76] Certainly, their histories are suspiciously similar: both were
important market towns on the Nupe frontier, both are said to have
been allied with Ilọrin in its revolt against Ọyọ in the 1820s and
1830s,[77] and both are reported to have been destroyed shortly afterwards.[78] If Ogodo can be identified with Raka, Johnson's otherwise
puzzling reference to the former as being 'situated at the confluence
of the river Niger' could be taken to refer to the confluence of the
Niger and the River Moshi.[79]

The greater part of Ọyọ trade with the north seems normally to
have been conducted, through Ogodo or Raka, with their north-
eastern neighbours, the Nupe. However, trade with the Bariba, to
the north-west, was also of some importance. In Borgu, the main
market for trade between north and south was Bussa.[80] The trade-
routes from Ọyọ via Nupe and Borgu joined up, at least in the early
nineteenth century, at the market town of Kulfo, in northern Nupe.[81]
From Kulfo, trade-routes led on to Hausaland and Bornu. In the
early nineteenth century, traders from Ọyọ were journeying as far as
Kulfo,[82] but apparently no further. But earlier, it appears that Ọyọ
traders had ventured further north. A quarter of the Hausa city of
Kano is currently inhabited by the descendants of traders from the
Ọyọ town of Ogbomọṣọ, who settled there during the eighteenth
century.[83] Hausa traders likewise travelled south into the Ọyọ

---

[75] Elphinstone, *Gazetteer of Ilorin Province*, 24–5.

[76] This identification was suggested to me by Mr. S. O. Babayẹmi.

[77] For the role of Ogodo in these wars, see Johnson, *History of the Yorubas*,
217, 259, 268; for the role of Raka, cf. Clapperton, *Journal of a Second Expedition*,
46, 204; R. and J. Lander, *Journal of an Expedition*, i. 189, 191.

[78] Ogodo is said to have been destroyed by forces from Ijaye after the fall of
Ọyọ Ile: Johnson, *History of the Yorubas*, 292; cf. Raka had been destroyed
some years before 1859: PRO, FO. 2/31, W. B. Baikie to Lord Malmesbury,
4 Mar. 1859.

[79] Cf. Johnson, *History of the Yorubas*, 292, links the destruction of Ogodo
with that of Gbajigbo, a town just upstream of the confluence of the Moshi with
the Niger.

[80] Cf. Robertson, *Notes on Africa*, 209, 282.

[81] Cf. the description of Kulfo by Clapperton, *Journal of a Second Expedition*.
135–8.   [82] Ibid. 138.

[83] R. A. Adelẹyẹ, 'Hausaland and Borno 1600–1800', in J. F. A. Ajayi and
M. Crowder (eds.), *History of West Africa*, i (2nd edn., London, 1976), 592.

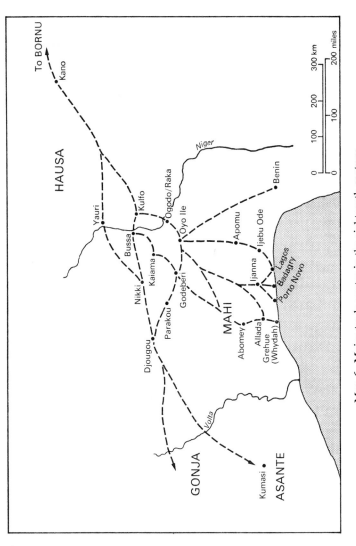

Map 6. Major trade-routes in the eighteenth century.

kingdom,[84] and even to the coast, being noticed at Lagos in the early nineteenth century.[85]

In the early nineteenth century, Ọyọ was importing a variety of commodities from the north. From Nupe came hides[86] and cotton cloth.[87] From Bornu came natron (sodium sesquicarbonate), a mineral salt used for medicinal purposes and (mixed with tobacco or snuff) as a stimulant.[88] From still further afield, from across the Sahara, came unwrought silk and beads of Venetian manufacture.[89] Some of these commodities, especially natron, were re-exported from Ọyọ to the areas closer to the coast.[90] Doubtless trade in these commodities dates back to an early period, though the assertion that this is so depends upon purely presumptive grounds.[91] However, two modern scholars have attempted to demonstrate the early existence of a substantial trade between Ọyọ and the north, and indeed, to explain the rise of Ọyọ power as a consequence of this trade and these suggestions require detailed consideration.

Morton-Williams seeks to connect the rise of Ọyọ with the development of trade (mainly in kola nuts) between Gonja in modern Ghana and Hausaland.[92] This trade, which is known from Hausa sources to have been pioneered during the fifteenth century,[93] linked the eastern commercial network, dominated by Hausa merchants, with the western network where Mande merchants, who had originally dispersed from the old kingdom of Mali, predominated. Morton-Williams suggests that Ọyọ occupied an important

[84] Clapperton, *Journal of a Second Expedition*, 137; cf. Johnson, *History of the Yorubas*, 190.

[85] S. Cock (ed.), *The Narrative of Robert Adams* (London, 1816), xxxvi; Robertson, *Notes on Africa*, 287.

[86] R. Lander, *Records of Captain Clapperton's Last Expedition*, ii. 205, 207. Lander observes that these hides were used for food: perhaps what he really saw was dried meat.

[87] Ibid. ii. 153.

[88] Clapperton, *Journal of a Second Expedition*, 59, 60, 133, 136; R. and J. Lander, *Journal of an Expedition*, i. 59.

[89] Clapperton, *Journal of a Second Expedition*, 137; for silk, cf. R. and J. Lander, *Journal of an Expedition*, i. 91.

[90] Clapperton, *Journal of a Second Expedition*, 59; R. and J. Lander, *Journal of an Expedition*, i. 59, 110.

[91] Cf. Ajayi and Smith, *Yoruba Warfare in the Nineteenth Century*, 3; Davidson, *Africa in History*, 167; I. A. Akinjogbin, 'The Expansion of Ọyọ and the Rise of Dahomey 1600–1800', in Ajayi and Crowder, *History of West Africa*, i. 380.

[92] Morton-Williams, 'The Influence of Habitat and Trade on Oyo and Ashanti'.

[93] Cf. the 'Kano Chronicle', in Palmer, *Sudanese Memoirs*, iii. 109–111.

position as middleman in the trade between Gonja and Hausaland, since traders approaching Hausaland from the west would choose to avoid the 'turbulent' conditions in the Bariba states of Nikki and Kaiama and to pass instead through Ọyọ before crossing the Niger at Jebba or Bussa.[94] As evidence for such early commercial links with the Mande west, Morton-Williams points to the fact that the usual Yoruba word for 'Muslim' is Imale, or 'man of Mali', which is best explicable if Islam was originally introduced into Ọyọ by Mande merchants.[95] The existence of a system of cowry enumeration related to one which operated in the Mande west might seem to point in the same direction.[96] But on the central point there is a dearth of convincing evidence that trade between Gonja and Hausaland ever passed regularly through Ọyọ in preference to Borgu. Our earliest detailed evidence on this, from the 1780s, is of a route passing through Djougou and Nikki and crossing the Niger at Yauri.[97] Bowdich at Kumasi in 1817 did hear of one route which avoided Nikki, but it equally avoided Ọyọ, passing from Djougou through Parakou, Tumbuya, Godeberi, Kaiama, and Wawa to cross the Niger at Bussa.[98] The Landers in 1830, it is true, found merchants travelling to Gonja via Kuṣu in the north-west of the Ọyọ kingdom (though not through the Ọyọ capital), but they observe that this was 'a new route, the road formerly taken being considered unsafe, on account of private broils and disturbances among the natives'.[99] Clearly, trade-routes were unstable, being readily altered in response to changing political conditions. It cannot be shown that trade between Gonja and Hausaland had not passed regularly through Ọyọ

[94] Morton-Williams, 'The Influence of Habitat and Trade on Oyo and Ashanti', 82, 89.

[95] Ibid. 92. There are several references to 'Imale' traders operating in the Dahomey area during the eighteenth century: e.g. Labat, Voyage du Chevalier des Marchais, ii. 273–4; Bulfinch Lambe to Baldwyn, 27 Nov. 1724, in W. Smith, A New Voyage to Guinea (London, 1744), 184; Snelgrave, New Account of Some Parts of Guinea, 79–80; Norris, Memoirs of the Reign of Bossa Ahadee, 102–3; BNRJ, 46, King of Allada (Porto Novo) to Prince Regent of Portugal, 16 Nov. 1804, quoted in Verger, Flux et Reflux de la Traite des Nègres, 270. In some of these references, the Imale seem to be distinct from the Ọyọ: presumably, therefore, the traders concerned were not Ọyọ Muslims, but some other group with Mande connections—possibly the Dendi of Borgu.

[96] Cf. above, p. 209.

[97] See the map, based on information collected by Lucas in Tripolitania in 1789, in Proceedings of the Association for Promoting the Discovery of the Interior Parts of Africa, vol. II, opp. p. 209.

[98] Bowdich, Mission from Cape Coast to Ashantee, 208–11.

[99] R. and J. Lander, Journal of an Expedition, i. 253; cf. ibid. 202.

in early times, but there seems to be no strong reason to believe that it did.

A somewhat more plausible argument has been advanced by Shaw.[100] He points out that the raw materials for the copper and brass sculptures which have been found in the Yoruba area, notably at Ile Ifẹ and at Jebba and Tada in Nupe country to the north-east of Ọyọ Ile, must have been imported from the countries to the north, and suggests that the trade-route along which they came would probably have passed through Ọyọ. The date at which these metal sculptures began to be made is as yet uncertain, but Shaw suggests that the trade which they attest may go back to the tenth century, and that the rise of Ọyọ was related to its control of this trade. However, although it is true that the copper for these sculptures must have been imported, this is not in itself evidence for substantial trade in other commodities, and it is not clear that the distribution of the sculptures is really such as to suggest specifically a trade-route passing through Ọyọ.

Other considerations suggest that the development of large-scale trade with the north might plausibly be placed considerably later. It will be recalled that the Ọyọ kingdom probably began to employ large numbers of cavalry in its armies during the sixteenth century, when the *Alafin* were at the temporary capital of Igboho.[101] The maintenance of a large cavalry force certainly presupposes a substantial northern trade, for most of the horses used were imported from the north, especially from Bornu.[102] Horse accoutrements, such as stirrups, bits, and saddles, were also imported from the north, Nupe being an important centre for their manufacture,[103] although by the nineteenth century, and probably earlier, these were also manufactured in Yorubaland.[104] While, therefore, trade with the north doubtless operated on a minor scale from very early times, a conservative evaluation of the evidence would suggest that a substantial trade developed only during the sixteenth century.

It is difficult to determine what the Ọyọ exported northwards to pay for the horses and other commodities which they imported. In the early nineteenth century the goods going north through Raka

[100] Shaw, 'A Note on Trade and the Tsoede Bronzes'.

[101] Cf. above, Ch. 3, p. 43.

[102] R. Lander, *Records of Captain Clapperton's Last Expedition*, ii. 13; cf. above, Ch. 9, pp. 184–5.

[103] Ibid. ii. 153.

[104] Oral evidence, from the *Kudẹfu* and the *Olokun Ẹṣin* of Ọyọ.

consisted mainly of re-exports of goods imported into Ọyọ from the coast—'all kinds of European goods, such as beads, woollen and cotton cloth, pewter and copper dishes, gunpowder, rum, &c.'[105] But these would not have been available before the seventeenth century. The Ọyọ could send north forest products, such as pepper, camwood (from Benin), and possibly kola nuts,[106] and also locally made cloth.[107] But it seems likely that the highly expensive importation of horses was financed in the sixteenth century by the northward export of slaves.[108] By the eighteenth century, far from exporting slaves northwards, Ọyọ was importing large numbers of Hausa slaves, both for domestic use[109] and for re-sale to the Europeans at the coast,[110] but this was a consequence of the reorganization of trading patterns which followed the involvement of Ọyọ in the Atlantic trade.

§4. LONG-DISTANCE TRADE: THE ATLANTIC TRADE

Ọyọ tradition indicates that the Ọyọ first established contact with the coast and the Europeans trading there during the reign of *Alafin* Ọbalokun. Johnson records that during his reign the Ọyọ for the first time imported salt (*iyọ*) whereas previously they had had only 'rock salt' (*obu*);[111] that a white man visited Ọyọ; and that Ọbalokun sent messengers with gifts (who, however, did not return) to a European king.[112] Both salt and white men might have come to Ọyọ as well from the north as from the south but the three events

[105] Denham and Clapperton, *Narrative of Travels and Discoveries*, Clapperton's Narrative, 87.

[106] For pepper and camwood, see Clapperton, *Journal of a Second Expedition*, 136. The northward kola trade is alluded to ibid. 137, but the principal source of kola nuts was probably Asante rather than Yorubaland.

[107] Ibid. 136 (referring specifically to Ijẹbu cloth).

[108] There is no direct evidence for this, but such an exchange of slaves for horses was a common pattern in trade between north and south: for the cases of Kwararafa and Nupe, cf. the 'Kano Chronicle', in Palmer, *Sudanese Memoirs*, iii. 109, 111. That slaves from Ọyọ might be found in the north is demonstrated by the fact that the Timbuktu scholar Aḥmad Baba commented on the legitimacy of enslaving Ọyọ in a work written in 1615/16: the passage is quoted in Hodgkin, *Nigerian Perspectives*, 156. But enslaved Ọyọ could have been brought north by capture as well as by trade.

[109] Cf. Johnson, *History of the Yorubas*, 193.

[110] Adams, *Remarks on the Country Extending from Cape Palmas*, 221-2.

[111] Johnson's use of the term 'rock salt' is misleading, since *obu* refers normally to salt obtained from vegetable ash: the use of such 'potash' as a substitute for salt in Ọyọ is noted by Adams, *Remarks on the Country Extending from Cape Palmas*, 84.

[112] Johnson, *History of the Yorubas*, 168.

recorded by Johnson evidently belong together and the story of an
embassy to a European king indicates a coastal provenance. It is
possible indeed, that the very name Ọbalokun, which appears to
mean 'King at the Sea', is an *oriki* commemorating this king's
establishment of contact with the coast. It is unlikely that any
European actually visited Ọyọ under Ọbalokun, but individual Ọyọ
probably met white men at the coast.

From his position in the Ọyọ king-list, Ọbalokun's reign appears
to have fallen during the first half of the seventeenth century.[113]
This date for the beginning of Ọyọ involvement in trade with the
Europeans is consistent with the evidence from European sources.
The Portuguese had, indeed, traded along the coast to the south of
the Ọyọ kingdom much earlier. They had made contact with Benin
in 1486,[114] and in the early sixteenth century briefly established
direct trade with the kingdom of Ijẹbu.[115] But it is unlikely that this
had any impact on Ọyọ. With Benin Ọyọ seems never to have traded
on a large scale. The jasper beads which Benin was selling to European traders in the seventeenth century may have come from Ọyọ,[116]
as may the horses used for ceremonial purposes by the kings and
chiefs of Benin.[117] There is also evidence, from the late eighteenth
century and early nineteenth century, for trade in other commodities,
tamarinds going from Ọyọ to Benin[118] and camwood from Benin to
Ọyọ.[119] These references hardly amount to a substantial trade: the
suggestion by Fage that Ọyọ originally exported slaves through
Benin, and that the establishment by Ọyọ of direct access to the
coast involved a diversion of trade away from Benin, which was a
factor in the decline of Benin power, seems altogether unwarranted.[120]
With Ijẹbu, Ọyọ certainly traded on a larger scale, but the market

[113] Cf. above, Ch. 4, p. 58.

[114] Ryder, *Benin and the Europeans*, 24–31.

[115] Pacheco Pereira, *Esmeraldo de Situ Orbis*, 117. In the seventeenth century,
however, the Ijẹbu seem to have traded with the Europeans only through Benin:
A. F. C. Ryder, 'Dutch Trade on the Nigerian Coast during the Seventeenth
Century', *JHSN* 3.2 (1965), 197–8.

[116] J. D. Fage, 'Some Remarks on Beads and Trade in Lower Guinea in the
Sixteenth and Seventeenth Centuries', *JAH* 3 (1962), 346.

[117] Benin tradition asserts that the first horse in Benin was brought from
Yorubaland by Ọranyan: Egharevba, *Short History of Benin*, 8. The provenance,
if not the date of introduction, is no doubt correct.

[118] Landolphe, *Mémoires*, ii. 85–7.

[119] Clapperton, *Journal of a Second Expedition*, 46, 136.

[120] Fage, *History of West Africa*, 99–100; Oliver and Fage, *Short History of
Africa*, 123.

for this trade, Apomu in the Ifẹ kingdom, appears to have been founded only during the latter half of the eighteenth century.[121]

Ọyọ trade initially passed to the coast by a more westerly route, through the kingdom of Allada in what is now the Republic of Benin. Allada had its own ports of Offra and Jakin, and also traded with the Europeans through the neighbouring kingdom of Hueda (Whydah), which had its port at Grehue.[122] The Portuguese began to trade with Allada much later than with Benin or Ijẹbu, probably only in the early seventeenth century.[123] And trade with Allada remained relatively unimportant until the general rise in the volume of the Atlantic slave trade after the 1630s, when the Dutch replaced the Portuguese as the principal traders. The earliest reference to the involvement of Ọyọ in the Atlantic trade is probably to be found in the work of the Dutch writer Dapper, published in 1668 but probably based on information relating to the 1640s.[124] Dapper refers to a large kingdom in the interior, north-east of Allada, called 'Ulkami', which sent large numbers of slaves for sale through Allada and imported salt, which was extracted locally from sea water, in exchange.[125] He also observes that the language of this kingdom was widely spoken in Allada, presumably as a result of these commercial contacts.[126] Later writers also refer to trade between the Allada area and a kingdom called 'Lucamee', and speak of the latter as a source of cloth as well as of slaves.[127] 'Ulkami', 'Lucamee', and

[121] A *Balẹ* of Apomu is said to have committed suicide during the reign at Ọyọ of *Alafin* Awolẹ, i.e. *c.* 1789–96: cf. Johnson, *History of the Yorubas*, 189. This *Balẹ* is identified in Apomu tradition as Atoyibi, the second ruler of the town: YHRS, D. A. Adeniji, 'History of Apomu', n.d.; Oral evidence, from the *Balẹ* and Chiefs of Apomu.

[122] The names given to the Slave Coast ports in the contemporary sources are somewhat confusing. The names Offra and Jakin were originally applied to two distinct towns situated close together, but eventually these towns expanded in area until they formed a single conurbation: cf. Labat, *Voyage du Chevalier des Marchais*, ii. 284. The name Hueda, or in the usual English transcription 'Whydah', referred originally to a kingdom, but after the Dahomian conquest in 1727 it was commonly applied to the port of Grehue, which is the 'Ouidah' of modern maps. In the present work, to avoid confusion, the kingdom is referred to by the name Hueda, the port by the name Whydah.

[123] Cf. Newbury, *The Western Slave Coast and its Rulers*, 3, 18.

[124] Dapper's information on the kingdom of Itsekiri, further east, relates to the year 1644: Dapper, *Naukeurige Beschrijvinge der Afrikaensche Gewesten*, 507.

[125] Ibid. 492, 494.

[126] Ibid. 491, A French missionary in 1640 similarly reported that the 'Licomin' language was spoken in Benin: Ryder, *Benin and the Europeans*, 100.

[127] PRO, T.70/7, Baldwyn, Mabyn, and Barlow to Company, 9 Aug. 1723 (abstract); Snelgrave, *New Account of Some Parts of Guinea*, 89; AHU, doc. da

other variants are probably to be equated with 'Olukumi', a name known to have been applied to Yoruba-speakers in other contexts.[128] Dapper's kingdom seems therefore to have been Yoruba, and it seems probable, though it is not demonstrable beyond doubt, that it is Ọyọ.

This pattern of trade, whereby Ọyọ exported slaves through Allada and Hueda, was disrupted in the early eighteenth century. In 1717–18 the kings of both Hueda and Allada attempted to tighten up royal control of the slave trade in their kingdoms. In Hueda, a royal monopoly of the slave trade was established, with the appointment of a royal agent to whom all slaves brought by the hinterland traders had to be sold.[129] In Allada the king attempted to enforce a more limited monopoly, reserving the purchase of firearms and cowry shells to himself.[130] These measures hit at the interests of the hinterland suppliers of slaves, and one of these, Dahomey, responded vigorously. In order to secure access to the Atlantic trade, Agaja, the king of Dahomey, sent forces to conquer Allada in 1724 and Hueda in 1727, thus securing control of the ports of Jakin and Grehue.[131] From the point of view of the Ọyọ traders, however, Dahomian control over the coastal ports was disastrous. Although the Dahomians could now export their own slaves freely, they were initially uninterested in operating as middlemen between other hinterland suppliers and the European traders.[132] Indeed, Agaja's military operations disrupted the trade-routes by which the other hinterland peoples had been accustomed to bring their slaves to the

---

Bahia, 797, Theodozio Rodriguez da Costa to Viceroy of Brazil, 27 May 1753 cited in Verger, *Flux et Reflux de la Traite des Nègres*, 191.

[128] Cf. above, Ch. 2, p. 16 and n. 20. Note also that 'Ulkami' and Ọyọ are associated if not identified, by Barbot, *Description of the Coasts of North and South Guinea*, 352.

[129] Akinjogbin, *Dahomey and its Neighbours*, 51–2.   [130] Ibid. 59.

[131] For this view of Agaja's motives, see APB, O.R. 21, doc. 58, Francisco Pereyra Mendes to Viceroy of Brazil, 4 Apr. 1727, quoted in Verger, *Flux et Reflux de la Traite des Nègres*, 145; Snelgrave, *New Account of Some Parts of Guinea*, 5–6; Pruneau de Pommegorge, *Description de la Nigritie*, 154; Norris, *Memoirs of the Reign of Bossa Ahadee*, x–xi; Dalzel, *History of Dahomy*, 7–8. However, a rival interpretation holds that Agaja's original intention was not to secure his own access to the Atlantic slave trade, but rather to bring the slave trade to an end: J. Atkins, *A Voyage to Guinea, Brasil, and the West Indies* (London, 1735), 119–22; elaborated by Akinjogbin, *Dahomey and its Neighbours*, 73–81.

[132] As Snelgrave observed in 1727, Agaja 'drives no regular Trade in Slaves, but only sells such as he takes in his Wars': Snelgrave, *New Account of Some Parts of Guinea*, 125.

coast.[133] Agaja may even have sought deliberately to discourage other slave-traders, so as to secure a monopoly of the supply of slaves for himself.[134] The Ọyọ, therefore, found their access to the Atlantic trade seriously threatened. Initially Jakin, though tributary to Dahomey, remained open to Ọyọ traders: Snelgrave in 1727 found that Jakin was receiving slaves from 'Lucamee', i.e. probably Ọyọ.[135] But in 1732 Jakin in turn was destroyed by the Dahomians.

This threat to the commercial interests of the Ọyọ was probably one motive for their intervention against Agaja in 1726–30.[136] In 1730 Dahomey itself became tributary to Ọyọ, and either then or later the Ọyọ were able to resume the supply of slaves to Whydah (Grehue) through Dahomey. Explicit evidence for the sale of slaves by Ọyọ to Dahomey is lacking before the 1770s,[137] but it is clearly implied in the fact that a European observer in 1754 explained the dullness of trade at Whydah by reference to the political troubles inside Ọyọ.[138] However, there were considerations which discouraged Ọyọ traders from dealing with Dahomey, and led them to seek new ports further east outside Dahomian control. One account asserts that trade in Dahomey was disrupted by maladministration during the last years of Agaja's reign, in the 1730s.[139] Another avers that trade was driven east by 'the King of Dahomey monopolising the trade in slaves in his own dominions'.[140] According to Dalzel, it was Kpengla, king of Dahomey in 1774–89, who attempted to establish a royal monopoly of the slave trade, and compelled inland traders to sell their slaves to his agents at fixed prices.[141] This is

[133] Ibid. 130; cf. the complaints by Portuguese officials in 1729–30, quoted in Verger, *Flux et Reflux de la Traite des Nègres*, 148–50.

[134] For Agaja's monopolistic intentions, cf. the observation in 1724 that 'he wants Ships to come to some Place only for his Slaves': Bulfinch Lambe to Baldwyn, 27 Nov. 1724, in Smith, *New Voyage to Guinea*, 174.

[135] Snelgrave, *New Account of Some Parts of Guinea*, 89.

[136] Fage, *History of West Africa*, 104.

[137] In 1773 'Yahoe' (Ọyọ) appears in a list of countries supplying slaves and ivory for sale at Whydah: PRO, T.70/1532, 'An Account of the Forts belonging to the British and Forreign Nations on that part of Africa called Guinea', 30 Nov. 1773. The reference by Norris, *Memoirs of the Reign of Bossa Ahadee*, 138, to the Ọyọ selling slaves to the Dahomian traders probably also relates to the 1770s.

[138] PRO, T.70/1523, W. Devaynes to T. Melvil, 22 Oct. 1754 (extract), quoted in T. Melvil to Committee, 30 Nov. 1754.

[139] Labarthe, *Voyage à la côte de Guinée*, 116.

[140] Adams, *Remarks on the Country Extending from Cape Palmas*, 219.

[141] Dalzel, *History of Dahomy*, 213–14. This royal monopoly of the slave trade was apparently abandoned after Kpengla's death in 1789: ibid. 223–4.

corroborated by other contemporary accounts from the 1780s, which report that the king of Dahomey had closed his dominions to Ọyọ traders,[142] and that the Ọyọ preferred the eastern ports because 'they are allowed to come to trade at the coast.'[143] Probably Ọyọ traders in Dahomey were not permitted to proceed beyond the hinterland market town of Cana, and were prevented from dealing directly with the Europeans. Dalzel also records that foreign traders in Dahomey were forbidden to purchase commodities of military value—muskets, gunpowder, and iron.[144]

The Dahomians at Whydah increasingly lost trade to the ports further east. In the early 1730s the main centre of trade in the east was Apa, which had escaped conquest by Agaja,[145] but from about 1736 Apa was replaced by the new port of Badagry.[146] Other important eastern ports were Epe, where slaves had already been sold in the 1720s,[147] and Porto Novo, the port of the new kingdom of Allada, which was opened up in the 1750s.[148] Further east, Lagos began to develop as a slaving port, initially on a smaller scale, from the 1760s.[149] The kingdom of Wemẹ, in the hinterland, became important as a staging post on the trade-route to the new ports in the east.[150] The diversion of trade eastwards is already illustrated by a list of Portuguese ships outward bound from the Slave Coast calling at the island of Principe between 1760 and 1770: they include twenty-nine from Whydah, thirteen from Epe, twelve from Porto Novo, fourteen from Badagry, and two from Lagos.[151] The process was considerably accelerated by the monopolistic policy of Kpengla of Dahomey after 1774.[152] The Ọyọ were known by European traders to be the principal suppliers of slaves to the eastern ports.[153]

---

[142] AN, C.6/26, de Champagny, 'Mémoire contenant des observations sur quelques points de la Côte de Guinée ... et sur la possibilité d'y faire des établissemens', 6 Sept. 1786.

[143] Labarthe, *Voyage à la côte de Guinée*, 104.

[144] Dalzel, *History of Dahomy*, 214.

[145] Snelgrave, *A New Account of Some Parts of Guinea*, 156.

[146] Cf. above, Ch. 8, p. 175 and note 167.

[147] Cf. ARA, NBKG, 94, Elmina Journal, entry for 8 May 1727, in van Dantzig, *Dutch Documents Relating to the Gold Coast and the Slave Coast*, 148.

[148] P. Verger, *Bahia and the West Coast Trade (1549–1851)* (Ibadan, 1964), 23–4; cf. id., *Flux et Reflux de la Traite des Nègres*, 194.

[149] Law, 'The Dynastic Chronology of Lagos', 51.

[150] Dalzel, *History of Dahomy*, 214; cf. ibid. 192.

[151] Verger, *Bahia and the West Coast Trade*, 25–6.

[152] Dalzel, *History of Dahomy*, 214.

[153] AN, C.6/26, Ollivier de Montaguère to Ministre de Marine, 6 Oct. 1777.

The Yoruba colony established at Porto Novo during this period was no doubt connected with this trade.[154] The Ọyọ colonization of southern Ẹgbado, which seems to have taken place during the 1770s and 1780s, was probably intended to secure the approaches to the new ports.[155]

Kpengla's response to the decline of trade at Whydah was to seek to eliminate its rivals in the east by military action.[156] His contemporary on the Ọyọ throne, Abiọdun, appears to have reacted to this threat, for by 1777 he was extending his protection to Porto Novo and Badagry.[157] Subsequently, after war had broken out between Porto Novo and Badagry in 1781, Abiọdun resolved to exploit the situation in order to concentrate the slave trade under his own control at Porto Novo. Kpengla was enlisted as an ally, in the belief that Abiọdun's intention was to concentrate trade at Whydah, and that slaves brought to Porto Novo would be sent by canoe through the lagoons for sale at Whydah.[158] With the active co-operation of Porto Novo and the encouragement of Ọyọ, the Dahomians destroyed Epe in 1782, Badagry in 1784, and Wemẹ in 1786. But instead of trade being diverted to Whydah, Kpengla found that 'the King of Ardrah [Allada, i.e. Porto Novo] . . . stopped all communication with Whydah . . . and the Dahoman traders, who had been accustomed to visit Ardrah, were no more allowed that liberty.'[159] The effect of Kpengla's actions had therefore been to encourage further trade at Porto Novo while Whydah continued to languish.

Abiọdun's policy probably involved a substantial increase in the level of slave exports as well as the concentration of trade at Porto Novo. It appears that the volume of slaves exported from Ọyọ reached a peak in the 1780s, though the 1790s, with the outbreak of a

---

and id. to id., 30 Dec. 1780; ibid., Ollivier de Montaguère, 'Project d'établissemens à la Côte d'Afrique', 25 June 1786; AN, C.6/27 bis, Chenevert and Bullet, 'Reflexions sur Juda', 1776, cited by Akinjogbin, *Dahomey and its Neighbours*, 146; PRO, T.70/1545, L. Abson to R. Miles, 26 Sept. 1783.
[154] Akindele and Aguessy, *Contribution à l'étude de l'histoire de l'ancien royaume de Porto-Novo*, 71, 73. These Yoruba settlers are said to have arrived in Porto Novo during the reign there of De Messe, dated by Akindele and Aguessy to 1752–7, but the accuracy of these dates is uncertain. The Yoruba colonists are said to have introduced Islam into Porto Novo: ibid. 131.
[155] Cf. above, Ch. 6, pp. 93–5.
[156] Dalzel, *History of Dahomy*, 166; cf. above, Ch. 8, pp. 176ff.
[157] AN, C.6/26, Baud-Duchiron, 'Mémoire pour servir à faire de nouveaux établissemens à la Côte de Guinée', 23 July 1777.
[158] Dalzel, *History of Dahomy*, 206–7.
[159] Ibid. 207.

European war (1793) and the temporary abolition of the slave trade by France (1794–1802), brought a serious depression in the slave trade. Curtin has estimated that the number of slaves exported from the Bight of Benin increased from 71,200 in the decade 1771–80 to 144,600 in 1781–90, but fell back again to 68,700 in 1791–1800.[160] At the same time, the main centre of European activity on the Slave Coast tended to move eastwards from Porto Novo to Lagos, which began to develop as the principal slaving port in the area from the 1790s.[161] Initially the principal supply of slaves at Lagos was brought by canoe through the lagoons from Porto Novo,[162] so that Ọyọ traders could continue to bring their slaves to Porto Novo. Lagos did, however, have a secondary supply of slaves, through the eastern lagoon ports of Ikosi and Ikorodu, from the Ijẹbu kingdom.[163] The slaves obtained here seem to have come mainly from domestic Ijẹbu sources,[164] but the Ijẹbu were by now also trading with the Ọyọ through the market of Apomu.[165] The measures of *Alafin* Abiọdun to check the kidnapping of Ọyọ traders at Apomu will be recalled:[166] no doubt such kidnappings were perpetrated to supply the European slave traders at Lagos. The town of Ilugun, in northern Ẹgbaland, also served as a market for trade between the Ọyọ and Ijẹbu.[167] But trade with Ijẹbu was open, for Ọyọ traders, to the same objections as trade with Dahomey: the Ijẹbu were notoriously jealous of their position as middlemen, and did not permit traders from the interior to proceed beyond their frontier markets.[168]

Slaves were virtually the only commodity the Ọyọ had to offer in which the European traders were interested. The Europeans may also have purchased some Ọyọ cloth for re-sale on the Gold Coast or in Brazil,[169] and the Ọyọ may have supplied some ivory.[170] Palm

---

[160] P. D. Curtin, *The Atlantic Slave Trade: A Census* (Madison, 1969), 227–8.

[161] Adams, *Remarks on the Country Extending from Cape Palmas*, 218–19; cf. ibid. 96.

[162] Ibid. 96, 219–20.   [163] Ibid. 96, 220.

[164] At least, they are said to have been 'principally of the Jaboo nation': ibid. 220.

[165] Cf. above, pp. 218–19 and note 121.

[166] Johnson, *History of the Yorubas*, 189.

[167] CMS, CA2/021, J. Barber, Journal, 23 Nov. 1853.

[168] Johnson, *History of the Yorubas*, 567; cf. Bowdich, *Mission from Cape Coast to Ashantee*, 224–5.

[169] In the 1680s cloth from 'Concomi' (a mistake for 'Loncomi', i.e. Olukumi, or Yorubaland) was being purchased at Whydah for re-sale on the Gold Coast: 'Relation du Sieur du Casse sur son voyage de Guynée' (1687/8), in P. Roussier, *L'Établissement d'Issiny 1687–1702* (Paris, 1935), 15. An early nineteeth-century

oil was also being purchased by European traders at Whydah by the 1780s,[171] but not in any substantial quantities, and probably solely from Dahomian sources. Of the commodities which the Ọyọ obtained in exchange for their slaves, the importance of salt, which was extracted at the coast from sea water,[172] is apparent from the citations already made of the Ọyọ traditions concerning *Alafin* Ọbalokun[173] and of Dapper's account of the kingdom of 'Ulkami'.[174] The Ọyọ also obtained a variety of goods of European and American origin. These were mainly luxury goods, such as cloth,[175] earthenware,[176] beads (especially coral),[177] rum,[178] and tobacco.[179] But there were some European manufactures of practical utility, notably firearms,[180] and one raw material of considerable importance, namely iron bars.[181] The Ọyọ also obtained from the European traders the cowry shells which served as their currency.[182]

Some consideration seems necessary of the sources from which the Ọyọ obtained the large numbers of slaves they sold at the coast. Dapper distinguishes two categories among the slaves brought to Allada from 'Ulkami' in the seventeenth century: enslaved criminals and war captives.[183] Richard Lander confirms that those found guilty in Ọyọ of serious thefts were sold as slaves to the coast.[184] But

---

source refers to the export of Ọyọ cloth through Badagry to Brazil; PRO, C.O.2/15, H. Clapperton, 'Journal of the African Mission from Badagry to Jennah', entry for 6 Dec, 1825. Other evidence, however, indicates that the Europeans normally purchased Ijẹbu rather than Ọyọ cloth: Adams, *Remarks on the Country Extending from Cape Palmas*, 97; Robertson, *Notes on Africa*, 301.

[170] However, the main source of ivory in Yorubaland was not Ọyọ, but the Ekiti area: cf. Ojo, *Yoruba Culture*, 249.

[171] Norris, *Memoirs of the Reign of Bossa Ahadee*, 146.

[172] For the manufacture of salt at the coast, see e.g. Dapper, *Naukeurige Beschrijvinge der Afrikaensche Gewesten*, 489; Snelgrave, *New Account of Some Parts of Guinea*, 20; Robertson, *Notes on Africa*, 280.

[173] Johnson, *History of the Yorubas*, 168.

[174] Dapper, *Naukeurige Beschrijvinge der Afrikaensche Gewesten*, 492.

[175] Clapperton, *Journal of a Second Expedition*, 57.

[176] Ibid. 14; cf. R. and J. Lander, Journal of an Expedition, i. 180.

[177] Dalzel, *History of Dahomy*, 208–9; R. and J. Lander, *Journal of an Expedition*, i. 110, 180.

[178] Clapperton, *Journal of a Second Expedition*, 57.

[179] Ibid.; Adams, *Remarks on the Country Extending from Cape Palmas*, 262.

[180] R. Lander, *Records of Captain Clapperton's Last Expedition*, ii. 222.

[181] Cf. Adams, *Remarks on the Country Extending from Cape Palmas*, 238.

[182] Ibid. 264.

[183] Dapper, *Naukeurige Beschrijvinge der Afrikaensche Gewesten*, 494.

[184] R. Lander, *Records of Captain Clapperton's Last Expedition*, i. 283–4.

it seems unlikely that enslaved criminals can ever have accounted for a very significant proportion of the slaves sold by the Ọyọ. War captives, however, were certainly available in large numbers. An Ọyọ invasion of the Mahi country in *c.* 1810 is reported to have yielded, probably with some exaggeration, no less than 20,000 slaves for sale at Lagos.[185] Abson, Governor of the British fort at Whydah in the late eighteenth century, seems to have believed that war captives formed the major source of the slaves sold by the Ọyọ: in 1783, explaining a failure of slave supplies to the coast by reference to the defeat of an Ọyọ raid against the Bariba, he describes the Ọyọ as 'the people whose excursions used to give life and commerce to Porto Novo and Badagree'.[186] Morton-Williams has suggested that the eastern Yoruba, the Ijẹṣa, Ekiti, and Yagba, formed the principal 'slave reservoir' from which the Ọyọ raided slaves.[187] This seems improbable, in view of the evidence that Ọyọ invasions of Ijẹṣa and Ekiti country were decisively defeated.[188] More probably, Ọyọ slave raids were directed primarily against their northern and western neighbours.

To Dapper's two categories two others can be added. First, slaves might be paid to Ọyọ as tribute by its subjects. Dahomey is reported to have presented 600 slaves to Ọyọ in 1730, during negotiations for peace,[189] and subsequently the annual tribute of Dahomey to Ọyọ is said to have included forty-one men and forty-one women.[190] It does not seem likely, however, that the number of slaves obtained as tribute was very large.[191] Second, slaves could be obtained by trade, being purchased from neighbouring states. Many slaves were purchased, specifically from the northern neighbours of Ọyọ, the Nupe and Bariba. European traders in the 1780s were aware that the slaves sold at Porto Novo were supplied not only by the Ọyọ, but also by the Nupe and Bariba.[192] The missionary Schön, writing in

---

[185] Bowdich, *Mission from Cape Coast to Ashantee*, 226.

[186] PRO, T.70/1545, L. Abson to R. Miles, 26 Sept. 1783.

[187] Morton-Williams, 'The Ọyọ Yoruba and the Atlantic Trade', 27–8.

[188] Cf. above, Ch. 7, pp. 127–32.

[189] ADLA, C.739, Mallet de la Mine to du Premenil, 8 Jan. 1732.

[190] Cf. above, Ch. 8, p. 165.

[191] Akinjogbin, 'Prelude to the Yoruba Civil Wars', 30, suggests that the 'tributary' states of Nupe and Borgu were the 'main source' of slaves for Ọyọ. These states certainly supplied many slaves, but by trade rather than as tribute. It is very doubtful whether they were in fact tributary to Ọyọ: cf. above, Chapter 8, pp. 146–50.

[192] AN, C.6/26, Ollivier de Montaguère, 'Projet d'établissemens à la côte

1842, similarly asserts that 'nearly all' the liberated slaves of Nupe and Kakanda origin in Sierra Leone had been sold from Nupe to Ọyọ and thence to the coast.[193] Slaves came to Ọyọ, indeed, from even further afield. Adams, who was active as a trader on the coast between 1786 and 1800, refers to the large numbers of Hausa slaves brought to Porto Novo by Ọyọ traders.[194] The sale of Hausa slaves to the Ọyọ and their re-sale to Europeans at the coast is also mentioned (and condemned) in the *Infāq al-Maisūr* of Muhammad Bello of Sokoto, written in 1812.[195] It will be recalled that there were also numerous Hausa slaves employed for domestic purposes within the Ọyọ kingdom. In the nineteenth century, the Ọyọ were obtaining a few slaves from as far away as Bornu.[196]

It is uncertain whether the Ọyọ had always been so heavily dependent on the north for its supplies of slaves. It is to be noted that two lists of the nationalities of slaves sold at Whydah during the first half of the eighteenth century do not include any of the northern peoples.[197] This is hardly conclusive evidence, since northerners might easily be concealed in such lists by a process of 'naturalization', being lumped together with the people who sold them.[198] It does seem probable, however, that the large-scale purchase of Hausa slaves began only with the increased scale of Ọyọ slave exports in the later eighteenth century.[199] The increased volume of exports could,

d'Afrique', 25 June 1786; ibid., de la Flotte, 'Situation de la côte d'Afrique', 1787.   [193] Schön and Crowther, *Journals*, 139.

[194] Adams, *Remarks on the Country Extending from Cape Palmas*, 221–2.

[195] Arnett, *The Rise of the Sokoto Fulani*, 16.

[196] e.g. Ali Eisami, originally enslaved by the Fulani in Bornu, was sold via Hausaland and Borgu to Ọyọ in *c.* 1813, and thence to Porto Novo in *c.* 1817: Koelle, *Native African Literature*, 252–3; Curtin, *Africa Remembered*, 212. In 1826 the Onìṣàrẹ of Ijanna possessed two slaves from Bornu: Clapperton, *Journal of a Second Expedition*, 16, 51.

[197] Labat, *Voyage du Chevalier des Marchais*, ii. 125–9, writing of the 1720s, includes, of the peoples to the north of Hueda and Allada, only the 'Foin' (Fon, i.e. Dahomians), 'Ayois' (Ọyọ), and 'Nago' (Anago, i.e. the western Yoruba); AN, C.6/25, Pruneau and Guestard, 'Mémoire pour servir à l'intelligence du commerce de Juda', 18 Mar. 1750, include the Fon, the Mahi, and the Anago (here probably the Yoruba in general, including the Ọyọ).

[198] Cf. Curtin, *Atlantic Slave Trade*, 186–7, suggests that the term Anago was used in the eighteenth century to refer not only to Yoruba slaves, but to all slaves handled by the Ọyọ.

[199] Curtin, ibid. 188, analysing the ethnic origins of slaves in Saint Domingue in 1760–1800, finds the Bariba and Tapa (Nupe) already represented in the 1760s, while the Hausa and 'Gambary' appear only in the 1780s. The 'Gambary' are not, as Curtin supposes, the Gbari: *Gambari* is the usual Yoruba name for the Hausa.

perhaps, only be attained by expanding the area from which slaves were recruited.[200] At the same time, the increased distances over which slaves were brought to the coast would account for the substantial increase in the price of slaves during the eighteenth century.[201]

The slaves and other commodities purchased from the north were paid for, it appears, mainly by the re-export northwards of goods obtained at the coast from the European traders.[202] The re-export of cowry shells, in particular, probably played a large part in financing imports from the north.[203] To a considerable extent, therefore, the Ọyọ functioned as middlemen between the north and the coast, trading in commodities (slaves from the north, European goods from the coast) produced by others. The expansion of the Atlantic trade, by creating at once an increased demand for slaves from the north and the means (imported European goods) to purchase them, thus stimulated a substantial expansion of the older system of long-distance trade between Ọyọ and the north. The Atlantic trade probably also stimulated local trade in the Ọyọ kingdom. Although some of the imports (cloth, earthenware, iron bars) were in competition with local products, there is no evidence that this competition led to the decline of local crafts,[204] and probably the imported goods entering the domestic economy served rather to stimulate local production, by increasing effective demand.[205] Certainly, the importance of the importation of cowry shells in the Atlantic trade is difficult to understand except in terms of an expanding scale of local trade.

§5. THE ECONOMIC BASIS OF ỌYỌ POWER

In the foregoing analysis of the economy of the Ọyọ empire, far more space has been given to commerce than to production. This disparity is due primarily to the greater amount of evidence available on commerce, but it also reflects what has been a conventional view, that the power of Ọyọ was based on trade, and in particular upon its

[200] The tendency for slave-recruiting areas to expand inland in West Africa has been noted by Johnson, 'The Cowrie Currencies of West Africa', Part 2, 348–9.

[201] For this increase in slave prices, cf. Fage, History of West Africa, 91.

[202] Denham and Clapperton, Narrative of Travels and Discoveries, Clapperton's Narrative, 87.

[203] Cf. P. R. Lovejoy, 'Interregional Monetary Flows in the Precolonial Trade of Nigeria', JAH 15 (1974), 569.

[204] As suggested by Ajayi, 'Aftermath of the Fall of Old Ọyọ', 137.

[205] Cf. Hopkins, Economic History of West Africa, 121.

involvement in the Atlantic slave trade.[206] Against this view, Ajayi has maintained that the importance of trade for Qyọ and for Yoruba states generally has been greatly exaggerated. The Yoruba economy, he argues, was based on agriculture, not on trade, and 'the basic ingredients of power were land and taxable peasants'.[207] This formulation is somewhat infelicitous. In pre-colonial Yorubaland, land being an abundant resource, control of labour was more important than control of land, and wealth consisted in the possession of slaves rather than in the accumulation of acres.[208] Equally, as will appear below, there was little taxation of individual 'peasants' or of individual 'peasant' lineages. But if it is reformulated to assert that the 'basic ingredients of power' were, first, the labour of slaves employed in agricultural production, and second, the levying of tribute from subject communities,[209] Ajayi's view may appear to have much plausibility. It will be evaluated here by a detailed examination, first, of the major sources of income available to leading Qyọ chiefs, and in particular to the *Alafin*, and second, of the precise ways in which income from these various sources was related to 'power'.

In analysing the income of the *Alafin*, it is necessary to consider both his official revenues, derived from taxation, and his personal income, derived from the activities of his household. In the almost total absence of figures,[210] any analysis of the *Alafin*'s revenues from taxation must be speculative and impressionistic, but it is at least possible to identify the major sources of revenue.[211] It is convenient to consider separately the taxes levied in the Qyọ capital and the revenues derived from the empire.

---

[206] See e.g. Fage, 'States of the Guinea Forest'.

[207] Ajayi and Smith, *Yoruba Warfare in the Nineteenth Century*, 124–5; cf. J. F. A. Ajayi and R. A. Austen, 'Hopkins on Economic Imperialism in West Africa', *Economic History Review*, 25 (1972), 304.

[208] A. G. Hopkins, 'Economic Imperialism in West Africa: A Rejoinder', *Economic History Review*, 25 (1972), 309; cf. id., *Economic History of West Africa*, 26.

[209] Ajayi himself goes on to observe that 'Each state sought to win control over as many towns and villages as possible, and to tax them . . . [and] to capture slaves in war who were valuable both for work on the farms and service in the ranks of the armies': Ajayi and Smith, *Yoruba Warfare in the Nineteenth Century*, 125.

[210] And also, given that much of the *Alafin*'s revenues was paid in kind rather than in cash.

[211] A very useful survey of state revenues in Yorubaland is given by Fadipẹ, *Sociology of the Yoruba*, 219–23.

In the capital, the *Alafin*'s revenues included judicial fees and fines, certain dues connected with the Ṣango cult,[212] and a share of the slaves and other booty taken by the Ọyọ army.[213] There seems to have been no regular direct taxation of the city population, beyond the gifts which the *Alafin* received from his chiefs at the annual Bẹrẹ festival.[214] There was, however, a death duty on the property of wealthy citizens.[215] There were also regular indirect taxes, levied on the trade of the city. As Richard Lander observed in 1827,

The King of Katunga levies a tax on every one that enters the gates of Katunga with a load, of whatever it may consist, and also appoints persons to collect tribute from every person attending the market with any saleable commodity. The amount of duty is always governed by the value of the beast or article sold, which is determined by accredited agents: for example, a handsome horse imported from Borgoo, or any other country, is liable in the market to a tax of two thousand cowries.[216]

Of these two taxes, the market dues were collected by the *Osi Iwefa*,[217] the gate taxes by the *ilari*.[218] It is to be noted that, according to Lander, the market dues were paid in money (cowry shells) rather than in kind. Later evidence suggests that the gate taxes also were levied principally in cash: the main revenue came from merchants, paid in cowries, while local farmers bringing their crops into the city made only small payments in kind, which were appropriated for the maintenance of the gate-keepers.[219]

Outside the capital, the *Alafin* received revenues from the subordinate towns of the Ọyọ kingdom and from the dependencies

---

[212] The *Alafin* as head of the Ṣango cult received fines from those whose compounds were struck by lightning: cf. Johnson, *History of the Yorubas*, 190.

[213] CMS, CA2/031a, the Revd. S. Crowther to T. J. Hutchinson, 10 Sept. 1856.

[214] These seem to have consisted mainly of *bẹrẹ* grass for the thatching of the palace roofs: Johnson, *History of the Yorubas*, 50.

[215] Fadipẹ, *Sociology of the Yoruba*, 221 and n.1.

[216] R. Lander, *Records of Captain Clapperton's Last Expedition*, ii. 223.

[217] Johnson, *History of the Yorubas*, 59, 61; Morton-Williams, 'The Yoruba Kingdom of Oyo', 63.

[218] Johnson, *History of the Yoruba*, 62. At New Ọyọ, of the nine city gates, only six paid taxes to the *Alafin*, one each being allotted to the *Arẹmọ*, the *Baṣọrun*, and the *Aṣipa*: Fadipẹ, *Sociology of the Yoruba*, 219. It is not known whether there was a similar division at Ọyọ Ile, where according to Clapperton (*Journal of a Second Expedition*, 58) there were in all ten city gates.

[219] Johnson, *History of the Yorubas*, 91–2; Bowen, *Central Africa*, 318; Fadipẹ, *Sociology of the Yoruba*, 219–20. Extraordinary gate taxes in kind were also levied to supply provisions for military expeditions: Campbell, *Pilgrimage to My Motherland*, 78–9.

outside the kingdom such as Dahomey and the Ẹgba. These normally paid a fixed annual tribute.[220] Trade taxes were levied locally, but for the most part were not paid to the *Alafin*. An important exception, however, was the Ẹgbado province of the Ọyọ kingdom, where the *Alafin* established an elaborate system of turnpikes, at which tolls were exacted on goods passing along the roads leading to and from the important coastal ports of Porto Novo and Badagry.[221] It is impossible to estimate what proportion of the *Alafin*'s imperial revenues came from these trade taxes as opposed to the fixed tributes. But even these fixed tributes did not, as Ajayi appears to suppose, represent taxes on agricultural production as opposed to trade. A considerable proportion of the tributes was paid in cash—for example, Dahomey paid 400 bags of cowries (about $4,000) annually.[222] And part was paid in the form of imported European goods—for example, the tribute of Dahomey included coral, European cloth, muskets, and gunpowder[223] and that of Porto Novo consisted of 'the richest European commodities',[224] while within the Ọyọ kingdom Ilaṣe paid gunpowder, flints, and tobacco[225] and Ifọnyin 'cloths and other articles of European manufacture'.[226] This preference for taxes in money and trade goods rather than in agricultural produce was probably related in part to the high cost of transport, which made it uneconomical to move large quantities of basic foodstuffs from the outlying areas of the empire. But it probably also reflects a judgement that money and trade goods were more useful to the *Alafin* than an accumulation of agricultural produce. At any rate, it is clear that even in areas where the *Alafin* levied only direct taxes, these taxes fell upon wealth derived from trade as well as upon agricultural production.

The *Alafin*'s personal income was derived from the activities of the members of his household, primarily his wives and slaves. It is clear that these activities included trade as well as farming: as Crowther remarked of the *Alafin* at New Ọyọ in the 1850s, 'he employs some

[220] Cf. above, Ch. 6, pp. 99–100; Ch. 7, p. 139; Ch. 8, pp. 165–7, 179–80, 181–2.
[221] Cf. above, Ch. 6, pp. 116–17.
[222] Le Herissé, *L'Ancien Royaume de Dahomey*, 319; Bertho, 'La Parenté des Yoruba aux peuplades de Dahomey et Togo', 126.
[223] Ibid.; cf. above, Ch. 8, p. 165.
[224] Dalzel, *History of Dahomy*, 207.
[225] Thomas, 'Historical Survey of the Towns of Ilaro, Ilobi, Ajilete, and Ilashe', 106.
[226] Johnson, *History of the Yorubas*, 179.

of his people in trade and others in agriculture.'[227] The *Alafin*'s commercial activities were also noted by Clapperton and the Landers in 1826–30. They were struck by the large numbers of the *Alafin*'s wives, in one case a party of as many as a hundred, whom they met trading along the roads of the Ọyọ kingdom.[228] Richard Lander explains: 'After they have reached a *certain* age, the king's wives are set at liberty, and permitted to trade up and down the country in the various articles of native produce and manufacture; the profits of which are uniformly given to the sovereign.'[229] Despite these comments, it seems likely that these trading women were not all wives of the *Alafin*, but that the term *ayaba*, 'King's wives', is here, as often, being used to include female palace slaves.[230] The women traders met by Clapperton and the Landers were engaged in petty trade, dealing in cloth, natron, and salt. Trade in slaves, an occupation hardly suited to women, was presumably conducted by the *Alafin*'s male slaves.

Simpson has suggested that long-distance trade was in some sense a monopoly of the *Alafin*: 'external trade was almost the prerogative of his wives and slaves.'[231] However, there seems to be no evidence for the operation of any such royal monopoly. On the contrary, various items of evidence attest trading by others. Princes of the royal lineage engaged in trade: three *Alafin* (Odarawu, Abiọdun, and Awolẹ) are said to have been traders *before* their accession to the throne.[232] So also did the non-royal chiefs: one anecdote tells of a son of *Baṣọrun* Gaha trading in Ẹgbado,[233] while Johnson observes that most of the Ọyọ chiefs sent members of their lineages to trade at Ogodo, the main market for trade with the Nupe.[234] The *Alafin* did, however, secure competitive advantages for his agents. The Landers in 1830 noted that the *Alafin*'s trading wives were exempted from the payment of 'tribute [market dues?] and turnpike dues', and also had the right to maintenance by the chiefs of the towns through which they passed. To identify them, their goods were

[227] CMS, CA2/031a, the Revd. S. Crowther to T. J. Hutchinson, 10 Sept. 1856.

[228] Clapperton, *Journal of a Second Expedition*, 21; R. and J. Lander, *Journal of an Expedition*, i. 109–10.

[229] R. Lander, *Records of Captain Clapperton's Last Expedition*, ii. 197; cf. R. and J. Lander, *Journal of an Expedition*, i. 196.

[230] Cf. Johnson, *History of the Yorubas*, 63.

[231] Simpson, 'Intelligence Report on the Oyo Division', §50.

[232] Johnson, *History of the Yorubas*, 169, 187, 189.

[233] Hethersett, in *Iwe Kika Ẹkẹrin*, 62.

[234] Johnson, *History of the Yorubas*, 217.

wrapped in a special type of cloth, imitation of which by others was punishable by enslavement.[235]

The *Alafin*'s income thus comprised, on the one hand, the food-stuffs produced by his farm slaves and the trading profits of his commercial agents, and on the other, a variety of taxes which were paid mainly in the form of money and trade goods. The relative importance of these different sources of income is uncertain, but it is at least clear that a substantial proportion of the *Alafin*'s income was derived, directly or indirectly, from trade. However, to resolve the issue raised by Ajayi, it is also necessary to consider the political purposes for which wealth was required. It may be suggested that the military power of Ọyọ depended in large part on the existence of a body of specialist soldiers, the war-chiefs and their retainers, whose efficiency derived from their ability to devote much of their time to training. Equally, the effective power of the *Alafin* within Ọyọ depended above all on the creation of a large staff of palace slaves, which provided both a following with which to overawe the Ọyọ chiefs and an administrative staff through which the empire could be governed. Clearly, in order to maintain a specialist army and a royal administrative staff, it was first of all necessary to feed them, which involved the use of a substantial force of agricultural slaves to produce a surplus of foodstuffs for consumption by the palace and the chiefly households. To this extent, Ajayi's assertion that agri-culture was more important than trade is justified. Trade, however, was far from being irrelevant to political power. The military efficiency of the Ọyọ army during the imperial period depended primarily on its use of cavalry, and cavalry mounts were obtained by trade, from the countries to the north. Moreover, this was not merely a question of securing one strategic import. Horses had to be purchased, in large measure, by the re-export northwards of imported goods, so that the maintenance of a cavalry force depended upon profits derived from the Atlantic slave trade. Trade was also crucial for the *Alafin*'s authority within Ọyọ. First, the superior standard of life which the *Alafin* and his palace enjoyed through their access to trade goods was an important source of prestige. But more import-antly, the loyalty of the *Alafin*'s palace slaves depended in large part upon his ability to reward his agents by the distribution of money and trade goods, while the opposition of the chiefs outside the palace might be bought off by the same means.

[235] R. and J. Lander, *Journal of an Expedition*, i. 110; cf. ibid., i. 196.

§6. ECONOMIC DETERMINANTS OF NATIONAL POLICY

Part of Ajayi's intention in denying the importance of trade for the power of Yoruba states was to suggest that 'political' factors were more important than 'economic' factors in determining the policies of these states. In so far as an economic motivation was involved, in Ajayi's view, this was essentially predatory—the desire to exact tribute. It is not proposed here to pursue the debate about the primacy of political or economic 'factors' in Ọyọ history, since it is ultimately sterile. In this and in analogous contexts, what is presented as a disagreement about the motives of statesmen might be better approached as complementary analysis at different levels—in Marxian terms, those of base and superstructure.[236] But if, for purposes of analysis, we seek to isolate the economic objectives of Ọyọ policy, it is necessary to examine whether commercial as well as purely predatory considerations did not influence the policies of the successive *Alafin*.

The question is of especial interest, since Akinjogbin has sought to explain the political struggle between *Baṣọrun* Gaha and the *Alafin* from Labisi to Abiọdun as a dispute between those advocating further imperial expansion by military means, headed by Gaha, and those advocating concentration upon commerce, led by the *Alafin*.[237] This interpretation should be rejected, not only because the evidence in support of it is weak, but also because the implied incompatibility between military and commercial expansion is altogether unrealistic. Successful wars produced slaves for the traders, while successful trading was needed to procure horses for the soldiers. The territorial expansion of the Ọyọ empire could certainly have been directed towards commercial objectives, and it will be argued here that this was in fact the case.

It must be admitted that any discussion of the motives behind Ọyọ policies has to rest largely upon conjecture, and frequently upon circular reasoning. Lacking direct evidence of the considerations which the *Alafin* and his advisers pondered in their minds and urged

---

[236] e.g. Fage, 'Slavery and the Slave Trade in the Context of West African History', 402, refutes the view that the Atlantic slave trade encouraged warfare in West Africa by citing statements by the kings of Dahomey and Asante that they went to war, not in order to capture slaves, but for reasons of glory, prestige, etc. But it is possible to believe both that kings went to war for non-economic *motives*, and that the prevalence of values which encouraged warfare was a consequence of the economic importance of war, as a source of slaves.

[237] Akinjogbin, 'The Oyo Empire in the Eighteenth Century'.

in their deliberations, we tend to infer their motives from the actions which they authorized, and then to 'explain' these actions by the motives inferred from them. Commercial objectives have often been attributed to the expansionist policies of African rulers, both in the sense that wars were launched for the specific purpose of capturing slaves for sale to the European traders, and in the sense that these rulers sought to expand in order to secure control of important trade 1outes, either to guarantee access to commercial opportunities or to levy taxes upon merchants. In the case of Ọyọ, while it may be suggested that wars were undertaken in order to capture slaves, it cannot be proved, or even supported by a single piece of convincing direct evidence. Though wars certainly produced slaves, there were doubtless other good reasons for waging them. The case for supposing that Ọyọ expanded in order to control important trade routes is rather stronger, but even here the argument depends in large part upon presumption rather than upon direct evidence.

It is, in the first place, striking that Ọyọ only began to expand towards the south under *Alafin* Ajagbo, during the latter half of the seventeenth century, after contact had been established with the European traders at the coast. Earlier, there had been wars against the Nupe and Bariba to the north, and attempts to expand into Ijẹṣa and Ekiti country to the east, but no recorded aggressions towards the south. It may be speculated that Ọyọ expanded towards the coast in order to control the new trade routes.[238] But it is difficult to find explicit evidence to this effect. For example, the Ọyọ invasion of Allada in 1698, which has been seen as commercially motivated,[239] is said by our source to have been provoked by the murder of an Ọyọ ambassador.[240] Similarly, in the case of the Ọyọ wars against Dahomey between 1726 and 1730, no source, contemporary or traditional, suggests that they were waged in order to keep open Ọyọ access to the trade ports of the Slave Coast, though it is true that they do not offer any other explanation either.

A somewhat better supported case can be made out for commercial motives in the Ọyọ colonization of the Anago and Ẹgbado areas in the south-west of the Ọyọ kingdom. Morton-Williams has argued that the colonization of the Anago area around 1700 was intended to secure the route by which Ọyọ traders approached

---

[238] Cf. Fage, *History of West Africa*, 101; Smith, *Kingdoms of the Yoruba*, 45.
[239] Fage, *History of West Africa*, 102.
[240] Bosman, *New and Accurate Description of the Coast of Guinea*, 397.

Allada, while the colonization of the Ẹgbado area under *Başọrun* Gaha and *Alafin* Abiọdun was similarly intended to secure the approaches to the new ports in the east, Porto Novo and Badagry.[241] This again is largely speculation, though plausible speculation. The motive of such colonization would not be merely to secure political control of the routes, but also to establish agricultural settlements which could provision traders passing along them.[242] The elaborate arrangements made for the taxation of trade in the Ẹgbado province certainly attest that the *Alafin* were well aware of the commercial importance of the area. There is, moreover, at least one piece of evidence that explicitly supports the view of Morton-Williams: a statement in the traditions of the Ẹgbado town of Tibọ that the founder of that town had been sent by *Alafin* Abiọdun 'to make a narrow road from Ọyọ to Tibọ and then to Porto Novo.'[243] And finally, there seems no reason to question the testimony of Dalzel and other European contemporaries that the policy of Abiọdun towards the coastal Egun states in the 1770s and 1780s was motivated by commercial interest, by the desire to protect Ọyọ access to ports independent of Dahomey, and later to concentrate the slave trade through his own tributary port of Porto Novo.

It may be that Abiọdun, described by Dalzel as 'a very close-fisted and shrewd monarch',[244] was unusually commercially minded among *Alafin*. He is one of the *Alafin* whom tradition records to have lived as a trader before his accession.[245] But it is at least clear that the Ọyọ empire attained its greatest power and extent under an *Alafin* whose policies were closely tied to commercial considerations.

[241] Morton-Williams, 'The Ọyọ Yoruba and the Atlantic Trade'.

[242] I owe this point to Marion Johnson.

[243] Abẹokuta Divisional Archives, 'The History of Tibo Town in the Egba District', 1 July 1938, encl. to petition of *Balẹ* of Tibọ and others, asking for separation from Imala, 17 July 1947.

[244] Dalzel, *History of Dahomy*, 207.

[245] Johnson, *History of the Yorubas*, 187.

CHAPTER 11

Retrospect: the Rise of the Ọyọ Empire

IT is now possible to look back, and attempt a synthesis of the detailed topical studies undertaken in the previous seven chapters, in order to present a general interpretation of the rise of the Ọyọ empire. A general survey of the expansion of the Ọyọ empire is first offered, together with some speculations about possible explanations of its rise. This is followed by a consideration of the character, origins, and outcome of the process of political change within the Ọyọ kingdom which can be discerned during the period of imperial expansion.

§1. THE EXPANSION OF THE ỌYỌ EMPIRE

The recovery of Ọyọ power after the disaster of the Nupe invasion under *Alafin* Onigbogi can be traced through the sixteenth century, with the establishment of a new capital at Igboho, the defeat of further invasions by the Bariba and Nupe, and finally the reoccupation of the old capital at Ọyọ Ile by *Alafin* Abipa around the beginning of the seventeenth century. The extent of the Ọyọ kingdom at this time is a matter of speculation, but perhaps by the reign of Abipa it already extended in the east into Igbomina territory, and in the south-east to the River Ọṣun. Expansion to the south-west, on the other hand, had probably not yet proceeded very far: perhaps not beyond the Ẹkun Ọtun province centred on Ṣaki.

What is clear is that the recovery of Ọyọ power attested by the reoccupation of Ọyọ Ile was also manifested in the beginnings of the kingdom's imperial expansion. Initially, Ọyọ expansion was directed towards the east and the south-east. The repulse of the Nupe invaders had probably involved the taking of some territory from the Nupe in the Igbomina area. The first major expansionist venture, however, was unsuccessful. Under Abipa's successor Ọbalokun the Ọyọ attempted an invasion of Ijeṣaland, in eastern Yorubaland, but were decisively defeated. At about the same time, and probably in close

connection with this Ijẹṣa expedition, the Ọyọ apparently attempted
to establish their control over other eastern Yoruba peoples—the
Ekiti, and the kingdoms of Ondo and Idanre. But here too, they
were eventually defeated, with the assistance of the rival imperial
power of Benin.

Successful expansion was resumed under Ọbalokun's successor
Ajagbo, in the latter half of the seventeenth century, who may be
accounted the founder of the Ọyọ empire. By this time Ọyọ expansion
had been redirected towards the south and south-west. In the south,
Ajagbo fought campaigns in Ẹgbaland and Ijẹbu, and perhaps
initiated the subjection of the former area to Ọyọ rule. In the south-
west his forces campaigned in the Onko area, perhaps effecting the
extension or consolidation of the Ọyọ kingdom in this region, and
raided the Egun state of Wemẹ. Either during or soon after the
reign of Ajagbo, Ọyọ power also began to be felt beyond Wemẹ.
Wars were fought against the coastal kingdom of Allada between the
1660s and 1690s, and against Dahomey, to the north of Allada, in
the late seventeenth or early eighteenth century. The Ọyọ coloniz-
ization of the Anago area in the extreme south-west of the Ọyọ
kingdom seems also to have taken place around the beginning of the
eighteenth century. To the same period, presumably, belongs the
establishment of Ọyọ control or influence over the immediate western
neighbours of the Ọyọ kingdom, the Yoruba states of Ṣabẹ and Ketu.

The translation of Ọyọ military domination west of the River
Wemẹ into effective rule seems to have been an achievement of the
eighteenth century. The kingdom of Dahomey, which had conquered Allada and emerged as the dominant power in the area, was
compelled to pay tribute to Ọyọ after a protracted war fought in
1726–30. The conquest of Dahomey is attributed by Ọyọ tradition
to *Alafin* Ojigi, who can be said to stand second to Ajagbo as a
creator of the Ọyọ empire. Ojigi is also credited with a campaign
into Igbomina country to the east. The importance of his role in the
creation of the empire is indicated by the story that he sent forces to
demonstrate Ọyọ suzerainty over 'the whole of the Yoruba country,
including Benin', by carrying out a circumnavigation of the area.[1]
This tradition is hardly historical, but it is likely enough that by the
reign of Ojigi the Ọyọ had already begun to claim the traditional
headship of the Yoruba area, by representing the *Alafin* as the true
successor to the kingship of the legendary Oduduwa of Ile Ifẹ. While

[1] Johnson, *History of the Yorubas*, 174.

this claim was never fully endorsed by the other Yoruba states, the *Alafin*'s seniority of status was eventually acknowledged by some important kingdoms in eastern and southern Yorubaland, including Ileṣa, Ila, and Ijẹbu.

Ojigi did not, however, carry the Ọyọ empire to its greatest power and extent. Dahomey revolted, and had to be reconquered in a war fought in 1739–48. Further campaigning was also necessary in Ẹgbaland, under Ojigi's successor Gberu. Expansion continued under *Baṣọrun* Gaha, who usurped effective power at Ọyọ in 1754–74, and who was responsible for the Ọyọ colonization of the Ẹwọn area of northern Ẹgbado. The period of Gaha's rule apparently also saw Ọyọ forces operating far away to the west, close to the River Volta, where they are reported to have inflicted a defeat on the Asante in 1764. It was under *Alafin* Abiọdun, who overthrew Gaha in 1774 and ruled until his death in 1789, that the Ọyọ empire attained its greatest extent. Abiọdun organized the Ọyọ colonization of the southern Ẹgbado area around Ilaro, and exacted tribute from the coastal kingdom of Porto Novo. He also campaigned in Ẹgbaland, and effected the conquest, in 1788, of the Mahi country between Ṣabẹ and Dahomey.

The Ọyọ kingdom at its greatest extent was bounded by the River Opara in the west, by the Rivers Moshi and Niger in the north, and by the River Ọṣun to the south-east. In the east it extended into Igbomina country, while to the south-west it included the Anago and Ẹgbado and extended almost to the coast. Beyond the boundaries of the Ọyọ kingdom proper, the *Alafin* received tribute from several states in the west, notably Dahomey, Porto Novo, and the Mahi, while the kingdoms of Ṣabẹ and Ketu were allies if not subjects. In the north, Ọyọ may possibly have levied tribute from the southern-most portions of Nupe and Borgu. Ọyọ power to the south-east, among the eastern and southern Yoruba, was more limited, but the Ẹgba were tributary and the Owu were allies, while other states such as Ila, Ileṣa, and Ijẹbu loosely acknowledged the dynastic seniority of the *Alafin* of Ọyọ.

The evidence is hardly adequate to determine with any precision or confidence the factors which led to the rise of the Ọyọ empire, but some speculations may be offered. It is natural to consider, first, purely military factors. The organization of the Ọyọ army, and its dependence upon highly trained cavalry and archers, has been discussed in detail above. The use of cavalry in particular has often been indicated by modern scholars as the crucial factor in the rise of the Ọyọ empire.[2] As has been seen earlier, it is possible that the Ọyọ adopted the use of cavalry during the sixteenth century, under the stimulus of the Nupe conquest, and that it was this adoption of cavalry which made possible the rapid recovery of Ọyọ power after that disaster. This is somewhat speculative, but it is clear enough that the possession of cavalry was an important factor in the success of Ọyọ expansion towards the south-west, in the late seventeenth and early eighteenth centuries. The dependence of Ọyọ upon cavalry can, indeed, be invoked to explain not merely the general success, but also the specific direction of Ọyọ expansion. The Ọyọ were thus able to impose their control in the south-west, where the country was open and suited to the operation of cavalry forces, but failed in their invasions of the forest area of Ijẹṣaland and the hilly country of Ekiti.[3]

Beyond military factors lie economic factors, and the rise of Ọyọ can also be connected with its participation in expanding long-distance commerce. Some modern scholars have tried to link the rise of Ọyọ with its involvement in trade with the major states of the Sudan, further north,[4] and this can be supported to the extent that the horses used by the Ọyọ cavalry from the sixteenth century onwards were imported from the north. However, a better-supported case can be made out for linking the rise of Ọyọ with its involvement in the Atlantic slave trade, which began during the seventeenth century. It is noteworthy that the establishment of contact with the European traders at the coast, under *Alafin* Ọbalokun, was quickly followed by the beginnings of imperial expansion, under Ọbalokun's successor Ajagbo. The connection between commercial and imperial expansion can be traced at two levels. First, the rulers of Ọyọ sought to extend their political control over areas of commercial importance, in order to enjoy the benefits of trade. Thus, the diversion of Ọyọ expansion towards the south-west may represent a desire to gain control of the new trade routes to the coast.[5] Second, and more important, the wealth derived from trade was itself a source of

[2] e.g. Ajayi and Smith, *Yoruba Warfare in the Nineteenth Century*, 3–4; Smith, *Kingdoms of the Yoruba*, 122–3; Webster and Boahen, *West Africa since 1800*, 92; cf. Law, 'A West African Cavalry State', 7–9.

[3] Ajayi and Smith, *Yoruba Warfare in the Nineteenth Century*, 4.

[4] Ibid. 3; Davidson, *Africa in History*, 167; Akinjogbin, 'The Expansion of Ọyọ and the Rise of Dahomey', 380.

[5] Fage, *History of West Africa*, 101; Smith *Kingdoms of the Yoruba*, 45.

power. This was so both in general terms, the revenues from trade and taxes on trade increasing the prestige and powers of patronage of the *Alafin*, and in the specific sense that vital military resources were secured through trade. Horses for the Ọyọ cavalry were purchased, as has been seen, from the north: but increasingly they were paid for with European goods obtained at the coast in exchange for slaves. The military successes of Ajagbo and his successors were thus financed directly out of the proceeds of the Atlantic slave trade.

§2. POLITICAL CHANGE

The newly acquired empire of the Ọyọ could be held only if an effective machinery could be created for its administration. Parallel with the process of territorial expansion, it is possible to trace a process of political change in Ọyọ during the seventeenth and eighteenth centuries. The essential character of this process was the progressive strengthening of the effective power of the *Alafin*, *vis-à-vis* both the *Ọyọ Mesi* in the capital and the subordinate rulers in the provinces, through the expansion of the staff of slave officials attached to the palace. The palace slaves were used above all in the administration of the expanding empire: the *ajẹlẹ* who resided in the provincial towns of the Ọyọ kingdom were recruited from the palace slaves, while the collection of tribute from outside the kingdom, for example in Ẹgbaland and Dahomey, seems to have been organized by the *ilari*, the *Alafin*'s palace messengers. The creation of the title of *Arẹ Ọna Kakamfo*, a post of *ilari* status, by *Alafin* Ajagbo, is to be seen as part of the same process, establishing royal control of the military forces of the provincial towns.

The process of centralization is probably closely connected with that of imperial expansion. The connection is twofold. First, the territorial expansion of the empire created administrative problems, to which centralization was a response.[6] And second, the process of imperial expansion created the resources which made centralization possible. Successful wars yielded slaves, who could be incorporated into the palace bureaucracy as well as being sold or put to work in the farms. And the revenues from tribute and the expanding slave trade yielded wealth in luxury goods which the *Alafin* could distribute in order to secure the loyalty of his personal staff.

This increasing centralization of power, it is suggested, is the explanation of the dissensions inside the Ọyọ capital which began

[6] Cf. Crowder, *Story of Nigeria*, 113–14.

under Ajagbo's successor Odarawu and continued throughout the imperial period. The *Ọyọ Mesi* sought to resist the growth in royal power, since it threatened their own status and power. They resisted to some effect, and in 1754 *Baṣọrun* Gaha was able to usurp effective power in the capital, take over the administration of the empire, and appropriate the imperial revenues. The *Alafin* was only able to recover power, in 1774, by invoking the aid of the *Arẹ Ọna Kakamfo* and the provincial towns against the capital. And even this, as will be seen in subsequent chapters, did not resolve the issue in the long term in the *Alafin*'s favour.

If the resentment of the *Ọyọ Mesi* is intelligible, it is perhaps less easy to understand how they were able to retain sufficient power to resist the growth of royal power so long and so effectively. It is important to note that the *Ọyọ Mesi* themselves were not wholly excluded from the profits of imperial expansion. There was no royal monopoly of the slave trade, and the *Ọyọ Mesi* shared with the *Alafin* in the booty taken by the Ọyọ army and in the tribute paid by the provincial towns of the Ọyọ kingdom, if not in that of the tributaries outside the kingdom. The *Ọyọ Mesi* also retained control of the principal military force of the capital, the seventy *Ẹṣọ* and their retainers. To cite these limitations of centralization as explanations of the failure of centralization would, however, be circular. For the question remains: why were the *Alafin* unable to exclude the *Ọyọ Mesi* altogether from wealth and power? This question, which is crucial to an understanding of the ultimate collapse of the Ọyọ empire, will be returned to in a concluding chapter, but here it may be repeated that one important constraint on the elimination of chiefly power was probably the dependence of Ọyọ upon the use of cavalry.[7] The purchase and maintenance of horses being highly expensive, the maintenance of a cavalry force was perhaps beyond the means of the *Alafin* alone, so that the *Ọyọ Mesi* could not easily be dispensed with in the raising of a powerful army.

The recovery of power by *Alafin* Abiọdun in 1774 had not, in fact, resolved the struggle for power in the capital, although the involvement of the *Arẹ Ọna Kakamfo* in the disputes had introduced a new and complicating factor into the situation. The further development of these political troubles will be the subject of the following chapters.

[7] Goody, *Technology, Tradition and the State in Africa*, 50–3; cf. Morton-Williams, 'The Influence of Habitat and Trade on Oyo and Ashanti', 91, 96; Ajayi, 'Aftermath of the Fall of Old Ọyọ', 139–40; Law, 'A West African Cavalry State', 11–13.

PART III

THE FALL OF THE ǪYǪ EMPIRE (*c*. 1790–*c*. 1836)

CHAPTER 12

Collapse at the Centre
c. 1790–*c.* 1823

IT has been shown in earlier chapters that the Ọyọ empire attained its greatest extent and power only in the 1780s, during the reign of *Alafin* Abiọdun. The greatness of Ọyọ was ephemeral, for the 1780s also saw the first signs of a weakening of the power of Ọyọ, in its relations with its northern neighbours, the Bariba and Nupe. In 1783 the Ọyọ suffered a crushing defeat in an attack on the Bariba kingdom of Kaiama. By the end of the 1780s Ọyọ was paying tribute to Nupe, and in 1790 an attempt to end this subjection was bloodily defeated.[1] In later Ọyọ tradition, indeed, Abiọdun is presented as the last *Alafin* to maintain the unity and strength of the empire.[2] His successor as *Alafin*, Awolẹ, was a weaker man, who was eventually overthrown by a rebellion of his own chiefs. The collapse of the Ọyọ empire is held to have begun with the overthrow of Awolẹ: specifically, the destruction of the Ọyọ kingdom is presented as the working out of a curse which Awolẹ pronounced upon his disloyal subjects.[3]

The traditions no doubt exaggerate the contrast between the state of Ọyọ under Abiọdun and its condition under Awolẹ: the weakening of Ọyọ on its northern frontiers certainly began during Abiọdun's reign. They also overemphasize the importance of the personal qualities of the two kings in determining the course of Ọyọ history. However, the picture they present is essentially accurate, in that the collapse of Ọyọ power began at the centre, with rebellion and civil war in the heart of the Ọyọ kingdom. The overthrow of Awolẹ was followed by the revolt of important provincial towns, notably Ilọrin under its ruler Afọnja. Subsequently there was also a rebellion, fomented by Afọnja, of the Muslim elements in the Ọyọ kingdom— pastoral Fulani, Hausa slaves, and Ọyọ converts: Afọnja himself was

---

[1] Cf. below, Ch. 13, pp. 261–6.

[2] Johnson, *History of the Yorubas*, 187; cf. Crowther, *Vocabulary of the Yoruba Language*, iv; Hethersett, in *Iwe Kika Ẹkẹrin*, 56.

[3] Johnson, *History of the Yorubas*, 192; cf. Hethersett, in *Iwe Kika Ẹkẹrin*, 59; Adeyẹmi, *Iwe Itan Ọyọ*, 10.

eventually killed by his Muslim allies, and control of Ilọrin passed to the Fulani. All these developments were essentially internal to the Ọyọ kingdom, and any consideration of the decline and fall of the Ọyọ empire must begin with an examination of this collapse at the centre.

§1. CHRONOLOGICAL PROBLEMS

Explanation and interpretation must be preceded by a determination of the actual sequence of events, but here as elsewhere in the history of Ọyọ, a precise chronology is exceedingly difficult to establish. Besides many minor problems, the major issue concerns the chronological relationship of Afọnja's original revolt against Ọyọ rule, which followed immediately after the overthrow of Awọlẹ, and the Muslim rebellion which he subsequently incited. At least two widely different reconstructions are possible.[4]

For a long time it was customary to place the overthrow of Awọlẹ, the revolt of Afọnja, and the Muslim rebellion closely together, in or about the year 1817.[5] The date 1817 appears to derive ultimately from Ilọrin sources, in which it is offered as the date of Afọnja's alliance with the Fulani and incitement of the revolt of the Hausa slaves.[6] Since the Muslims of Ilọrin will probably have kept written records in Arabic, it is possible that this date derives from contemporary or nearly contemporary written sources. Certainly, other evidence suggests that it is accurate. In particular, there is the testimony of Ali Eisami (recorded *c.* 1850), who was resident at Ọyọ as a slave at the time, that at a date which can be calculated as around 1817, 'a war arose: now, all the slaves who went to the war, became free; so when the slaves heard these good news, they all ran there', a circumstance which caused Ali Eisami's owner to sell him to the European traders at the coast before he too should run away.[7] This must be an allusion to the revolt of Hausa slaves incited by Afọnja. The dating of this revolt to *c.* 1817 is also consistent with the testimony of Samuel Crowther, that his home town Ọṣogun was destroyed by an army of Fulani, Muslim Ọyọ, and runaway slaves in

[4] For fuller discussion of the chronological problems of this period, see Law, 'Chronology of the Yoruba Wars'; for earlier reconstructions, cf. Bascom, 'The Fall of Old Oyo'; Smith, *Kingdoms of the Yoruba*, 148–52; I. A. Akinjogbin, 'A Chronology of Yoruba History, 1789–1840', *Odu*, 2nd series, 2.2 (1966), 81–6.

[5] This reconstruction appears first in Temple, *Notes on ... the Northern Provinces of Nigeria*, 446–7.

[6] Burdon, *Northern Nigeria*, 15; Elphinstone, *Gazetteer of Ilorin Province*, 15.

[7] Koelle, *Native African Literature*, 252–3; Curtin, *Africa Remembered*, 212–13.

1821, and that similar raids had been going on for 'some years' previously.[8] Clapperton, however, was told in January 1826 that the Hausa slaves at Ilọrin had been in revolt for two years.[9] Since, in view of the evidence of Ali Eisami and Crowther, this can hardly refer to the original slave revolt, probably Clapperton's informants meant to date the subsequent overthrow of Afọnja and seizure of power in Ilọrin by the Fulani and Hausa, which can therefore be placed in c. 1823–4.[10]

It has commonly been believed that Afọnja's incitement of the rebellion of Fulani, Hausa slaves, and Ọyọ Muslims followed soon after the overthrow of *Alafin* Awọlẹ, which has therefore also been placed in 1817. However, this date is inconsistent with evidence recently discovered by Akinjogbin relating to the death of Awọlẹ's predecessor Abiọdun. As has already been seen, a contemporary European source reports the death of a king of Ọyọ, who must be identified with Abiọdun, in April 1789.[11] The nineteenth-century sources, beginning with Crowther in the 1840s, agree that Awọlẹ reigned for seven years,[12] which would indicate that his reign ended in c. 1796 rather than in 1817. It is necessary, therefore, either to reject the evidence suggesting that Abiọdun died in 1789, or to accept that an interval of about twenty years separated Afọnja's overthrow of Awọlẹ and his initial revolt against Ọyọ from his incitement of the Muslim rebellion.

The report of an *Alafin*'s death in 1789 cannot be treated as sacrosanct, since, although contemporary, it is based on hearsay, and might merely be repeating a false rumour. However, it should only be rejected if it is felt that an interval of twenty years between the death of Awọlẹ and the Muslim rebellion is unacceptable in the light of our other evidence. Samuel Johnson certainly places the alliance of Afọnja with the Muslim elements immediately after the death of Awọlẹ,[13] but it is noteworthy that our earliest account of these events, that compiled by Crowther in the 1840s, makes no

[8] Schön and Crowther, *Journals*, 371–2; Curtin, *Africa Remembered*, 299.

[9] Clapperton, *Journal of a Second Expedition*, 28; cf. R. Lander, *Records of Captain Clapperton's Last Expedition*, i. 96.

[10] Cf. Smith, *Kingdoms of the Yoruba*, 148–9.

[11] AN, C.6/26, Gourg to Ministre de Marine, 8 June 1789; Akinjogbin, *Dahomey and its Neighbours*, 175, n.1; cf. above, Ch. 4, p. 54.

[12] Crowther, *Vocabulary of the Yoruba Language*, v; Hethersett, in *Iwe Kika Ẹkẹrin*, 69; Johnson, *History of the Yorubas*, 192.

[13] Johnson, *History of the Yorubas*, 193–4; cf. Hethersett, in *Iwe Kika Ẹkẹrin*, 73.

reference to the Muslim elements in connection with the overthrow of Awọlẹ and its immediate aftermath, and mentions Afọnja's alliance with them only in a later context.[14] In the light of Crowther's evidence, it seems permissible to accept both 1789 for the date of the death of Abiọdun (and hence c. 1796 for that of Awọlẹ) and 1817 for the date of the Muslim rebellion, and these dates will be adopted in the account that follows.

§2. THE REIGN OF AWOLẸ (1789–c. 1796)

At the death of Abiọdun in April 1789, it immediately became apparent that the political dissensions inside the Ọyọ capital were far from being over. It might have appeared that Abiọdun, by using force to overthrow Baṣọrun Gaha in 1774, had finally crushed the power of the Ọyọ Mesi and secured a royal autocracy. But the selection of a new Alafin to succeed Abiọdun provided an opportunity, which was not neglected, for the Ọyọ Mesi to reclaim their influence. Abiọdun's Arẹmọ, Adeṣina, put forward a claim to the throne, possibly believing that the restoration of succession by primogeniture was the logical corollary to the establishment of royal power in 1774. The Ọyọ Mesi, however, rejected Adeṣina, alleging that he had poisoned his father Abiọdun, and conferred the throne instead upon Awọlẹ. Adeṣina was obliged to commit suicide,[15] and Abiọdun's other children were driven out of Ọyọ.[16]

Awọlẹ is presented in the traditions as a weak character, 'too weak for the times',[17] easily overborne against his better judgement by his advisers, and even by his wives. It seems probable, indeed, that he was made Alafin precisely because of his weakness: the Ọyọ Mesi may have felt that they would be able to dominate him. Awọlẹ was a son of Agboluaje, the pliant Alafin who had allowed Baṣọrun Gaha to become the effective ruler of Ọyọ,[18] and this was no doubt remembered.

However, although weak, Awọlẹ appears to have been dominated by his personal advisers, his kinsmen and senior eunuchs, rather than by the Baṣọrun and the Ọyọ Mesi. Certainly, he was soon at odds with his chiefs. He quarrelled with the Baṣọrun, Aṣamu, when the

---

[14] Crowther, *Vocabulary of the Yoruba Language*, v–vii.

[15] For Adeṣina's claim to the succession and suicide, see Johnson, *History of the Yorubas*, 187; Hethersett, in *Iwe Kika Ẹkẹrin*, 59–60; cf. Oyerinde, *Iwe Itan Ogbomọṣọ*, 23.

[16] Johnson, *History of the Yorubas*, 274.   [17] Ibid. 188.

[18] For Awọlẹ's parentage, see Adeyemi, *Iwe Itan Ọyọ*, 9.

latter instigated or connived at the robbing of a Hausa trader at Ọyọ, on the pretext that 'he was bringing bad charms into the city': Awọlẹ ordered restitution of the stolen goods, but the trader's Quran, which had no doubt been the principal cause of offence, was not returned. Awọlẹ also quarrelled with Lafianu, the *Owota* (one of the senior *Ẹsọ*), by ordering the execution of a man whom the *Owota* had taken under his protection.[19]

The experience of 1774 had shown that an *Alafin* could overcome the hostility of the chiefs of the capital, if he commanded the loyalty of the provinces. But Awọlẹ was unfortunate or foolish enough to quarrel also with the *Arẹ Ọna Kakamfo*, who at this time was Afọnja, the ruler of Ilọrin. Afọnja's family had played a prominent part in the recent disturbances in the Ọyọ kingdom: his grandfather, Paṣin, had died in revolt against *Baṣọrun* Gaha,[20] and his father, Alagbin, had joined the army which overthrew Gaha in 1774.[21] Afọnja was also connected in the female line with the royal family of Ọyọ.[22] He had apparently been appointed to the title of *Arẹ Ọna Kakamfo* by *Alafin* Abiọdun shortly before the latter's death.[23] Awọlẹ had an old grievance against Afọnja, because he had been punished by him for misbehaviour at Ilọrin on a visit there before his accession to the throne.[24] Moreover, Afọnja, by virtue of his relationship to the royal family of Ọyọ, had apparently conceived an ambition to become *Alafin* himself in place of Awọlẹ.[25]

The event that finally provoked Awọlẹ's chiefs into revolt had its origins in a machiavellian plan to destroy Afọnja. Awọlẹ was persuaded by his advisers to order Afọnja to attack the reputedly

[19] Johnson, *History of the Yorubas*, 190–1. Awọlẹ is also said to have executed a chief called Ẹdun Awonnu: Adeyẹmi, *Iwe Itan Ọyọ*, 9.

[20] Johnson, *History of the Yorubas*, 199–200.   [21] Ibid. 194.

[22] For differing versions of Afọnja's connection with the Ọyọ royal family, see Ojo, *Short History of Ilorin*, 9; Hermon-Hodge, *Gazetteer of Ilorin Province*, 64. Crowther, *Vocabulary of the Yoruba Language*, v, calls Afọnja the 'nephew' of Awọlẹ. Another version, which probably derives from the propaganda of Afọnja's enemies, denies that Afọnja was of royal ancestry and claims that his mother was merely a palace slave: Johnson, *History of the Yorubas*, 200.

[23] Ojo, *Short History of Ilorin*, 10. This seems more plausible than the statement of Crowther, *Vocabulary of the Yoruba Language*, v, that Afọnja had been appointed by Awọlẹ himself.

[24] J. B. Wood, *Historical Notices of Lagos, West Africa* (2nd edn., Lagos, 1933), 24; Hethersett, in *Iwe Kika Ẹkẹrin*, 67.

[25] Crowther, *Vocabulary of the Yoruba Language*, v; cf. the Hausa manuscript translated in Mischlich and Lippert, 'Beiträge zur Geschichte der Haussastaaten', 241. However, Johnson, *History of the Yorubas*, 193, denies that Afọnja aspired to the Ọyọ throne.

impregnable town of Iwere, in the Onko province of the kingdom,[26] allegedly on the calculation that Afọnja would be defeated, and would thereby be obliged to commit suicide. The choice of Iwere was unfortunate, since it was the town of Abiọdun's mother, and Afọnja was able to remind the Ọyọ war-chiefs that many of them owed their titles to Abiọdun.[27] A mutiny was arranged between Afọnja and the *Onikoyi* of Ikoyi, Adegun, among the provincial chiefs, and *Baṣọrun* Aṣamu and *Owota* Lafianu among the metropolitan chiefs. Instead of besieging Iwere, the army marched to Ọyọ, and presented a demand for Awọlẹ's suicide. Awọlẹ, having pronounced his curse upon his disloyal subjects, took poison. The army entered Ọyọ and ransacked the palace, and then dispersed.[28]

§3. THE REVOLT OF ILỌRIN

The *coup d'état* against Awọlẹ quickly evolved into a rebellion by the provinces against the capital. Afọnja had supported the *Ọyọ Mesi* in removing Awọlẹ in the expectation that he himself would be chosen as *Alafin* in his place. However, the *Ọyọ Mesi* selected instead a prince called Adebo. This is hardly surprising: the *Ọyọ Mesi* could have no interest in appointing a strong man such as Afọnja as *Alafin*. But Afọnja declined to accept his disappointment meekly. He at once repudiated his allegiance to Ọyọ, and set about carving out an independent kingdom for himself. He formed an alliance with the *Olupo* of Ajaṣẹ Ipo, the principal ruler in the Igbomina province of the Ọyọ kingdom, and in co-operation with him began the reduction of the towns of the Igbomina province, expelling the *Alafin*'s *ajẹlẹ* and installing his own.[29] Afọnja's example was followed by at least one other important provincial ruler. Ọpẹlẹ, the *Balẹ* of Gbogun, who had played a leading role in the mutiny at Iwere, also revolted, and began attacking and reducing

---

[26] For the location of Iwere, cf. R. Law, 'Iwere', *JHSN* 6.2 (1972), 239–41.

[27] Adeyẹmi, *Iwe Itan Ọyọ*, 9; cf. Crowther, *Vocabulary of the Yoruba Language*, v. Johnson by an error describes Iwere as the 'maternal town' not of Abiọdun but of *Alafin* Ajagbo: Johnson, *History of the Yorubas*, 192.

[28] For the *coup d'état* against Awọlẹ, see Crowther, *Vocabulary of the Yoruba Language*, v; Hethersett, in *Iwe Kike Ẹkẹrin*, 66–9; Johnson, *History of the Yorubas*, 191–3; Adeyẹmi, *Iwe Itan Ọyọ*, 9–10. What seems to be an account of this *coup* was heard by Bowdich at Kumasi in 1817: Bowdich, *Mission from Cape Coast to Ashantee*, 209.

[29] For Afọnja's revolt, see Johnson, *History of the Yorubas*, 193–4; Crowther, *Vocabulary of the Yoruba Language*, v. For his campaigns in Igbomina, cf. also Ojo, *Short History of Ilorin*, 15; Hethersett, in *Iwe Kika Ẹkẹrin*, 74–5.

neighbouring towns. After taking Idofian and Igbo Owu, however, Ọpẹlẹ was killed while besieging Igboho.[30]

At this crisis the situation was further complicated by the intervention at Ọyọ of a son of *Baṣọrun* Gaha called Ojo Agunbambaru, who had escaped the massacre of Gaha's kinsmen in 1774 and taken refuge among the Bariba. Ojo now appeared at Ọyọ with a force of Bariba archers and, ostensibly espousing the cause of the *Alafin*, proceeded to a massacre of chiefs alleged to be friendly to Afọnja, including for good measure many of his late father's enemies. About a hundred chiefs are said to have been killed, including *Owota* Lafianu. Ojo then summoned the loyal provincial forces and marched against Ilọrin. After early successes, however, he was defeated, largely through the treachery of Adegun, the *Onikoyi*, who feared that he too might be marked down for destruction. Ojo was then obliged to retire again to the Bariba country.[31]

Ojo having departed, *Alafin* Adebo tried his own hand at reducing the rebel towns. He sent forces to besiege Gbogun, but before this town could be taken, Adebo died at Ọyọ, having reigned for only 120 days. Rumour claimed that he had died by poison, either by suicide or murder.[32] The *Ọyọ Mesi* then conferred the throne upon Maku. One account describes Maku as a 'friend of Afọnja',[33] and his election may have been intended to conciliate Afọnja. If so, however, it was ineffective, for Afọnja declined to acknowledge Maku's authority.[34]

Meanwhile, it appears that even the threat of Afọnja's revolt had not sufficed to end the tension within the capital between the *Alafin* and the *Ọyọ Mesi*. Details of the struggles inside the capital at this period are lost, but it is recorded that during the brief reigns of Adebo and Maku there were no less than three holders of the *Baṣọrun* title. Aṣamu, who had taken part in the overthrow of Awole, was succeeded by a certain Alobitoki, who significantly is said to have belonged to a different lineage. Presumably, as in the time of *Alafin*

---

[30] Johnson, *History of the Yorubas*, 193. A somewhat different account of Ọpẹlẹ's death is given by Crowther, *Vocabulary of the Yoruba Language*, vi.

[31] Johnson, *History of the Yorubas*, 194–5; cf. Hethersett, in *Iwe Kika Ẹkẹrin*, 71–3.

[32] Johnson, *History of the Yorubas*, 196. For rumours of poisoning, cf. Crowther, *Vocabulary of the Yoruba Language*, v; Ojo, *Short History of Ilorin*, 16.

[33] Crowther, *Vocabulary of the Yoruba Language*, v.

[34] Cf. the exchange of messages between Afọnja and Maku, recorded by Johnson, *History of the Yorubas*, 196; Hethersett, in *Iwe Kika Ẹkẹrin*, 70.

Gberu and *Baṣọrun* Jambu,[35] this was an attempt by the *Alafin* to secure a co-operative *Baṣọrun*. However, Alobitoki apparently held the title only briefly, and on his death or removal the title was recovered by the old line, being conferred on a grandson of *Baṣọrun* Gaha called Ojo Aburumaku.[36] In these circumstances, *Alafin* Maku apparently had little confidence in the loyalty of the metropolitan chiefs, and decided to command the Ọyọ army in person, a practice long in abeyance. For reasons not indicated, Maku attacked a town called Iworo, in the south-east, of the kingdom, but was defeated. The *Ọyọ Mesi* made this an excuse for demanding his suicide, and Maku was obliged to comply, having reigned for only three months.[37]

The rapid removal of Adebo and Maku was followed by an interregnum at Ọyọ, during which *Baṣọrun* Ojo Aburumaku ruled as Regent.[38] The reason for this interregnum is unclear. One source suggests that no prince was willing to accept election,[39] but it is possible that the interregnum was engineered by the *Baṣọrun* in order to perpetuate his power. At any rate, the continued political tensions inside the capital made it impossible to take effective measures against Afọnja at Ilọrin. Afọnja was left to consolidate and expand his independent state undisturbed. He proceeded to reduce several important towns in the north-east of the kingdom, including Irẹsa and Igbọn, and extended his raids into the Epo province.[40]

§4. CAUSES OF THE REVOLT

The overthrow of an *Alafin* by military force was by no means unparalleled in the history of Ọyọ. Before Awọle, *Alafin* Karan had died in an insurrection, and other *Alafin* had been compelled to commit suicide or even murdered. From one point of view, the overthrow of Awọle was no more than the latest episode in the struggle for power between the *Alafin* and the *Ọyọ Mesi* which had

[35] Cf. above, Ch. 5, p. 79.

[36] Johnson, *History of the Yorubas*, 72.

[37] Ibid. 196; cf. Crowther, *Vocabulary of the Yoruba Language*, v–vi; Hethersett, in *Iwe Kika Ẹkẹrin*, 69–70.

[38] Crowther, *Vocabulary of the Yoruba Language*, vi; cf. Johnson, *History of the Yorubas*, 197.

[39] Ojo, *Short History of Ilorin*, 17: possibly here, as often, Chief Ojo is merely rationalizing the traditions.

[40] Johnson, *History of the Yorubas*, 196, 197, 200. Igbọn was situated near to Ilọrin. The date of these campaigns is uncertain, and they may have occurred later, after the Muslim rebellion in 1817.

been going on since the beginning of the eighteenth century. But whereas these earlier troubles had apparently not put in jeopardy the control of the capital over the Ọyọ kingdom, the overthrow of Awọlẹ was followed by the collapse of the *Alafin*'s authority over the provincial towns.

What requires explanation, then, is why in *c.* 1796 the deposition of an unpopular *Alafin* should have led on to provincial rebellion. Part of the answer lies in the process whereby, in the second half of the eighteenth century, the provincial rulers had been drawn into the political quarrels of the capital. When *Bașọrun* Gaha seized effective power in Ọyọ in 1754, he had taken over the management of the empire, appropriating the imperial revenues and replacing the *Alafin*'s *ajẹlẹ* in the provincial towns by his own kinsmen.[41] The traditions allege that Gaha's kinsmen misgoverned the kingdom: certainly, there was at least one revolt, by the town of Ilọrin, then ruled by Afọnja's grandfather Pașin.[42] Whether because of resentment at Gaha's misgovernment or because of loyalty to the royal house, Abiọdun in 1774 had been able to overthrow Gaha by calling in the military assistance of the provincial towns, under the then *Arẹ Ọna Kakamfo*, Ọyabi of Ajașẹ.[43] The European writer Dalzel, recording Abiọdun's use of force to overthrow Gaha, expressed the opinion that this action would provide a useful precedent for his successors on the throne of Ọyọ.[44] In the event, it was rather the *Alafin*'s enemies who drew the lessons from this episode. The provincial towns, and in particular the *Arẹ Ọna Kakamfo*, now held the key to power in the capital: but if the *Arẹ* could be induced to support the *Ọyọ Mesi* rather than the *Alafin*, the decision of 1774 might be reversed.

What went wrong with these calculations was that Afọnja declined to serve merely as an instrument of the *Ọyọ Mesi*. He supported the *coup d'état* against Awọlẹ in the expectation that he would be made *Alafin*, and revolted when his ambition was thwarted. It had clearly been foolish to place a potential claimant to the Ọyọ throne in a position of such power as that of *Arẹ Ọna Kakamfo*.[45] However,

---

[41] Ibid. 180.   [42] Ibid. 199–200.

[43] Ibid. 183–4; cf. Hethersett, in *Iwe Kika Ẹkẹrin*, 63.

[44] Dalzel, *History of Dahomy*, 157.

[45] However, there is no evidence that it was an 'accepted rule' that the post of *Arẹ Ọna Kakamfo* 'should not go to a royal', as suggested by Morton-Williams, 'The Yoruba Kingdom of Oyo'; and id., 'The Fulani Penetration into Nupe and Yoruba', 13.

when Afǫnja was appointed to the post, his claim to the throne was probably not envisaged. Afǫnja's claim was, after all, exceedingly weak, as he was of royal descent only through the female line. It seems probable that Afǫnja's pretensions to the throne were themselves a function of the progressive erosion of political norms through a century of strife in the capital: only in a context where so many traditional rules were already being broken was a man in Afǫnja's position likely to aspire to the throne.[46]

The personal ambition of Afǫnja, however, cannot be a complete explanation of what happened. The other provincial rulers, after all, might have supported the *Alafin* in suppressing Afǫnja's revolt, rather than abetting it actively or by neutrality. For the disaffection of the provinces in the 1790s, the sources offer no clear explanation. Johnson, indeed, does report of the reign of Awolę that 'the provinces were groaning under the yoke of oppression.'[47] The claim is vague, and it is not clear why oppression should have been greater in the 1790s than earlier. It may perhaps be speculated that the provincial rulers had come to realize that their power and importance, no less than that of the *Ǫyǫ Mesi*, were threatened by the expansion of the *Alafin*'s staff of palace slaves and the tightening of his control over the administration of the kingdom. These tensions might have become evident before the 1790s, but perceptions may have been clouded by the episode of Gaha's rule. The provinces had, in a sense, already revolted against metropolitan misrule in 1774, but since power in the metropolis was for the moment in the hands of the *Basǫrun*, this first rebellion had taken a legitimist, monarchist form. By the 1790s, it may have become clear that, from the point of view of the provinces, a strong *Alafin* was no better than a strong *Basǫrun*. *Alafin* Abiǫdun's organization of the new Ęgbado province, moreover, will have provided a warning of the lengths to which centralization could be carried.[48]

There may have been, in addition to these long-term considerations, more immediate cause of provincial disaffection in the 1790s.

[46] Afǫnja might well have used the argument which is recorded to have been employed by *Balogun* Ibikunle of Ibadan in defending a later irregularity in the Ǫyǫ royal succession (viz. the succession of the *Aręmǫ*, Adelu, in 1859), that 'as many of the Yoruba laws were broken through the late wars, and we had come to a new time, he did not see why the law concerning the successor should not be broken too': CMS, CA2/049, the Revd. D. Hinderer to H. Venn, 25 Apr. 1860.

[47] Johnson, *History of the Yorubas*, 188.

[48] Cf. Morton-Williams, 'The Fulani Penetration into Nupe and Yoruba', 11; id., 'The Yoruba Kingdom of Oyo', 43.

The collapse of the volume of slave exports in the 1790s[49] is likely to have cut deep into the *Alafin*'s revenues, and Awolẹ may have responded by stepping up demands for taxes from within the kingdom.[50] It is recorded that the tribute of Dahomey was raised in this period,[51] and it seems quite likely that this increase in tribute was a general phenomenon. It is also noteworthy that the lead in the rebellion was taken by towns in the north-east of the Ọyọ kingdom, notably Ilọrin and Gbogun. As will be seen in the next chapter, the north-eastern provinces of the kingdom had suffered severely from raids by the Nupe during the 1780s,[52] and there may have been a feeling in this area that the rulers of the capital had failed to provide adequate defence for the provincial towns.

§5. THE MUSLIM REBELLION

The interregnum at Ọyọ is said to have lasted for five years, that is until *c.* 1802.[53] A new *Alafin*, Majotu, was then installed. With a measure of central direction restored, action was taken to reassert Ọyọ power, at least in some areas. In the south-west, during the first decade of the nineteenth century, action was taken to secure Ọyọ interests in Porto Novo and in the Mahi country.[54] It does not appear, however, that any effective action was taken against Ilọrin. Presumably, the *Alafin* still did not command sufficient support from the other provincial rulers to be able to confront the power of Afọnja.

The stalemate between Ọyọ and Ilọrin was eventually resolved when Afọnja, in 1817, decided to invoke a Muslim rebellion in his support. The background to this decision was, of course, the seizure of political power in Hausaland by a group of militant Muslims, mainly Fulani, led by 'Uthmān dan Fodio, in the great *jihad* (holy war) which began in 1804. The end result had been the creation of a Muslim Caliphate controlling most of Hausaland, with its capital at Sokoto.[55] Within a few years, the Sokoto *jihad* had begun to affect

---

[49] Cf. above, Ch. 10, p. 224.
[50] As suggested by Lloyd, *Political Development of Yoruba Kingdoms*, 14–15.
[51] Cf. below, Ch. 13, p. 268.   [52] See below, Ch. 13, pp. 264–5.
[53] Crowther, *Vocabulary of the Yoruba Language*, vi. Akinjogbin, 'Chronology of Yoruba History', 82, suggests that the interregnum lasted much longer than Crowther indicates, perhaps to *c.* 1817 or *c.* 1822: on this, see Law, 'Chronology of the Yoruba Wars', 213–14.   [54] Cf. below, Ch. 13, pp. 269–70.
[55] For the *jihad* of 'Uthmān dan Fodio, see esp. Last, *Sokoto Caliphate*; M. Hiskett, *The Sword of Truth: The Life and Times of the Shehu Usuman dan Fodio* (London, 1973).

Nupe, the north-eastern neighbour of Ǫyǫ, where local Fulani joined with Nupe Muslims in rebellion against the Nupe king.[56] Here, evidently, was a military force of considerable power, which Afǫnja might hope to harness to his own ends.

In Ǫyǫ, as in Nupe, there were important groups which were likely to respond to the call for a *jihad*. There were, first, the pastoral Fulani, of whom there were many in the northern areas of the kingdom: indifferent Muslims, but likely, as in Hausaland, to support the Muslim Fulani leaders in a confrontation with the indigenous authorities. There were also numerous slaves of northern origin, Hausa and others, who were Muslims, and for whom a successful *jihad* would mean liberation. And in addition to these alien, unassimilated groups there were by the early nineteenth century a significant number of Ǫyǫ converts to Islam. Islam had been established in the Ǫyǫ capital as early as the seventeenth century, and by the early nineteenth century the city contained a substantial Muslim quarter.[57] Concern at the increasing influence of Islam in the city is attested by the tradition that under *Alafin* Awolę a visiting Hausa trader was accused of bringing 'bad charms' into Ǫyǫ and robbed of his Quran.[58] There were also substantial Muslim quarters in some of the provincial towns, such as Igboho and Isęyin.[59]

There were also potential leaders for a *jihad*, in a number of *mallams*, or Muslim scholars, of northern origin who were already active in the Ǫyǫ kingdom, preaching and selling charms. The most important of these *mallams* was one Sālih, better known in Ǫyǫ tradition as 'Alimi',[60] a Fulani from Hausaland, who undertook a mission of preaching to the Muslim communities in the Ǫyǫ towns, and visited Ogbomǫsǫ, Ikoyi, and Kuwǫ.[61] Sālih seems to have

---

[56] For the *jihad* in Nupe, see Mason, 'The Nupe Kingdom', 53–79: the *jihad* here had begun by 1810, when the Muslim rebels are recorded to have received assistance from the Sokoto leadership.

[57] Cf. above, Ch. 5, pp. 75–6.

[58] Johnson, *History of the Yorubas*, 190. However, there is no evidence to support the suggestion of Akinjogbin, 'Prelude to the Yoruba Civil Wars', 36–7, that Awolę himself had been converted to Islam.

[59] Gbadamǫsi, 'The Growth of Islam among the Yoruba', 10–11.

[60] From the Arabic *'ālim*, meaning 'scholar'. The name Sālih is supplied by the Arabic history of Ilǫrin written by Aḥmad b. Abī Bakr (Abū Ikǫkǫrǫ): see Martin, 'A New Arabic History of Ilorin', 24; and the quotation from Abū Ikǫkǫrǫ's history in Hodgkin, *Nigerian Perspectives*, 280.

[61] Sālih's visits to these towns are recorded by Abū Ikǫkǫrǫ: see Martin' 'A

begun preaching in the Ọyọ kingdom in about 1813.[62] He was presumably inspired by the Sokoto *jihad*, though the exact nature of his connection with Sokoto is unclear.[63] Another *mallam*, an Arab called Muhammad Gumso, with four companions preached Islam in the Ọyọ capital itself. Eventually the *Alafin* (Majotu?), instigated by his pagan priests, arranged the assassination of the Muslim preachers, only Gumso escaping, through the assistance of one of the *Alafin*'s wives who secretly favoured Islam.[64] Other northern *mallams* are said to have penetrated as far south as Ijanna, in Ẹgbado, and the coastal town of Badagry.[65]

Ajọnja himself was not a Muslim. He believed, however, in the efficacy of the Muslim charms which a man like Sālih could provide for success in war,[66] and he presumably knew of the military-successes of the *jihad* in the north. He invited Sálih from Kuwọ to Ilọrin, and induced him to bring his sons and other followers with him. Sālih proceeded to proclaim a *jihad* against Ọyọ, and quickly attracted widespread support. Many, though not all, of the pastoral Fulani responded.[67] So, too, did many Ọyọ Muslims, headed by a

---

New Arabic History of Ilorin', 24; Hodgkin, *Nigerian Perspectives*, 280. Kuwọ was apparently in the Ilọrin area. Hermon-Hodge, *Gazetteer of Ilorin Province*, 66, claims that Sālih also visited the Ọyọ capital, while Ojo, *Short History of Ilorin*, 10, adds a visit to Ṣaki: these accounts are probably spurious.

[62] Sālih is said to have spent three months in Ogbomọṣọ, one year at Ikoyi, and three years at Kuwọ before going to Ilọrin, presumably in 1817: Abū Ikọkọrọ, in Hodgkin, *Nigerian Perspectives*, 280.

[63] Some Ilọrin sources claim that Sālih was sent to Yorubaland by 'Uthmān dan Fodio: Burdon, *Northern Nigeria*, 15; cf. Mischlich and Lippert, 'Beiträge zur Geschichte der Haussastaaten', 241. There is no corroboration of this, however, from Sokoto sources.

[64] R. Lander, *Records of Captain Clapperton's Last Expedition*, i. 277–9. Gumso's misfortunes at Ọyọ are also alluded to in Denham and Clapperton, *Narrative of Travels and Discoveries*, Clapperton's Narrative, 87. Current Ilọrin tradition apparently attaches the experience of Gumso at the Ọyọ court to Sālih: an almost identical story, but with Sālih as the hero, was told to the present writer by al-Hajj Adam al-Ilūrī, a local historian of Ilọrin.

[65] R. Lander, *Records of Captain Clapperton's Last Expedition*, i. 279–80.

[66] Oral evidence, from al-Hajj Adam al-Ilūrī. Sālih's making of charms for Afọnja is also mentioned by A. F. Mockler-Ferryman, *Up the Niger* (London, 1892), 172; Hermon-Hodge, *Gazetteer of Ilorin Province*, 65.

[67] There were still many pastoral Fulani groups in the Ọyọ kingdom in 1826–30 who had not joined the *jihad*, but remained at peace with the Ọyọ: Clapperton, *Journal of a Second Expedition*, and R. and J. Lander, *Journal of an Expedition*, vol. i, *passim*. The account of Abū Ikọkọrọ, in Hodgkin, *Nigerian Perspectives*, 281, indicates that some pastoral Fulani were with Afọnja at Ilọrin even before the arrival there of Sālih and the proclamation of *jihad*.

chief of Kuwọ called Ṣọlagberu.[68] And, perhaps most damaging to Ọyọ, there was a widespread revolt of the northern slaves held by Ọyọ slave-owners.[69]

It would be an oversimplification to see the events of 1817 as a simple confrontation between Muslim and pagan elements in the Ọyọ kingdom. The *jihad* was, after all, sponsored by the opportunism of a non-Muslim, Afọnja. Moreover, by no means all Muslims supported the *jihad*. One account asserts that the response of the Ọyọ to the rebellion of 1817 was to 'put all Mahometans to death, whether natives or in caravans trafficking'.[70] Some such reaction is likely enough, and would account for the treatment of Muhammad Gumso at the Ọyọ capital. However, the evidence of Clapperton and the Landers in 1826–30 shows that there were still Muslims to be found in the areas of the kingdom loyal to the *Alafin*. By 1830 Hausa *mallams* were once more permitted to sell charms at the capital, though regarded with great suspicion,[71] while at Ilaro, in Ẹgbado, Islam had been adopted as the official cult.[72] Islam was, however, central to the rebellion of 1817, inasmuch as it provided a basis upon which disparate elements—Fulani, Hausa, and Yoruba—could be united in a common loyalty for an assault upon the established order.

The Muslim rebellion of 1817 greatly increased the intensity and territorial extent of the disturbances within the Ọyọ kingdom. Before the rebellion Afọnja's military operations seem to have been confined to the eastern provinces of the kingdom, but now his Fulani and Hausa allies extended their activities across the River Ogun into the western provinces. By 1821 the town of Isẹyin was serving as a base for extensive raiding in the Ibarapa province of the kingdom, in the course of which Samuel Crowther's town Ọṣogun was destroyed.[73] The Fulani and Hausa are also said to have attacked the

---

[68] For Ṣọlagberu, see esp. Johnson, *History of the Yorubas*, 193–4; cf. Hethersett, in *Iwe Kika Ẹkẹrin*, 74 (where the text by an error gives the name as Ṣọlagbemi); Abū Ikọkọrọ, in Hodgkin, *Nigerian Perspectives*, 281.

[69] For the outbreak of the *jihad*, see esp. Johnson, *History of the Yorubas*, 193–4; Crowther, *Vocabulary of the Yoruba Language*, vi–vii. For accounts based on Ilọrin sources, cf. Mockler-Ferryman, *Up the Niger*, 172; Mischlich and Lippert, 'Beiträge zur Geschichte der Haussastaaten', 241–2; Burdon, *Northern Nigeria*, 15; Abū Ikọkọrọ, in Hodgkin, *Nigerian Perspectives*, 280–1.

[70] Clapperton, *Journal of a Second Expedition*, 204.

[71] R. and J. Lander, *Journal of an Expedition*, i. 182.

[72] Ibid. i. 77.

[73] Schön and Crowther, *Journals*, 371–2; Curtin, *Africa Remembered*, 299–304.

Ọyọ capital itself, and to have burned a part of the city before being beaten off.[74]

It quickly became evident that, in seeking to make use of militant Islam for opportunist ends, Afọnja had gravely miscalculated. Alarmed at the increasing power and unruliness of his Muslim allies, and apparently hoping to conciliate opinion in the Ọyọ capital so that he might yet secure the Ọyọ throne,[75] Afọnja sought to remove the Fulani and Hausa from Ilọrin. By this time, Sālih himself was probably dead, and the principal leader of the Ilọrin Muslims was Sālih's son 'Abd al-Salām (called in Yoruba, Abudusalami).[76] Afọnja attempted to persuade the Fulani and Hausa to leave Ilọrin and settle separately to the east. They responded by an insurrection, and Afọnja was killed. This was probably, as has been seen, in *c.* 1823–4.[77] 'Abd al-Salām now became the ruler of Ilọrin, and it was perhaps at this point that he declared his allegiance to the Caliph at Sokoto. He was formally recognized by Sokoto as the 'Emir of Yoruba', and placed under the immediate authority of the Emir of Gwandu, who was responsible for the western emirates of the Sokoto Caliphate.[78] Not long after, the destruction of Yoruba power in Ilọrin was completed by the liquidation of the Yoruba Muslim leader, Ṣọlagberu.[79] Some of Afọnja's Yoruba followers

[74] Clapperton, *Journal of a Second Expedition*, 204; R. and J. Lander, *Records of Captain Clapperton's Last Expedition*, ii. 13.

[75] Cf. Crowther, *Vocabulary of the Yoruba Language*, vii.

[76] Sālih is said to have lived at Ilọrin for six years, which would place his death in *c.* 1823: Abu Ikọkọrọ, in Hodgkin, *Nigerian Perspectives*, 281; Hermon-Hodge, *Gazetteer of Ilorin Province*, 65. Johnson, *History of the Yorubas*, 202, and Burdon, *Northern Nigeria*, 15, place the death of Sālih after that of Afọnja, but according to Abu Ikọkọrọ, loc. cit., Sālih in fact predeceased Afọnja, and this latter version is to be preferred. The dating of Sālih's death to 1831, first found in Elphinstone, *Gazetteer of Ilorin Province*, 16, cannot be correct. On these problems, cf. Law, 'Chronology of the Yoruba Wars', 218–19.

[77] For the overthrow of Afọnja, see esp. Crowther, *Vocabulary of the Yoruba Language*, vii; Hethersett, in *Iwe Kika Ẹkẹrin*, 76–7; Johnson, *History of the Yorubas*, 198–9; Burdon, *Northern Nigeria*, 15; Abū Ikọkọrọ, in Hodgkin, *Nigerian Perspectives*, 282.

[78] The account in Mischlich and Lippert, 'Beiträge zur Geschichte der Haussastaaten', 241, claims that Ilọrin was placed under the Emir of Gwandu by 'Uthmān dan Fodio during the lifetime of Sālih, but local traditions cited by Hermon-Hodge, *Gazetteer of Ilorin Province*, 69, indicate that a flag of authority from Sokoto was received only after Sālih's death by 'Abd al-Salām. It is possible that the recognition of 'Abd al-Salām as Emir of Ilọrin preceded the overthrow of Afọnja, and in fact provoked Afọnja's attempt to eliminate the Fulani.

[79] Johnson, *History of the Yorubas*, 204; cf. Abū Ikọkọrọ, as reported by Martin, 'A New Arabic History of Ilorin', 25.

left Ilọrin,[80] but most remained in the city, now subject to Fulani rule.[81]

[80] One of Afọnja's chiefs, Ojo Amepo, left Ilọrin and set himself up as an independent raider in the Epo area, while a son of Afọnja, Oluyedun, is later found at Ibadan: Johnson, *History of the Yorubas*, 234, 244.

[81] Ilọrin comprised four quarters, each with its own *Balogun* (war-chief), occupied by the Fulani, the Hausa, the 'Imale' (Ọyọ Muslims), and the 'Yoruba' (non-Muslim Ọyọ?): Martin, 'A New Arabic History of Ilorin', 27; cf. Lloyd, *Political Development of Yoruba Kingdoms*, 42.

CHAPTER 13

Disintegration at the Periphery

THE collapse of the Ọyọ empire has sometimes been attributed to its having become 'overstretched', to its having grown too large for effective control to be maintained over its remoter areas.[1] This view ignores the actual course of the empire's collapse. The Ọyọ empire did not shrink gradually through the defection of its outlying dependencies. The collapse, as has been seen, began at the centre, in the heart of the Ọyọ kingdom, with the revolt of Ilọrin in *c*. 1796. The outlying areas were, for the most part, lost later, and arguably as a direct result of the collapse at the centre. In the present chapter attention will be for the moment directed away from the civil wars at the centre of the Ọyọ kingdom, to trace the disintegration of Ọyọ power at the periphery of the empire. This process involved, first, the deterioration of the situation along the northern frontier of the kingdom from the 1780s, and later, the loss of the Ọyọ dependencies —Dahomey, Ẹgba, and Ẹgbado—in the south-west.

§1. THE NORTHERN FRONTIER

The first clear signs of a decline in the power of Ọyọ appeared in the 1780s, in the relations of the kingdom with its northern neighbours, the Bariba and Nupe. After the defeat of the Nupe and Bariba invasions of the sixteenth century, Ọyọ had apparently enjoyed two centuries of security on its northern frontiers. It is, indeed, possible, though not certain, that during its period of imperial greatness in the seventeenth and eighteenth centuries Ọyọ was able to exact tribute from some of the southernmost Bariba and Nupe communities.[2] But in the last two decades of the eighteenth century, the Ọyọ were once more in serious difficulties in the north.

To take first the Bariba, an English trader at the coast heard in September 1783 that 'The Ihos [Ọyọ] have received 2 months agoe a

[1] e.g. A. A. B. Aderibigbe, 'Peoples of Southern Nigeria', in J. F. A. Ajayi and I. Espie (eds.), *A Thousand Years of West African History* (Ibadan, 1965), 191; Gann and Duignan, *Africa and the World*, 350; cf. B. Davidson, *A History of West Africa, 1000–1800* (London, 1965), 201.

[2] Cf. above, Ch. 8, pp. 145–50.

total overthrow from a country by name Barrabbas [Bariba], having
lost in the battle 11 umbrellas & the generals under them.'[3] This
disastrous defeat is (perhaps not surprisingly) not recorded in Ọyọ
tradition, though there is some recollection of fighting against the
Bariba around this time in the traditions of the provincial town of
Ogbomọṣọ.[4] The war is, however, recalled in Bariba tradition, which
identifies the adversaries of the Ọyọ specifically as the people of
Kaiama. A large army of Yoruba is said to have invaded the kingdom
of Kaiama from Gwanaguru on the upper Moshi, but to have been
repulsed in a battle just south of the town of Kaiama.[5] One account
attributes this victory to a king of Kaiama called Sabi Agba.[6] Since
Sabi Agba's grand-nephew and third successor on the throne of
Kaiama, Yaru, was reigning in 1826–30,[7] there is no difficulty in
identifying his defeat of the Yoruba invaders with the war of 1783.[8]
The Bariba traditions do not explain the circumstances leading to
this war. One account connects it with the transfer of the Kaiama
capital from Vobera (to the south-east) to its present site,[9] but it is
not made clear why the Ọyọ should have intervened. Akinjogbin has
suggested that the war of 1783 was a revolt of the Bariba against
Ọyọ rule, and that Johnson has therefore committed a slight error in
placing the loss of Borgu to the Ọyọ empire after instead of before the
death of *Alafin* Abiọdun in 1789.[10] The evidence that Kaiama or

[3] PRO, T.70/1545, L. Abson to R. Miles, 26 Sept. 1783; cf. Akinjogbin, *Dahomey and its Neighbours*, 164.

[4] Ologolo, who was *Balẹ* of Ogbomọṣọ in the time of *Alafin* Abiọdun, is said to have campaigned against the Bariba before his accession as *Balẹ*: Oyerinde, *Iwe Itan Ogbomọṣọ*, 22.

[5] Duff, *Gazetteer of Kontagora Province*, 28; Hermon-Hodge, *Gazetteer of Ilorin Province*, 144–5; NAK, DOB/HIS/35, H. L. Norton Traill, 'South Borgu', 1908.

[6] NAK, DOB/HIS/35, H. L. Norton Traill, 'South Borgu', 1908; Hermon-Hodge, *Gazetteer of Ilorin Province*, 144.

[7] Clapperton, *Journal of a Second Expedition*, 62 etc.; R. and J. Lander, *Journal of an Expedition*, i. 221 etc. For Yaru's relationship to Sabi Agba, cf. Duff, *Gazetteer of Kontagora Province*, 29.

[8] Estimates of the date of this war based solely on Bariba tradition agree in placing it during the second half of the eighteenth century: NAK, DOB/HIS/35, H. L. Norton Traill, 'South Borgu', 1908, followed by Hermon-Hodge, *Gazetteer of Ilorin Province*, 145, gives the date c. 1800; Talbot, *Peoples of Southern Nigeria*, i. 286, gives c. 1760; cf. Duff, *Gazetteer of Kontagora Province*, 29, dates Sabi Agba's reign to 1775–85.

[9] NAK, DOB/HIS/35, H. L. Norton Traill, 'South Borgu', 1908; Hermon-Hodge, *Gazetteer of Ilorin Province*, 144.

[10] Akinjogbin, *Dahomey and its Neighbours*, 164; Johnson, *History of the Yorubas*, 187.

any other part of Borgu was subject to Ọyọ before the 1780s is slight,[11] but the suggestion seems nevertheless plausible.

If it is uncertain whether the war of 1783 marked the end of an Ọyọ domination of Kaiama, it is very probable that the defeat of the Ọyọ in this war resulted in the loss of some territory to the Bariba. The location of the boundary between Borgu and Ọyọ was discussed in an earlier chapter.[12] It was there concluded that originally the boundary probably followed the main stream of the River Moshi along its entire length, but that later the towns of Kenu, Ileṣa, and Okuta, to the south of the Moshi, passed into the possession of the Bariba. The evidence of Bowdich in 1817 indicates that the area had already changed hands by that date.[13] In fact, it appears from local traditions that the Bariba dynasty which now rules in Kenu was established, by a man from Nikki, towards the end of the eighteenth century.[14] It is claimed that the transfer took place peacefully, the first Bariba king inheriting sovereignty over the town from the indigenous dynasty through the female line, but this is probably simply an attempt to disguise and legitimize foreign usurpation. It is more likely that the loss of this area to the Bariba was a consequence of the war of 1783.

Bariba pressure on the Ọyọ kingdom continued for many years after 1783. The intervention of Bariba forces in support of Ojo Agunbambaru's attempt to recover power in Ọyọ in c. 1796–7 has been mentioned in the previous chapter.[15] Thirty years later, in 1826, Clapperton found that raiders from Kaiama were infesting the roads in the north-west of the Ọyọ kingdom,[16] and that Kaiama had lately taken from Ọyọ the town of 'Algi' on the south bank of the River Moshi.[17]

During the same period, the Ọyọ also came under pressure from the Nupe to the north-east. The English trader Norris, writing in 1789, reports that Ọyọ had become tributary to the Nupe: 'Of the

[11] Cf. above, Ch. 8, p. 149.
[12] Cf. above, Ch. 6, pp. 85–6.
[13] Bowdich, *Mission from Cape Coast to Ashantee*, 208.
[14] NAK, DOB/HIS/35, H. L. Norton Traill, 'South Borgu', 1908, followed by Hermon-Hodge, *Gazetteer of Ilorin Province*, 145, places the establishment of the Bariba dynasty at Kenu at about the same time as Sabi Agba's victory over the Yoruba, in c. 1800. Okuta and Ileṣa received their Bariba dynasties later, but these towns had apparently earlier been under Kenu.
[15] Cf. above, Ch. 12, p. 251.
[16] Clapperton, *Journal of a Second Expedition*, 33.
[17] Ibid. 61–2.

Tappas [Tapa, i.e. Nupe], but little is known . . . This nation, however, must have acquired considerable importance, as they drew a regular tribute from the *Eyos*.'[18] A little later Dalzel gives an account of an attempt by the Ọyọ to end this subjection to the Nupe, in 1790:

Eyeo . . . appears to be tributary to a neighbouring and more powerful Prince, called *Tappah*, of whose history little is known. The King of Eyeo, desirous, it seems, to throw off the yoke, had ordered the buffalo's hide to be twice trodden,[19] in order to give Tappah a hearty drubbing. His army, however, numerous as it was, met with a complete overthrow, and was under the necessity of submitting to the victor's terms, having lost thirteen umbrellas in the action.[20]

Akinjogbin has argued that this account is confused, and that the war of 1790 was in fact a successful revolt by the Nupe against their previous subjection to Ọyọ, this being the loss of Nupe which Johnson records as having occurred after the death of *Alafin* Abiọdun.[21] But Johnson's testimony seems altogether too weak a basis upon which to reject the contemporary evidence of Norris and Dalzel. There is, indeed, no direct confirmation in Ọyọ or Nupe tradition that Ọyọ was at this period tributary to Nupe. There is, however, evidence in Nupe tradition that the Nupe kingdom was especially strong under *Etsu* Mu'azu and *Etsu* Majiya I, who reigned during the latter half of the eighteenth century.[22] The war of 1790 itself is not recalled in Ọyọ tradition, but Nupe tradition records that *Etsu* Mu'azu fought against the Yoruba,[23] and this probably alludes to the defeat of the Ọyọ in 1790.

Ọyọ appears to have suffered not only the imposition of tribute,

[18] Norris, *Memoirs of the Reign of Bossa Ahadee*, 139.

[19] i.e. he sent an army of twice the normal size: cf. above, Ch. 9, p. 196.

[20] Dalzel, *History of Dahomy*, 229.

[21] Akinjogbin, *Dahomey and its Neighbours*, 175; Johnson, *History of the Yorubas*, 187.

[22] Nadel, *Black Byzantium*, 76, states that Nupe 'reached its greatest power' under *Etsu* Mu'azu; while according to W. B. Baikie, 'Notes of a Journey from Bida in Nupe, to Kano in Haussa, performed in 1862', *J. of the Royal Geographical Society*, 37 (1867), 105, it was Majiya whose reign was 'the most flourishing in Nupe'. Mu'azu reigned twice, and Majiya's reign fell between the two reigns of Mu'azu, but the dates are uncertain: Baikie dates Majiya to *c*. 1760–85, while Nadel gives 1759–67 for Mu'azu's first reign, 1767–77 for Majiya, and 1778–95 for Mu'azu's second reign; however, Schön and Crowther, *Journals*, 190, implies that Mu'azu died as late as *c*. 1818.

[23] NAK, BIDDIV. 2/1, B.375, E. V. Rochfort Rae, 'Introduction to Certain Notes Collected from Various Native Authorities, on the Origins of the Bini, Kedawa, Agabi, Badeggi, Ebe and Gbwagbwazhi', 1921, Information from Jebba and Alkali Jebba, §2.

but also raids by Nupe forces. Local traditions in the north-eastern provinces of the Ọyọ kingdom recall a period of extensive and destructive raiding by the Nupe king Majiya. In the Igbomina province, the Nupe raiders are said to have destroyed the town of Ajaṣẹ Ipo, killing the *Olupo*,[24] and to have burned Isanlu Iṣin and Oke Aba.[25] The Nupe also penetrated beyond Igbomina, raiding in the Afọn area to the south of Ilọrin[26] and harrying the people of Ọfa.[27] The Nupe domination of Ọyọ presumably ended when the Nupe kingdom itself disintegrated in civil war (later complicated by the outbreak of the *jihad*) after the death of *Etsu* Mu'azu, probably in the early nineteenth century.[28]

The weakening of Ọyọ in its relations with the Bariba and Nupe in the late eighteenth century, and in particular the catastrophic defeats of 1783 and 1790, have sometimes been held to mark the beginning of the decline of the Ọyọ empire.[29] This view needs qualification, since the collapse of Ọyọ power from the 1790s was not related in any obvious way to the troubles on the northern frontier, but evolved, as has been seen, out of an internal crisis, beginning with the overthrow of *Alafin* Awolẹ in *c.* 1796.[30] It is difficult, on the available evidence, to account satisfactorily for the weakening of Ọyọ *vis-à-vis* its northern neighbours at this period. It has been suggested that the increasing involvement of Ọyọ in the Atlantic trade had involved a diversion of Ọyọ economic interest away from the north and towards the coast, with a consequent neglect of the kingdom's northern frontiers.[31] This view ignores the interdependence of the northern and southern trade of Ọyọ, discussed in an

[24] NAK, SNP.10/4, 746P/1916, V. F. Biscoe, 'Assessment Report, Ajasse Po District', 1916, §§2–3; cf. Elphinstone, *Gazetteer of Ilorin Province*, 11.

[25] NAK, SNP.7/13, 4705/1912, V. F. Biscoe, 'Assessment Report, Omu-Isanlu District', 1916, §§28, 40.

[26] NAK, ILORPROF.4, 766/1912, C. S. Burnett, 'Assessment Report, Afon District, Ilorin Province', 1912, §12.

[27] NAK, ILORPROF.4/1, 266/1918, 'Notes collected by Alfa Aliu from an aged historian', supplied by H. B. Hermon-Hodge, included as an appendix in P. A. Benton, 'Assessment Report, Offa District', 1918; cf. Hermon-Hodge, *Gazetteer of Ilorin Province*, 97.

[28] For the Nupe civil wars, see Mason, 'The Nupe Kingdom', 53–79.

[29] Allison, 'The Last Days of Old Oyo', 26; Smith, *Kingdoms of the Yoruba*, 50, 138; Akinjogbin, 'Prelude to the Yoruba Civil Wars', 29–30.

[30] Unless the disaffection of the north-eastern provinces of the Ọyọ kingdom in the 1790s was due in part to resentment at the failure of the *Alafin* to defend them adequately against the Nupe raids: cf. above Ch. 12, p. 255.

[31] Allison, 'The Last Days of Old Oyo', 26; cf. Smith, *Kingdoms of the Yoruba*, 137.

earlier chapter:[32] since many slaves came from the north, the Atlantic slave trade will have increased rather than diminished the economic importance to Ọyọ of its northern connections. Akinjogbin has suggested that after 1774 *Alafin* Abiọdun had deliberately weakened the military forces of Ọyọ, in order to undermine the influence of the *Ọyọ Mesi*.[33] But there is no evidence for this, and it is far from clear that Abiọdun had any interest in weakening the military power of Ọyọ, though he might have wished to build up the importance of the provincial army under the *Arẹ Ọna Kakamfo* against that of the metropolitan army under the *Ọyọ Mesi*. Probably the weakening of Ọyọ in the 1780s was due simply to its internal dissensions, which had led to civil war in 1774 and were soon to precipitate the kingdom's total collapse.

§2. THE REVOLT OF THE ẸGBA

The first of the Ọyọ dependencies in the south-west to assert its independence was probably Ẹgbaland. According to Ẹgba tradition, the liberation of the Ẹgba from Ọyọ rule was effected by a revolt led by Lisabi, a war-chief of Igbein in the Alake province of Ẹgbaland. The revolt began with a massacre of the *Alafin*'s representatives who had come to collect the annual tribute, over 600 of whom are said to have been killed. The Ọyọ then sent a punitive expedition, which invaded Ẹgbaland from Ẹgbado across the River Ogun, but was completely defeated by Lisabi at Igbein.[34] Lisabi himself was shortly afterwards killed while fighting against the Dahomians,[35] but the freedom of Ẹgbaland survived the death of its architect.

The date of Lisabi's revolt is uncertain, although a context towards the end of the eighteenth century seems, in the light of the other evidence relating to the decline of Ọyọ power, most likely. Biobaku was unable to find any evidence in Ẹgba or Ọyọ tradition to fix the date, but speculated that the Ẹgba might have taken the

---

[32] Cf. above, Ch. 10, pp. 226–8.

[33] Akinjogbin, 'Prelude to the Yoruba Civil Wars', 28; cf. id., 'The Oyo Empire in the Eighteenth Century', 458.

[34] The earliest account of Lisabi's revolt is that in Bowen, *Central Africa*, 107. For more detailed accounts, see George, *Historical Notes on the Yoruba Country*, 71–5; Ajiṣafẹ, *History of Abẹokuta*, 14–17; Loṣi, *History of Abẹokuta*, 4–9.

[35] George, *Historical Notes on the Yoruba Country*, 75; Loṣi, *History of Abẹokuta*, 9. Chief Ojo, *Short History of Ilorin*, 13, claims that the Dahomians undertook this campaign against the Ẹgba at the request of the Ọyọ, who wished to punish the Ẹgba for their revolt: this is not supported by any other source, and is probably merely rationalization by Chief Ojo.

opportunity for revolt offered by the civil war at Ọyọ between *Alafin* Abiọdun and *Baṣọrun* Gaha in 1774.[36] Akinjogbin has suggested that the revolt is more likely to have taken place during the 1780s, when Ọyọ was in difficulty on its northern frontiers, against the Bariba and Nupe.[37] Chief Ojo, however, places the revolt of the Ẹgba during the brief regency of *Baṣọrun* Aṣamu between the death of *Alafin* Awolẹ and the installation of his successor Adebo, that is in c. 1796.[38] Chief Ojo's chronological computations are always subject to suspicion, since they are frequently based upon guesswork rather than upon any explicit evidence in the traditions: but in this case his date is at least as plausible as those of Biobaku and Akinjogbin.

The revolt under Liṣabi did not altogether end Ọyọ interference in Ẹgbaland. After the death of Liṣabi, the Ẹgba confederacy, never very real, disintegrated in a series of civil wars. In one of these wars, the *Alake*, Okikilu, called in the assistance against his enemies of a war-chief of Ijanna, in the Ẹgbado province of the Ọyọ kingdom, called Agbaje. But Okikilu and Agbaje were defeated, and both were killed.[39] No successor to Okikilu as *Alake* was elected, and the Ẹgba confederacy ceased to have even a nominal existence. These troubles may have enabled the Ọyọ to retain or regain control over a part of Ẹgba territory, for an account obtained from a slave of Ijẹbu origin describing conditions in c. 1820 describes 'Ekba-Ikeya', presumably Ẹgba Ikija, i.e. the town of Ikija in the Oke Ọna province of Ẹgbaland, as a 'dependency' of Ọyọ.[40] However, it is certain that the greater part of Ẹgbaland was never brought back under Ọyọ rule.

§3. THE REVOLT OF DAHOMEY

As was seen in an earlier chapter, the kingdom of Dahomey had become increasingly restive against its subjection to Ọyọ from the 1770s onwards.[41] During the reign in Dahomey of Kpengla (1774–89), which coincided with that of Abiọdun in Ọyọ, Dahomian

---

[36] Biobaku, *The Egba and their Neighbours*, 9.

[37] Akinjogbin, 'The Oyo Empire in the Eighteenth Century', 458.

[38] Ojo, *Short History of Ilorin*, 13; accepted by Smith, *Kingdoms of the Yoruba*, 84–5.

[39] George, *Historical Notes on the Yoruba Country*, 78; Ajiṣafẹ, *History of Abẹokuta*, 48–9; Loṣi, *History of Abẹokuta*, 14–15. However, current Ijanna tradition does not recall this war, or the existence of an Ijanna war-chief called Agbaje: Oral evidence, from the *Balẹ* of Ijanna.

[40] d'Avezac-Maçaya, *Notice sur le Pays et le Peuple des Yébous*, 35.

[41] Cf. above, Ch. 8, pp. 174–9.

resentment had never gone as far as open revolt, but the weakening of Ọyọ power after the 1780s evidently encouraged the Dahomians to believe that a successful revolt was now possible. The first attempt at liberation probably came under Kpengla's successor Agonglo (1789–97). It is unfortunate, however, that the detailed documentation from European sources which we have on Dahomian relations with Ọyọ in the 1770s and 1780s becomes much sketchier after *c.* 1790. The course of events has in consequence to be reconstructed to a much greater degree from traditional evidence, and is therefore considerably more uncertain.

The immediate object of Dahomian resentment in the 1770s and 1780s had been the coastal Egun kingdom of Allada (Porto Novo), which was competing successfully with the Dahomian port of Whydah for the Atlantic slave trade, and which enjoyed the protection of Ọyọ. In 1791 Dahomian forces again raided the beach at Porto Novo, but this did not represent defiance of Ọyọ, since Agonglo had sought and obtained the *Alafin*'s permission for the raid before undertaking it.[42] Of the reasons for the *Alafin*'s consent, there is no record, but perhaps this concession to Dahomian pressure should be seen as a first sign of the weakening of Ọyọ *vis-à-vis* Dahomey. Certainly, so soon after the catastrophic defeat of the Ọyọ at the hands of the Nupe (1790), the *Alafin* was in no position to coerce Dahomey, and threats to invade Dahomey would have carried little conviction. Later in his reign, if we can believe Dahomian tradition, Agonglo openly revolted, and refused to pay tribute to Ọyọ. An Ọyọ army was therefore despatched against Dahomey, and the Dahomian capital Abomey was again sacked, after which the tribute was reimposed.[43] We may speculate that this revolt was provoked by the Ọyọ decision, recorded in another Dahomian tradition, to raise the tribute of Dahomey once more to the level at which it had stood before the reduction under Kpengla in 1784.[44] The revolt of Agonglo is not confirmed by any extant contemporary source, and the story is rejected by Akinjogbin as due to a confusion in the traditions.[45] However, the tradition of Agonglo's revolt against Ọyọ was already current in Dahomey within little more than half a

[42] AN, C.6/27, Denyau de la Garenne to Ministre de Marine, 2 Mar. 1791.

[43] Dunglas, 'Contribution à l'histoire du Moyen-Dahomey', t.II, 31–2.

[44] Le Herissé, *L'Ancien Royaume de Dahomey*, 319. This tradition is also reflected in the earlier statement of Skertchly, *Dahomey As It Is*, 451, that under Agonglo 'the Eyeos imposed heavy taxes on his people'.

[45] Akinjogbin, *Dahomey and its Neighbours*, 178, n.1.

century of Agonglo's reign, for Forbes was told it at Abomey in 1850: 'Agon-groo . . . appears to have been a weak monarch, and during his reign he had to flee from the Eyeos.'[46] The story is also supported by the traditions of Ṣabẹ, which recall that around this period Akikanju, the king of Ṣabẹ, fought with success against the Dahomians when they revolted against Ọyọ:[47] the Ṣabẹ presumably made war against Dahomey in alliance with or on behalf of the Ọyọ. It seems probable enough that the Dahomians would have seen an opportunity for revolt in the weakening of Ọyọ power which had been demonstrated by the defeats of the Ọyọ by the Bariba (1783) and the Nupe (1790). It is rather more surprising that the Ọyọ should have been able to reply effectively to the revolt, but a few years after the disaster of 1790 might have sufficed for the reorganization of the Ọyọ army, and much of the burden of the war against Dahomey may have been carried by the Ṣabẹ allies. In any case, as will be seen below, there is other evidence that the Ọyọ retained military dominance in the west even after the beginning of their troubles at home.

Agonglo's successor Adandozan (1797–1818) appears to have avoided an open confrontation with Ọyọ. Dahomian tradition maintains that Adandozan himself did refuse to pay tribute to Ọyọ, and defied the messengers sent by the *Alafin* to demand it, but that the chiefs of Dahomey, fearing an Ọyọ invasion, arranged for it to be paid without his knowledge.[48] This story at least finds a plausible context, in the fact that Adandozan, having succeeded to the throne as a minor, ruled together with a council of regents until 1804.[49] Adandozan's defiance of Ọyọ certainly took the more usual form of military pressure against Ọyọ's protégé, Porto Novo. From 1803 onwards Dahomian forces launched a series of raids upon the territory of Porto Novo.[50] In 1805 the authorities at Ọyọ stirred themselves to deliver a warning to Adandozan to leave Porto Novo alone,[51] but it does not appear that Dahomian pressure was more than temporarily relaxed. By 1807 these Dahomian raids were reported to have seriously disrupted trade between Ọyọ and Porto

---

[46] Forbes, *Dahomey and the Dahomans*, ii. 89.
[47] George, *Historical Notes on the Yoruba Country*, 23–4: Akikanju was the predecessor of Ikọṣoni, who was the ruler of Ṣabẹ at the time of the successful Dahomian revolt in 1823.
[48] Le Herissé, *L'Ancien Royaume de Dahomey*, 312–13.
[49] Akinjogbin, *Dahomey and its Neighbours*, 187.
[50] Ibid. 188.
[51] AN, C.6/27, Goupil, untitled report, n.d. (received in France, Feb. 1806).

Novo, forcing Ọyọ traders to take their slaves instead to Lagos, further east and beyond the range of Dahomian raids.[52] Ọyọ traders travelling to Porto Novo in this period had to go in caravans, protected by cavalry and archers, for fear of Dahomian attacks.[53]

However, although relations between Dahomey and Ọyọ must have become very strained at this period, there was no open rupture. A contemporary source attests the presence of an Ọyọ embassy at Abomey in 1808, though in what connection is not indicated.[54] It appears, moreover, that Adandozan continued to pay tribute to Ọyọ, though towards the end of his reign payment of this tribute is reported to have become 'irregular'.[55] The reason for Adandozan's failure to venture as far as open revolt is clear enough, since the Ọyọ demonstrated during his reign that they were still capable of effective military action in the west. In about 1810 Ọyọ forces are reported to have operated successfully in the adjoining territory of the Mahi. According to Bowdich, who had the story from a British officer resident at Lagos at the time, the Ọyọ 'entirely conquered the Mahees', capturing large numbers of slaves who were brought for sale at Lagos.[56] We would gladly know more of this campaign, but no other source throws any light on it. The Mahi country, or parts of it, had been tributary to Ọyọ since 1788,[57] and the Ọyọ may have been suppressing a local revolt. Alternatively, the expedition may have been a reaction to Dahomian encroachment upon the Ọyọ sphere in the Mahi country. At any rate, the campaign will have provided a salutary warning to Adandozan and the Dahomians. There is, indeed, some suggestion that Ọyọ forces in this period actually raided Dahomey itself. A circumstantial story recorded in 1849 asserts that during Adandozan's reign an Ọyọ army invaded Dahomian territory and ambushed and destroyed a small party of Dahomian soldiers.[58] The incident was evidently minor, and appar-

[52] APB, O.R. 143, f. 109, Governor of Bahia to Secretary of State, 14 Oct. 1807, quoted in Verger, *Flux et Reflux de la Traite des Nègres*, 271.

[53] Robertson, *Notes on Africa*, 282.

[54] PRO, T.70/1163, Day Book, William's Fort Whydah, entry for 10 Mar. 1808. Akinjogbin, *Dahomey and its Neighbours*, 188, 196, assumes that this was a tribute-collecting mission, but it might equally have come to complain about Dahomian raids on Porto Novo, or on some other business of which we know nothing.

[55] Robertson, *Notes on Africa*, 268.

[56] Bowdich, *Mission from Cape Coast to Ashantee*, 226: the campaign is dated to 'about nine years ago'.

[57] Cf. above, Ch. 8, pp. 181–2.

[58] PP, 1850 (1291), vol. lv, p. 7, J. Duncan to Lord Palmerston, 22 Sept. 1849:

ently led to no large-scale fighting, but it too will have served to discourage Dahomian inclinations to revolt.

Dahomey was, therefore, still tributary to Ọyọ when Adandozan was deposed and replaced on the Dahomian throne by Gezo in 1818.[59] It has been suggested, indeed, that one reason for Adandozan's deposition may have been precisely his failure to liberate Dahomey from Ọyọ rule.[60] Certainly, Gezo proceeded to achieve what Adandozan had failed to achieve. Gezo's task was easier than Adandozan's, since the outbreak of the Muslim rebellion in 1817 had further weakened the power of Ọyọ, a fact of which Gezo was no doubt aware.[61] The revolt of Dahomey seems to have come finally in 1823. A contemporary report of that year refers to the impending outbreak of war between Dahomey and Ọyọ, occasioned by a Dahomian attack on territory tributary to Ọyọ.[62] The identity of this tributary is not indicated: perhaps it was Mahi, which had certainly come under Dahomian pressure in recent years.[63] Unfortunately the contemporary account breaks off before any actual fighting had begun. According to Dahomian tradition, Gezo refused to pay tribute to Ọyọ, and finally murdered the Ọyọ ambassadors sent to demand it. An Ọyọ army was therefore dispatched against Dahomey. The Ọyọ had the assistance of at least some of the Mahi,[64] and also of Ṣabẹ, now ruled by Akikanju's successor Ikọṣoni.[65] Gezo, however, met and repulsed the invaders at Paouignan, in the Mahi country. A second, and larger, Ọyọ force was then mustered,

two Ọyọ who had commanded (or perhaps acted as guides to) the Ọyọ forces on this raid, and who were regarded as traitors since they had earlier resided in Dahomey, were captured by the Dahomians and recognized many years later and executed, at the age of about eighty, in 1849.

[59] There seems to be no evidence for this date earlier than Burton, *Mission to Gelele*, ii. 104, who presumably calculated it from the information that Gezo, who died in 1858, had reigned for 40 years: this looks like an approximation, but no doubt it is approximately correct.

[60] Akinjogbin, *Dahomey and its Neighbours*, 201; cf. the confused story in Forbes, *Dahomey and the Dahomans*, ii. 23–5, that Adandozan was deposed for refusing to attack the Ẹgbado town of Ijanna.

[61] Cf. Burton, *Mission to Gelele*, i. 198 and ii. 118.

[62] *Royal Gold Coast Gazette and Commercial Intelligencer*, 21 Jan., 11 Feb., 18 Mar. 1823.

[63] Cf. Robertson, *Notes on Africa*, 269.

[64] Cf. J. Duncan, *Travels in Western Africa in 1845 and 1846* (London, 1847), ii. 41–2.

[65] Dunglas, 'Contribution à l'histoire du Moyen-Dahomey', t.II, 57; cf. Duncan, *Travels in Western Africa*, ii. 41–2, refers to the king of 'Anago' as an ally of Ọyọ.

under the command of a general called Ajanaku. Gezo forestalled an invasion of the Dahomian homeland by himself again invading the Mahi country and besieging the Mahi town of Kpaloko, which was allied to Oyo. Ajanaku marched to the relief of Kpaloko, but was defeated by Gezo before the town. The Oyo forces fled in retreat across the River Weme, Ajanaku was taken prisoner and put to death, and Kpaloko was taken by the Dahomians.[66]

The victory of Gezo in the war of 1823 was by no means a foregone conclusion. Despite their internal distractions, the Oyo had mustered a strong army under Ajanaku: it is said to have numbered no less than 4,000 men,[67] and to have included a strong contingent of cavalry.[68] Gezo, according to one account, nullified the threat of the dreaded Oyo cavalry by attacking Ajanaku's camp at night.[69] However, once Gezo had defeated the invaders, Dahomey was free, for the Oyo no longer commanded sufficient resources to maintain a protracted war against Dahomey.

The successful revolt of Dahomey also destroyed what remained of Oyo control over its other dependencies in the west. When Clapperton reached Oyo in 1826, he was told that Dahomey, Mahi, Porto Novo, and Badagry were all tributary to Oyo,[70] but except in the case of Badagry, this claim was evidently mere nostalgia. Some at least of the Mahi had remained loyal to Oyo down to the time of Gezo's revolt, but the defeat of Oyo left the Mahi at the mercy of the Dahomians, who had largely conquered the

[66] For Gezo's revolt, see esp. Le Herissé, L'Ancien Royaume de Dahomey, 319–22; and cf. the accounts derived from local tradition in the Mahi country given by Duncan, Travels in Western Africa, ii. 41–2, 56–7, and Skertchly, Dahomey As It Is, 326. The account given by Dunglas, 'Contribution à l'histoire du Moyen-Dahomey', t.II, 56–9, conflates the battle at Paouignan and the siege of Kpaloko into a single campaign. Ross, 'The Autonomous Kingdom of Dahomey', 37–9, argues that Gezo's opponents in Ajanaku's invasion were the Mahi, Sabe, and Ketu and that the implication of the Oyo in this campaign by Dahomian tradition is a patriotic elaboration, but the account of Duncan, recorded as early as the 1840s, confirms that the Oyo were involved at Kpaloko as well as at Paouignan. Burton, Mission to Gelele, ii. 406, followed by Skertchly, Dahomey As It Is, 118–19, refers to a great battle between Gezo and the Oyo at Cana: for the problems raised by this account, cf. above, Ch. 8, p. 169.

[67] Le Herissé, L'Ancien Royaume de Dahomey, 321.

[68] Dunglas, 'Contribution à l'histoire du Moyen-Dahomey', t.II, 57.

[69] Ibid. It is noteworthy that the Ibadan similarly employed a night attack against the cavalry of Ilorin at the battle of Osogbo in c. 1838, according to Johnson, History of the Yorubas, 286–7: no doubt the Ibadan commanders had heard of Gezo's tactics at Kpaloko.

[70] Clapperton, Journal of a Second Expedition, 56; cf. ibid. 39.

territory by the 1840s.[71] Gezo also attacked and destroyed Ṣabẹ, killing Ikọṣoni,[72] and induced the other major western Yoruba kingdom, Ketu, to accept Dahomian protection.[73] The coastal kingdom of Porto Novo had probably fallen away from Ọyọ even before 1823. The Ọyọ warning to Adandozan to cease raiding Porto Novo territory in 1805 was the last recorded Ọyọ intervention in protection of that kingdom, and Porto Novo had probably felt obliged to make its peace with Dahomey. In 1823, the king of Porto Novo is said to have advised Gezo to make peace with Ọyọ.[74] Dahomian tradition represents this as a friendly act, the king of Porto Novo being fearful for Dahomey's safety: while this may distort the original significance of the action, clearly the king of Porto Novo did nothing to assist the Ọyọ. Ọyọ influence over Badagry was perhaps maintained for rather longer. In *c.* 1821, Badagry came under the rule of Adele, the exiled king of Lagos.[75] Adele had to defend Badagry against attacks from Dahomey and Porto Novo, and perhaps in consequence sought a rapprochement with Ọyọ. In 1825, Clapperton was told at Badagry as well as at Ọyọ that Badagry was tributary to the *Alafin*.[76] Later however, Adele exploited the decline of Ọyọ power to repudiate his allegiance, and in the 1830s he went to war against the subjects of Ọyọ in Ẹgbado.[77]

§4. THE OWU WAR AND THE POWERS IN THE SOUTH

While the Ọyọ kingdom was disintegrating in civil war, and its tributaries in the west were falling away, a series of wars was being waged in southern Yorubaland which was to destroy the main ally of Ọyọ in the south, the kingdom of Owu, and establish new centres of

[71] Duncan, *Travels in Western Africa*, ii, esp. 81; cf. Forbes, *Dahomey and the Dahomans*, ii. 181.

[72] Dunglas, 'Contribution à l'histoire du Dahomey', t.II, 67; Le Herissé, *L'Ancien Royaume de Dahomey*, 327–8. The skull of 'Kohcharnee [Ikọṣoni], king of Anagoo' was exhibited at Abomey in 1850: PP, 1852 (1455), vol. liv, p. 67, Journal of Lt. Forbes, on his Mission to Dahomey, entry for 15 June 1850.

[73] Forbes, *Dahomey and the Dahomans*, i. 20; but cf. Parrinder, *Story of Ketu*, 49–50.

[74] Le Herissé, *L'Ancien Royaume de Dahomey*, 321–2; Dunglas, 'Contribution à l'histoire du Moyen-Dahomey', t.II, 19, n.3.

[75] For the date of Adele's arrival at Badagry, see Law, 'The Dynastic Chronology of Lagos', 48, 50. For his repulse of a Dahomian-Porto Novo attack on Badagry, see PRO, C.O.2/15, H. Clapperton, 'Journal of the African Mission from Badagry to Jennah', entry for 6 Dec. 1825; Loṣi, *History of Lagos*', 20–21.

[76] PRO, C.O.2/15, H. Clapperton, 'Journal of the African Mission from Badagry to Jennah', entry for 6 Dec. 1825; cf. Clapperton, *Journal of a Second Expedition*, 39, 56. [77] Cf. below, p. 277.

power which would ultimately eclipse the Ọyọ capital. Since these events were only tangentially connected with the collapse of the Ọyọ empire itself, they will be dealt with here only briefly.[78]

The events that led up to the destruction of Owu were in large part a consequence of the decline of Ọyọ power. The ultimate origin of the war was the shift of the main centre of the Atlantic slave trade from Porto Novo eastwards to Lagos. The rise of Lagos as an important slaving port began in the 1790s, when the outbreak of war between Britain and France interfered with European activities at Porto Novo. At first this shift did not alter the patterns of trade in the interior, since the main supply of slaves at Lagos was brought by canoe through the lagoon system from Porto Novo.[79] However, the Dahomian raids on Porto Novo after 1803 severely disrupted the trade-routes between Ọyọ and Porto Novo. In 1804 the Ọyọ were still bringing large numbers of slaves to Porto Novo,[80] but by 1807 the disruption of the trade routes by Dahomian raids had forced the Ọyọ traders to take their slaves instead direct to Lagos.[81] Some slaves were probably brought from Ọyọ to Lagos through Ẹgbado and Ọta, but others were taken to the new market town of Apomu, in the Ifẹ kingdom, to be sold to Ijẹbu traders, who re-sold them to Lagos through the lagoon ports of Ikosi and Ikorodu. In the 1790s, the Ijẹbu were supplying only a small proportion of the slaves sold at Lagos,[82] but by 1819 it could be reported that Lagos was entirely dependent upon the Ijẹbu port of Ikosi for its supplies of slaves.[83] However, the supply of slaves from Ọyọ through Apomu probably declined with the decay of Ọyọ power in the early nineteenth century. After 1817 the exacerbation of civil strife inside the Ọyọ kingdom was to yield a new supply of slaves, but before the Muslim rebellion in Ọyọ there was probably increasing pressure of Lagos demand upon Ijẹbu supplies of slaves. The Ijẹbu apparently responded by inciting local slave-raiding in the Apomu area by the towns of the western portion of the Ifẹ kingdom: certainly, in the 1810s there

---

[78] For fuller treatment, see Mabogunjẹ and Omer-Cooper, *Owu in Yoruba History*; Law, 'The Owu War in Yoruba History'.

[79] Adams, *Remarks on the Country Extending from Cape Palmas*, 218–19.

[80] BNRJ, 46, King of Allada (Porto Novo) to Prince Regent of Portugal, 18 Nov. 1804, quoted in Verger, *Flux et Reflux de la Traite des Nègres*, 270.

[81] APB, O.R. 143, f. 109, Governor of Bahia to Secretary of State, 14 Oct. 1807, quoted in Verger, *Flux et Reflux de la Traite des Nègres*, 271.

[82] Adams, *Remarks on the Country Extending from Cape Palmas*, 96; cf. ibid. 220.

[83] Bowdich, *Mission from Cape Coast to Ashantee*, 224–5.

was a serious outbreak of kidnapping there, from which Ọyọ traders travelling to Apomu suffered.[84]

Alarmed by the breakdown of order in the Apomu area, two of the leading provincial rulers of the Ọyọ kingdom, Adegun, the *Onikoyi* of Ikoyi, and Toyejẹ, the *Balẹ* of Ogbomọṣọ, sent a request to the *Olowu* of Owu, Akijọbi, for action to suppress local slave-raiding. *Olowu* Akijọbi complied, and attacked and subjected several western Ifẹ towns, including Apomu itself. This action provoked a war with Ifẹ (*c.* 1812?[85]), in which the Owu were victorious. A few years later, however, the Ijẹbu were drawn in on the side of the Ifẹ. This shifted the military balance against the Owu, since the involvement of the Ijẹbu in the Atlantic slave trade had enabled them to equip their troops with imported European muskets. With these they were able to defeat the Owu in battle (*c.* 1817), and the Ifẹ and Ijẹbu forces began a long siege of the town of Owu.[86]

The Ọyọ made no effort to assist *Olowu* Akijọbi in the war which he had undertaken on their behalf.[87] This is hardly surprising, since after 1817 the Ọyọ kingdom was distracted by the Muslim rebellion incited by Afọnja. Indeed, large numbers of refugees and adventurers displaced by the civil wars inside the Ọyọ kingdom joined the besieging army before Owu, and the final fall of Owu, in *c.* 1822, was in large measure due to this reinforcement of the Ifẹ-Ijẹbu forces.[88] After the destruction of Owu, the Ifẹ and Ijẹbu, together with the Ọyọ refugees, proceeded to invade Ẹgbaland, and one by one to destroy almost all the old Ẹgba towns. Many of the Ẹgba eventually rallied and established a new city at Abẹokuta on the River Ogun, in the far west of Ẹgba territory, while the Ọyọ refugees occupied the town of Ibadan, in the Gbagura province of Ẹgbaland.[89] A few years later another group of Ọyọ refugees, displaced from the Epo

---

[84] PP, 1887 (c. 4957), vol. lx, p. 4, A. Moloney to Sir S. Rowe, 12 May 1881; Johnson, *History of the Yorubas*, 206–7.

[85] For the chronology of these events, see Law, 'Chronology of the Yoruba Wars', 219–20.

[86] Johnson, *History of the Yorubas*, 206–8.

[87] Ojo, *Iwe Itan Ọyọ*, 82–4, states that *Olowu* Akijọbi did in fact send to the *Alafin* (anachronistically identified by Chief Ojo as Oluewu: in fact, Majotu was reigning at this time) for aid, but was rebuffed, and that later, when some years after the fall of Owu Akijọbi was finally captured and put to death by the Ibadan (probably *c.* 1833/4), he pronounced a curse on the city of Ọyọ in vengeance for this desertion. This makes a nicely moral story, analogous to that of the curse of *Alafin* Awolẹ (cf. above, Ch. 12, p. 245), but it is probably an invention.

[88] Johnson, *History of the Yorubas*, 208–10.

[89] Ibid. 223–6.

K

province of the Ọyọ kingdom, seized possession of another Gbagura town, Ijaye.[90] There followed, in the 1830s, a series of wars in which the Ọyọ at Ibadan, with support from Ijaye and Ijẹbu, attempted unsuccessfully to eliminate the new centre of Ẹgba power at Abẹo-kuta.[91] By c. 1835, both Ibadan and Ijaye appear to have acknow-ledged the overlordship of the *Alafin* of Ọyọ, and forces from these towns played some part in the last campaigns against Ilọrin.[92]

<h2>§5. THE LOSS OF ẸGBADO</h2>

Through all the troubles from the 1790s to the 1820s, the most remote province of the Ọyọ kingdom, Ẹgbado, appears to have remained firmly in Ọyọ hands. Ẹgbado was still clearly very much under effective Ọyọ control when Clapperton and Richard Lander travelled through it on their way to Ọyọ in 1825–6, and if by 1830 Richard and John Lander could observe some signs of a loosening of the Ọyọ grip, notably in the fact that the post of *Onisarẹ* at Ijanna had been left unfilled for fifteen months,[93] this was evidently due to lassitude at the capital rather than to any challenge to Ọyọ rule locally. However, the collapse at the centre of the Ọyọ kingdom was eventually to lead to the destruction of Ọyọ power in Ẹgbado also.

The first challenge to Ọyọ authority in Ẹgbado appears to have come from the revolt of a certain Dẹkun, an *ilari* posted by the *Alafin* to the town of Ijanna, who is probably to be identified with the 'Dorkun', described as the 'head man' of the 'Governor' of Ijanna, whom the Landers met in 1830.[94] According to Johnson, Dẹkun took advantage of the distracted state of the Ọyọ kingdom after the Muslim rebellion, to 'make himself great at Ijanna, by appropriating all taxes and tribute he should have forwarded to Ọyọ.'[95] During the 1820s Dẹkun went to assist the army of Ọyọ refugees which was devastating Ẹgbaland, but later returned to Ijanna. Subsequently, presumably in the early 1830s, Dẹkun and Aṣade, the *Balogun* (principal war-chief) of Ijanna, took their followers out of Ijanna and founded their own town at Rẹfurẹfu,

---

[90] Ibid. 236.

[91] Ibid. 248–56; cf. Ajiṣafẹ, *History of Abẹokuta*, 65–8.

[92] Cf. below, Ch. 14, p. 294.

[93] R. and J. Lander, *Journal of an Expedition*, i. 81.

[94] 'Dorkun' is not mentioned in the published *Journal* of the Landers, but in a brief note at the end of the manuscript Journal of Richard Lander (Wellcome Historical Medical Library, MS. 1659).

[95] Johnson, *History of the Yorubas*, 228.

west of the River Yewa. Dẹkun and Aṣade later quarrelled, and Dẹkun was exiled from Rẹfurẹfu. He ultimately made his way to Dahomey, where he persuaded Gezo to attack and destroy Rẹfurẹfu.[96]

By the time Rẹfurẹfu fell to the Dahomians, Ọyọ power in Ẹgbado had been destroyed by another invader. In the wars of the early 1830s between the new powers of Ibadan and Abẹokuta, the towns of the Ẹgbado province apparently assisted Ibadan. The Ẹgba of Abẹokuta responded, in c. 1833, by invading Ẹgbado, where they attacked and destroyed the principal towns, Ilaro and Ijanna. Aṣade Agunloye, the *Olu* of Ilaro, and Abinuwọgbo, the *Oniṣarẹ* of Ijanna, were both killed.[97] Adele, the exiled king of Lagos then ruling at Badagry, assisted the Ẹgba in this war, and himself sent forces which besieged and destroyed the town of Ilobi.[98] A couple of years later, in c. 1835, the Ẹgba completed the liquidation of Ọyọ power in the Ẹgbado area by attacking and subjecting the town of Ọta.[99] The Ọyọ, who by the 1830s were distracted by the final struggles against Ilọrin, are not recorded to have taken any action to protect their Ẹgbado subjects.

[96] For Dẹkun's career, see esp. Johnson, *History of the Yorubas*, 228–9; Adewale, 'The Ijanna Episode in Yoruba History', 252–4. An appallingly confused account of Dẹkun and Rẹfurẹfu is given by Forbes, *Dahomey and the Dahomans*, ii. 24–7: Ijanna and Rẹfurẹfu are confused, and the events of the 1830s confounded with Gezo's revolt against Ọyọ in 1823. An allusion in Johnson, *History of the Yorubas*, 250, shows that Rẹfurẹfu had been founded by c. 1833; its destruction by the Dahomians occurred at an uncertain date before 1849, when this event is first alluded to, by Forbes, *Dahomey and the Dahomans*, i. 31, 68.

[97] Johnson, *History of the Yorubas*, 248–50.

[98] Fọlayan, 'Ẹgbado to 1832', 31–2.

[99] Johnson, *History of the Yorubas*, 255–6; for the chronology of these events, see Law, 'Chronology of the Yoruba Wars', 221–2.

K*

CHAPTER 14

The Fall of Ọyọ (*c.* 1823 – *c.* 1836)

THE overthrow of Afọnja at Ilọrin in *c.* 1823 brought to an end the period in which the disturbances in the Ọyọ kingdom could be seen as no more than a struggle for power between rival factions among the Ọyọ. Ilọrin, incorporated as an emirate into the Sokoto Caliphate, now represented an alien power whose object was the complete destruction of the Ọyọ kingdom. The aim of the new rulers of Ilọrin was no less than to 'dip the Koran into the sea',[1] i.e. to carry the *jihad* throughout Yorubaland to the coast. While this larger objective was never realized, the destruction of Ọyọ power was effected in no more than thirteen years. This final phase of the decline and fall of Ọyọ (*c.* 1823–36) is the subject of the present chapter.

§1. THE SITUATION IN *c.* 1823

We may begin by attempting to describe the situation facing the rulers of Ọyọ at the fall of Afọnja. Thanks mainly to the evidence of Clapperton and the Landers, it is possible to reconstruct the situation in the 1820s, at least in outline, with some confidence.

Even by 1823 the *Alafin* retained at least the nominal allegiance of much of the Ọyọ kingdom. The original revolt had been largely confined to the eastern provinces of the kingdom—the Ẹkun Osi, Ibọlọ, Epo, and Igbomina provinces. Afọnja had detached the Igbomina from allegiance to Ọyọ,[2] and Ilọrin forces had raided into the Ibọlọ and Epo provinces, destroying some important towns, such as Irẹsa, Igbọn, and Ejigbo.[3] Also in possession of the Fulani, and in alliance with Ilọrin, was the important commercial town of Raka, to the north-east of Ọyọ.[4] The attitude of some important towns in the Ẹkun Osi which had supported Afọnja's original revolt—such as Ikoyi, Ogbomọṣọ, and Gbogun—during the last years of Afọnja's

---

[1] Johnson, *History of the Yorubas*, 288; cf. ibid. 338.

[2] Ojo, *Short History of Ilorin*, 15; cf. Johnson, *History of the Yorubas*, 194, 196.

[3] Johnson, *History of the Yorubas*, 194, 197, 200.

[4] Clapperton, *Journal of a Second Expedition*, 46, 204; R. and J. Lander, *Journal of an Expedition*, i. 189.

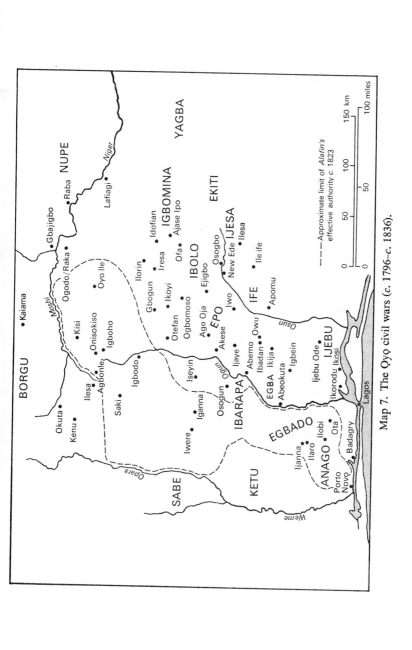

Map 7. The Ọyọ civil wars (c. 1796–c. 1836).

life is unclear. While there is no evidence that they actively supported
Afọnja, it is likely that they equally paid little attention to the
capital.[5] One provincial ruler who seized the opportunity presented
to make himself independent was Kubọlaje, the *Timi* of Ẹdẹ, who
moved his town southwards across the River Ọṣun as a precaution
against Fulani raids and set about attacking and reducing neighbouring towns in the Ibọlọ province.[6] Two other independent
principalities had been established in the Epo province. After the
death of Afọnja, one of his subordinate chiefs, Ojo Amepo, left
Ilọrin and established himself at Akesẹ in the Epo province, from
which he conducted widespread raids.[7] A rival raider, Ọja, settled in
the same area at Agọ Ọja ('Ọja's Camp'), the later New Ọyọ, where
he was joined by a renegade son of *Alafin* Abiọdun called Atiba.[8]
During the same period, other bands of Ọyọ refugees and adventurers
were settling beyond the boundaries of the Ọyọ kingdom, in Ifẹ and
Ẹgba territory, and the Ẹgba town of Ibadan, as has been seen,
became the centre of another independent Ọyọ power.[9]

However, although almost the whole of the eastern provinces was
either in revolt or of doubtful loyalty, the *Alafin*'s power in the
western provinces was still strong. To the west of the River Ogun,
the town of Iseyin had adhered to the Muslim cause, and had become
a base for raids in the Ibarapa province of the kingdom, in the
course of which the important town of Oṣogun was destroyed.[10]
But elsewhere, there had apparently been little disturbance. Clapperton and the Landers in 1825–6 and 1830 were able to journey from
Badagry through Ẹgbado, western Ibarapa, western Onko, and the
Ẹkun Ọtun to Ọyọ through towns which still acknowledged the
Alafin's authority, and found no evidence of Fulani raids until they
reached the north-eastern area of the Ẹkun Ọtun, beyond Ṣaki.[11]

    [5] Toyejẹ, the *Balẹ* of Ogbomọṣọ, who was *Ọtun Kakamfo*, seems to have
continued to co-operate with Afọnja after the latter's revolt: cf. Johnson, *History
of the Yorubas*, 197. Fagbohun of Jabata, the *Osi Kakamfo*, quarrelled with
Afọnja, but there is no suggestion that he sought to uphold the *Alafin*'s authority
against him: ibid., 198.   [6] Olunlade, *Ẹdẹ: A Brief History*, 18.
    [7] Johnson, *History of the Yorubas*, 234.
    [8] Ibid. 276. Ọja may also have been a former follower of Afọnja: Johnson,
ibid., describes him as 'an officer on the staff of the [Arẹ Ọna] Kakanfo', but
does not state which holder of this title Ọja served under.
    [9] For the settlement of Ọyọ refugees in Ifẹ territory, and the foundation of the
Ọyọ town of Modakẹkẹ, close to Ile Ifẹ, see ibid. 230–2. For the Ọyọ occupation
of Ibadan, cf. above, Ch. 13, p. 275.
    [10] Schön and Crowther, *Journals*, 371–2; Curtin, *Africa Remembered*, 299–304.
    [11] Clapperton, *Journal of a Second Expedition*, 28 etc.

Moreover, even many of the eastern towns, such as Ikoyi, Ogbomọṣọ, Gbogun, and Ẹdẹ, were to rally to the *Alafin* after the removal of Afọnja.

It remained uncertain, however, whether the Ọyọ capital was capable of providing effective leadership for the loyal provincial towns, for the city continued to suffer from its internal dissensions. The *Alafin* at this time was apparently still Majotu.[12] Little is known of the political history of the capital during his reign, but it appears that tension between the *Alafin* and the *Baṣọrun* continued. This, at least, is suggested by the fact that when Ojo Aburumaku, the *Baṣọrun* who had ruled as Regent during the interregnum of *c.* 1797–*c.* 1802, died, *Alafin* Majotu once more transferred the title to a new lineage, conferring it upon a certain Akioṣo.[13] Moreover, Majotu was by now an old man,[14] and the effective power of the throne fell increasingly to his *Arẹmọ*, Adewusi, who behaved tyrannically and clashed violently with the *Baṣọrun*.[15] The political troubles of the capital thus continued to divide and weaken the central leadership of the kingdom.

In addition to metropolitan dissension and provincial rebellion, Ọyọ seems by the 1820s to have been suffering a severe commercial depression. It has been seen in an earlier chapter that the volume of slave exports from Ọyọ, after reaching a peak in the 1780s, fell dramatically in the 1790s.[16] By the 1820s the situation had deteriorated further. The lack of success of the Ọyọ armies meant that there was no longer any substantial supply of war captives for sale to the Europeans, while the disturbances consequent upon the decline of Ọyọ power disrupted the major trade routes. In the south Dahomian pressure had interfered with the supply of slaves to Porto Novo, driving the main centre of the slave trade eastwards to Lagos.[17] By the 1820s the principal suppliers of slaves to Lagos were the Ijẹbu, and they were receiving their slaves not from Ọyọ, but from its dissident vassals, such as Ilọrin,[18] and from the wars in southern

---

[12] Johnson, *History of the Yorubas*, 210; Law, 'Chronology of the Yoruba Wars', 213–14. [13] Johnson, *History of the Yorubas*, 72.

[14] Johnson, ibid. 212, states that Majotu was 'well advanced in age' at his accession: this is unlikely if (cf. above, Ch. 12, p. 255) he came to the throne as early as *c.* 1802.

[15] Ibid. 213–15; cf. Crowther, *Vocabulary of the Yoruba Language*, vi.

[16] Cf. above, Ch. 10, p. 224.   [17] Cf. above, Ch. 13, pp. 269–70 274.

[18] For the sale of war captives by Afọnja, cf. Johnson, *History of the Yorubas*, 200. An example is Samuel Crowther, enslaved at the capture of Oṣogun in 1821, and sold via the Ẹgba country and Ikosi to Lagos.

Yorubaland, in the Owu and Ẹgba countries.[19] In the north also the trade-routes had been disrupted, and the supply of slaves from the countries to the north of Ǫyǫ substantially reduced. Clapperton in 1826 found that the traditional northern market of the Ǫyǫ, Raka on the Nupe frontier, was in Fulani hands, and the road to it was considered unsafe.[20] Clapperton was therefore obliged to travel to the north instead through Borgu, crossing the Niger at Bussa. Ǫyǫ trade with the north had evidently also been diverted through Borgu, for Clapperton learned that Raka had been replaced by a new market town to the west of the Ǫyǫ capital, called 'Agolly' or 'Ajoolly', probably to be identified with Agbǫnle.[21] It appears, moreover, that most of the slaves coming from the north were by-passing Ǫyǫ altogether, being taken through Borgu and Dahomey for sale at Whydah. Clapperton was struck by the abundance of imported European goods in Borgu, in contrast with their paucity in Ǫyǫ. At Kaiama he observed: 'I have seen more European articles, such as earthenware jugs, brass and pewter dishes, pieces of woollen and cotton cloth, within these two days that I have been in Kiama, than I saw during the whole time I was in Yourriba.'[22] These European goods, he learned, were imported into Borgu from Dahomey, in exchange for slaves.[23] This pattern of trade was a consequence of the troubles inside the Ǫyǫ kingdom, for Clapperton was told that the importation of large quantities of European goods into Borgu had only begun 'since the war between the Fellatas [Fulani] and the people of Yourriba'.[24]

The loss of income resulting from this commercial depression must have considerably weakened the capacity of the Ǫyǫ to respond effectively to the threat of Ilǫrin. In particular, it may have been

---

[19] For the sale of the captives taken in these wars to the Ijẹbu traders, see CMS, CA2/O52, E. G. Irving, 'Journal of a Visit to the Ijebbu Country in the Months of Dec. 1854 and Jany 1855'.

[20] Clapperton, *Journal of a Second Expedition*, 46.

[21] Clapperton's manuscript 'Journal', in PRO, CO.2/16, Part 1, 'Missions to the Interior of Africa', vol. 2, p. 92, observes that 'Agolly is one day south of Ensookoso [Onisokiso] and is now resorted to instead of Rakah'; cf. Clapperton, *Journal of a Second Expedition*, 135, 137. 'Agolly' is no doubt identical with the town described earlier by Bowdich, *Mission from Cape Coast to Ashantee*, 208, as 'Aquallie . . . the frontier town of Yariba, second only to the capital', which seems to be Agbǫnle: however, a slip on Clapperton's part must be assumed, since Agbǫnle was west rather than south of Onisokiso.

[22] Clapperton, *Journal of a Second Expedition*, 68.

[23] Ibid. 83–4, 123.

[24] Ibid. 93.

responsible for the virtual disappearance of the cavalry force upon which the military power of Ǫyǫ had earlier rested. The Ǫyǫ army which attempted to suppress the revolt of Gezo of Dahomey in 1823 is said to have included a strong cavalry contingent,[25] but this was apparently the last occasion on which the Ǫyǫ disposed of a large cavalry force. Ǫyǫ tradition records that in the wars between Ǫyǫ and Ilǫrin after Afǫnja's death, the Ǫyǫ were at a serious disadvantage because their enemies possessed cavalry, while they themselves evidently did not.[26] This is corroborated by the evidence of Clapperton and the Landers. Clapperton in 1826 reports that the Ǫyǫ feared the Fulani of Ilǫrin because 'they have a great number of horses',[27] while in the Ǫyǫ kingdom horses were 'scarce'.[28] The Landers in 1830 similarly heard that Ilǫrin possessed 'upwards of three thousand horses', while Ǫyǫ did not have 'as many hundreds'.[29] The small cavalry force which still existed in Ǫyǫ, Clapperton did not find very impressive:

> The horsemen . . . are but ill mounted: the animals are small and badly dressed, their saddles so ill secured, and the rider sits so clumsily on his seat, that any Englishman, who ever rode a horse with an English saddle, would upset one of them the first charge with a long stick.[30]

The reasons for the decline of the Ǫyǫ cavalry are a matter of controversy. It has been suggested that the revolt of the Hausa slaves in 1817 deprived the Ǫyǫ of their supplies of skilled grooms.[31] This is very probable: indeed, the revolt may have robbed the Ǫyǫ of skilled horsemen as well as grooms, since at least some of the mounted retainers of the Ǫyǫ war-chiefs were northern slaves.[32] However, it is clear that the Ǫyǫ in the 1820s lacked not only skilled grooms and riders, but also horses. Evidently the importation of good cavalry mounts from the north had been drastically reduced. It has been suggested that this was due to an embargo on the sale of horses to Ǫyǫ imposed, for military reasons, either by the Nupe and Bariba in the late eighteenth century[33] or by Ilǫrin in the early

---

[25] Dunglas, 'Contribution à l'histoire du Moyen-Dahomey', t.II, 57.

[26] Johnson, *History of the Yorubas*, 202, 263, 286; cf. Bowen, *Central Africa*, 198.

[27] Clapperton, *Journal of a Second Expedition*, 28.

[28] Ibid. 56.

[29] R. and J. Lander, *Journal of an Expedition*, i. 190.

[30] Clapperton, *Journal of a Second Expedition*, 34.

[31] Ajayi, 'Aftermath of the Fall of Old Ǫyǫ', 143.

[32] Cf. above, Ch. 9, p. 189.

[33] Akinjogbin, 'Prelude to the Yoruba Civil Wars', 30.

nineteenth century.[34] But there is no evidence for such an embargo, and it seems more probable that the decline of horse imports into Ọyọ was simply a consequence of the depression in trade discussed above. Horses had earlier been bought primarily by the northward re-export of European manufactures: with the shift of the slave trade to Dahomey and Lagos, the Ọyọ no longer had the purchasing power, in terms of imported European goods, with which to buy horses.

The penetration of European firearms, which had first been used effectively in Yorubaland by the Ijẹbu against the Owu in c. 1817,[35] might appear to have promised an alternative basis for an Ọyọ military recovery. Firearms were both cheaper than horses, and more easily available to Ọyọ than to Ilọrin. Richard Lander in 1827 did find that muskets were being imported into Ọyọ in some numbers, but observed: 'they are of comparatively little use to the people, who know not how to handle them with effect; and it is not unusual for them to carry these weapons to battle without either powder or ball.'[36] Effective use of muskets was only beginning to spread among the Ọyọ in the 1830s, and the first to adopt the new weapons were the new centres of Ọyọ power in the south. Thus, the securing of supplies of gunpowder had become a crucial factor in the wars between Ibadan and Abẹokuta by the early 1830s,[37] and muskets were by then also being used by the troops of Atiba of Agọ Ọja.[38] Firearms therefore served to strengthen the dissident vassals of Ọyọ rather than contributing to the military strength of the Ọyọ kingdom.

§2. THE ỌYỌ COUNTER-ATTACK AND ITS FAILURE
(c. 1823–c. 1831)

The fall of Afọnja, by making explicit the significance of the Muslim rebellion in Ọyọ, at least temporarily united the surviving Ọyọ towns in resistance to Ilọrin. The eastern provincial towns whose loyalty had been doubtful, such as Ikoyi, Ogbomọṣọ, Gbogun, and Ẹdẹ, now rallied again to the *Alafin*. To replace Afọnja as *Arẹ Ọna Kakamfo*, *Alafin* Majotu appointed Toyejẹ, the *Balẹ* of Ogbomọṣọ, who had been *Ọtun Kakamfo* under Afọnja.[39] With a unified military

---

[34] Ajayi, 'Aftermath of the Fall of Old Ọyọ', 147.
[35] Cf. above, Ch. 13, p. 275.
[36] R. Lander, *Records of Captain Clapperton's Last Expedition*, ii. 222.
[37] Cf. Johnson, *History of the Yorubas*, 251–2; Ajiṣafẹ, *History of Abẹokuta*, 66; Loṣi, *History of Abẹokuta*, 36.
[38] Johnson, *History of the Yorubas*, 260, 266.   [39] Ibid. 201.

command whose legitimacy was unquestioned thus restored, the Ọyọ then organized a concerted attempt to crush the rising power of Ilọrin.

A first attack was beaten back at the battle of Ogele, near Ilọrin, and the Ilọrin forces followed up their victory by raiding into the Ibọlọ province.[40] In this extremity, the Ọyọ sought external assistance against Ilọrin, and secured the alliance of the king of Nupe, *Etsu* Majiya II. In Nupe, as in Ọyọ, there had been an insurrection of the local Fulani, led by *Mallam* Dendo, who were able to exploit a civil war between rival segments of the Nupe royal lineage. Majiya, having come to power in Nupe with Fulani assistance, had broken with the Fulani and expelled them from his kingdom. Dendo and the other Fulani leaders had then sought refuge with 'Abd al-Salām at Ilọrin. Majiya therefore had a common interest with the Ọyọ in eliminating Ilọrin. For the Ọyọ, the main advantage of the alliance with Majiya may have been that he could supply a substantial force of cavalry, for Nupe tradition records that his army included 4,000 mounted troops.[41] Majiya and the Ọyọ now attacked Ilọrin, and were apparently able to lay siege to the city: the campaign became known as the Mugbamugba ('Locust Fruit') War, because both besiegers and besieged were reduced to living upon the locust fruit (*igba*). However, in the end the Ọyọ and Nupe forces were decisively defeated before Ilọrin (c. 1825?). Majiya fled back to Nupe, but was followed there by *Mallam* Dendo and the Fulani, who were now able to seize control of the Nupe capital at Raba and become the effective rulers of the kingdom.[42] This establishment of Fulani control in Nupe meant that the Ọyọ could no longer look to Nupe for aid against Ilọrin: in fact, in future it was rather the Ilọrin who were to receive assistance from their Fulani allies in Nupe.[43] The Ilọrin meanwhile followed up their victory in the Mugbamugba War by taking the important town of Ọfa, in the Ibọlọ province.[44]

[40] Ibid.

[41] Nadel, *Black Byzantium*, 78.

[42] For the Mugbamugba War, see esp. Johnson, *History of the Yorubas*, 201–2. For the involvement of *Etsu* Majiya and the Nupe, cf. Burdon, *Northern Nigeria*, 52; E. G. M. Dupigny, *Gazetteer of Nupe Province* (London, 1920), 9–10; Elphinstone, *Gazetteer of Ilorin Province*, 30–1; Hermon-Hodge, *Gazetteer of Ilorin Province*, 103; Nadel, *Black Byzantium*, 78–9; Mason, 'The Nupe Kingdom', 69–72.

[43] Cf. below, p. 294.

[44] Johnson, *History of the Yorubas*, 202; Hermon-Hodge, *Gazetteer of Ilorin Province*, 98.

After the defeat of the Ọyọ in the Ogele and Mugbamugba campaigns, the counter-attack against Ilọrin was in effect abandoned. Instead, the major Ọyọ provincial towns turned to fighting against each other, and soon began to look upon Ilọrin less as a common enemy than as a potential ally against their rivals. The first major conflict was between Toyejẹ of Ogbomọṣọ, the *Arẹ Ọna Kakamfo*, and Adegun, the *Onikoyi* of Ikoyi. The implicit tension between the rival claims of the *Arẹ Ọna Kakamfo* and the *Onikoyi* to the first place among the provincial rulers of the Ọyọ kingdom[45] now became overt, with disastrous effects. Toyejẹ was supported by the important towns of Iwo and Ẹdẹ, and also secured the assistance of forces from Ilọrin. Ikoyi was besieged, but the *Onikoyi* was able to detach the Ilọrin from the attackers by declaring his own allegiance to Ilọrin, and the besieging forces were defeated by the Ikoyi and Ilọrin at Pamọ, south-west of Ikoyi. The *Timi* of Ẹdẹ, Kubọlaje, was killed in this war.[46] The *Onikoyi* then demonstrated his claim to independence from Ọyọ by creating his own *Arẹ Ọna Kakamfo* as a rival to Toyejẹ, conferring the title upon Ẹdun, the *Balẹ* of Gbogun.[47]

After his defeat at Pamọ, Toyejẹ's authority over the other provincial towns began to crumble. The new *Timi* of Ẹdẹ, Bamigbaiye, repudiated his allegiance to Toyejẹ, but was compelled to submit after a long siege of Ẹdẹ.[48] Soon after this, however, it appears that Toyejẹ died. Ẹdun of Gbogun was thus briefly left as the sole claimant to the title of *Arẹ Ọna Kakamfo*, but his right to the title was soon challenged by Ojo Amepo, the independent raider established at Akesẹ in the Epo province, who assumed it on his own initiative.[49] A little later, indeed, a third claimant to the title appeared, when Oluyedun, a son of Afọnja who was among the Ọyọ refugees who had occupied Ibadan, and who eventually emerged as the leading chief in that town, also assumed his father's title.[50] The dissolution of the Ọyọ kingdom could hardly be better illustrated than by this simultaneous existence of three claimants to its senior military title, none of whom had been appointed by the *Alafin*.

During these quarrels among the provincial rulers, it appears

[45] Cf. above, Ch. 9, p. 192.
[46] Johnson, *History of the Yorubas*, 203–4; Olunlade, *Ẹdẹ: A Brief History*, 19.
[47] Johnson, *History of the Yorubas*, 210.
[48] Ibid. 211–12; Olunlade, *Ẹdẹ: A Brief History*, 21–2.
[49] Johnson, *History of the Yorubas*, 234.
[50] Ibid. 244.

that no attempt was made to dislodge the Fulani from Ilọrin. *Alafin* Majotu in the Ọyọ capital seems to have been quite unable to impose his authority over, or even mediate effectively between, his erstwhile vassals, and in these conditions it was clearly impossible to organize further campaigns against Ilọrin. Clapperton in 1826 found Majotu living in vain expectation of being delivered from his troubles by aid from outside, perhaps from the British,[51] perhaps from Benin.[52] The Landers in 1830 were amazed at the lack of effort, and apparent lack of concern, evinced by the *Alafin* in the face of the Fulani threat. They observe of the situation in the Ọyọ capital:

The walls of the town have been suffered to fall into decay; and are now no better than a heap of dust and ruins; and such unconcern and apathy pervade the minds of the monarch and his ministry, that the wandering and ambitious Falatah [Fulani] has penetrated into the very heart of the country, made himself master of two of its most important and flourishing towns [sc. Ilọrin and Raka], with little, if any, opposition; and is gradually, but very perceptibly, gaining on the lukewarm natives of the soil, and sapping the foundations of the throne of Yarriba. The people cannot, surely, be fully aware of their danger, or they never would be unconcerned spectators of events which are rapidly tending to root out their religion, customs, and institutions, and totally annihilate them as a nation.[53]

The Landers, indeed, suggest that some sort of formal accommodation had been effected between Ọyọ and Ilọrin. They report that *Alafin* Majotu had come to terms with Ilọrin, recognizing its independence and permitting trade with it on condition that no more Fulani were admitted to the town.[54] There is no trace of this episode in any of the available traditions, but the report is so specific that it is difficult to believe that the Landers were mistaken. It must be supposed that this reconciliation between Ọyọ and Ilọrin was very short-lived.

Alafin Majotu's complacency was all the more remarkable, in that by 1830 the subversive forces in his kingdom were beginning to receive substantial backing from outside. Up to this time, the *jihad* in Ọyọ had been sustained entirely by local forces, but now the Emir of Gwandu, the immediate overlord of Ilọrin within the Sokoto Caliphate, began to take an active interest in the Ọyọ area. Gwandu sources assert that Muhammad Wani, the second Emir of Gwandu,

[51] Clapperton, *Journal of a Second Expedition*, 39.
[52] Ibid. 41.
[53] R. and J. Lander, *Journal of an Expedition*, i. 178.
[54] Ibid. i. 189, 190.

who ruled from 1829 to 1833, sent an expedition to the Yoruba country which captured a town called 'Kwajobi'.[55] This expedition can probably be identified with one which occurred during the visit to Ǫyǫ of the Landers in 1830. The Landers heard that the Caliph of Sokoto, Muhammad Bello, had sent a party of Fulani to the Ǫyǫ area to collect tribute from Ilọrin and Raka. This party attacked and captured an Ǫyǫ town situated on the River Moshi, and then proceeded to Raka, but the people of Ilọrin were reported to have refused their demand for tribute, and 'declared themselves independent of the Falatahs.'[56] The belief of the Landers that the expedition came from Sokoto rather than from Gwandu is an understandable confusion, since like other European observers the Landers did not grasp that immediate authority over the western emirates of the Caliphate had been delegated by Sokoto to Gwandu. Ilọrin's alleged defiance of Gwandu, the report of which was perhaps embroidered by the wishful thinking of the Ǫyǫ, can have represented no more than a temporary difficulty in relations between the two emirates. The identity of the town captured by Muhammad Wani's forces is uncertain, but the name 'Kwajobi' might perhaps represent Gbajigbo, which was situated on the left bank of the Niger close to its confluence with the Moshi.

At the end of *Alafin* Majotu's reign, perhaps in *c.* 1830–1, the power of Ǫyǫ was further weakened by a natural calamity. A failure of the rains produced a severe famine in the savanna areas of the kingdom.[57] This disaster probably substantially accelerated the depopulation of the northern areas of the kingdom, already devastated by the protracted civil wars. It is, at any rate, noteworthy that traditions attribute the abandonment of several Ǫyǫ towns in this period to famine rather than to destruction by the Fulani.[58]

§3. THE FULANI CONQUEST OF ǪYǪ (c. 1831–c. 1833)

Alafin Majotu apparently died soon after the visit to Ǫyǫ of the Landers, probably in *c.* 1831.[59] Majotu's *Arẹmọ*, Adewusi, attempted to claim the throne, but he was rejected by the *Ǫyǫ Mesi* and obliged to commit suicide.[60] Instead, a prince called Amodo was installed as

---

[55] Arnett, *Gazetteer of Sokoto Province*, 38.
[56] R. and J. Lander, *Journal of an Expedition*, i. 181, 191, 259.
[57] Johnson, *History of the Yorubas*, 215.
[58] Abimbọla, 'The Ruins of Ǫyǫ Division', 17.
[59] Law, 'Chronology of the Yoruba Wars', 218.
[60] Johnson, *History of the Yorubas*, 216.

Alafin. Amodo's brief reign (c. 1831–3) saw the establishment of Fulani dominance over virtually the whole of the Ọyọ kingdom.

At first the removal of the senile and ineffectual Majotu appeared to promise a more vigorous leadership from the Ọyọ capital. The new *Alafin* set about attempting to organize renewed resistance to Ilọrin, and sought to strengthen his position by forming an alliance with Lanloke, the ruler of the important market town of Ogodo. As has been noted in an earlier chapter, it is possible that Ogodo should be identified with Raka,[61] and if so Amodo may have been attempting to exploit the apparent breach between Ilọrin and Raka which is suggested by their differing attitudes towards the expedition from Gwandu in 1830, mentioned above. However, in the end Lanloke instead allied with Ilọrin, and forces from Ogodo and Ilọrin laid siege to the Ọyọ capital. Amodo was eventually compelled to capitulate, and the Ilọrin forces entered and plundered Ọyọ. The inhabitants of the city were forced to make a profession of Islam, and Ọyọ became tributary to Ilọrin.[62]

The shock of the Ilọrin conquest of the capital, like that of the overthrow of Afọnja eight years earlier, produced a temporary unity among the surviving provincial rulers of the Ọyọ kingdom. *Alafin* Amodo was thus able to organize another attempt to defeat Ilọrin, and to secure the support of several important provincial rulers who had earlier been in rebellion, including Adegun of Ikoyi, Ẹdun of Gbogun, and Ọja and Atiba of Agọ Ọja. It was, however, a ram-shackle coalition, undermined by jealousies between the rival provincial rulers. The principal tension was again between the *Arẹ Ọna Kakamfo* and the *Onikoyi*, the rival claimants to primacy among the provincial rulers: although Ẹdun of Gbogun had been appointed to the former title by *Onikoyi* Adegun, he nevertheless saw himself as a rival for the latter's primacy. Consequently, at the battle of Kanla Ẹdun turned traitor and withdrew his forces without fighting, and the Ọyọ were decisively defeated, both Adegun and Ọja being killed.[63]

The Ilọrin victory at Kanla destroyed *Alafin* Amodo's hopes of regaining independence, and the Ọyọ capital remained tributary to Ilọrin. Moreover, the Ilọrin forces quickly went on to gain control of Ikoyi and Gbogun. After the death of Adegun succession to the Ikoyi throne was disputed between claimants supported by Ọyọ and

---

[61] Cf. above, Ch. 10, p. 212.
[62] Johnson, *History of the Yorubas*, 217–18.   [63] Ibid. 218–19.

Ilọrin, and Ilọrin forces intervened to secure the installation of the Ilọrin candidate.[64] A section of the pro-Ọyọ forces in Ikoyi, led by the war-chiefs Dado and Kurunmi, left and went to join Ojo Amepo at Akesẹ in the Epo province.[65] Ikoyi thus became subject to Ilọrin, but the depopulation caused by the departure of the pro-Ọyọ chiefs very much diminished its military power and importance.[66] Ẹdun of Gbogun then provoked a clash with Ilọrin by attacking Ikoyi. An Ilọrin army besieged and captured Gbogun, and Ẹdun, having fled to Igbodo, was killed by the people of that town, out of fear of Ilọrin.[67]

The Ilọrin next turned their attention to the Epo province in the south. The major powers in this area were Akesẹ, under the self-styled *Arẹ Ọna Kakamfo* Ojo Amepo, and Agọ Ọja, now ruled by Ẹlẹbu (the brother of Ọja) and Atiba. Ẹlẹbu and Atiba formed an alliance with Ilọrin, and made a profession of Islam,[68] but Ojo Amepo, although also a Muslim,[69] continued to defy Ilọrin, and had now been reinforced by the refugees from Ikoyi led by Dado and Kurunmi. With the assistance of Agọ Ọja, the Ilọrin forces began operations against the towns allied to Ojo Amepo. Ojo Amepo was killed in a minor skirmish, and Akesẹ surrendered. The main body of Ojo's war-chiefs, however, under Ayọ, together with the Ikoyi refugees led by Dado and Kurunmi, escaped and withdrew south into Ẹgba territory, where they seized possession of the town of Ijaye. Subsequently, quarrels among these chiefs led to the exile of Dado, and to the departure of Ayọ and his followers to occupy the nearby town of Abemọ, leaving Kurunmi as the undisputed ruler of Ijaye.[70]

At about the same time the Ilọrin were also establishing their control over the Ọyọ provinces to the west of the River Ogun. The town of Ṣaki was reduced, and compelled to accept an Ilọrin *ajẹlẹ*.[71] Further south, the town of Iganna, in the Onko province, came to terms with Ilọrin,[72] but the Ibarapa province was overrun by Ilọrin

[64] Ibid. 219-20.
[65] Cf. ibid. 220, 234-8.
[66] Later, at an uncertain date, Ikoyi was destroyed and abandoned, and the *Onikoyi* sought refuge in Ogbomọṣọ, but the town was reoccupied in 1906: ibid. 13, 76 and n.2.
[67] Ibid. 221.
[68] Ibid. 234; cf. ibid. 277.
[69] Ibid. 386.
[70] Ibid. 234-8.
[71] Ojo, *Iwe Itan Ṣaki*, 41.
[72] NAI, IBAPROF. 3/4, H. Childs, 'A Report on the Western District of the Ibadan Division of Oyo Province', 1934, §97.

forces, who destroyed several towns.[73] The Ilọrin on this occasion apparently raided as far south as Abẹokuta.[74] The only check to Ilọrin expansion in this period came when an Ilọrin army attempted an invasion of the Ijẹṣa country: like the Nupe and the Ọyọ before them,[75] they found that the forests of Ijẹṣaland were unsuited to the operation of their cavalry, and the invasion was decisively repulsed.[76]

Thus, by c. 1833 the Ilọrin had either destroyed or subjected almost all the important Ọyọ towns. Ọfa, Ikoyi, Gbogun, Ṣaki, and Iganna, and the new towns of Akẹṣe and Agọ Ọja, had all fallen or submitted, while the Ọyọ capital itself was tributary to Ilọrin. Of the other major provincial towns, we hear nothing at this period of Ogbomọṣọ, but probably it too had made its submission to Ilọrin. Only Ẹdẹ, in the Ibọlọ province, which was shielded from direct attack by the River Ọṣun, apparently preserved its independence. Apart from Ẹdẹ, the only independent Ọyọ powers were the newly established states in the south: Ijaye, under Kurunmi, Abemọ, under Ayọ, and Ibadan, where after the death of Oluyedun a man called Oluyọle eventually emerged as the leading chief. The success of the Ilọrin in overrunning the Ọyọ kingdom had been due in part to the superiority of their cavalry in the open savanna, but also to the disunity of the Ọyọ, which allowed them to overthrow the Ọyọ towns one by one without meeting concerted resistance.

§4. THE END OF ỌYỌ (c. 1833–c. 1836)

In c. 1833 *Alafin* Amodo died, and was succeeded by Oluewu, a son of *Alafin* Awolẹ.[77] At about the same time, it appears that 'Abd al-Salām, the Emir of Ilọrin, also died, and was succeeded by his brother Shi'ta.[78] Under Oluewu and Shi'ta were fought the last battles

[73] Ibid. *passim.*

[74] Cf. Biobaku, *The Egba and their Neighbours*, 24.

[75] Cf. above, Ch. 3, pp. 38–9; Ch. 7, p. 127.

[76] Johnson, *History of the Yorubas*, 222.

[77] For the date, see Law, 'Chronology of the Yoruba Wars', 217–18. For Oluewu's parentage, see Adeyẹmi, *Iwe Itan Ọyọ*, 11.

[78] 'Abd al-Salām is said to have reigned for nine years by Mockler-Ferryman, *Up the Niger*, 173, and for eleven years by Burdon, *Northern Nigeria*, 15, and later sources: since his father Sālih died in c. 1823 (cf. above, Ch. 12, p. 259, n.76), the former figure would indicate that 'Abd al-Salām died in c. 1832, while the latter gives a date of c. 1834. Burdon, loc. cit., and sources deriving from him state that 'Abd al-Salām was Emir of Ilọrin at the time of the fall of Ọyọ Ile (c. 1836), but Johnson, *History of the Yorubas*, 222 ff., shows that he had by then already been succeeded by his brother Shi'ta. The conventional dating of 'Abd

in the war between Ọyọ and Ilọrin, which led to the final destruction of the Ọyọ kingdom and the abandonment of the capital at Ọyọ Ile.

At the accession of Oluewu, Ọyọ was still subject to Ilọrin, and the new *Alafin* was required to go to Ilọrin to pay homage to the Emir Shi'ta. Indignant at his treatment there, Oluewu resolved to reassert the independence of Ọyọ, and refused a subsequent demand that he should return to Ilọrin to make a profession of Islam. Oluewu's decision brought to a head once more the political tensions inside the capital, since the *Ọyọ Mesi* favoured a policy of accommodation with Ilọrin, and the *Baṣọrun* Akioṣo and the *Aṣipa* Ailumọ undertook a mission to Ilọrin against the *Alafin*'s wishes. Shi'ta, however, was not appeased by this action of the Ọyọ chiefs, and dispatched an army under Lanloke, the chief of Ogodo, to attack Ọyọ.[79]

In this crisis the Ọyọ again decided to seek outside assistance, and Oluewu appealed for aid to his north-western neighbours, the Bariba of Borgu. A large Bariba army arrived in Ọyọ to support Oluewu. Ọyọ sources name the commander-in-chief of this army as 'King Eleduwẹ', which is apparently a stock name used for any Bariba king.[80] Bariba tradition identifies him as Siru Kpera, the king of Nikki.[81] Under Siru Kpera, there were also contingents from Kaiama and Wawa, commanded by the kings of those towns, while Kitoro, the king of Bussa, sent a force under his nephew Gajere.[82] This alliance between the Bariba and the Ọyọ represented a remarkable reversal of attitudes since the 1820s, when the Bariba had sought rather to exploit Ọyọ's difficulties by raiding into the north-west of the Ọyọ kingdom,[83] and the Bariba kings apparently looked forward to the impending fall of Ọyọ to the Ilọrin with equanimity.[84] In

---

al-Salām's death to 1842, first found in Elphinstone, *Gazetteer of Ilorin Province*, 16, is incorrect.   [79] Johnson, *History of the Yorubas*, 258–9.

[80] Schön and Crowther, *Journals*, 318; Johnson, *History of the Yorubas*, 260; Hethersett, in *Iwe Kika Ẹkẹrin*, 78; Adeyẹmi, *Iwe Itan Ọyọ*, 11. Ilọrin sources call the Bariba leader Ikoko, a nickname meaning 'hyena': Mockler-Ferryman, *Up the Niger*, 173; Burdon, *Northern Nigeria*, 15; Elphinstone, *Gazetteer of Ilorin Province*, 16.

[81] P. Mercier, 'Histoire et légende: la bataille d'Illorin', *Notes africaines*, 47 (1950), 92–5.

[82] NAK, DOB/HIS/55, T. Hoskyns-Abrahall, 'History of Bussa' (1925), §20; cf. Hermon-Hodge, *Gazetteer of Ilorin Province*, 129.

[83] Cf. above, Ch. 13, p. 263.

[84] Cf. Clapperton, *Journal of a Second Expedition*, 90, reporting a conversation with the king of Wawa: '. . . he added, the sultan of Boussa could take Yourriba whenever he chose, but, says he, the Fellatas will take it now.'

recent years, however, the Bariba themselves had suffered invasions by forces from Gwandu,[85] and Siru Kpera had apparently had to suppress a rebellion by the Muslim elements in Nikki.[86] A rival claimant to the Nikki throne, who had perhaps been implicated in this abortive Muslim rebellion, is said to have taken refuge at Ilọrin.[87] In these circumstances it was easier for Siru Kpera and the other Bariba rulers to recognize that they had a common interest with the Ọyọ in resisting the *jihad*. The Bariba forces which they brought to Ọyọ are said to have been distinguished principally by their skill in archery, but they probably also included a substantial contingent of cavalry,[88] which would be especially valuable in view of the decline of the cavalry strength of the Ọyọ.

With the support of the Bariba, Oluewu first crushed the opposition inside his own capital, murdering the *Aṣipa* and placing *Baṣọrun* Akioṣo under house arrest pending the outcome of the war: the *Baṣọrun* was, however, then murdered by his own kinsmen, to avoid the disgrace of a public execution.[89] Finding the Ọyọ reinforced by the Bariba, the Ilọrin army under Lanloke withdrew from before the city. At the same time, some of the Ọyọ provincial towns, presumably encouraged by the arrival of the Bariba, apparently declared for the *Alafin*: such revolts against Ilọrin seem to have occurred at Ṣaki[90] and at Igbodo.[91] The Ilọrin, with the support of some of the Ọyọ provincial chiefs, notably Ẹlẹbu and Atiba of Agọ Ọja, next laid siege to Igbodo. However, the Ọyọ and Bariba forces marched to the relief of Igbodo, and drove off the Ilọrin (*c.* 1834).[92] Ẹlẹbu was killed in this battle, leaving Atiba in effective control of Agọ Ọja: soon after, Atiba defected to the Ọyọ side.[93]

After their victory at Igbodo, Oluewu and Siru Kpera resolved to

[85] Arnett, *Gazetteer of Sokoto Province*, 38; Hermon-Hodge, *Gazetteer of Ilorin Province*, 122–3; R. and J. Lander, *Journal of an Expedition*, ii. 9–10; Laird and Oldfield, *Narrative of an Expedition*, ii. 310.

[86] M. B. Idris, 'The History of Borgu in the Nineteenth Century' (uncompleted Ph.D. Thesis, University of Birmingham, 1973), Ch. 7.

[87] Mercier, 'La bataille d'Ilorin'.

[88] Johnson, *History of the Yorubas*, 261, describes the Bariba as 'good archers'. Bariba tradition recalls that Siru Kpera accumulated over 400 horses in preparation for the Ilọrin war: Idris, 'History of Borgu', Ch. 2.

[89] Johnson, *History of the Yorubas*, 259–60.

[90] Ojo, *Iwe Itan Ṣaki*, 42.

[91] Cf. Johnson, *History of the Yorubas*, 260.

[92] Ibid. 260–1; for the date, cf. Schön and Crowther, *Journals*, 318.

[93] Johnson, *History of the Yorubas*, 261; for Atiba's change of side, cf. ibid. 262.

attempt an attack upon Ilọrin itself. They first marched south through the Ẹkun Ọtun province, picking up forces from Ṣaki, Iganna, and Isẹyin, and then crossed the River Ogun to Ọtẹfan, where they were joined by Atiba from Ogọ Ọja.[94] Faced with this threat, Shi'ta of Ilọrin in turn sought outside assistance, and appealed to his overlord, Khalil, the Emir of Gwandu. According to Gwandu sources, Khalil sent an army to assist Ilọrin which was commanded by Bukhari dan Shehu and Muhammad Sambo.[95] While there is no reason to doubt this, it appears that the bulk of the forces sent were in fact drawn from Nupe. Johnson asserts that the army was commanded by 'Eṣugoyi of Rabbah'.[96] 'Eṣugoyi' is a Yoruba version of the Nupe title Etsu Goy, 'the Fulani Etsu', which is normally applied in Nupe to 'Uthmān Zaki, the successor of Mallam Dendo at Raba.[97] However, Johnson's informants appear to have been in error on this point, since Nupe tradition indicates that the ruler who aided the Ilọrin in this war was in fact Manzuma, the ruler of the minor Fulani emirate of Lafiagi, south of the River Niger.[98] Reinforced by Manzuma's army, the Ilọrin attacked the Ọyọ–Bariba army at Ọtẹfan, but were again beaten off.[99]

During the following rainy season (1835?), the Ọyọ and Bariba forces advanced from Ọtẹfan to Ogbomọṣọ, where they received further reinforcements. Bamigbaiye, the Timi of Ẹdẹ, brought a contingent, as did the chiefs of the new powers in the south, Kurunmi of Ijaye, Ayọ of Abemọ, and Oluyọle of Ibadan.[100] Of the major Ọyọ towns, apparently only Ikoyi still held to its alliance with Ilọrin.[101] However, the imposing army now assembled at Ogbomọṣọ was riven by dissensions. There was tension between the Ọyọ and the Bariba, due largely to the past reputation of the latter as robbers and kidnappers along their frontier with Ọyọ. There were also the by now customary disagreements and jealousies among the Ọyọ. Alafin

[94] Ibid. 261–2.
[95] Arnett, Gazetteer of Sokoto Province, 38–9.
[96] Johnson, History of the Yorubas, 263.
[97] Mason, 'The Nupe Kingdom', 217.
[98] Elphinstone, Gazetteer of Ilorin Province, 33; Hermon-Hodge, Gazetteer of Ilorin Province, 105; cf. Mason, 'The Nupe Kingdom', 217–19.
[99] Johnson, History of the Yorubas, 263.
[100] Ibid.
[101] Johnson, ibid., states that before the battle of Ọtẹfan only Ikoyi and Ogbomọṣọ had held aloo ffrom the alliance against Ilọrin: Ogbomọṣọ had now been occupied by the allied army, but there is no suggestion that Ikoyi had rallied to the Alafin.

Oluewu quarrelled with the metropolitan Oyo chiefs, who had been left behind to guard the capital, about the strategy to be pursued in the war, and also gave offence to some of his provincial chiefs, notably Bamigbaiye of Ede and Atiba of Ago Oja.[102] Atiba, in particular, as a son of *Alafin* Abiodun, felt that he had a claim to the Oyo throne, and plotted to secure it by betraying Oluewu. To this end, he secured the support of Kurunmi of Ijaye and Oluyole of Ibadan, by promising them the titles of *Are Ona Kakamfo* and *Basorun*, respectively, if he should become *Alafin*.[103] When, therefore, the army finally advanced against Ilorin in the following dry season (1835–6?), several of the Oyo chiefs, led by Atiba and Bamigbaiye, turned traitor and withdrew without offering to fight. Although the Ilorin were at first hard pressed, the attackers were eventually decisively defeated.[104] Siru Kpera and the rulers of Wawa and Kaiama were all killed, though the Bussa commander Gajere survived.[105] Oluewu himself is said to have been taken prisoner, and later put to death at Ilorin.[106]

Lanloke of Ogodo seized this opportunity to attack the Oyo capital, but was repulsed. The citizens of Oyo, however, fearing that the main Ilorin army would soon join Lanloke, now abandoned the city, fleeing to neighbouring towns such as Igboho and Kisi. Lanloke's troops were then able to plunder the empty city without opposition.[107]

It was not immediately clear that the Oyo empire had come to an end. The surviving members of the *Oyo Mesi* at Igboho and Kisi resolved to fill the vacant throne. However, one prince who was offered the throne declined, and the chiefs were reduced to offering it to the renegade prince Atiba at Ago Oja, who at least seemed to command sufficient resources to make the royal power a reality again. This was done on the understanding that Atiba would lead the Oyo back to the old capital, but instead Atiba established his court at Ago Oja, making it a new Oyo.[108] The old capital at Oyo

[102] Ibid. 263–6.
[103] Ibid. 279; Hethersett, in *Iwe Kika Ekerin*, 78.
[104] Johnson, *History of the Yorubas*, 266–7; cf. Schön and Crowther, *Journals*, 318; Adeyemi, *Iwe Itan Oyo*, 12–13; Mockler-Ferryman, *Up the Niger*, 173; Burdon, *Northern Nigeria*, 15; Elphinstone, *Gazetteer of Ilorin Province*, 16; Hermon-Hodge, *Gazetteer of Ilorin Province*, 123–5.
[105] Hermon-Hodge, *Gazetteer of Ilorin Province*, 125.
[106] Johnson, *History of the Yorubas*, 287. Other accounts imply that Oluewu was killed in battle at Ilorin.
[107] Ibid. 268.
[108] Ibid. 279.

Ile was never reoccupied.[109] In accordance with his promise at Ogbomọṣọ, Atiba conferred the title of *Arẹ Ọna Kakamfo* on Kurunmi of Ijaye, and that of *Baṣọrun* on Oluyọle of Ibadan.[110] (The third of the new Ọyọ powers in the south, Abemọ, had been destroyed, and its chief Ayọ killed, by Kurunmi and Oluyọle soon after their return from Ilọrin.[111]) Although this seemed to institutionalize the subordination of these new powers to Ọyọ, in practice their allegiance to the *Alafin* was nominal, and there was no longer an Ọyọ empire. The Ilọrin advance was finally checked, by the Ibadan at the battle of Oṣogbo in c. 1838,[112] but the Ilọrin emirate was not destroyed, and Ọyọ power was never re-established in the north-east. The history of the Ọyọ area during the rest of the nineteenth century revolved around, first, the struggle for power between Ibadan and Ijaye, eventually resolved by the destruction of Ijaye in 1862, and second, the ultimately unsuccessful attempt of Ibadan to consolidate an empire incorporating most of central Yorubaland.[113] The role of the *Alafin* in these events was that of an ineffectual mediator, increasingly resentful of his nominal vassal Ibadan. After the establishment of British rule over Yorubaland in the 1890s, there was an attempt to reconstruct the Ọyọ empire, by subordinating Ibadan to Ọyọ, but this broke down in the 1930s.[114] The *Alafin* of Ọyọ remained a ruler of immense prestige and considerable influence, but the Ọyọ empire had been broken beyond recall in the wars of the 1820s and 1830s.

§5. THE FALL OF THE ỌYỌ EMPIRE

The causes of the fall of the Ọyọ empire have been discussed at great length by several modern scholars.[115] A large part of the present writer's interpretation has been given already, in earlier chapters.

---

[109] The proposal to reoccupy the abandoned capital remained a live issue in the 1840s: cf. ibid. 297–8.

[110] Ibid. 281–2; Hethersett, in *Iwe Kika Ẹkẹrin*, 78.

[111] Johnson, *History of the Yorubas*, 271–2.

[112] Ibid. 285–8; for the date, cf. Schön and Crowther, *Journals*, 318.

[113] For the history of the Ibadan empire, see Awẹ, 'The Ajele System', and id., 'The End of an Experiment'. For its collapse, see also S. A. Akintoye, *Revolution and Power Politics in Yorubaland 1840–1893: Ibadan Expansion and the Rise of Ekitiparapo* (London, 1971).

[114] Atanda, *The New Ọyọ Empire*.

[115] See e.g. Akinjogbin, 'Prelude to the Yoruba Civil Wars'; Smith, *Kingdoms of the Yoruba*, 136–9; J. A. Atanda, 'The Fall of the Old Ọyọ Empire: A Re-Consideration of its Causes', *JHSN* 5.4 (1971), 477–90; Ajayi, 'Aftermath of the fall of Old Ọyọ', 136–45.

Evidently, explanation must concentrate upon two main factors—the dissensions between the *Alafin* and his chiefs, both in the capital and in the provincial towns, which culminated in the revolt of Ilọrin under Afọnja; and the outbreak of the *jihad*, or Muslim rebellion, in 1817. Much of the debate, indeed, has been precisely over the relative importance of these two factors in the fall of Ọyọ.

The two factors were closely interconnected, inasmuch as the political divisions of the Ọyọ were a condition of the success of the *jihad*. The tensions which had led to the revolt of Afọnja also operated to prevent the Ọyọ from combining against Ilọrin after Afọnja's death: as Johnson observes, the disloyalty of the provincial chiefs in the 1830s was due to the calculation that the destruction of Ilọrin would lead to their own re-subordination to the *Alafin*.[116] This is not, however, to suggest that the dissensions of the Ọyọ chiefs were a more important or more fundamental cause of the collapse of the empire than the *jihad*. It is ultimately unprofitable to attempt to determine which of these two factors was 'decisive' for the fall of Ọyọ. To borrow a comparison used by another historian in an analogous context, when a sick man dies after being knocked down by a bus, it is possible to argue with equal plausibility that he was killed by the bus; that, being ill, he would have died soon anyway; and that, if he had not been ill, the impact of the bus would not have been fatal.[117] If the Ọyọ had not been divided, they might not have succumbed to the *jihad*; but conversely, if the *jihad* had not supervened, they might have been able to resolve their dissensions. The combination of metropolitan dissension, provincial disaffection, and Muslim rebellion, however, was certainly fatal to the empire.

It should be stressed, however, that it is misleading to contrast the dissensions of the Ọyọ and the *jihad* as an 'internal' and an 'external' factor.[118] The *jihad* in Ọyọ was not a 'Fulani invasion',[119] but an insurrection by local elements—Fulani pastoralists, Hausa slaves, and Ọyọ Muslims. For the Muslim Ọyọ, moreover, it may be that their participation in the *jihad* is best understood as a continuation

---

[116] Johnson, *History of the Yorubas*, 218, 264.

[117] T. Wilson, *The Downfall of the Liberal Party 1914–35* (2nd edn., London, 1968), 20–1.

[118] This terminology is used, e.g. by Smith, *Kingdoms of the Yoruba*, 138; Atanda, *The New Ọyọ Empire*, 35.

[119] The phrase is used, e.g. by Akinjogbin, 'Prelude to the Yoruba Civil Wars', 44; cf. Davidson, *Africa in History*, 219, invents 'an invasion of Muslim-led cavalry from the new Fulani empire in Hausaland'.

and a consequence of the earlier troubles. Their readiness to place
religious above national loyalty, it may be suggested, had its origins
in the progressive erosion of loyalty to the traditional political system
which had been evident for several years before 1817.

The history of Yorubaland after the 1830s served only to confirm
the finality of the dissolution of Ǫyǫ power. The Fulani could not be
dislodged from Ilǫrin, since their cavalry continued to dominate the
savanna areas of northern Yorubaland.[120] But equally, the 'Emir of
Yoruba' at Ilǫrin could not make good his claim to be the inheritor
of the Ǫyǫ kingdom, since the Fulani cavalry were ineffective in the
southern forests where the centres of Ǫyǫ power were now located.
Moreover, the constitutional problems of the Ǫyǫ kingdom remained
unresolved. By 1836 the shift of effective power from the capital to
the provincial towns had gone so far that Atiba was able to succeed
where Afǫnja had failed, in using his position as the ruler of a
provincial town to grasp the Ǫyǫ throne. But the accession of Atiba,
and the transfer of the capital to New Ǫyǫ, made little difference to
the situation. Atiba was merely one of a number of successful free-
booters in the south, and far from the most successful: both Ijaye
and Ibadan were larger, and therefore more powerful, towns than
New Ǫyǫ.[121] This disparity was accentuated when the Atlantic slave
trade was replaced by trade in palm oil from the 1840s, since Ǫyǫ
was situated north of the area where the oil palms grew and was
therefore less able than Ijaye or Ibadan to participate in the new
export trade. Atiba's only advantage over Kurunmi and Oluyǫle
was a plausible claim to the royal title. Traditional legitimacy and
effective power therefore remained separated after 1836 as they had
been before. Only the establishment of an *Alafin* at Ibadan might
have resolved the problem. The possibility existed, since Oluyǫle,
who like Afǫnja could claim a connection with Ǫyǫ royalty through
the female line, put forward a claim to the Ǫyǫ throne in the 1840s.[122]
But jealousy of Ibadan brought this to nothing, and after Oluyǫle's
death in 1847 Ibadan developed along highly decentralized lines
which excluded the possibility of any chief with royal ambitions
gaining a similar position of predominance in the city.[123] The

[120] Johnson, *History of the Yorubas*, 288.

[121] In the 1850s, the population of New Ǫyǫ was estimated to be 25,000, while
that of Ibadan was about 70,000 and that of Ijaye about 35,000: Bowen, *Central
Africa*, 218.

[122] Johnson, *History of the Yorubas*, 297: Oluyǫle was the son of a daughter
of *Alafin* Abiǫdun.   [123] Cf. ibid. 367.

ambiguous position of Ibadan, as the strongest Yoruba power but lacking a crowned ruler, was one important cause of the failure of its imperial ambitions later in the nineteenth century.[124]

[124] Awẹ, 'The End of an Experiment', 229–30.

PART IV

EPILEGOMENA

CHAPTER 15

Comparisons

A great part of this book has been concerned, either directly or indirectly, with two major themes in the history of the Ọyọ empire: the consequences of the involvement of Ọyọ in the Atlantic slave trade, and the process of political change which occurred in Ọyọ during its imperial period. Ọyọ was only one of a number of West African states which flourished during the period of the Atlantic slave trade, and it may be illuminating to consider how far the experience of Ọyọ was typical, and how far it refutes or supports some of the conventional generalizations of West African historiography. Of particular interest for such comparison are the other large territorial empires which emerged in the Lower Guinea area. Among these, detailed studies already exist of Benin,[1] Dahomey,[2] and Asante,[3] and this concluding chapter will concentrate upon comparisons with these states. To proceed in this way from local study to comparison and generalization is, it should be stressed, more than a little misleading. The author's conclusions on the history of Ọyọ were in many instances suggested or moulded by perceptions of parallels with other states, or by general models. This final chapter, therefore, in order to avoid the imputation of circularity, might best be presented as making more explicit the models and parallels implicit in the main body of the work.

§1. THE ATLANTIC SLAVE TRADE

As has been noted by Fage, the history of Ọyọ is closely paralleled by that of Dahomey and Asante.[4] All three empires were created during the seventeenth and eighteenth centuries, when the Atlantic slave trade was at its height. All three became large exporters of slaves (though Asante also exported gold). And all three began as hinterland states and subsequently sought to extend their control

[1] Ryder, *Benin and the Europeans*; cf. also Bradbury, *Benin Studies*.
[2] Akinjogbin, *Dahomey and its Neighbours*; cf. also Argyle, *The Fon of Dahomey*.
[3] Fynn, *Asante and its Neighbours*; Wilks, *Asante in the Nineteenth Century*.
[4] Fage, *History of West Africa*, 97.

southwards, over the coastal areas where the European traders operated. The fourth of the great empires of Lower Guinea, Benin, presents a quite different pattern. Benin was situated near the coast, and was already a considerable power when the first European traders arrived in the 1480s. Moreover, it was much less involved in the slave trade than the others, and for some time even operated a total ban on the sale of male slaves to the Europeans.[5]

The rise of Ọyọ, Asante, and Dahomey was no doubt linked to the development of the Atlantic slave trade by more than coincidence in time. Asante and Dahomey, like Ọyọ, expanded coastwards in order to secure access to the Atlantic trade,[6] and wealth from this trade was a factor in the power of Asante and Dahomey, as it was in that of Ọyọ. Indeed, the link between trade and politics is more immediately obvious in the cases of Asante and Dahomey than in that of Ọyọ, since the military forces of these states were equipped, from the late seventeenth century, with imported European firearms.[7] The armies of Ọyọ, it will be recalled, were also dependent upon imported resources, but in this case horses imported from the interior: the Atlantic trade was only indirectly relevant, as a source of trade goods which could be exchanged against horses in the north.

It is not, of course, suggested that there was any simple relationship between participation in the Atlantic trade (or in long-distance trade generally) and political power. Manning has attacked the supposition that there was such a relationship, and sought to show that there is no observable correlation between volumes of trade and degrees of power, so that the Atlantic trade can be taken as neither a necessary nor a sufficient condition of the flourishing of West African empires.[8] There is no doubt that this is an entirely valid point, but hardly a surprising or even a very interesting one. Even those who believe the Atlantic trade to have been the most important determinant of the 'power' of the coastal empires are unlikely to hold that it is the only relevant variable. And once this is conceded, it is no longer to be expected that the simple correlations which

[5] Ryder, *Benin and the Europeans*, 45.

[6] For Asante, see Fynn, *Asante and its Neighbours*, 108. In the case of Dahomey, Akinjogbin, *Dahomey and its Neighbours*, 73–80, attempts to refute the 'commercial' interpretation of Dahomian expansion to the coast, but cf. above, Ch. 10, pp. 220–1.

[7] Fynn, *Asante and its Neighbours*, 32–3, 39, n.5, 55, etc.; Akinjogbin, *Dahomey and its Neighbours*, 82, 94, 103, etc.

[8] P. Manning, 'Slaves, Palm Oil and Political Power on the West African Coast', *African Historical Studies*, 2 (1969), 279–88.

Manning seeks and fails to find should be observable. It is, indeed, not necessary to resort to Manning's quasi-quantitative methods to make his point, since the case of Benin, an empire won by the bow and arrow a generation before the beginning of the Atlantic trade, is itself a sufficient refutation of the view which Manning sets up in order to overthrow. However, it can hardly be denied that the Atlantic trade provided opportunities for the amassing of wealth, and more particularly of munitions, which could be and were utilized in the process of state-building. Possibly the empires of Ọyọ, Dahomey, and Asante might have been created even without the Atlantic trade, but in the event they were not.

If it has been conventional to see the Atlantic trade as an important stimulant to the growth of the Guinea empires, it has equally been conventional to present the Atlantic slave trade as a destructive influence. This has been argued, in particular, in a general survey by Davidson,[9] and in studies by Rodney of the Gold Coast[10] and by Akinjogbin of the Aja area.[11] Asante and Dahomey have to be regarded, of course, as states which succeeded in avoiding or minimizing the deleterious effects of participation in the slave trade, since these kingdoms continued to flourish throughout the period of the Atlantic slave trade. The case of Ọyọ, on the other hand, is of especial interest for this issue, since it collapsed in the early nineteenth century.

The decline and fall of Ọyọ has long been attributed to the effects of the slave trade. As early as 1826 Clapperton assured the king of Bussa that 'Yourriba presented nothing but ruined towns and villages, and all caused by the slave trade.'[12] The implication, presumably, is that the civil wars in the Ọyọ kingdom in the early nineteenth century were fought in order to procure slaves for sale to the Europeans. A more elaborate version of the same interpretation was propounded in the 1850s by the abolitionist writer Wilson, in a comparative study of Ọyọ, Dahomey, and Benin. According to Wilson's model, African states at first satisfied the demands of the Atlantic slave trade by raiding their weaker neighbours, but when these external sources began to fail the required slaves were found inside the exporting states, mainly by abuse of judicial procedures.

[9] Davidson, *Black Mother*.
[10] W. Rodney, 'Gold and Slaves on the Gold Coast', *Transactions of the Historical Society of Ghana*, 10 (1969), 13–28.
[11] Akinjogbin, *Dahomey and its Neighbours*, Ch. 1.
[12] Clapperton, *Journal of a Second Expedition*, 102.

Competition for access to the European trade, combined with this internal slave recruitment, led to the disintegration of centralized authority and political fragmentation. In the case of Ọyọ, although the *jihad* of 1817 is recognized as an independent factor, the collapse of the kingdom into civil war is thus attributed primarily to the impact of the slave trade.[13] Among modern scholars, the destructive effect of the slave trade on Ọyọ has been similarly stressed by Akinjogbin, though he points rather to its economic than to its political consequences. Arguing from comparison with Kongo, Benin, and the Aja states, Akinjogbin asserts that participation in the slave trade inevitably weakened the exporting states, since the export of slaves sapped the productive labour force, while local slave-raiding led to insecurity which hampered other economic activities.[14]

On the face of it, it is difficult to sustain this gloomy picture of the conditions caused by the slave trade from a study of Ọyọ during the seventeenth and eighteenth centuries. Throughout this period, it appears that Ọyọ continued to recruit most of the slaves which it sold to the Europeans externally, both by raiding neighbours such as the Mahi and by purchasing slaves from the north. The Ọyọ kingdom itself therefore suffered neither depopulation nor insecurity. Indeed, the population of the kingdom probably increased, since many of the slaves purchased from the north were retained in the kingdom for domestic use. In this, it may be noted, Ọyọ did not differ from Asante or Dahomey, which also obtained many of the slaves which they sold at the coast by purchase from the interior.[15] All three states, it appears, were able to escape the social costs of the slave trade, by operating largely as middlemen and transferring the burden of supplying the slaves onto others.[16]

Certainly, there is no evidence that the domestic economy of Ọyọ declined through loss of labour and insecurity. Local crafts, such as the manufacture of cloth, continued to flourish. It seems likely, indeed, that participation in the slave trade acted as a stimulus to

[13] J. L. Wilson, *Western Africa: Its History, Conditions, and Prospects* (New York, 1856), 189–93.

[14] Akinjogbin, 'Prelude to the Yoruba Civil Wars', 28: Benin will hardly stand as an example of the destructive impact of the slave trade, in the light of Ryder's study, *Benin and the Europeans*.

[15] Fynn, *Asante and its Neighbours*, 116–17; Akinjogbin, *Dahomey and its Neighbours*, 140, 145.

[16] Cf. Rodney, 'Gold and Slaves on the Gold Coast', 24–6.

local trade and manufacturing. It is sometimes suggested that the Atlantic trade was essentially a state-managed sector which had no direct links with the domestic economy,[17] and it is certainly the case that the slave trade tended to be dominated by a small number of large-scale entrepreneurs, normally the political and military chiefs, with the mass of the population unable to participate directly.[18] Perhaps the only opportunity for ordinary people to benefit directly from the slave trade was in the supply of foodstuffs to trading caravans. The conception of long-distance trade as an enclave largely isolated from the rest of the economy seems especially applicable to the northern trade of Ọyọ, in which the principal imports, horses, were used only by the chiefs. But the Atlantic trade yielded a greater variety of imported goods, and in particular masses of cowry shells for currency. Much of the trade goods and cowries which the chiefs received in return for their slaves was not consumed or hoarded within the chiefly households, but was exchanged for local products, thus spreading the wealth from the Atlantic trade more widely. It is, it may be suggested, not merely a reflection of the point of view of the Ọyọ chiefs that the reign of *Alafin* Abiọdun, the peak of Ọyọ involvement in the Atlantic slave trade, was remembered as a time of great wealth, and more specifically as a time when cowries were abundant.[19]

However, it might perhaps be argued that by the late eighteenth century Ọyọ had reached the point at which, in Wilson's model, slave traders were beginning to turn to the internal recruitment of slaves, with the consequence of political disintegration. Rather than the exhaustion of external sources, the cause might be found in the massive increase in the volume of slave exports in the 1780s. Some support for such a view can be found in the admittedly vague statement of Johnson, describing the misgovernment which provoked the overthrow of *Alafin* Awọlẹ in *c.* 1796, that 'slavery for the slightest offence' had become normal.[20] However, it seems that the great expansion of slave exports in the 1780s was achieved primarily through increased purchases of slaves from the north, so that any

[17] See e.g. K. Polanyi, *Dahomey and the Slave Trade: An Analysis of an Archaic Economy* (Seattle, 1966).
[18] Hopkins, *Economic History of West Africa*, 104–5, 120.
[19] *L'aiye Abiọdun l'a fi igba wọn 'wo*, In Abiọdun's time we weighed money (cowries) by calabashes: traditional poem quoted by Johnson, *History of the Yorubas*, 188.
[20] Ibid. 188.

political consequences should be sought in Hausaland rather than in Ọyọ.[21] If the Wilson model has any application to Ọyọ, the crucial point should be placed not in the 1790s, but in the 1810s or 1820s. External recruitment of slaves had by then failed, owing to the military weakness of Ọyọ and the disruption of the northern trade routes: in consequence, European demand for slaves had to be satisfied from within Yorubaland. This factor has long been recognized as one part of the background to the outbreak of the Owu war in southern Yorubaland in c. 1817.[22] It is probably equally relevant to the exacerbation of the civil wars inside the Ọyọ kingdom which followed the Muslim rebellion of 1817.

§2. POLITICAL CHANGE

It has been argued in detail above that the imperial expansion of Ọyọ was accompanied by a process of political change, the essential character of which was the growth of effective royal power at the expense of that of the non-royal chiefs (the *Ọyọ Mesi*), through the expansion of the *Alafin*'s staff of palace slaves. Similar processes can be seen in the histories of Asante and Benin. In Asante, Wilks has traced the subversion of the power of the hereditary chiefs of Kumasi through the creation of what he terms a 'bureaucracy' of new chiefs under royal control, a process which began in earnest under Osei Kwadwo (1764–77): succession to the new offices was regularly patrilineal, in contrast to the matrilineality of Asante society, thus separating them from the control of the old descent groups.[23] In Benin the power of the king was confronted and checked by that of a council of hereditary chiefs analogous to the *Ọyọ Mesi*, the *Uzama*: the destruction of their power appears to have been effected in the late fifteenth century by *Ọba* Ẹwuare, who created both a series of offices associated with the palace and an alternative, non-hereditary range of 'town' chiefs.[24] It is less easy to trace a similar process in Dahomey, which seems to appear already

[21] Enslavement was one of the principal grievances in the period of unrest which preceded the *jihad* of 'Uthmān dan Fodio in Hausaland in 1804: Hiskett, *The Sword of Truth*, 77–9.

[22] Biobaku, *The Egba and their Neighbours*, 13; Law, 'The Owu War in Yoruba History', 145–6.

[23] Wilks, *Asante in the Nineteenth Century*, esp. Ch. 11.

[24] R. E. Bradbury, 'Patrimonialism and Gerontocracy in Benin Political Culture', in M. Douglas and P. M. Kaberry (eds.), *Man in Africa* (London, 1969), 27–9; id., *Benin Studies*, 138–40.

ıs a highly centralized monarchy at the beginning of the eighteenth century. But here too there are hints of conflict between the king ınd his senior chiefs,[25] and the king built up a staff of palace slaves,[26] ıs well as employing as his agents his numerous wives[27] and male members of his own lineage.[28]

The essential character of political change in all these kingdoms ıas the creation of an administrative staff appointed by and responsble to the king, upon which he could therefore rely to carry out his vishes even against the opposition of the hereditary chiefs, who ince they did not owe their position to the king were better placed o defy him. Wilks terms this process, borrowing a concept from Weber, 'bureaucratization',[29] but if Weberian categories are to be mployed, a more appropriate one than 'bureaucracy' would be patrimonialism', which Bradbury applies in the case of Benin.[30] The principal difference between the various kingdoms lay in the source from which the royal administrative staff was drawn: in Ọyọ, mainly from slaves; in Benin and Asante, mainly from free citizens; ın Dahomey, partly from slaves, partly from the palace women, and partly from relatives of the king.

The process of political change is related to that of imperial expansion, to which it was a response. First, imperial expansion created new administrative problems which could not be satisfactorily resolved within the existing system. As Wilks observes of Asante, government had to be extended in *range*, to control areas far distant from the metropolitan region; in *scope*, to regulate spheres of activity previously untouched by central authority; and in *proficiency*, beyond the managerial resources of the hereditary aristocracy of the

[25] Notably, the revolt of the *Mehu*, the principal non-royal chief, in *c.* 1735: Akinjogbin, *Dahomey and its Neighbours*, 105; cf. also the abortive royal monopoly of the slave trade instituted in the 1780s by Kpengla, as recorded by Dalzel, *History of Dahomy*, 213–15.

[26] Argyle, *The Fon of Dahomey*, 65–9.

[27] For complaints about the increasing power of the king's wives in the 1780s, cf. Dalzel, *History of Dahomy*, 224. Later, king Gezo (1818–58) created a large force of soldiers from among his wives: Le Herissé, *L'Ancien Royaume de Dahomey*, 58; Foa, *Le Dahomey*, 255–6.

[28] This practice was also initiated by Gezo (1818–58): Le Herissé, *L'Ancien Royaume de Dahomey*, 33, 44.

[29] Wilks, *Asante in the Nineteenth Century*, Ch. 11; cf. id., 'Aspects of Bureaucratization in Ashanti in the Nineteenth Century', *JAH* 7 (1966), 215–32.

[30] Bradbury, 'Patrimonialism and Gerontocracy in Benin'. For the concepts of 'bureaucracy' and 'patrimonialism', see M. Weber, *The Theory of Social and Economic Organization*, translated by A. M. Henderson and T. Parsons (New York, 1964), 324–58.

pre-imperial period'.[31] At the same time, as Lloyd stresses with regard to Ọyọ, imperial expansion (and expanding trade) provided kings with new sources of revenue which might be used to reward and secure the loyalty of their agents, and to entice followers away from the hereditary chiefs.[32]

The major difference between Ọyọ and the other Lower Guinea empires was that in Ọyọ this process of centralization was not carried to a successful conclusion.[33] Instead, the unresolved struggle for power between the *Alafin* and the *Ọyọ Mesi* proved to be a crucial factor in the collapse of the Ọyọ empire. In this, it may be noted, Ọyọ was not altogether unique. The fall of the kingdom of Hueda to the Dahomian invaders in 1727 was similarly facilitated by the disaffection of the Hueda chiefs, a consequence of the king's attempts to centralize administration under his own control.[34] However, the contrast with Asante, Dahomey, and Benin is sufficiently striking to prompt consideration of why the Ọyọ kingdom should have fared so differently in this respect.

It has been argued above that it was the drawing of the provincial chiefs of the Ọyọ kingdom into the conflict inside the capital which created irresolvable contradictions: *Alafin* Abiọdun's *coup d'état* of 1774 pointed the way to the disastrous *coup* against Awọlẹ in *c.* 1796. However, this explains how rather than why, for the provincial rulers were drawn into parallel conflicts in other kingdoms without similarly disastrous results. In Asante, in 1748, the king crushed a revolt of the Kumasi chiefs with the aid of the *omanhene*, the confederate rulers of the Asante state.[35] And in Benin, in a major civil war in the 1690s, royal victory seems to have been secured through assistance from outside the capital.[36] It is therefore necessary to consider further the reasons for the persistence of chiefly power in the Ọyọ capital.

Comparison with other states does suggest some tentative explanations, though most are open to some sort of objection. Bradbury, in a comparison of Ọyọ with Benin, suggested that centralization in

---

[31] Wilks, *Asante in the Nineteenth Century*, 127.

[32] Lloyd, *Political Development of Yoruba Kingdoms*, 1–8.

[33] Cf. Fage, *History of West Africa*, 151.

[34] Akinjogbin, *Dahomey and its Neighbours*, 47, 51–2, 68–72.

[35] Dupuis, *Journal of a Residence in Ashantee*, 235; Fynn, *Asante and its Neighbours*, 84–5.

[36] Bosman, *New and Accurate Description of the Coast of Guinea*, 467; Bradbury, 'Chronological Problems in Benin History', 272–4; id., *Benin Studies*, 28–9.

Ọyọ was inhibited by the existence there of large, powerful corporate descent groups, whereas in Benin descent groups were weaker (land rights, for example, being vested in village authorities rather than in descent group heads).[37] However, this involves assuming that descent group structures in the two kingdoms have remained constant, while other institutions have changed. Lloyd pertinently asks whether the strength of descent groups in Ọyọ and their weakness in Benin may not be rather a consequence than a cause of the failure of centralization in the former and its success in the latter.[38] Lloyd himself points out that the method adopted to build up the royal administrative staff in Ọyọ, where the king's officials were recruited largely from slaves, did not directly weaken the chiefly descent groups: whereas in Asante and Benin, where the king's staff was recruited from free men, individuals were detached from their allegiance to their descent groups, or at least faced with problems of divided loyalties.[39]

It is also noteworthy that whereas in Dahomey and Benin at least (the position in Asante is less clear), the king controlled the Atlantic trade very closely,[40] in Ọyọ there was nothing approaching a royal monopoly of external trade. From one point of view, of course, this simply represents one facet of the incomplete centralization of power in Ọyọ, but perhaps the lack of royal control over trade can be explained independently, and seen as a causal factor in the political situation. It can at least be suggested that the geographical location of Ọyọ, in the interior at some distance from the coast, which precluded direct contacts between the *Alafin* and the European traders, inhibited the establishment of close royal control over the Atlantic trade.[41]

Another possible constraint on centralization in Ọyọ was its military organization. It is, at any rate, clear that the armed forces

[37] R. E. Bradbury, 'The Historical Uses of Comparative Ethnography, with special reference to Benin and the Yoruba', in J. Vansina, R. Mauny, and L. V. Thomas (eds.), *The Historian in Tropical Africa* (London, 1964), 145–60; also in Bradbury, *Benin Studies*, 3–16.

[38] P. C. Lloyd, 'The Political Development of West African Kingdoms', *JAH* 9 (1968), 329; id., *Political Development of Yoruba Kingdoms*, 50–1.

[39] Lloyd, 'Political Development of West African Kingdoms', 328.

[40] Ryder, *Benin and the Europeans*, passim; Akinjogbin, *Dahomey and its Neighbours*, 103, 127–8; Fynn, *Asante and its Neighbours*, 117–20.

[41] Lloyd, *Political Development of Yoruba Kingdoms*, 48; cf. Goody, *Technology, Tradition and the State in Africa*, 52. Asante, however, was for most of its history equally a hinterland state, not directly in control of the coastal ports.

L

of the Ọyọ capital remained under the control of the *Ọyọ Mesi*. In Dahomey and Asante, in contrast, considerable royal armies were built up, though mainly in the nineteenth century, as a final phase in the process of centralization.[42] It has been suggested that the reason for this contrast lies in the use of cavalry by the army of Ọyọ, and of firearms by those of the coastal states. Goody, noting the relative decentralization of hinterland kingdoms such as Ọyọ, the Bariba states, and Gonja, and the centralization of Benin, Dahomey, and Asante, argues that whereas firearms, being cheap and easily stored, were readily centralizable, horses were too expensive to purchase and maintain for royal control to be feasible. A cavalry army is best raised through an estate of independent chiefs, who undertake the acquisition of horses for themselves.[43] A similar argument is put forward by Morton-Williams, in a comparison of Ọyọ and Asante.[44] There is something in this, although it appears that the constraint on centralization was less the expense of horses (since the *Alafin* in fact supplied horses to his chiefs) than the cost of maintaining them: a question of labour (i.e. slaves) rather than of purchasing power (trade goods).[45]

Ultimately, perhaps, explanations are to be sought in specific historical contingencies, though the evidence on Ọyọ is hardly adequate for a detailed reconstruction of the course of its political struggles. But the accumulation of constraints—descent group structures, the use of foreign slaves rather than free men as royal agents, the inability to control access to the Atlantic trade, and the difficulty of centralizing a cavalry army—may be held to go a long way towards explaining the failure of the *Alafin* of Ọyọ to eliminate the power of their chiefs, and thereby to consolidate the empire which they had conquered.

[42] For Asante, see Wilks, *Asante in the Nineteenth Century*, 527–8, 616, 676–7. For Dahomey, see Le Hérissé, *L'Ancien Royaume de Dahomey*, 58.

[43] Goody, *Technology, Tradition and the State in Africa*, 47–56. Benin can hardly stand as an example of centralization through firearms, since firearms only became numerous there at the end of the seventeenth century, by which time Benin's centralized political institutions were already established.

[44] Morton-Williams, 'The Influence of Habitat and Trade on Oyo and Ashanti', esp. 95–6.

[45] Cf. Law, 'A West African Cavalry State', 11–13.

Appendix: Sources and Bibliography

1. ORAL EVIDENCE

Oral evidence was collected by the present writer in various areas of Yorubaland during 1968–9 and in 1973. Details of the informants whose evidence has been made use of in the present work are as follows:

A. New Ọyọ

Aṣiru Alabi, the *Parakoyi*, interviewed 3 Apr. 1969.

Members of the *Agunpopo* lineage, interviewed 3 Apr. 1969.

Oriki (praise-names) of certain *Alafin* of Ọyọ, collected in the *afin* (palace) on behalf of the author, by Mr. B. Ajuwọn, in Apr. 1969.

The *Kudefu*, the *Ọna Iwefa*, the *Ọtun Iwefa*, the *Osi Iwefa*, the *Ilusinmi*, the *Olokun Ẹsin*, and the *Arẹ Agọ* (palace officials), interviewed on various occasions between 30 July and 13 Aug. 1973.

B. *Provincial towns of the Ọyọ kingdom*

Ṣaki: Chief S. Ojo, the *Bada*, a local historian, interviewed 7 Mar. 1968.

Iwere: H. H. Labọde, the *Oniwere*, and his Chiefs, interviewed 4 Feb. 1969.

Iganna: H. H. Adegoke Adegun, the *Ṣabiganna*, and his Chiefs, interviewed 4 Feb. and 2 Mar. 1969.

Iwoye: H. H. Emmanuel Oyebanji, the *Oluwoye*, and his Chiefs, interviewed 4 Mar. 1969.

Iwo: D. A. Adeniji, a local historian, interviewed 13 May 1969.

Ilaro: H. H. Samuel Idowu Okunade, the *Olu*, and others, interviewed 4 and 8 June 1968.

Ijanna: Chief Daniel Oniyitan, the *Balẹ*, and Mr. Amos Egunlẹti, interviewed 4 June 1968.

C. *Towns in the West Yagba area*

Ẹgbẹ: (Oke Ẹgbẹ quarter) Joseph Babalọla Denki, the *Ẹlẹgbẹ*, interviewed 22 June 1968.

(Odo Ẹgbẹ quarter) J. O. A. Olokuntu, the *Balẹ*, interviewed 24 June 1968.

Ere: (Oke Ere, or Akata, quarter) Samuel Aro, the *Balẹ*, interviewed 24 June 1968.

(Odo Ere quarter) Akolo Fatọla, Ogungbẹmi Soga Meduna, and Onitede Ajibọla, the *Ogagun*, interviewed 23 June 1968.

Ẹri: (Oke Ẹri quarter) M. D. Olu, the *Olu* and Chief of West Yagba, and Ekusagba Ọdọfin, interviewed 23 June 1968.

(Odo Ẹri quarter) M. T. Olupinla, the *Ẹlẹri*, and Audu Salami, the *Olukosi*, interviewed 22 June 1968.

Obo Ile: Adeyẹmi, the *Ọwal'Obo*, interviewed 23 June 1968.

D. *Towns in the Owu area*

Owu Ipole: H.H. Adeleke, the *Olowu*, interviewed 6 Mar. 1968.
Ẹrunmu: Sani Oyelẹṣẹ, the *Balẹ*, interviewed 4 Mar. 1969.
Apomu: Bẹlọ Oyetunji, the *Alapomu* (*Balẹ*), interviewed 6 Mar. 1968.

E. *Ijẹbu Ode*

Chief Odubanjọ Odutọla, the *Olotu'fore*, a local historian, interviewed 17 and 18 Feb. 1968.

F. *Badagry*

T. O. Avoseh, a local historian, proprietor of Ajeromi Public School, Ajegunlẹ, Apapa (Lagos), interviewed at Ajegunlẹ, 15 and 22 Mar. 1969.

G. *Ilọrin*

Al-Hajj Adam al-Ilūrī, a local historian, proprietor of the Arabic Training School, Agege, interviewed at Surulere, Lagos, 21 Feb. 1968.

2. UNPUBLISHED WRITTEN SOURCES

A. *Archives*

(1) Public Record Office, London

The main documents consulted here were those in the T.70 series, comprising the records of the chartered companies involved in trade with Africa, viz. the Royal African Company (1672–1750) and the Company of Merchants Trading to Africa (1750–1821).

In addition, selective use has been made of documents from the following nineteenth-century Foreign Office and Colonial Office series: FO.2 (Consular Correspondence, Africa); FO.97 (Niger Expedition); CO.2 (African Exploration); CO.147 (Colony of Lagos).

(2) Archives Nationales, Paris

The documents consulted here were those in the Archives des Colonies, Série C, 6/25–27bis, comprising the records of the Compagnie des Indes and (after 1767) the Ministère de Marine relative to the French fort at 'Juda' (Whydah) and neighbouring areas.

(3) Archives Départementales de la Loire-Atlantique, Nantes

Selective use was made here of the records of the Chambre de Commerce of Nantes (Série C).

(4) National Archives, Ibadan

The documents preserved here consist of the records of the administration of the Western Region of Nigeria, and also of the central Colonial Secretary's Office (the CSO series). The documents consulted comprised primarily the relevant Intelligence Reports and Assessment Reports in the CSO.26 series, and the records relating to the administration of the Ọyọ Province (the OYOPROF. series) and the Ibadan Province (the IBAPROF. series). In addition, selective use has been made of documents relating to the Abẹokuta Province and the Abẹokuta District, in the ABEPROF. and ABEDIST. series.

(5) National Archives, Kaduna

These contain the records of the administration of the Northern Region of Nigeria. The documents consulted here comprised primarily the relevant Assessment Reports in the records of the Secretariat of the Northern Provinces (in the SNP.7 and SNP.10 series), and the records relating to the administration of the Ilọrin Province (the ILORPROF. series). In addition, selective use has been made of documents relating to the District of Borgu (DOB. series), the Bida Division (BIDDIV. series), and the Minna Province (MINPROF. series).

(6) Abẹokuta Divisional Archives, Abẹokuta

Only selective use was made of these documents, which comprise the records of the Abẹokuta Divisional Council, and are preserved in the Council Offices at Ake, Abẹokuta.

(7) Church Missionary Society Archives, London

The documents consulted here were those relating to the Yoruba Mission, established in 1842. Systematic work was done on the CA2 series (1842–80), and more selective work on the G.3, A2 series (after 1880).

B. *Records of the Yoruba Historical Research Scheme*

The records of the Scheme, which operated in 1957–64, under the directorship of Professor S. O. Biobaku, are now preserved in the University of Lagos. Both local historians and academically trained scholars were employed to collect oral traditions. The following Reports by members and associates of the Scheme have been used in the present work:

D. A. Adeniji, 'History of Apomu', n.d.

D. A. Adeniji, 'The History of Ikirun', 1957.

I. A. Akinjogbin, 'Report on Idanre History', n.d.

H. U. Beier, 'Notes on Dassa Zoume, A Yoruba Kingdom in French Dahomey', n.d.

Chief S. Ojo (the *Bada* of Ṣaki), 'Report on Ọyọ Yoruba History', n.d.

C. *Unpublished theses*

Aṣiwaju, A. I., 'The Impact of French and British Administrations on Western Yorubaland 1889–1945', Ph.D. Thesis, University of Ibadan, 1971.

Biobaku, S. O., 'The Egba State and its Neighbours, 1842–1872', Ph.D. Thesis, University of London, 1951.

El Masri, F. H., 'A Critical Edition of Dan Fodio's *Bayān wujūb al-hijra 'alā'l-'ibād*', Ph.D. Thesis, University of Ibadan, 1968.

Gbadamọsi, G. O., 'The Growth of Islam among the Yoruba, 1841–1908', Ph.D. Thesis, University of Ibadan, 1968.

Idris, M. B., 'The History of Borgu in the Nineteenth Century', uncompleted Ph.D. Thesis,* University of Birmingham, 1973.

---

* This thesis was left uncompleted at the tragic death of Musa Idris in a motor accident in 1973: it is now being prepared for publication by Michael Crowder, Paulo Farias, and Marion Johnson.

Mason, M. D., 'The Nupe Kingdom in the Nineteenth Century: a political history', Ph.D. Thesis, University of Birmingham, 1970.

Oroge, E. A., 'The Institution of Slavery in Yorubaland, with particular reference to the nineteenth century', Ph.D. Thesis, University of Birmingham, 1971.

Pallinder-Law, A., 'Government in Abẹokuta 1830–1914, with special reference to the Ẹgba United Government 1898–1914', Fil.Dr. Thesis, University of Göteborg, 1973.

Ross, D. A., 'The Autonomous Kingdom of Dahomey, 1818–94', Ph.D. Thesis, University of London, 1967.

D. Miscellaneous unpublished sources

Barbot, J., 'Description des Côtes d'Affrique, depuis le Cap Bojador jusques à celui de Lopo Gonzales', 1688, unpublished manuscript in the Ministry of Defence Navy Library, London (MS. 63).

Lander, R., Manuscript diary for 31 March to 30 October 1830, in the Wellcome Historical Medical Library, London (MS. 1629).

Simpson, J. MacRae, 'An Intelligence Report on the Oyo Division of the Oyo Province', 1938, in the Rhodes House Library, Oxford (MSS. Afr. s.526).

Thomas, E. V. S., 'Historical Survey of the Towns of Ilaro, Ilobi, Ajilete, and Ilashe in the Ilaro Division', 1933, microfilm copy in the Library of the University of Ibadan.

3. PUBLISHED SOURCES

The following bibliography is selective only, and does not include all the works cited in the footnotes to the main body of the work.

A. Contemporary works

For convenience, the category 'contemporary' is extended to include all works written before 1845, i.e. within ten years of the end of the Ọyọ empire.

(1) Works in European languages:

Adams, J., *Remarks on the Country Extending from Cape Palmas to the River Congo*, London, 1823.

Atkins, J., *A Voyage to Guinea, Brasil, and the West Indies*, London, 1735.

D'Avezac-Maçaya, M., *Notice sur le pays et le peuple des Yébous en Afrique*, Paris, 1845.

Barbot, J., *A Description of the Coasts of North and South Guinea*, London, 1732.

Bosman, W., *A New and Accurate Description of the Coast of Guinea*, London, 1705.

Bowdich, T. E., *A Mission from Cape Coast to Ashantee*, London, 1819.

Clapperton, H., *Journal of a Second Expedition into the Interior of Africa*, London, 1829.

de Clodoré, J., *Relation de ce qui s'est passé dans les isles et terre-ferme de l'Amérique*, 4 vols., Paris, 1671.

COCK, S. (ed.), *The Narrative of Robert Adams*, London, 1816.

CROWTHER, S., *A Vocabulary of the Yoruba Language*, London, 1843.

DALZEL, A., *A History of Dahomy*, London, 1793.

DAPPER, O., *Naukeurige Beschrijvinge der Afrikaensche Gewesten*, Amsterdam, 1668.

DENHAM, D., and H. CLAPPERTON, *Narrative of Travels and Discoveries in Northern and Central Africa*, London, 1826.

DU CASSE, J.-B., 'Relation du Sieur du Casse sur son voyage de Guynée . . . en 1687 et 1688', in P. Roussier (ed.), *L'Établissement d'Issiny 1687–1702* (Paris, 1935), 1–47.

DUPUIS, J., *Journal of a Residence in Ashantee*, London, 1824.

LABARTHE, P., *Voyage a la Côte de Guinée*, Paris, 1803.

LABAT, J.-B., *Voyage du Chevalier des Marchais*, 4 vols., Paris, 1730.

LAIRD, M., and R. A. K. OLDFIELD, *Narrative of an Expedition into the Interior of Africa*, 2 vols., London, 1837.

LANDER, R., *Records of Captain Clapperton's Last Expedition to Africa*, 2 vols., London, 1830.

LANDER, R., and J. LANDER, *Journal of an Expedition to Explore the Course and Termination of the Niger*, 3 vols., London, 1832.

LANDOLPHE, J. F., *Mémoires du Capitaine Landolphe*, edited by J. S. Quesne, 2 vols., Paris, 1823.

NORRIS, R., *Memoirs of the Reign of Bossa Ahadee, King of Dahomy*, London, 1789.

PACHECO PEREIRA, DUARTE, *Esmeraldo de Situ Orbis*, edited by A. E. de Silva Dias, Lisbon, 1905.

Proceedings of the Association for Promoting the Discovery of the Interior Parts of Africa, 2 vols., London, 1810.

PRUNEAU DE POMMEGORGE, –, *Description de la Nigritie*, Paris, 1789.

RABAN, J., *The Eyo Vocabulary*, 3 vols., London, 1830–2.

ROBERTSON, G. A., *Notes on Africa, particularly those parts which are situated between Cape Verde and the River Congo*, London, 1819.

Royal Gold Coast Gazette and Commercial Intelligencer, Cape Coast, 1822–3.

SANSON D'ABBÉVILLE, N., *L'Affrique en plusieurs cartes nouvelles et exactes*, Paris, 1656.

SCHÖN, J. F., and S. CROWTHER, *Journals of the Rev. James Frederick Schön and Mr. Samuel Crowther, who . . . accompanied the Expedition up the River Niger in 1841*, London, 1842.

SMITH, W., *A New Voyage to Guinea*, London, 1744.

SNELGRAVE, W., *A New Account of Some Parts of Guinea*, London, 1734.

(2) Works in Arabic:

MUHAMMAD BELLO, *Infāq al-Maisūr* (written 1812), translated by E. J. Arnett, as *The Rise of the Sokoto Fulani*, Kano, 1922.

'UTHNĀN DAN FODIO, *Tanbīh al-ikhwān 'alā aḥwāl arḍ al-Sudān* (written 1811), translated by H. R. Palmer, as 'An Early Fulani Concept of Islam', 3 parts, *Journal of the African Society*, 13 (1914), 407–14, and 14 (1915), 53–9 and 185–92.

B. *Parliamentary Papers*

These have recently been reprinted by the Irish Universities Press. The following volumes have been used in the present work:

1850 (1291), vol. lv, Correspondence . . . relating to the Slave Trade, 1 April 1849 to 31 March 1850 (in IUP edn., Slave Trade, vol. 37).

1852 (1455), vol. liv, Papers relative to the Reduction of Lagos by Her Majesty's Forces on the West Coast of Africa (in IUP edn., Slave Trade, vol. 90).

1887 (c. 4957), vol. lx, Correspondence respecting the War between the Native Tribes in the Interior and the Negotiations for Peace conducted by the Government of Lagos (in IUP edn., Colonies: Africa, vol. 63).

1887 (c. 5144), vol. lx, Further Correspondence respecting the War between the Native Tribes in the Interior and the Negotiations for Peace conducted by the Government of Lagos (in IUP edn., Colonies: Africa, vol. 63).

C. *Local histories*

These works are based primarily on oral traditions.

ABIỌLA, J. D. E., BABAFẸMI, J. A., and ATAIYERO, S. O. S., *Iwe Itan Ijẹṣa-Obokun*, Ileṣa, 1932.

ADEMAKINWA, J. A., *Ifẹ, Cradle of the Yorubas: A Handbook on the History of the Origin of the Yorubas*, Parts 1 and 2, Lagos, 1958.

ADEYẸMI, M. C., *Iwe Itan Ọyọ–Ile ati Ọyọ Isisiyi abi Agọ–d'Ọyọ*, Ibadan, 1914.

AJIṢAFẸ, A. K., *History of Abẹokuta*, 1st edn. 1916; 2nd edn. 1924; 2nd edn. reprinted, Abẹokuta, 1964.

——, *Iwe Itan Abẹokuta*, 1st edn. (?) 1916; 2nd edn., Abẹokuta, 1972.

AKINYẸLE, I. B., *Iwe Itan Ibadan ati Iwo, Ikirun, ati Oṣogbo*, 1st edn. 1911; 3rd edn., Exeter, 1950.

ATUNDAOLU, H., 'A Short Traditional History of the Ijesas and Other Hinterland Tribes', serialized in 6 parts in *Lagos Weekly Record*, June–July 1901.

AVOSEH, T. O., *A Short History of Badagry*, Lagos, 1938.

EGHAREVBA, J., *A Short History of Benin*, 1st edn. 1934; 3rd edn., Ibadan, 1960.

FỌLARIN, A., *Short Historical Review of the Life of the Egbas, from 1829 to 1930*, Abẹokuta, 1931.

GEORGE, J. O., *Historical Notes on the Yoruba Country and its Tribes*, Lagos, 1895.

HETHERSETT, A. L., and others, *Iwe Kika Ẹkẹrin li Ede Yoruba*, 1st edn. 1911; 2nd(?) edn., Lagos, 1952.

JOHNSON, S., *The History of the Yorubas*, edited by O. Johnson, London, 1921; reprinted, London, 1966.

KẸNYỌ, E. A., *Founder of the Yoruba Nation*, Lagos, 1959.

——, *Yoruba Natural Rulers and their Origins*, Ibadan, 1964.

LEIGH, J. A., *The History of Ondo*, Ondo, 1917.

LIJADU, E. M., 'Fragments of Ẹgba National History', serialized in *Ẹgba Government Gazette*, 1904–5.

Loṣi, J. B. O., *History of Lagos*, 1st edn. 1914; 2nd edn., Lagos, 1967.
——, *History of Abẹokuta*, Lagos, 1923.
Odutọla, O. (the *Olotu'fore* of Ijẹbu), *Iwe Kini Ilọsiwaju Ẹkọ Itan Ijẹbu*, Ijẹbu Ode, 1946.
Oguntuyi, A., *A Short History of Ado-Ekiti*, Akurẹ, n.d. (*c.* 1957).
Ojo, S. (the *Bada* of Ṣaki), *Iwe Itan Ṣaki*, 1st edn. 1937; 4th edn., Ṣaki, n.d. (*c.* 1967).
——, *Iwe Itan Ondo*, 1st edn. 1940; 4th impression, Ondo, 1962.
——, *Short History of Ilorin*, Ṣaki, n.d. (*c.* 1958).
——, *Iwe Itan Ọyọ, Ikoyi, ati Afijio*, Ṣaki, n.d. (*c.* 1961).
Oluganna, D., *Oshogbo*, Oṣogbo, 1959.
Olunlade, E. A., *Ẹdẹ: A Brief History*, translated by I. A. Akinjogbin, edited and annotated by H. U. Beier, Ibadan, 1961.
Oni, J. O., *A History of Ijeshaland*, Ileṣa, n.d. (*c.* 1970).
Oyerinde, N. D., *Iwe Itan Ogbomọṣọ*, Jos, 1934.
Reindorf, C. C., *History of the Gold Coast and Asante*, Basel, 1895.
Ṣopẹin, F., 'A Chapter in the History of the Yoruba Country', in *Nigerian Chronicle*, 17 Sept. 1909.
Wood, J. B., *Historical Notices of Lagos, West Africa*, 1st edn. 1878; 2nd edn., Lagos, 1933.

D. *Other works* (*selective list*)

Abimbọla, W., 'The Ruins of Ọyọ Division', *African Notes*, 2.1 (1964), 16–19.
Abraham, R. C., *Dictionary of Modern Yoruba*, London, 1958.
Adewale, T. J., 'The Ijanna Episode in Yoruba History', in *Proceedings of the Third International West African Conference, Ibadan 1949* (Lagos, 1956), 251–6.
Agiri, B. A., 'The Ogboni among the Ọyọ–Yoruba', *Lagos Notes and Records*, 3.2 (1972), 50–9.
——, 'Early Oyo History Reconsidered', *History in Africa*, 2 (1975), 1–16.
Ajayi, J. F. A., 'Samuel Johnson, Historian of the Yoruba', *Nigeria Magazine*, 81 (1964), 141–6.
——, 'The Aftermath of the Fall of Old Ọyọ', in J. F. A. Ajayi and M. Crowder (eds.), *History of West Africa*, vol. ii (London, 1974), 129–66.
——, and R. Smith, *Yoruba Warfare in the Nineteenth Century*, 2nd edn., Cambridge, 1971.
Akindele, A., and C. Aguessy, *Contribution à l'étude de l'histoire de l'ancien royaume de Porto-Novo*, Dakar (Mémoires de l'IFAN, no. 25), 1953.
Akinjogbin, I. A., 'The Prelude to the Yoruba Civil Wars of the Nineteenth Century', *Odu*, 2nd series, 1.2 (1965), 24–46.
——, 'A Chronology of Yoruba History, 1789–1840', *Odu*, 2nd series, 2.2 (1966), 81–6.
——, 'The Oyo Empire in the Eighteenth Century—A Reassessment', *JHSN* 3.3 (1966), 449–60.
——, *Dahomey and its Neighbours, 1708–1818*, Cambridge, 1967.
——, 'The Expansion of Ọyọ and the Rise of Dahomey, 1600–1800', in

J. F. A. Ajayi and M. Crowder (eds.), *History of West Africa*, vol. i (2nd edn., London, 1976), 373–412.

ALLISON, P., 'The Last Days of Old Oyo', *Odu*, 1st series, 4 (n.d.), 16–27.

ARGYLE, W. J., *The Fon of Dahomey*, Oxford, 1966.

ARNETT, E. J., *Gazetteer of Sokoto Province*, London, 1920.

AṢIWAJU, A. I., 'A Note on the History of Ṣabẹ', *Lagos Notes and Records* 4 (1973), 17–29.

ATANDA, J. A., 'The Fall of the Old Ọyọ Empire: A Re-Consideration of its Causes', *JHSN* 5.4 (1971), 477–90.

——, *The New Ọyọ Empire: Indirect Rule and Change in Western Nigeria 1894–1934*, London, 1973.

——, 'The Yoruba Ogboni Cult: Did it Exist in Old Oyo?', *JHSN* 6.4 (1973), 365–72.

AWẸ, B., 'The Ajele System: A Study of Ibadan Imperialism in the Nineteenth Century', *JHSN* 3.1 (1964), 47–60.

——, 'The End of an Experiment: The Collapse of the Ibadan Empire, 1877–1893', *JHSN* 3.2 (1965), 221–30.

BABAYẸMI, S. O., 'Ọyọ Ruins', *African Notes*, 5.1 (1968), 8–11.

——, 'Upper Ogun: An Historical Sketch', *African Notes*, 6.2 (1971), 72–84.

——, 'Bẹrẹ Festival in Ọyọ', *JHSN* 7.1 (1973), 121–4.

BAIKIE, W. B., 'Notes of a Journey from Bida in Nupe, to Kano in Haussa, performed in 1862', *J. of the Royal Geographical Society*, 37 (1867), 92–108.

BASCOM, W., 'The Fall of Old Oyo or Katunga', *Présence africaine*, 24–5 (1959), 321–7.

——, 'Les Premiers fondements historiques de l'urbanisme Yoruba,' *Présence africaine*, 23 (1959), 22–40.

——, 'Lander's Routes through the Yoruba Country', *The Nigerian Field*, 25.1 (1960), 12–22.

——, *The Yoruba of Southwestern Nigeria*, New York, 1969.

BERTHO, J., 'La Parenté des Yoruba aux peuplades de Dahomey et Togo', *Africa*, 19 (1949), 121–32.

BIOBAKU, S. O., *The Egba and their Neighbours, 1842–1872*, Oxford, 1957.

—— (ed.), *Sources of Yoruba History*, Oxford, 1973.

BIVAR, A. D. H., and M. HISKETT, 'The Arabic Literature of Nigeria to 1804: A Provisional Account', *Bulletin of S.O.A.S.*, 25 (1962), 104–148.

BOWEN, T. J., *Central Africa: Adventures and Missionary Labours in Several Countries in the Interior of Africa, from 1849 to 1856*, Charleston, 1857.

BRADBURY, R. E., 'Chronological Problems in the Study of Benin History', *JHSN* 1.4 (1959), 263–87.

——, 'The Historical Uses of Comparative Ethnography, with special reference to Benin and the Yoruba', in J. Vansina, R. Mauny, and L. V. Thomas (eds.), *The Historian in Tropical Africa* (London 1964), 145–60.

——, 'Patrimonialism and Gerontocracy in Benin Political Culture', in

M. Douglas and P. M. Kaberry (eds.), *Man in Africa* (London, 1969), 17–36.

——, *Benin Studies*, edited by P. Morton-Williams, London, 1973.

BRAY, J. M., 'The Organization of Traditional Weaving in Iseyin, Nigeria', *Africa*, 38 (1968), 270–80.

BURDON, J. A., *Northern Nigeria: Historical Notes on Certain Emirates and Tribes*, London, 1909.

BURTON, R. F., *A Mission to Gelele, King of Dahome*, 2 vols., London, 1864.

CAMPBELL, R., *A Pilgrimage to My Motherland*, New York, 1861.

CLARKE, J. D., 'Ilorin Stone Bead Making', *Nigeria Magazine*, 14 (1938), 156–7.

——, 'A Visit to Old Oyo', *The Nigerian Field*, 7.3 (1938), 139–42.

——, 'Carved Posts at Old Oyo, *Nigeria Magazine*, 15 (1938), 248–9.

——, 'Ancient Pottery from Old Oyo', *Nigeria Magazine*, 18 (1939), 109.

CLARKE, W. H., *Travels and Explorations in Yorubaland (1854–1858)*, edited by J. A. Atanda, Ibadan, 1972.

COISSY, A., 'Un Règne de femme dans l'ancien royaume d'Abomey', *Études dahoméennes*, 2 (1959), 5–8.

CORNEVIN, R., *Histoire du Dahomey*, Paris, 1962.

——, *Histoire du Togo*, 3rd edn., Paris, 1969.

CROWDER, M., *The Story of Nigeria*, 2nd edn., London, 1966.

——, *Revolt in Bussa: A Study of British 'Native Administration' in Nigerian Borgu, 1902–1935*, London, 1973.

CURTIN, P. D. (ed.), *Africa Remembered: Narratives by West Africans from the Era of the Slave Trade*, Madison, 1967.

——, *The Atlantic Slave Trade: A Census*, Madison, 1969.

DAVIDSON, B., *Black Mother: Africa, The Years of Trial*, 2nd edn., London, 1970.

——, *Africa in History: Themes and Outlines*, 3rd edn., London, 1974.

DEBIEN, G., and J. HOUDAILLE, 'Les Origines des esclaves aux Antilles: No. 32, Sur une sucrerie de la Guyane en 1690', *Bulletin de l'IFAN*, Série B, 26 (1964), 166–94.

DENNETT, R. E., *Nigerian Studies, or the Religious and Political System of the Yoruba*, London, 1910.

DODWELL, C. B., 'The Tim-Tim Makers of Oyo', *Nigeria Magazine*, 42 (1953), 126–31.

DUFF, E. C., *Gazetteer of Kontagora Province*, London, 1920.

DUNCAN, J., *Travels in Western Africa in 1845 and 1846*, 2 vols., London, 1847.

DUNGLAS, E., 'Contribution à l'histoire du Moyen-Dahomey', 3 vols., *Études dahoméennes*, 19–21 (1957–8).

——, 'Adjohon: étude historique', *Études dahoméennes*, new series, 8 (1966), 57–73.

——, 'Origine du royaume de Porto-Novo', *Études dahoméennes*, new series, 9–10 (1967), 29–62.

DUPIGNY, E. G. M., *Gazetteer of Nupe Province*, London, 1920.

ELLIS, A. B., *The Yoruba-Speaking Peoples of the Slave Coast of West Africa*, London, 1894.

ELPHINSTONE, K. V., *Gazetteer of Ilorin Province*, London, 1921.

FADIPẸ, N. A., *The Sociology of the Yoruba*, edited by F. O. and O. O. Okediji, Ibadan, 1970.

FAGE, J. D., 'Some Remarks on Beads and Trade in Lower Guinea in the Sixteenth and Seventeenth Centuries', *JAH* 3 (1962), 343–7.

——, 'States of the Guinea Forest', in R. Oliver (ed.), *The Dawn of African History*, 2nd edn. (London, 1968), 68–74.

——, *A History of West Africa: An Introductory Survey*, Cambridge, 1969.

——, 'Slavery and the Slave Trade in the Context of West African History', *JAH* 10 (1969), 393–404.

FLINT, J. E., *Nigeria and Ghana*, New Jersey, 1966.

FOA, E., *Le Dahomey*, Paris, 1895.

FỌLAYAN, K., 'Ẹgbado to 1832: The Birth of a Dilemma', *JHSN* 4.1 (1967), 15–33.

FORBES, F. E., *Dahomey and the Dahomans*, 2 vols., London, 1851.

FORDE, D., *The Yoruba-Speaking Peoples of South-Western Nigeria*, London (Ethnographic Survey of Africa: Western Africa, Part IV), 1951.

FROBENIUS, L., *The Voice of Africa*, translated by R. Blind, 2 vols., London, 1913.

FYNN, J. K., *Asante and its Neighbours, 1700–1807*, London, 1971.

GANN, L. H., and P. DUIGNAN, *Africa and the World: An Introduction to the History of Sub-Saharan Africa from Antiquity to 1840*, San Francisco, 1972.

GBADAMỌSI, G. O., 'The Imamate Question among Yoruba Muslims', *JHSN* 6.2 (1972), 229–37.

GOODY, J., *Technology, Tradition and the State in Africa*, London, 1971.

HAIR, P. E. H., 'Ethnolinguistic Continuity on the Guinea Coast', *JAH* 8 (1967), 247–68.

HERMON-HODGE, H. B., *Gazetteer of Ilorin Province*, London, 1929.

HISKETT, M., *The Sword of Truth: The Life and Times of the Shehu Usuman dan Fodio*, London, 1973.

HODGKIN, T., *Nigerian Perspectives: An Historical Anthology*, 2nd edn., London, 1975.

HOPKINS, A. G., *An Economic History of West Africa*, London, 1975.

JOHNSON, M., 'The Cowrie Currencies of West Africa', 2 parts, *JAH* 11 (1970), 17–49 and 331–53.

KEA, R. A., 'Firearms and Warfare on the Gold and Slave Coasts from the Sixteenth to the Nineteenth Centuries', *JAH* 12 (1971), 185–213.

KEAY, R. W. J., 'Notes on the Vegetation of Old Oyo Forest Reserve', *Farm and Forest* (1947), 36–46.

KOELLE, S. W., *Native African Literature*, London, 1854.

KRAPF-ASKARI, E., *Yoruba Towns and Cities*, Oxford, 1969.

LAST, M., *The Sokoto Caliphate*, London, 1967.

LAW, R., 'The Dynastic Chronology of Lagos', *Lagos Notes and Records*, 2.2 (1968), 46–54.

——, 'The Fall of Allada, 1724—An Ideological Revolution?', *JHSN* 5.1 (1969), 157–63.

——, 'The Chronology of the Yoruba Wars of the Early Nineteenth Century: A Reconsideration', *JHSN* 5.2 (1970), 211–22.

——, 'The Constitutional Troubles of Ọyọ in the Eighteenth Century', *JAH* 12 (1971), 25–44.

——, 'Iwere', *JHSN* 6.2 (1972), 239–41.

——, 'The Heritage of Oduduwa: Traditional History and Political Propaganda among the Yoruba', *JAH* 14 (1973), 207–22.

——, 'The Ọyọ Kingdom and its Northern Neighbours', *Kano Studies*, new series, 1 (1973), 25–34.

——, 'The Owu War in Yoruba History', *JHSN* 7.1 (1973), 141–7.

——, 'A West African Cavalry State: the Kingdom of Oyo', *JAH* 16 (1975), 1–15.

——, 'Early Yoruba Historiography', *History in Africa*, 3 (1976), 69–89.

LE HERISSÉ, A., *L'Ancien Royaume de Dahomey*, Paris, 1911.

LLOYD, P. C., 'The Yoruba Lineage', *Africa*, 25 (1955), 235–51.

——, 'Sacred Kingship and Government among the Yoruba', *Africa*, 30 (1960), 221–37.

——, *Yoruba Land Law*, London, 1962.

——, 'The Political Development of West African Kingdoms', *JAH* 9 (1968), 319–29.

——, *The Political Development of Yoruba Kingdoms in the Eighteenth and Nineteenth Centuries*, London (Royal Anthropological Institute, Occasional Paper no. 31), 1971.

LOVEJOY, P. E., 'Interregional Monetary Flows in the Precolonial Trade of Nigeria', *JAH* 15 (1974), 563–85.

MABOGUNJẸ, A. L., *Yoruba Towns*, Ibadan, 1962.

——, and J. OMER-COOPER, *Owu in Yoruba History*, Ibadan, 1971.

MACROW, D. W., 'Natural Ruler—A Yoruba Conception of Monarchy', *Nigeria Magazine*, 47 (1955), 233–45.

MANNING, P., 'Slaves, Palm Oil and Political Power on the West African Coast', *African Historical Studies*, 2 (1969), 279–88.

MARTIN, B. G., 'A New Arabic History of Ilorin', Centre of Arabic Documentation, University of Ibadan, *Research Bulletin*, 1.2 (1965), 20–7.

MERCIER, P., 'Histoire et légende: la bataille d'Illorin', *Notes africaines*, 47 (1950), 92–5.

MISCHLICH, A., and J. LIPPERT, 'Beiträge zur Geschichte der Haussa-staaten', *Mittheilungen des Seminars für orientalische Sprachen zu Berlin*, 6 (1903), Dritte Abtheilung, 137–242.

MOCKLER-FERRYMAN, A. F., *Up the Niger: Narrative of Major Claude MacDonald's Mission to the Niger and Benue Rivers*, London, 1892.

MORTON-WILLIAMS, P., 'The Yoruba Ogboni Cult in Ọyọ', *Africa*, 30 (1960), 362–74.

——, 'An Outline of the Cosmology and Cult Organization of the Ọyọ Yoruba', *Africa*, 34 (1964), 243–61.

——, 'The Ọyọ Yoruba and the Atlantic Trade, 1670–1830', *JHSN* 3.1 (1964), 25–45.

——, 'The Yoruba Kingdom of Oyo', in D. Forde and P. M. Kaberry (eds.), *West African Kingdoms in the Nineteenth Century* (London, 1967), 32–69.

——, 'The Fulani Penetration into Nupe and Yoruba in the Nineteenth Century', in I. M. Lewis (ed.), *History and Social Anthropology* (London, 1968), 1–24.

——, 'The Influence of Habitat and Trade on the Polities of Oyo and Ashanti', in M. Douglas and P. M. Kaberry (eds.), *Man in Africa* (London, 1969), 79–98.

MOULERO, T., 'Histoire et légende de Chabe (Save)', *Études dahoméennes*, new series, 2 (1964), 51–92.

NADEL, S. F., *A Black Byzantium: The Kingdom of Nupe in Nigeria*, London, 1942.

NEWBURY, C. W., *The Western Slave Coast and its Rulers*, Oxford, 1961.

NIVEN, C. R., *A Short History of the Yoruba Peoples*, London, 1958.

ỌBAYẸMI, A., 'The Yoruba and Edo-Speaking Peoples and their Neighbours before 1600', in J. F. A. Ajayi and M. Crowder (eds.), *History of West Africa*, vol. i (2nd edn., London, 1976), 196–263.

OJO, G. J. A., *Yoruba Culture*, London, 1966.

——, *Yoruba Palaces*, London, 1966.

OLIVER, R., and B. M. FAGAN, *Africa in the Iron Age*, Cambridge, 1975.

——, and J. D. FAGE, *A Short History of Africa*, 3rd edn., London, 1970.

PALMER, H. R., *Sudanese Memoirs, being mainly Translations of a Number of Arabic Manuscripts relating to the Central and Western Sudan*, 3 vols., Lagos, 1928.

PARRINDER, G., *The Story of Ketu*, 2nd edn., edited by I. A. Akinjogbin, Ibadan, 1967.

RATTRAY, R. S., *Ashanti Law and Constitution*, London, 1929.

RODNEY, W., 'Gold and Slaves on the Gold Coast', *Transactions of the Historical Society of Ghana*, 10 (1969), 13–28.

RYDER, A. F. C., 'Dutch Trade on the Nigerian Coast during the Seventeenth Century', *JHSN* 3.2 (1965), 195–210.

——, *Benin and the Europeans, 1485–1897*, London, 1969.

SHAW, T., 'A Note on Trade and the Tsoede Bronzes', *West African J. of Archaeology*, 3 (1973), 233–8.

SKERTCHLY, J. A., *Dahomey As It Is*, London, 1874.

SMITH, H. F. C., 'Arabic Manuscript Material bearing upon the History of the Western Sudan: A Seventeenth Century Writer of Katsina', Historical Society of Nigeria, *Bulletin of News*, Suppl. to 6.1 (1961).

SMITH, R., 'The Alafin in Exile: A Study of the Igboho Period in Oyo History', *JAH* 6 (1965), 57–77.

——, 'List of Alafin of Ọyọ', *The African Historian*, 1.3 (1965), 52–5.

——, 'The Bara, or Royal Mausoleum, at New Oyo', *JHSN* 3.2 (1965), 415–20.

——, 'Yoruba Armament', *JAH* 8 (1967), 87–106.

——, *Kingdoms of the Yoruba*, London, 1969.

——, and D. WILLIAMS, 'A Reconnaissance Visit to Ọyọ-Ile', *Odu*, 2nd series, 3.1 (1966), 56–60.

STEVENS, P., 'The Kisra Legend and the Distortion of Historical Tradition', *JAH* 16 (1975), 185–200.

TALBOT, P. A., *The Peoples of Southern Nigeria*, 4 vols., London, 1926.

TEMPLE, O., *Notes on the Tribes, Emirates and States of the Northern Provinces of Nigeria*, 2nd edn., London, 1922.

TOWNSEND, H., 'Abbeokuta and its Inhabitants', *Church Missionary Intelligencer*, 1.6 (1849), 136–42.

VAN DANTZIG, A., *Dutch Documents relating to the Gold Coast and the Slave Coast (Coast of Guinea) 1680–1740*, cyclostyled, Legon, 1971.

VANSINA, J., *Oral Tradition: A Study in Historical Methodology*, translated by H. M. Wright, London, 1965.

VERGER, P., *Bahia and the West Coast Trade (1549–1851)*, Ibadan, 1964.

——, *Flux et reflux de la traite des nègres entre le golfe de Bénin et Bahia de Todos os Santos*, Paris, 1968.

WATTERS, R. G., 'A Visit to Old Oyo', *Nigeria Magazine*, 44 (1958), 346–9.

WEBSTER, J. B., and A. A. BOAHEN, *The Revolutionary Years: West Africa since 1800*, London, 1967.

WESCOTT, J., and P. MORTON-WILLIAMS, 'The Symbolism and Ritual Context of the Yoruba *Laba Shango*', *J. of the Royal Anthropological Institute*, 92 (1962), 23–37.

WHEATLEY, P., 'The Significance of Traditional Yoruba Urbanism', *Comparative Studies in Society and History*, 12 (1970), 393–423.

WILKS, I., *Asante in the Nineteenth Century: The Structure and Evolution of a Political Order*, Cambridge, 1975.

WILLETT, F., 'A Terra-Cotta Head from Old Oyo, Western Nigeria', *Man*, 59 (1959), 286.

——, 'Investigations at Old Oyo, 1956–1957: An Interim Report', *JHSN* 2.1 (1960), 59–77.

——, *Ife in the History of West African Sculpture*, London, 1967.

WILSON, J. L., *Western Africa: Its History, Conditions, and Prospects*, New York, 1856.

Index